FACETS OF TAOISM

Facets of Taoism

ESSAYS IN CHINESE RELIGION

edited by

Holmes Welch   Anna Seidel

New Haven and London   Yale University Press   1979

Designed by Thos. Whitridge
and set in Bembo type
Printed in the United States of America.

*Published in Great Britain, Europe, Africa, and Asia (except Japan) by Yale University
Press, Ltd., London. Distributed in Australia and New Zealand by Book & Film Services,
Artarmon, N.S.W., Australia; and in Japan by Harper & Row, Publishers, Tokyo
Office.*

Library of Congress Cataloging in Publication Data

International Conference on Taoist Studies, 2d, China, Japan, 1972.
   Facets of Taoism: Essays in Chinese Religion

   Includes bibliographical references and index.
   1.   Taoism—Congresses.   2.   China—Religion—
Congresses.   I.   Welch, Holmes.   II.   Seidel, Anna K.   III.   Title.
BL1899.5.I.57   1972   299'.514   77–28034
ISBN 0–300–01695–6

Contents

Introduction

CONFUCIANISM, BUDDHISM, AND TAOISM are sometimes called the three "great traditions" of China. They shared—and interacted with —many elements of popular religion. They were often united and combined in syncretistic sects, particularly after the Sung dynasty (960–1278).

They were also combined in the daily reality of Chinese life. During the last millennium most Chinese, including many of the literati, were Confucians in their social life and Buddhists or Taoists in self-cultivation and religious observances. There is only limited truth in the idea (implanted by the literati in Western residents in China and in scholars of China) that Confucianism was the doctrine of the ruling class, whereas Buddhism and Taoism appealed solely to the ignorant masses.[1] Furthermore, each of the three traditions had borrowed so much from the others that, except for terminology, there was little that was unique to any one of them.

Of these three traditions Taoism was, until recently, the one on which the least research had been done. The Bellagio Conference in 1968 brought scholars together for the first time to discuss Taoist studies.[2] It was felt by all participants to have been a successful harvest in a whole new field of investigation into Chinese culture, and plans were soon made for a sequel to it.

To begin with, because no senior Japanese specialists on Taoism had come to Bellagio and because research on Taoism was most developed in Japan (where the Taoist Studies Society had some three hundred members), the organizers preferred a Japanese site for the second conference. A budget ceiling made this impossible until Professor Tadao Sakai offered to raise the funds that were needed. He set up a committee that assumed

1. For a description of how this implantation succeeded with respect to Buddhism, see Holmes Welch, *The Buddhist Revival in China* (Cambridge, Mass., 1968), pp. 202–53.

2. The first Taoism Conference, held at Bellagio, Italy, in September 1968, was sponsored by the American Council of Learned Societies. Some of its papers were published in *History of Religions* (Chicago), 9.2–3:107–279 (1969/70).

responsibility for all local arrangements and expenses. Funds came from several generous donors including the Ministry of Education and the Mitsubishi Corporation. International House of Japan provided a secretariat under the able direction of Mikio Kato. The selection of participants, however, and the conduct of the actual sessions remained the responsibility of the steering committee representing the sponsors, namely, the American Council of Learned Societies, the Center for the Study of World Religions, and the East Asian Research Center (both of Harvard University). The following scholars participated: T. Sakai and H. Miyakawa (Japan), J. Needham (Great Britain), M. Kaltenmark, R. A. Stein, C. L. Hou, and K. M. Schipper (France), A. Seidel (Ecole française d'Extrême-Orient), M. Porkert (Germany), J. L. Dull, R. B. Mather, N. Sivin, M. Strickmann, and H. H. Welch (United States).

The conference sessions were held during the first week of September 1972, in Tateshina, Nagano prefecture. The task of English-Japanese interpretation was very competently dealt with by Miss Chie Adachi, assisted, as far as specific Taoist terminology was concerned, by the expert and polyglot skills of the two scholars Fumimasa and Shigemasa Fukui. Professor Tetsurō Noguchi kindly assumed the task of tape-recording the discussions.[3]

A word must be said about an empty chair. Taoism is Chinese, and yet no senior Chinese scholar was among those present. L. S. Yang of Harvard had originally accepted the invitation, but ill health kept him away. For two years efforts had been made to invite Ch'en Kuo-fu, probably the leading authority on Taoism in mainland China. These efforts proved unsuccessful.[4] Other Chinese scholars were invited or considered, but time

3. The rapporteurs were Anna Seidel, Farzeen Hussein, and Donald B. Wagner, with assistance from Judith Berling. A set of their abstracts of the conference discussions has been deposited with the East Asian Research Center, 1737 Cambridge Street, Cambridge, Mass. 01238.

4. In 1940–41 Ch'en Kuo-fu 陳國符 coauthored two articles in English on Chinese alchemy with Tenney L. Davis, Professor of Organic Chemistry at the Massachusetts Institute of Technology (1919–42). By 1942 he was back in China teaching chemistry and studying the Taoist Canon under Lung Ch'üan-chen 龍泉鎮. In 1949 he published *Tao-tsang yüan-liu k'ao* 道藏源流考 (Studies in the Evolution of the Taoist Canon), the scope of which was broader than the title indicates. It is, still today, regarded by many students of Taoism as the most valuable Chinese study of Taoist scriptures together with Fu Ch'in-chia 傅勤家, *Chung-kuo Tao-chiao shih* 中國道教史 (The History of Taoism in China [Shanghai, 1937]). In December 1963, just as the political relaxation of the early sixties was coming to an end, Ch'en brought out a new and enlarged edition of his history of the canon, published in Peking. In 1972 he was reported to be teaching chemistry at the University of Tientsin.

In hopes of getting approval to invite a scholar of Ch'en's caliber to attend the second

or other obstacles made it impossible for any of them to attend. So, much to the regret of the sponsors and participants, no senior Chinese scholar came to Tateshina. Also regretted was the absence of the eminent scholar Yoshitoyo Yoshioka, whose participation had been one of the purposes of holding the conference in Japan. The editors were, however, fortunate to obtain his permission to include in this volume a translation of his article dealing with his experiences in a Taoist monastery in Peking. The only other Japanese to have had extended personal experience of Taoist monastic life is the Reverend Kenryū Igarashi, a Shingon priest, who attended the conference as a specially invited guest, bringing along his Taoist monk's robe and black cap of the Ch'üan-chen sect which he had received in the T'ai-ch'ing Kung in Shen-yang in the late 1930s.

Most of the conference papers were submitted in preliminary form. There were two additional studies to be translated from Japanese. The editorial process was therefore long and difficult. Of the thirteen papers contributed, six have, for different reasons, not been included in this volume.[5] They have, however, been published in the counterpart volume in Japanese.[6]

The Focus of the Conference

Taoism is often thought of as originating with the philosophical writings

---

Taoism conference, Frederick Burkhardt, the president of the ACLS, wrote twice to Kuo Mo-jo, president of the Chinese Academy of Sciences, first on September 23, 1971, and second on March 3, 1972. This was just after the Sino-American agreement of February 27, 1972 regarding the facilitation of cultural exchanges. Unfortunately, this initiative did not produce any results, and no scholar from China attended the Taoism conference at Tateshina. It is also to be noted that no new research in the field of specifically religious studies has been published in mainland China for many years.

5. The papers omitted are: J. Needham, "The Social Aspects of Taoist Alchemy" (sections of which have appeared in Science and Civilisation in China, vol. 5, pt. 3 [Cambridge, 1976]). T. Sakai, "The Morality Books (shan-shu) and the Educated Commoners of Late Ming and Early Ch'ing Society"; J. L. Dull, "Taoist Trends among Confucian Thinkers"; M. Porkert, "The Ethical Make-up of the Taoist Insurgent according to the P'ing-yao chuan" (cf. Patrick Hanan, "The Composition of the P'ing yao chuan," Harvard Journal of Asiatic Studies 31: 201–19 [1971]); K. M. Schipper, "Some Remarks on the Function of the 'Inspector of Merits' "; N. Sivin, "Folk Medicine and Classical Medicine in Traditional China: a Contribution to the Definition of 'Taoist.' " The publication in this volume of a different paper by M. Strickmann will be explained below, as will the addition of articles by T. Sakai, N. Ōfuchi, and Y. Yoshioka.

6. Tadao Sakai, ed., Dōkyō no sōgō teki kenkyū 道教の總合的研究 (A synthesis of studies on Taoism; Tokyo, 1977). This volume includes all the papers contributed to the conference except that of Hou Ching-lang. In addition, it contains a study by Yoshitoyo Yoshioka on the Ho-shang kung Commentary of the Lao tzu ("Rōshi Kajōkō hon to dōkyō" 老子河上公本と道教) and an article by T. Sakai and Fumimasa Fukui entitled "What is Taoism?" ("Dōkyō to wa nani ka—Dōkyō, dōka, dōjutsu, dōshi" 道教とは何か—道教・道家・道術・道士).

of Lao-tzu and continuing in modern times with the parish priests of the Celestial Master's sect and the celibate monks whose life is described toward the end of this volume. Some scholars now find in the *Lao-tzu* not merely philosophy but political science, instructions on self-cultivation, descriptions of trance, and traces of shamanism. In the second century of our era, several hundred years after the *Lao-tzu* (or *Tao-te ching*) was written, it became the sacred scripture of Taoist rebels who set up an independent state in western China. Their movement was known as the "Way of the Five Pecks of Rice," these five pecks being the annual tithe its followers paid to their leaders.

At the same time (A.D. 184) Taoist rebels in eastern China were threatening to overthrow the central government. They were called the "Yellow Turbans" (from their headgear) and their sacred text was the *T'ai-p'ing ching* or "Scripture of Great Peace." A text with the same title survives, but it appears to have been connected not so much with the Yellow Turbans in the east, who called their movement the "Way of Great Peace," as with the Five Pecks of Rice in the West. This *T'ai-p'ing ching* is the subject of the opening article in the present volume, by M. Kaltenmark. Readers who find themselves becoming confused by the maze of similar names in separate movements (names of leaders as well as of texts) may be helped by what Kaltenmark has written about the subject in his popular book on Taoism.[7]

Some passages Kaltenmark quotes from the *T'ai-p'ing ching* are sui generis. Others are a mixture of ideas that sound like naïve echoes of Confucians, Mohists, cosmologists, and different schools of Buddhism. One passage, for example, states that merchants belong to the lowest social class. The idea is Confucian, but not its rationale—namely, that there must be circulation among Heaven, Earth, and Man, and among men there must be circulation of goods with which merchants interfere by hoarding (see Kaltenmark's article, p. 34). Offerings to the dead must be modest (p. 36), not for the Mohist reason that exorbitant offerings mean waste, but, first, because it is wrong to make *yin* (the realm of the dead) superior to *yang* (the realm of the living);[8] second,

7. See M. Kaltenmark, *Lao tseu et le taoisme* (Paris, 1965), pp. 142–43; translated in Kaltenmark, *Lao-tzu and Taoism* (Stanford, 1969), pp. 113–15. The English edition omits all the splendid illustrations of the French. On the Taoist movements discussed in Kaltenmark's article, see also Holmes Welch, *Taoism, the Parting of the Way* (Boston, 1965), pp. 113–18; and, for the fullest treatment, see R. A. Stein, "Remarques sur les mouvements du taoïsme politico-religieux au IIᵉ siècle ap. J.-C.", *T'oung Pao* 50.1–3 :1–78 (1963).

8. Compare the place where "the bad young men" sit, the South-Western direction where the *yin* is increasing and the *yang* is decreasing (p. 33). In the *T'ai-p'ing ching* we see that *yin* and *yang* have already begun to evolve from complementary forces to good versus evil.

because the dead live in peace and joy below the earth (an archaic, pre-Buddhist concept) so that to lavish offerings on them would be to disturb them with the thought of returning to their soul tablets (as good Confucians hoped they would); and third, because if the spirits of dead ancestors could not eat up all the offerings put out for them, the unconsumed surplus would attract dangerous demons who might harm the community (early evidence of the Chinese people's preoccupation with the danger of demons).

The *T'ai-p'ing ching* states, like the *Mencius*, that when the ruler is good, all other nations hasten to submit to him of their own accord (Kaltenmark, p. 28), but the respect that it shows for other nations and their barbarian inhabitants is the reverse of what we find in Mencius.[9]

At a good many points the book seems Buddhistic. A slave can become a god (Kaltenmark, n. 20) just as a dog can become a buddha. Those who refuse to teach the Tao are condemned (p. 33) like *pratyeka* buddhas in Mahāyāna texts. The Taoist notion of *ch'eng-fu*—inherited merit or guilt (p. 24)—has something in common with the Buddhist concept of karma, just as Buddhist reincarnation can be compared with the return to life of an ancestor's *ch'i* (n. 24). In the same way that Buddhist texts of the T'ien-t'ai school explain the apparent contradictions in the Buddha's teachings, so the *T'ai-p'ing ching* explains that Heaven teaches each of us only what we are capable of understanding and this is why different sages wrote different things (p. 25). The section entitled *Shih-t'se wen* (especially p. 39, b and g) advocates something like the Buddhist practice of reciting the name of Amitābha (introduced in the sixth century) and the incantation of mantras (introduced with Tantric Buddhism somewhat later). Yet none of these apparent similarities with Buddhism meant anything more than the fact that Buddhist ideas, as they reached the Chinese, seemed much less strange and more acceptable and offered a stronger challenge to indigenous systems. When it condemns "the four pernicious kinds of conduct" (p. 35), the *T'ai-p'ing ching* clearly displays a hostile rejection of Buddhism in whatever form Buddhism existed in China when the passage was written.

At other points the scripture sounds almost Marxist. All goods belong to the state (p. 35); the individual receives them according to his needs (p. 35) and produces them according to his means (p. 21). The ruler collects and distributes the opinions of the populace (pp. 28–29) rather as the People's Government did during the Great Leap Forward of 1958–59. This may be one reason why the *T'ai-p'ing ching* is one of the few ancient

---

9. For example, see *Mencius* III, 1. iv (Legge, pp. 253–54).

texts that has been collated, edited, and published in China since 1949 (see Kaltenmark, n. 2). Kaltenmark, however, is as skeptical of parallels with modern ideologies as with Buddhism. The *T'ai-p'ing ching* is not an antecedent of Mao's "little red book." Rather, it is a thesaurus of religious ideas that were current among the commoners of China in the period when they—the commoners—were becoming religiously conscious and active for the first time. This is what makes it so important: the book springs from a different social milieu from that of most other writings surviving from that period. It gives us an early glimpse outside the curtained orthodox world of the literati.

Kaltenmark, although he studied the *T'ai-p'ing ching* for more than twenty years, refrained from publishing any of the results of his research until he wrote this article. That was due to the nature of the book. It is written in a peculiar language, often colloquial and repetitious. Some passages (like the *Shih-ts'e wen*) are so cryptic that Kaltenmark leaves them untranslated. Clearly he feels that the *T'ai-p'ing ching* is comprehensible only after the whole of it has been examined and considered. Yet even after doing so he has remained hesitant to draw conclusions about it. Some of his conclusions did not emerge until the conference discussion, which is reproduced after his article. The article itself is the fullest treatment of the *T'ai-p'ing ching* to appear so far in a Western language.[10]

In the two centuries following the end of their first rebellions, the Taoists became respectable citizens—so respectable that they seem to have been trying to outdo the Confucians in their condemnation of heresy and heterodoxy. Yet much of what they condemned can barely be distinguished from what they embraced. This anomaly is the theme of the next article, by R. A. Stein. He points out that there was continuous interpenetration of belief and practice among the different levels of society. This created a problem for people in the upper levels who wished to distinguish themselves from hoi polloi in matters of religion as in other matters. One lower-level practice was the "bloody sacrifice" of uncooked

10. It is briefly discussed in Vincent C. Y. Shih, "Some Chinese Rebel Ideologies," *T'oung Pao* 44:150–226 (1956); in Timoteus Pokora, "On the Origins of the Notions T'ai-p'ing and Ta-t'ung in Chinese Philosophy," *Archiv Orientalni* 29:448–54 (1961); in Wolfgang Bauer, *China und die Hoffnung auf Glück* (Munich, 1971), pp. 175–86; and in Yü Ying-shih, "Life and Immortality in Han China," *Harvard Journal of Asiatic Studies* 25:84–86 (1964–65). Yü agrees with Kaltenmark about the early composition of the *TPC*, whereas Shih, Stein, and others date it as Six Dynasties. The controversy about whether it is an early work with later accretions or a later work incorporating earlier sections reminds one of the story about "Three in the Morning" in *Chuang-tzu* 2, 4.

meat to the divinities being worshipped. This kind of sacrifice was characteristic of what the upper-level Taoists called *yin-ssu* 淫祀, which Stein prefers to render as "excessive cults." (Another translation might be "promiscuous cults.")

Bloody sacrifices were not the only practice to which upper-level, orthodox Taoists objected. Like the Confucians, they believed that a man should worship solely his own ancestors and the gods of his own locality, and that he should eschew the worship of "foreign" gods or of any gods at all on days other than the appointed festivals (see Stein, pp. 66–67, 68, 78). Both these principles were flouted in the "excessive cults"; and so, when the orthodox Taoists had the power, they sometimes suppressed them and actually destroyed their temples (pp. 58, 67–68, 81). Sometimes they did not; and little difference can be seen in those they suppressed and those they allowed to continue. When suppression did occur, they justified it by saying that the offending cults had exacted from the people ruinous expenditures for sacrifice. (This is the same argument used for the same purpose today by government officials in both Taiwan and the Chinese mainland.)

Orthodox Taoists felt that such cults not only competed with their own but were embarrassingly similar. Yet they could not successfully resist the upward force of penetration of lower-level practices. Stein shows how a few such practices, such as religious banquets, were probably borrowed from the heterodox Taoists by the orthodox. Recalling Kaltenmark's article, one might ask: to which of the two categories— orthodox or heterodox—did the author or authors of the *T'ai-p'ing ching* belong? Stein, who dates it later than Kaltenmark, does not offer an opinion. He notes in passing that the *T'ai-p'ing ching*, like the *Pao-p'u-tzu*, condemns sacrifices to the divinities who cause illness or take possession of people, especially sacrifices to local, uncanonical gods (p. 62). On the other hand, it seems significant that whereas the *T'ai-p'ing ching* looks favorably on barbarians, some of the texts quoted by Stein warn against the mixing of Chinese with foreigners (p. 63). Perhaps future research will identify the social milieu which produced works as different as the *T'ai-p'ing ching*, the *San-t'ien nei-chieh ching*, the *Shen-chou ching*, and other Taoist scriptures frequently referred to by the authors of this volume.

The third article is by H. Miyakawa, an eminent authority on religion in the Six Dynasties, especially Taoism. He originally submitted to the conference a longer paper entitled "The Origin of Sun En's Rebellion and its Relation to the Local Cults in the Lake P'o-yang Region." The editors felt that it comprised two separate articles on rather different topics, and so they decided, with the author's permission, to publish the second part only. One reason was that Sun En's rebellion had already been described in Western literature,[11] whereas the cults discussed by Miyakawa in this volume will be unfamiliar to readers who do not have access to the original Chinese sources.

The rebellion of Sun En in A.D. 304 was the third great uprising in Chinese history in which Taoists played a leading role. It offers another illustration of the elusive affinity between Taoism and rebellion, an affinity that has worried Chinese governments down through the early 1950s. Miyakawa suggests that Sun En's brand of Taoism was connected with the thaumaturgy of his father's master, Tu Chiung, and argues that this in turn was related to the cults of the tutelary divinities of the great P'o-yang Lake, which lies in northern Kiangsi and has its mouth on the Yangtze River. In the Six Dynasties especially, this lake afforded communication by water between east and west, north and south. Merchants and other travelers of the time believed that they could only cross it after propitiating the deities under whose authority it fell. Describing these deities takes Miyakawa into some curious byways of the history of religion in China. There was, for example, a belief in pythons as dangerous as the Scylla of the *Odyssey*—except that whereas Scylla had to thrust her long neck down to snap up the crewmen of Odysseus, the Chinese python could inhale them from a distance, or it could appear as a five-colored cloud onto which the victim would decorously step. Thus the horrible content of a legend was lost in its decoration, rather as in modern Chinese opera.

Miyakawa's conclusions can be read at the end of his article, but it may be helpful to supplement them with what he stated in the course of correspondence. The Sun En rebellion, he wrote, was a fratricidal war "fought between members of the orthodox Cheng-i Taoist school and its dissenters, a heterodox sect led by the Suns. . . . The Suns' religion had many points in common with shamanism, but it was at the same time reinforced by the Taoist doctrine transmitted from Tu Chiung." Here again is the theme explored by R. A. Stein: conflict between orthodox and heterodox Taoists. In this case, the heterodox Taoists do not seem to

11. See Werner Eichhorn, "Description of the Rebellion of Sun En and Earlier Taoist Rebellions," *Mitteilungen des Instituts für Orientforschung* 2.2:325–52 (1954) and "Nachträgliche Bemerkungen zum Aufstande des Sun En," ibid. 2.3:463–76 (1954). Miyakawa disagrees with Eichhorn on several points.

have favored bloody sacrifices of uncooked meat, nor does Miyakawa cite any instance in which their temples were destroyed by orthodox Taoists. Rather, the latter—or orthodox Buddhists—seem to have taken over certain temples and evicted the deities who "resided" there.

Taoist orthodoxy reached one of its peaks—of official acceptance, at least—under the Northern Wei ruler T'ai-wu (424–452). For the first time in Chinese history Taoism became the established religion of the land, espoused by the emperor himself.[12] Soon after he took the throne, T'ai-wu grew interested in the revelations of a Taoist recluse named K'ou Ch'ien-chih, and in 425 he bestowed on K'ou the title of "Celestial Master." This title had originally been used by the Three Changs who led the Five-Pecks-of-Rice in western China two centuries earlier. In 440 T'ai-wu himself assumed the reign-name "Perfect Ruler of Great Peace" (T'ai-p'ing Chen-chün 太平眞君), thus appropriating the T'ai-p'ing phraseology that had been used by the other Three Changs, who had led the Yellow Turban rebellion in eastern China. By now, the descendants of the two groups had merged in a common religion, and Taoist priests (tao-shih)[13] led the same kind of parishes in the same kinds of practice throughout much of China, east and west.

To this religion K'ou Ch'ien-chih added a superstructure of elaborate state rites designed to make the Northern Wei capital into the New Zion of Taoism. Naturally this brought him into competition with the Buddhists, who had been favored and supported by the two previous rulers of the dynasty. The emperor's closest adviser was Ts'ui Hao, the man who had originally recommended K'ou Ch'ien-chih to the court and remained his friend and patron. Ts'ui saw in Buddhism an obstacle to his dream of recreating an ideal Confucian society with everyone in his place. Therefore he persuaded the emperor to issue the series of decrees (A.D. 444–446) that brought about the first great persecution of Buddhism in China, when many monks were killed and monasteries destroyed. Some scholars have characterized Ts'ui as a narrow Confucian, but in fact he had many links with Taoism too—including an ancestor who was brother-in-law and successor to the Taoist rebel Sun En!

The intricate details of this story are clearly and elegantly presented by R. B. Mather in his article "K'ou Ch'ien-chih and the Taoist Theocracy

12. Earlier emperors like Wen-ti and Ching-ti had been interested in the teachings of Lao-tzu. In A.D. 166 the Emperor Huan personally made a sacrifice to the god Lao-tzu in the imperial palace: see Anna K. Seidel, *La divinisation de Lao tseu dans le taoïsme des Han* (Paris, 1969), pp. 36–38.

13. There is no satisfactory uniform translation of tao-shih 道士. It can refer to either married priests or celibate monks. The editors have usually left the term romanized.

at the Northern Wei Court 425–451," of which many of the details will be new to Western readers. The article's particular merit is that it utilizes an unusual episode in Chinese court history to flesh out what had been happening to Taoism as a whole from the third through the fifth centuries. Among the people there were communal religious feasts, rites of penitence, and sexual rites. On the part of the Taoist orthodox—the new orthodox—there were the promulgation of codes of conduct and the suppression of heterodox cults and practices (sexual rites as well as wayside shrines). At various levels of society there were utopian longings, sometimes focused on the notion of an ideal society in the West, toward which Lao-tzu had supposedly disappeared a thousand years earlier.

One current of Taoism that has not been mentioned so far is alchemy. The most famous early authority on Chinese alchemy was Ko Hung (fourth century), a part of whose *Pao-p'u-tzu* has now appeared in English translation.[14] Another somewhat later alchemist was T'ao Hung-ching (456–536). He is usually thought of as a great scholarly compiler and codifier of Taoist texts, particularly of the Mao Shan school. The beginnings of the Mao Shan school were described in a paper contributed to the Tateshina conference by Michel Strickmann, "The Mao San Revelations: Taoism and the Aristocracy," which is to be published in the sinological journal *T'oung Pao*. The paper published here, "On the Alchemy of T'ao Hung-ching," is complementary to that article, and the two together open up the whole field of Mao Shan studies, which until recently has almost been terra incognita for the Western reader—almost, but not entirely. G. Bertuccioli, who was unable to attend the conference, has published an account of his visit to Mao Shan in 1947, fully annotated and illustrated both with his own photographs and woodcuts from the *Mao-shan chih* 茅山志 of 1671.[15]

As the centuries passed, Taoism became ever more intertwined with popular practices such as divination, geomancy, and astrology. Until now scholars have emphasized the utilization of astrology in the art of government. It is stated in the classics that the imperial astrologer observed the stars and planets connected with the different fiefs so that "their pros-

14. J. R. Ware, *Alchemy, Medicine, and Religion in the China of +320; the Nei P'ien of Ko Hung (Pao P'u Tzu)* (Cambridge, Mass., 1969). The fullest treatment of Chinese alchemy is in Joseph Needham, *Science and Civilisation in China*, vol. 5, pt. 2 and 3 (Cambridge University Press, 1974, 1976). The bibliography directs the reader to almost everything available on the subject in Western languages, including the article by Strickmann here introduced.

15. See G. Bertuccioli, "Reminiscences of Mao Shan," *East and West* (Rome), n.s. 24.3–4:3–16 (September–December 1974).

perity or misfortune could be ascertained. He made prognostications, according to the twelve years (of the Jupiter cycle), of good and evil in the terrestrial world . . . . In general he concerned himself with the five kinds of phenomena, so as to warn the emperor to come to the aid of the government, and to allow for variations in the ceremonies according to the circumstances."[16] What this passage represents is the *ideal* of astrology in the Han dynasty. Then and later the *practice* was a little different. Its purpose was not "to warn the emperor to come to the aid of the government," but to enable his ministers better to restrain him from folly. That is, they would cite heavenly portents as arguments against imperial actions of which they disapproved.

Yet astrology was important to the common people too. This is demonstrated for the first time by C. L. Hou's article, "The Chinese Belief in Baleful Stars," in which he discusses three such stars or constellations. With regard to each, he first describes the modern beliefs and practices in Taiwan and then traces their history back to the Han dynasty. As a sinologist native to Taiwan (though trained in Paris), Hou is able to offer rich and authentic details of local customs. One of the more striking passages in the present volume is his description of how the Taoist priest addresses the gods of the baleful stars—with scarcely veiled contempt, as if they were silly children rather than great and dangerous divinities (Hou, pp. 198–99). The priest's contemptuous manner is surely meant to show that he is stronger and superior to the demons—otherwise would they not take revenge on him? Here we see, perhaps, one of the ways in which the Taoist priesthood reinforced both its status in the community and the need for its services.

At other points in Hou's article the data presented suggest how exorcism could serve as a premodern form of psychotherapy. Suppose, for example, that a peasant who is worried about his wife's approaching confinement hears the yelp of a dog and recognizes it as a sign of the approach of White Tiger, the demon-star who devours foetuses in the womb (p. 210) and who "lies in wait by the bed and the door . . . behind the stove and in front of the well" (p. 212). Perhaps the peasant then goes to an almanac or a soothsayer and gets confirmation of the danger. All his fears for the safety of his wife and child come to the surface of his mind and

16. Joseph Needham, *Science and Civilisation in China*, 5:190. Needham is here quoting *Chou-li* 周禮 5:86 translated by Edouard Biot, in *Le Tchou-Li ou Rites des Chou* (Paris, 1851), 2:113–16. The editors have changed the tense. Needham has little to say in volume 3 about the political use of astrology. He refers his readers to H. Bielenstein, "An Interpretation of the Portents in the *Ts'ien Han Shu*," *Bulletin of the Museum of Far Eastern Antiquities* 22:127 (1950) and Ho Peng Yoke, *The Astronomical Chapters of the Chin Shu* (Paris, 1966).

coagulate, as it were, around White Tiger. He may feel more afraid than he did before, but after he has performed a rite like "Leave-taking outside" (p. 199), he feels less afraid. Thus his belief (or half-belief) in White Tiger has helped him to exteriorize and cope with an inner fear that he had no other means of coping with. Hou himself suggests this when he speaks of a rite's "efficacy in allaying those anxieties of which the demons are no more than personifications created by the popular imagination" (p. 227).

At the other end of the Taoist spectrum from peasants and soothsayers lay the celibate monks of the Ch'üan-chen sect, whose monasteries began to be set up on a Buddhist model in the thirteenth century. The most important was the White Cloud Monastery (Po-yün Kuan) in Peking. How it operated in the 1940s is described by Y. Yoshioka in his article "Taoist Monastic Life." Yoshioka lived there himself as a lay guest from 1940 to 1946, gaining experience unequaled among those who have written about Taoist monasticism in Western languages.[17] What he gives us is not a theoretical picture based on textual research, but the actual practice as he observed it at this monastery in specific years. After his return to Japan, he read newspaper accounts of the bizarre event he reports at the end of his article: the monks of the White Cloud Monastery burned their abbot alive.

G. Bertuccioli was in Peking at the time and visited the monastery ten days after this happened. He was told that both the abbot and the prior had been killed by the other monks and then cremated in a pyre in the temple courtyard. The civil authorities sentenced the two instigators to life imprisonment, but the rest of the monks involved were allowed to return to the monastery. This was because they could cite a clause in its code of rules stating that if the abbot sold off monastic property without the consent of the monks, he should be burned. In this case the abbot was said to have been selling monastic property to maintain an expensive concubine. Such behavior would have been as shocking to Taoists as to Buddhists, not only to other celibate monks but to their lay supporters.[18]

17. Peter Goullart's *Monastery of the Jade Mountain* (London, 1961) and John Blofeld's *The Secret and the Sublime* (London, 1973) were not intended to be scholarly treatments of Taoist monasticism. The authors neither made nor recorded any systematic observations of the monasteries they stayed in. H. Hackmann's *Die Dreihundert Mönchsgebote des Chinesischen Taoismus* (Amsterdam, 1931) includes detailed materials but does not reflect much if any personal observation.

18. Lay devotees gave financial support to monks partly in order to share in the merit the latter accumulated through their abstinence. Therefore monastic licentiousness was a

Because of the importance of the White Cloud Monastery, we offer below some further information about its history in recent years.

J. B. Pratt recorded in the notebook of his travels through China in 1924 that the White Cloud Monastery then had three hundred monks. Many of them did not stay there all the time but came and went, and they included not only celibate monks but married priests of the sect of the Celestial Master. Pratt was also told that the monastery was headquarters for training monks of the Lung-men sect and held examinations on the basis of which it appointed officers to serve at other monasteries of the sect in many parts of China.[19] (Yoshioka states that it had no administrative authority over the other monasteries.)

Good photographs of the White Cloud Monastery appeared in a book published soon after Pratt wrote his notebook.[20] They show that it must have been prosperous and well-managed, for no grass can be seen growing between the paving stones or on the roof. The roof tiles are all in place, and everything looks neat as a pin. In those days a temple fair was held there annually. On the 19th of the first lunar month, Immortals and perfected men (*chen-jen*) were supposed to be among the crowds who thronged the monastery. During the whole period from the 1st through the 19th, one of the monks sat in an artificial cave under a bridge over a dry pond inside the entrance (7 and 8 on the key to Yoshioka's floor plan, p. 250). Visitors would try to hit the monk with coins they tossed from the bridge to see if he was really in trance—and as a pious contribution to his income.[21]

Little was published about the White Cloud Monastery in the first years after 1949, but when the Chinese Taoist Association was set up in 1957, its headquarters were installed there and its president, Yüeh Ch'ung-tai 岳崇岱 was the abbot. In 1934 Yüeh had been guest prefect of the T'ai-ch'ing Kung in Shen-yang, the only other Taoist monastery of which a full systematic account has been written by an outsider who lived there for a long period.[22] This outsider was a Japanese, and in 1957 he went back to China to tour

betrayal of trust. Similar cases of misconduct and the sale of property by *Buddhist* abbots were reported during the Republican period. For example, at the Ching-an Ssu 靜安寺 in Shanghai, well known to foreigners as the "Bubbling Well Monastery," the abbot was impeached for selling monastic property to maintain his mistresses; the monks complained about it to a member of the Shanghai Municipal Council (who is the source of this information). Parallels are reported from other cities and even Buddhist sacred mountains. Yet it is also true that some laymen took a certain pleasure in attributing sensuality and greed to monks and nuns, perhaps in order to relieve their own feelings of lesser virtue; and China is a land where rumors flourish.

19. J. B. Pratt's notebooks are in the Williams College Library, Williamstown, Massachusetts.

20. In the section by John C. Ferguson in *The Mythology of All the Races*, ed. John Arnott MacCulloch and George Focte Moore (Boston, 1928), vol. 8, facing pp. 22 and 50.

21. H. H. Welch heard this from a resident of Peking who often went to the fair, but almost the same information is given in L. C. Arlington and William Lewisohn, *In Search of Old Peking* (Peking, 1935), p. 247, and Juliet Bredon, *Peking* (Shanghai, 1931), pp. 263 ff.

22. See Igarashi Kenryū 五十嵐賢隆 *Taiseikyū shi* 太清宮志 (Annuals of the T'ai-ch'ing Kung; Feng-t'ien [Shen-yang], 1938). The Reverend Igarashi, a Shingon priest, lived in the T'ai-ch'ing Kung for two years, starting in 1933, and was ordained there as a tao-shih in 1935 or 1936. Like Yoshioka at the White Cloud Monastery, he stayed in a superior guest

the country as a member of a Buddhist delegation. While in Peking he visited the White Cloud Monastery, and whom should he meet but his old friend and teacher from Shen-yang, Yüeh Ch'ung-tai! He learned from him that a government subsidy of 550,000 JMP (about US $220,000) had been provided for the renovation of the buildings, which was two-thirds completed. (He had to enter by a side door because of the scaffolding still around the main gate.) On the other hand, the monastery's greatest treasure, the only surviving copy of the Ming edition of the Taoist Canon (see below, p. 247), had been moved to the Peking National Library. As to concrete details about the operation of the monastery, he was told little.[23]

A European who visited White Cloud a few months later in the spring of 1958 wrote that "everything was spotless, ready for display. . . . A few old monks moved about amid this well-swept disenchantment like vigilant museum custodians."[24]

In 1965, according to *Nagel's Guide*, there were still over twenty *tao-shih* in residence, wearing their hair in the traditional topknot. The temple fair was held on New Year's Day and several thousand people came to it. Since the Tung-yüeh Miao (the famous Temple of the Eastern Peak)[25] had been converted into a secondary school, this was the only Taoist temple left in use in Peking.[26]

---

room 上客堂 and took his meals with the abbot and guest-prefect, separately from the main body of monks.

23. He was told that in Peking there were 150–60 tao-shih and 65 Taoist temples, but not how many tao-shih were residing in the White Cloud Monastery itself. See Igarashi Kenryū, "Hō Chū Nihon Bukkyō shinzen shi-dan hōkokusho" 訪中日本佛教親善使動報告書 (Report of a visit to China by the Japanese Buddhist Friendship Delegation), *Nitchū Bukkyō* 日中佛教 (Buddhism in Japan and China) 1.3:20–21 (May 20, 1958). Igarashi visited the White Cloud Monastery on December 4, 1957, when the anti-rightist campaign had made the atmosphere much tenser than it had been when the Chinese Taoist Association was set up the preceding April. The secretary of the association was listed as Li Yün-hang 李運航 of Mao Shan.

24. Martin Hürlimann, *Traveller in the Orient* (London, 1960), p. 202. On p. 188 there is a clear photograph of the altar and images. *Pei-ching tsai chien-she chung* 北京在建設中 (Peking under construction; Peking, 1958, unpaginated) reproduced a photograph captioned in English the "Paiyunkuan Taoist Temple under repair." It shows only the entrance *p'ai-lou*. Despite its renovation at government expense, the White Cloud Monastery was not listed among the 77 ancient buildings placed under central government protection by the regulations promulgated March 4, 1961. Two other Taoist edifices were: the Yung-le Kung 永樂宮 in Shansi (with its famous murals) and the Chin-tien 金殿 at Wu-tang Shan, Hupeh, where cadres had destroyed so many Taoist art treasures in 1955–56.

25. On this temple, noted for its vivid depictions in statuary of the tortures of hell, see Anne Swann Goodrich, *The Peking Temple of the EasternPeak* (Nagoya, 1964).

26. See *Nagel's Encyclopedia—Guide: China* (Geneva, 1968), pp. 569–71. The description given here of the monastery is worth comparing with Yoshioka's. On pp. 231–32 he states that during land reform its 27,000 *mou* of farmland outside the city were confiscated and it received 51 *mou* (about 8 acres) in return. Income from performing ceremonies and donations during festivals were cut off because ceremonies and festivals had ceased to be held after Liberation. Because of the drop in income, the number of monks dropped from 250 to 25. Yoshioka cites a Communist source for this information: the Hong Kong *Ta-kung pao* of October 12, 1950.

It may be true that, as *Nagel's Guide* states, thousands of people came to the White Cloud fair on New Year's Day, 1965 (presumably meaning January 1). On lunar New Year's in 1961 (February 15), no one at all came to the monastery, according to a reliable observer,

The religious use of the White Cloud Monastery may not have ended until the Cultural Revolution in 1966, when all urban monasteries in China were closed and their monks sent home. A Westerner who visited it in November 1971 found its name still above the gate, but there was a soldier in a guardhouse just outside who refused him admission. Even Chinese could enter only if they had a pass. No Taoist monks were in evidence. The same Western visitor had been to Kiangsi and seen an exposition in Nanchang of the decorative arts of the province—an exhibit not open to the general public. On display was porcelain decorated with traditional themes, including statues of the Buddha, Kuan-yin, and Lao-tzu. Such, perhaps, will be the terminal manifestation of religious Taoism in China.

The last two articles in this volume are bibliographical. First comes "The Formation of the Taoist Canon" by N. Ōfuchi. This is not intended to be a complete history of the canon in all its editions, but rather a compact description of how it took the form it has today. Its complete history may be found in two books, one in Chinese, one in Japanese.[27] Many Westerners interested in Taoism have been hesitant about using the canon because it appears to be such a hodgepodge—a small wall-full of books in no apparent order and seeming to lack dates and authors. For finding one's way through it, Ōfuchi provides valuable orientation; he explains the relationship between the Taoist Canon and the Buddhist; and he helps to answer the question: when did the Taoists first become aware that they were Taoists?

The concluding article, "Taoist Studies in Japan" by T. Sakai and T. Noguchi, originated in a request that certain conference participants from Europe, America, and Asia report on the "state of the art" in their respective areas. Sakai did much more. He wrote a bibliographical history of the development of Taoist studies in Japan over the past century.[28] It was expanded by his colleague, T. Noguchi, so that it can be utilized as a select, annotated bibliography of works on Taoism in Japanese. It also testifies to the scope and depth of Taoist studies in Japan and to the strength of the tradition that Japanese participants brought to the conference table at Tateshina. Sakai distributed at the conference a much longer classified bibliography (94 pages) of books and articles on Taoism

---

who entered the deserted premises that day and took photographs. This observer was told by an old Peking resident that the festival at the White Cloud Monastery on the 19th of the first lunar month had not been held since the Japanese took Peking.

27. Ch'en Kuo-fu, *Tao-tsang yüan-liu k'ao* (see n. 3), and Y. Yoshioka, *Dōkyō kyōten shiron* 道教經典史論 (On the history of Taoist scriptures; Tokyo, 1955).

28. The period covered by his article is longer than that covered by Goto Kimpei 後藤均平, "Studies on Chinese Religion in Post-war Japan," in *Monumenta Serica* 15.2:466–75 (1956). The latter, however, provides very useful information (in English) about the research published and the opinions held on particular problems.

in Japanese, which was published late in 1972.[29] This may be regarded as complementary to the bibliography of Western literature on Taoism published by M. Soymié and F. Litsch.[30]

At the final session of the Tateshina conference useful information was given on the state of Taoist studies in France. K. M. Schipper mentioned plans at the Centre National de la Recherche Scientifique to publish Taoist manuscripts from Tun-huang and the publication of a series of reference works on Taoism by the Ecole française d'Extrême-Orient. Already out in this series were a concordance to titles in the Taoist Canon, an annotated liturgical text (on the *fen-teng* 分燈 ritual), and a concordance to the *Huang-t'ing ching* 黃庭經.[31] Schipper referred to a glossary of Taoist terms that had long been in preparation by Bernard Saby, Isabelle Robinet, and others under the direction of M. Kaltenmark.

R. A. Stein described the photographs of religious phenomena that had been collected in the preceding ten years at the Centre de Documentation d'Histoire des Religions (19, avenue d'Iéna, Paris 16). The collection already exceeded 10,000 photographs of temples, images, festivals, rites, and so on, largely in China, Japan, Vietnam, and Tibet. All are identified, annotated, and entered in an index. In order to assure copyright protection to past and future donors, the photographs are available for study only, not for publication.

Schipper explained that the center also served as repository for most of the tapes and photographs he had made in Taiwan. His manuscripts, paintings, altar trappings, and other paraphernalia connected with Taoism were (at that time) stored in Holland. He told the conference that his manuscripts, like his photographs, would be made available (on microfilm) to any serious student of Taoism who needed them for research. Schipper added that the Musée Guimet had a collection of 150 small statues of deities from Taiwan, all of them identified. He ended his report by calling for closer collaboration and the exchange of students among specialists in Taoist studies in different countries.

---

29. *Dōkyō Kenkyū bunken mokuroku (Nihon)* 道教研究文獻目錄 (日本) (A bibliography of studies of Taoism in Japan; Tokyo, 1972).

30. This is the fullest classified bibliography of Western language publications on Taoism. It appeared in *Dōkyō Kenkyū* 道教研究 (Taoist studies; Tokyo) 3:247–317 (1968) and 4:225–89 (1971).

31. Compare the publication plans discussed by Schipper in 1968 at the Bellagio conference, *History of Religions* 9.2–3:132. Numerous studies on Taoism have been completed in France since 1972. See list of French publications following this introduction.

Help in preparing this volume of papers has come from many persons, some of whom should be mentioned by name. Dr. Barbara Kandel made the initial translation into English of Kaltenmark's article. Farzeen Hussein was the *rapporteur* who recorded the Kaltenmark discussion. Michel Strickmann translated the articles by Hou and Ōfuchi, Martin C. Collcutt the Yoshioka chapter. Cynthia K. McLean typed or retyped five sections of the manuscripts and made useful editorial suggestions. Suggestions were also gratefully accepted from Timothy E. Connor. Thanks are due, above all, to the authors, who have patiently endured the editors' requests for emendations, additions, and fuller citations. It is as difficult, perhaps, for a senior Japanese scholar to write about his findings for the benefit of an American college student as it is for a French scholar to write between the two modes to which he is accustomed (the mode of rigorous monographs to be read by other specialists and the mode of popularization to be read by the general public). This is why explanatory material such as dates has occasionally been supplied in brackets. The editors have preferred not to clutter the text with cross-references, just as they have preferred not to impose rigorous consistency on the authors. For example, Mather translates *chen jen* 眞人 as "Realized Man" whereas Strickmann renders it "Perfected Man."

It is our hope that, as Taoist studies progress and more articles like these appear, it will become easier to see what Taoism was and what it meant in Chinese history and life.

H.W.
A. S.

September 1, 1976

French publications on Taoism from 1972 to 1977

Bergeron, Ina. "La mystique taoïste." *Encyclopédie des mystiques orientales.* Paris: Laffont, 1975.
——. *Wang Pi, philosophe du non-avoir.* To be published in the series Variétés Sinologiques, nouvelles éditions, Institut Ricci. Taipei, 1977.
Despeux, Cathérine. *T'ai-ki k'iuan, technique de longue vie, technique de combat.* Mémoires de l'Institut des Hautes Etudes Chinoises, vol. 3. Paris, 1976.
Hou, Ching-lang. *Monnaies d'offrande et la notion de trésorerie dans la religion*

chinoise. Mémoires de l'Institut des Hautes Etudes Chinoises, vol. 1. Paris, 1975.

Kaltenmark, M. "Miroirs magiques." *Mélanges de sinologie offerts à Monsieur Paul Demiéville*, vol. 2. Bibliothèque de l'Institut des Hautes Etudes Chinoises, vol. 20, pp. 151–66. Paris, 1974.

Larre, Claude. "La bannière funéraire de Tch'ang-cha." *Actes du colloque international de sinologie de Chantilly*. Cathasia: Belles-Lettres, 1976.

————. *Les aspects subtils et légers; traduction, analyse et commentaire de la partie doctrinale du chapitre 7 de Houai-nan tseu.* To be published in the series Variétés Sinologiques, nouvelles éditions, Institut Ricci. Taipei, 1977.

Robinet, Isabelle. *Les commentaires du Tao tö king jusqu'au VIIe siècle.* Mémoires de l'Institut des Hautes Etudes Chinoises, vol. 5. Paris, 1977.

————. "Les randonnées extatiques des taoïstes dans les astres." To be published in *Monumenta Serica* 32 (1978).

Schipper, K. M. *Concordance du Houang-t'ing king.* Publication de l'Ecole française d'Extrême-Orient, vol. 104. Paris, 1975.

————. *Concordance du Tao-tsang.* Publication de l'Ecole française d'Extrême-Orient, vol. 102. Paris, 1975.

————. *Le Fen-teng, rituel taoïste.* Publications de l'Ecole française d'Extrême-Orient, vol. 103. Paris, 1975.

————. "Taoisme." *Encyclopaedia Universalis*, vol. 15, pp. 738–44. Paris, 1973.

The professors of the Ecole Pratique des Hautes Etudes and the Collège de France publish annual reports on their research seminars in their institutes' "annuaires." For the work in progress of Michel Soymié, cf. *Annuaire de l'Ecole Pratique des Hautes Etudes, IVe section, Sciences hist. et philol.*, under "Histoire et philologie de la Chine médiévale et moderne." For summaries of the seminars given by M. Kaltenmark and K. M. Schipper, cf. *Annuaire de l'EPHE, V^e section, Sciences religieuses*, under "Religions de la Chine." For R. A. Stein's lectures, cf. *Annuaire du Collège de France*, under "Etude du monde chinois: institutions et concepts."

1 The Ideology of the T'ai-p'ing ching

Max Kaltenmark

AS IS THE CASE with so many ancient Chinese books, the question of the authenticity of the *T'ai-p'ing ching* (*TPC*) is controversial and difficult to resolve. It is well known that the book appears in the *Tao-tsang* (*TT*) in two forms: the *TPC* that consisted originally of 170 chapters, of which there remain the 57 chapters that fill *TT* fascicles 748–55; and, secondly, the summarized text entitled *TPC ch'ao* 鈔 of *TT* 746–47, whose ten chapters are headed respectively by the ten stems (*chia* 甲, *i* 乙, *ping* 丙, *ting* 丁 etc.). The discovery of a manuscript from Tun-huang (S. 4226) which contains the complete table of contents of the *TPC* in 170 chapters proves that the text now preserved in the *TT* is identical with that which circulated at the end of the sixth century. As for the *TPC ch'ao*, it is a condensation of the same text made by Lü-ch'iu Fang-yüan 閭丘方遠, who lived at the end of the T'ang.

It is not my intention to repeat here the details of the problems which are posed by the history of the text and which have been superlatively treated by Fukui, Ōfuchi, and Yoshioka.[1] We are obliged to the last-mentioned scholar for the publication of Tun-huang S. 4226 and for the thorough study with which it is accompanied. The question which, of course, one would like most of all to be able to answer is whether or not our text in the *TT* remains faithful to the original *TPC*—that is, to either of the two lost writings which bore that title during the Han. An earlier *TPC* entitled *T'ien-kuan li pao-yüan t'ai-p'ing ching* 天官歷包元太平經 in twelve chapters was presented to Emperor Ch'eng 成帝 (32–7 B.C.) by a certain Kan Chung-k'o 甘忠可 from Ch'i 齊. It was written in

---

1. Fukui Kōjun 福井康順, *Dōkyō no kisoteki kenkyū* 道教の基礎的研究 (Tokyo, 1958), pp. 214–55; Ōfuchi Ninji 大淵忍爾, "Taiheikyō no shisō ni tsuite" 太平經の思想について, *Tōyōgakuhō* 東洋學報 28.4:145–68 (1941); Yoshioka Yoshitoyo 吉岡義豊, *Dōkyō to Bukkyō* II 道教と佛教 (Tokyo, 1970), pp. 9–161.

that book that the House of Han stood at the end of one historical-cosmological cycle, that its mandate was on the point of being revived, and that Heaven had here below delegated the *chen-jen* 眞人 named Ch'ih-ching tzu 赤精子 to reveal the Tao [of *t'ai-p'ing*]. Later, under the Emperor Shun 順帝 (A.D. 126–145) another book entitled *T'ai-p'ing ch'ing-ling shu* 太平清領書 was presented to the throne by Kung Ch'ung 宮崇 from Lang-ya 瑯邪, who said he had got it from his master Yü Chi 于吉 (or Kan Chi 干吉). It was this book that is said to have been later utilized by Chang Chüeh 張角, the leader of the Yellow Turbans and of the T'ai-p'ing Tao. It was based, according to what Hsiang Chieh 襄楷 said in his famous memorial of A.D. 166, on respect for Heaven and Earth and on conformity with the Five Elements. It contained recipes to assure the prosperity of the state and numerous descendants.[2] Finally, there was a *T'ai-p'ing tung-chi ching* 太平洞極經 revealed to the Celestial Master by T'ai-shang Lao-chün 太上老君.

Does our text of the *TPC* originate from the sect of the Five Pecks of Rice? At first glance it does show similarities with the sect, at least in those parts which portray a Celestial Master (T'ien-shih 天師) and a group of six disciples called *chen-jen*. The parts where a "Lord of Heaven" (T'ien-chün 天君) appears instead of the Celestial Master do not diverge from the others as to doctrine, although they are written in a different style. If, therefore, our text probably originates from the Celestial Masters, there arises the question of its connection with the *TP ch'ing-ling shu*, with a *Tung-chi ching*, and with the *Cheng-i meng-wei ching* 正一盟威經, which was also revealed to Chang Tao-ling 張道陵. But the problem is insoluble because, although a *Tung-chi ching* is mentioned in the *TPC* (as we shall see), no fragments of it seem to be preserved there; and, as regards the *Cheng-i meng-wei ching*, it no longer exists except for short citations in some works.[3]

Yet we shall find indications which make it possible to believe that one

---

2. The title seems to refer to one detail of the physical appearance of the book. *Ch'ing-ling* 清領 is probably the equivalent of *ch'ing-shou* 青首, which can be found in the *TPC*: "the best of my books—i.e., those that the Celestial Master reveals—always have to have the head green and the title red" 青首丹目 (*TPC*, p. 647: here and below, *TPC* and *TPC ch'ao* chapter numbers and pagination refer to the reconstituted text and chapter numbering established by Wang Ming 王明, who has collated all text fragments of the various *TPC* in his text edition and study: *T'ai-p'ing ching ho-chiao* 太平經合校 [Peking, 1960]; his edition lacks only the Tun-huang ms [S. 4226] of the table of contents of the *TPC* in 170 chapters). See also the text of the biography of Hsiang Chieh 襄楷 in the *Hou Han-shu* 後漢書, cited in *TPC ho-chiao*, p. 747. The meaning of *shou* 首 is uncertain.

3. For instance, in *Tao-chiao i-shu* 道教義樞 (*TT* 762–63); *Yao-hsiu k'o-i chieh-lü ch'ao* 要修科儀戒律鈔 (*TT* 204–07); *Yün-chi ch'i-ch'ien* 雲笈七籤 (*TT* 677–702).

part of our text does go back to the Han and even to a period prior to the Five Pecks of Rice or the T'ai-p'ing Tao of Chang Chüeh. In this part the Celestial Master is a really celestial being and not the leader of a sect. Most important of all is the fact that the element symbolizing the prince is Fire and that his color is Red. This stands in contrast to the Yellow that was the color whose advent was announced by the Yellow Turbans and probably also by the leaders of the Five Pecks of Rice (we should not forget that the Wei chose Yellow to symbolize their dynasty). This shows how, besides the similarities between the system of the *TPC* and the organization of the Five Pecks of Rice, one notices differences that cannot be explained if our text had first been written by the historical Celestial Masters of the Five Pecks of Rice or if it had been produced at a later date.

The Ideal of T'ai-p'ing

As the titles themselves suggest, the various *TPC* of the Han claimed to reveal the proper methods for establishing an era of Great Peace or Great Equality (both ideas are implied by the word "*p'ing*"). This is an idea which probably goes back to the period of the Warring States, because "*t'ai-p'ing*" or "*ta-p'ing*" 大平 or simply "*p'ing*" appear in many pre-Han texts. The *Ta-hsüeh* 大學 5 states that once his kingdom is well governed, the prince shall see the whole world in peace 國治而后天下平. In *Li-chi* 禮記 25 (*Chung-ni yen-chü* 仲尼燕居), we read that when the sage understands the nature of rites and music and when he reigns facing south, then the world knows the Great Peace 天下太平. *Chuang-tzu* 13 calls a government conforming to the order of nature "*t'ai-p'ing*." *Hsün-tzu* 4 says that a society is perfectly balanced when each individual has the place which suits him and fulfills his task according to his capacities— an idea frequently expressed in the *TPC*. According to *Lü-shih ch'un-ch'iu* 1 (*Kuei-kung* 貴公) when the communal spirit reigns, the world is in peace 公則天下平. According to ibid., 5 (*Ta-yüeh* 大樂), thanks to the music of the ancient kings, the world knew *t'ai-p'ing* and all creatures were at peace 天下太平萬物安寧.[4]

During the Han the notion becomes very common. Thus we read in *Huai-nan tzu* 淮南子 2 that he who establishes *t'ai-p'ing* deserves to remain in the Great Hall (meaning in the Ming-t'ang 明堂, according to the

4. W. Eichhorn has collected some ancient texts on the idea of T'ai-p'ing in his article "T'ai-p'ing und T'ai-p'ing Religion," *Mitteilungen des Instituts für Orientforschung* 5.1:113–40 (1957). Cf. R. A. Stein on the utopias of T'ai-p'ing and Ta Ch'in 大秦, in "Remarques sur les mouvements du taoïsme politico-religieux au IIe siècle ap. J.-C.," *T'oung Pao* 50.1–3:8–21 (1963).

commentary)—in other words to reign as the Son of Heaven;[5] and in ibid., 20, that the ancient generations cultivated the root [the essential] whereas the recent ones attend to the branches [items of secondary importance], which is the reason why *t'ai-p'ing* cannot arise. *Ch'un-ch'iu fan-lu* 春秋繁露 17 states that when among the people everyone obtains the place that suits him, the prince establishes *t'ai-p'ing* through non-action (*wu-wei* 無爲). According to *Yen-t'ieh lun* 鹽鐵論 36, in the times of Chou-kung 周公, when the world had *t'ai-p'ing*, there were no premature deaths, no bad harvests, the climate was so friendly that the rain did not break the clods of earth and the wind did not whistle in the branches 雨不破塊風不鳴條.[6] There are several relevant passages in the *Lun-heng* 論衡, particularly in 19, with regard to the government of Emperor Kuang-wu 光武: at that time there was *t'ai-p'ing*, harmony of the Breaths (*ho-ch'i* 和氣), and multiplication of auspicious prodigies. In general the idea prevailed that *t'ai-p'ing* had been realized by the ancient sages Yao, Shun, Chou-kung and Confucius. In addition, Wang Ch'ung 王充 upholds the thesis that the Han emperors, particularly Wen and Kuang-wu, established *t'ai-p'ing*. According to the *Po-hu t'ung* 白虎通, the Feng and Shan 封禪 sacrifices were aimed at announcing *t'ai-p'ing* to Heaven and Earth. In the view of Confucian authors, it was essentially owing to rites and music that *t'ai-p'ing* could be established.

For the authors of the *TPC*, who divided history into "three antiquities" (*san-ku* 三古),[7] only the "high antiquity" (*shang-ku* 上古) knew *t'ai-p'ing*, but not the following ages (*chung-ku* 中古 and *hsia-ku* 下古), during which morals became more and more depraved. "In [high] antiquity the sages governed while nourishing themselves on breath. They remained in the depths of a dark abode in order to think of the Tao and to reflect on the signs announcing success and failure. They did not dare to deviate however slightly from the celestial norm. They remained in a pure and quiet place, and, as soon as they were in accord with the will of Heaven, their government established Peace and was equal to that of Heaven and Earth."[8]

5. In the *TPC* the Ming-t'ang is also the residence of the celestial judges to whom the interior spirits of each individual denounce his misdeeds (see, for example, 112:569; 114:624). Cf. Jao Tsung-i 饒宗頤, *Lao-tzu Hsiang-erh chu chiao-chien* 老子想爾注校牋 (Hongkong, 1956), p. 80.

6. The expression originated from Tung Chung-shu 董仲舒, according to a citation of the *Hou-ch'ing lu* 侯鯖錄 translated by Eichhorn, "T'ai-p'ing und T'ai-p'ing Religion," p. 120.

7. The notion of "three antiquities" was current in the Han but with different explanations. In the *TPC ku* 古 seems to designate historical times, and *hsia ku* 下古 seems to include the period in which the authors are writing.

8. 古者聖賢飲食氣而治，深居幽室思道，念得失之象；不敢離天法銖分之間也，居清靜處，已得其意，

"High antiquity" was in fact the time of the "princes of T'ai-p'ing" 太平之君, who knew how to bring about a "Breath of T'ai-p'ing" 太平之氣. When this "Breath" reigned, not a single being suffered and everyone was in his place. If one single being suffered, there was inequality and injustice 不平 (93:398). The "princes of T'ai-p'ing" were content with satisfying three essential needs of their subjects, that is, food, the union of the sexes, and clothing (36:42 ff.). They reigned by confining themselves in an attitude of *wu-wei*. In the following generations the government became increasingly complicated and intervened more and more (36:46). It ended by reaching the extreme of decadence (*hsia-chi* 下極, 47:144) with a proliferation of fickle and harmful doctrines. When this point is reached, one has to return to the Tao in order to rediscover *t'ai-p'ing*, and for that it is necessary to turn one's thoughts to the essential (*pen-ken* 本根). That expression refers to the origin of the *ch'i* 氣之元, or the Primordial Breath (*yüan-ch'i* 元氣). This original element of man is in his own interior parts, and for rediscovering it the TPC recommends an exercise of spiritual concentration which consists in "retaining the One" (*shou-i* 守一) or "retaining the light of the One" (*shou-i-ming* 明). The question is how to bring back to the interior of oneself the spirits which have become externalized, and thus to obtain an enlightenment (pp. 12 and 15 ff., *TPC ch'ao, i* 乙).

Although the TPC, as we shall see, deals extensively with morals and politics, it is still thoroughly Taoist in the importance it accords to spiritual exercises and the other methods of long life. In it we read, just as in the *Hsün-tzu* and in the *Ch'un-ch'iu fan-lu*, that in order to have *t'ai-p'ing* each creature should be in his place and the rulers should keep in accord with the will of Heaven (*t'ien-hsin* 天心). Yet it is no longer by means of the rites that this is possible. The only Confucian virtues adopted by the authors of the TPC are filial piety and *jen* 仁, and they are, moreover, understood in a very peculiar fashion. Music is accepted providing it is tuned so as to influence favorably the cosmic rhythms and the spirits of the internal organs (50:183–84). Yet the originality of the TPC rests above

---

其治立平與天地相似哉 (36:48). The *p'ing* 平 of *t'ai-p'ing* is explained as alluding to the equity of government 其治太平均 and to the horizontality, the exact equilibrium, of earth (48:148; and p. 718). In the *Erh-ya* 爾雅, *t'ai-p'ing* is defined as the place out of which the sun rises in the far east. That idea is taken up again in the *Cheng-i fa-wen T'ien-shih chiao-chieh-k'o ching* 正一法文天師教戒科經 13a (*TT* 563): the revelation of a 太平之道 to Kan 干 [= Yü 于] Chi 吉 took place in Lang-ya; it is therefore in the east that the Tao of T'ai-p'ing has begun its work of rescuing the people immersed in distress . . . 於瑯琊以授干吉太平之道起於東方, 東方始欲濟民於塗炭. T'ai-p'ing has also the sense of a good harvest: more precisely, a year with three harvests is 泰平 (*Han-shu pu-chu* 漢書補注 24A:7a [1900 ed.]); the TPC *ch'ao, keng* 庚, p. 638 contrasts the years of T'ai-p'ing, when all the plants grow well, to the inauspicious years 凶年之歲, when the harvests are bad.

all on the fact that it does not present *t'ai-p'ing* solely as a state of the more or less distant past, but as a state that will come about in the near future, thanks to the revelation brought forth by the Celestial Master.

The Revelation and the Texts

The *TPC* is in fact a religious book which teaches a doctrine of salvation. Evil has accumulated for innumerable generations through the inheritance of sins (*ch'eng-fu* 承負).[9] The Celestial Master presents himself as a "divine man" (*shen-jen* 神人) sent by Heaven to save mankind by means of a celestial scripture (*t'ien-shu* 天書), which teaches how one can return to a method of ideal government and assist the imminent arrival of the "Breath of T'ai-p'ing." The Celestial Master, whose advent is temporary (that he will definitely leave again is stated at the beginning of 46:126), delivers to the *chen-jen* texts which are "celestial words" or "celestial and terrestrial words" 天談, 天談地語 The *chen-jen* are requested to transmit the texts to a prince of high virtue 上德之君. Heaven and Earth do, in fact, not speak directly to men, and therefore they periodically arrange for the birth of a Saint 聖人 or a Master 聖師 to transmit the proper doctrine (p. 651). The disciples (the *chen-jen*) who interrogate the Master do this likewise under the inspiration of Heaven (102:461).

If the *TPC* were simply one or several texts with which Heaven inspired the Celestial Master, the question of its revelation would be simple. But matters are complicated by the fact that there have been manifold revelations and that mankind has had good and bad texts. The authors of the *TPC* lavishly denounce the "perverse texts" (*hsieh-wen* 邪文) which obviously also presented themselves as revelations.[10] Among the texts that the present *TPC* considers a true revelation there are the songs of children inspired from above, there are *shen-shu* 神書, which Heaven sends to rescue the world from its faults (50:174); there are "Celestial Tesserae" (*t'ien-ch'üan* 天券 or *ch'üan-wen* 券文), which seem to be talismanic texts of the same kind as the *Ho-t'u* 河圖 and *Lo-shu* 洛書; there are

---

9. In spite of its importance in the *TPC*, I shall not dwell here on this theory, which has already been explained by several authors. It is treated in *TPC ch'ao, i* 乙 pp. 22 ff.; 37:57 ff.; 39:70. There has been a tendency to see a Buddhist influence here, even though the idea of *ch'eng-fu* is really quite different from that of karma. Moreover *ch'eng-fu* not only involves the inheritance of good or evil by successive generations but also all those cases where the consequences of an act or an event have repercussions on beings other than those who caused them.

10. This doubtless refers to religious texts of other sects, Taoist or not, with Buddhist texts perhaps among them. On the other hand, the Confucian classics are rejected solely on the grounds that they are superficial and do not contain recipes for long life (65:230).

imprecatory formulas (*shen-chou* 神祝) also sent by Heaven. The *chou* 祝 are the "original texts" (*pen-wen* 本文) of the deities, which are useful for curing diseases; collected in one volume, they are named *chou-ch'an shu* 祝讖書 (50:181). There are characters engraved by Heaven 天刻之文字 named *tan-ming yao* 丹明耀, thanks to which one can eliminate perversities 禦邪 (50:172). Under these circumstances what is the exact status of the book that the Celestial Master brought to the *chen-jen*, so that they might deliver it to a virtuous prince? I admit that I have not yet been able to solve that question. Yet its status is partly explained by the term *tung-chi*.

The Celestial Master's book itself is often called a *Tung-chi* 洞極 *ching*, and its doctrine is called "the correct Tao of the (celestial) *tung-chi*" (天之) 洞極正道 (91:361) or 皇天洞極政事 (91:354 and 348), or again 大洞極 天之政事 (41:87). What we are dealing with here is actually not so much a title, properly speaking, as a qualifying term. "*Tung-chi*" figures also in other expressions. Thus the entirety of walking, living beings is said to belong to the world of *tung-chi*, above and below 上下洞極萬物蚑行之屬 (73–85:303). The "Breath of T'ai-p'ing" that is on the point of arriving is called 洞極上平之氣 (92:378). One passage, where it is said that "the *Book of Tung-chi* is called *T'ai-p'ing* [*ching*]" 洞極之經名曰太平, suggests that the true title is *T'ai-p'ing ching* and not *Tung-chi ching* (112:576). It also has to be noted that the Celestial Master is sometimes called 洞極之師 (118:668).[11] In an explanation of the rather strange expression 大洞極天之 政事, it is specified that *tung* 洞 signifies that the good and the bad (*sic*) in Tao 道 and in Te 德 are in communication and union 洞治 with the Yin and the Yang of Heaven and Earth in such a way that there is response throughout the universe and each being obtains his proper place.

Whether the term *tung-chi* is applied to the doctrine or to the book of the Celestial Master, it has a well-defined sense. Since high antiquity numerous texts have been written by the sages of the past, but because the latter had only partial knowledge, Heaven revealed to each only what he was capable of understanding. That is the reason for the differences that can be found in the books of diverse periods. The sages were not sufficiently gifted to understand the perfect and complete truth which is called *tung-chi chih i* 洞極之意. That is why Heaven sent the Celestial Master to "collect and examine the celestial, terrestrial, and human texts and those of the gods in order to extract the best from them and make a *tung-chi chih ching*" 洞極之經.[12]

11. Cf. the expression 上下六方洞極 for indicating the immensity of the world (93:397).
12. 其爲道迺拘校 . . . 天文地文人文神文, 皆撰簡得其善者以爲洞極之經 (41:87).

He not only gathered sacred texts, including those of the *Ho-t'u* and *Lo-shu* type, but also the utterances of the people 凡民—those of the slaves 奴婢 and those of the barbarians far away 夷狄. As these latter texts might be very far away, he installed "Houses of T'ai-p'ing" 太平之宅 in the local districts and on the roads, so that the inhabitants of the more remote regions would place their texts and their formulas there (91:348). It is not quite clear what the procedure is conceived to be in case of the collection organized by the Celestial Master, nor is it any clearer in the case of the analogous collection which the disciples are requested to make for their part (91:348 ff.). But the prince has to do the same thing, and for him the *TPC* gives more details, which I shall explain further on.

First I must draw attention to another "title" of the book of the Celestial Master, namely, the *San-tao hsing-shu* 三道行書 or *San-tao wen-shu* 文書 or again *San-tao hsing wen-shu*. These "titles" are actually the same kind of qualifying terms as *tung-chi ching*. On the other hand, in one passage in 118:672 the title *San-tao hsing-shu* designates a register kept by the celestial spirits on those people who misbehave (in this case those who devote themselves to hunting and who kill).[13] It is said besides that similar registers are kept by the terrestrial spirits and by human beings (118:672). The idea is to record transgressions and make up a sort of moral code. *San-tao* 三道 refers to Heaven, Earth, and mankind; these three ways must communicate among themselves and with the whole universe 三道通行八方. The Breaths of Yin and of Yang and the mixture of the two (*chung-ho* 中和) must reciprocally communicate (*hsiang-t'ung* 相通).

It is indeed one of the basic ideas of the *TPC* to assert that for establishing an era of *t'ai-p'ing* it is necessary to have harmonious communication between different domains grouped in threes: the great Yin, the great Yang, and the *chung-ho* or Central Harmony 太陰太陽中和; Heaven, Earth, and man 天地人; Sun, Moon, and Stars 日月星; Mountains, Rivers, and Plains 山川平土; Father, Mother, and Child 父母子; Prince, Minister, and People 君臣民; Tao, Te, and Jen 道德仁.

There is an affinity, term for term, among these triads: for example, the Prince is Heaven, Tao, Father; the People is Central Harmony and Jen 仁. As the Minister is similar to Earth, which aspires to rise in order to be of one heart with Heaven 與天合心, his only concerns are with what is above, with the Prince. It is the People's mission to harmonize the ten thousand beings, which refers essentially to cultivated plants. The Prince, the Minister, and the People form one family whose members must

13. At the moment when the fair "Breath of Peace" 良善平氣 arrives, Heaven fears lest the people violate the "seasonal ordinances" 時令 and indulge in hunting (118:672).

communicate among themselves by means of oral and written utterances. The three Breaths will then be united and form one great harmony out of which comes the Breath of T'ai-p'ing 太平之氣.[14]

But when one of the Breaths is interrupted and does not communicate any more 不善相通, there is neither harmony 太和 nor T'ai-p'ing (pp. 18–19, *TPC ch'ao, i* 乙). It is essentially for establishing such communication that the Master teaches his *San-tao hsing-shu*. This book must be used for the examination of the celestial texts 天文, the sacred books of Earth 地神書, the utterances of men 人辭 of olden times and of today (96:421). That is what the *chen-jen* teach the "virtuous prince." He in his turn has to encourage the circulation of ideas and of the wisdom that can be found in all social strata of his empire, and even among the barbarians beyond the frontiers.

It is inauspicious that fear should prevent the people from speaking because of the severity of the emperor or of the major and minor officials, from those of the commandery down to the heads of a *t'ing* 亭長. If no one dares to forward his good ideas to the top of the hierarchy, the Tao is interrupted. Those who interrupt the Tao commit a great sin and incur the wrath of Heaven and Earth, which results in natural disasters and bad harvests.

Therefore people must be able to present reports (*hsing-shu*), but this should not be the action of isolated persons, because the utterance of a single individual can be treacherous and deceptive.[15] It is necessary that a large number of sages deliberate together (*chi-i* 集議), so that those who present reports may then watch one another, rendering lies impossible.

14. The *TPC* frequently employs the expression *san-ho* 三合 to indicate the union of the three Breaths of Yin, of Yang, and of Chung-ho 中和. It is an ancient usage since it can be found already in the *T'ien-wen* 天問 (*Ch'u-tz'u pu-chu* 楚辭補注 3:2a [Kyoto, 1972 ed.]) and in the *Ku-liang chuan* 穀梁傳 (Chuang 莊 3d year, in *Ch'un-ch'iu ku-liang chuan chu-shu* 春秋穀梁傳注疏 5:4a [*Shih-san ching chu-shu* 十三經注疏 ed.]). Its germ is in the *Lao-tzu* 42: 萬物負陰而抱陽, 沖氣以爲和; see Jao Tsung-i, "Hsiang-erh chiu-chieh yü san-ho i" 想爾九戒與三合義, *Ch'ing-hua hsüeh-pao* 清華學報 4.2:80–81 (1964). Later on *san-ho* and *san-tao* 三道 have another meaning in connection with the theory of Lao-tzu's conversion of the barbarians (*hua-hu* 化胡); cf. Yoshioka (n. 1), pp. 147 ff.

15. "One cannot trust the words of one man" 不可聽信一人之言——一人之言不可獨從 (70: 279). "The word of one man can be untrue and deceitful. . . . An assembly of great sages is never too numerous. If two or three men get together, there will certainly be something fallacious [in their utterances]" 一人言或妄僞佞欺, 名爲使上失實. . . . 上士之人衆集者, 常病不多兩三人集, 固々有奸僞 (86:318). I slightly emend the text and the punctuation of Wang Ming. One reads in 86:317 that when the mandarin 長吏 in a *chou* 州 is feared and when the people do not dare to express themselves, the sages should agree to go for deliberation to another *chou* and present their report there; and the same applies in a *chün* 郡, a *hsien* 縣, etc. Those who want to prevent them from expressing themselves will be severely punished.

In this way, when nothing of what goes on in the local districts 州郡縣鄉亭 is concealed, Heaven is satisfied, and disasters are averted (86:319).

In order to know if the reports are in good accord with the divinities 究治於神靈, the prince will send confidential emissaries to make investigations among the people. His purpose will be to learn whether there is any anthrax, leprosy, and itch 疽癘疥 and how much there is. If there are pests who devour the people, this is due to petty officials without Tao-te who continue to be rampant and are similar to pests. If there are no diseases, this signifies that good people are in office (86:319–20).

There are also strange or calamitous phenomena 災變泽異 that can occur in a country, generally in rural areas, where the common folk are the first to perceive them. If they do not dare reveal them to their superiors and the latter do not dare reveal them to the sovereign, all of them will be interrupting the transmission of the word of Heaven and Earth. Therefore the minor local officials and the people should stand in awe of one another, so that the truth reaches the sovereign. That is one proper method for immediately establishing T'ai-p'ing (86:322).

The "good texts" (shan-shu 善書) that should reach the prince may be too far away to be brought by those who have them. This is particularly so in the case of the barbarians who are acquainted with "extraordinary texts, excellent ideas, remarkable recipes" 奇文善策殊方. In order to obtain that universal wisdom, the sovereign shall order that in the chou 州 and in the chün 郡, and as far away as in the border regions, "huts of kindness be constructed on the main roads, which from four sides lead to the capital" 宜各作一善好宅於都市四達大道之上也 (86:322). These huts[16] shall be three chang 丈 high, and their sides shall likewise be three chang (? one modern chang is about three meters). Toward the top of the front wall, at eye level, an opening shall be made large enough to put one's hand through. The hut's door shall be hermetically sealed. A notice shall be put on the outside inviting anyone to make a memorandum of what he knows and thinks and to throw it into the interior of the hut, also putting down his name 姓字.

The best texts shall be rewarded by promotions or gifts. Thanks to that process the whole world will become good; the sages in hiding and the hermits 隱士穴處人 will come to the capital; the good men, the sages, and the saints of the eighty-one barbarian territories, noticing that China has a prince of such high virtue, will hasten in successive columns to submit joyfully, carrying the most precious of their goods and products.

16. They are called by different names in the same chapter 88: 太平來善之宅, 四方來善宅 (88:333), 皇平之宅 (88:334), 上皇良平之氣宅 (88:335), 大樂之宅 (88:336).

The prince shall then examine the texts that were collected in this way and have the best of them extracted, which will form a *Tung-chi chih ching* entirely like the *TPC* of the Celestial Master.[17] This text, which represents the quintessence of universal wisdom, shall in its turn be redistributed among the people so that they shall become converted to the good 俱化善 and be ignorant of the evil: "That is called completely obtaining the heart of Heaven, of Earth, of Man, and of the Barbarians, so that great joy appears day by day, so that the world becomes one family and together constitutes a total order" (88:333).[18]

In another chapter, where the subject under discussion is the gifts which the king should liberally bestow, it is stated that he gives food to the hungry, clothes to those who feel cold, and texts to the sages. These texts are a celestial book (*t'ien-ching* 天經) made up of the best writings of all times (of the *san-ku* 三古). The texts are useful to improve 化 men, "nourish their vital principle, and assure their tranquility" 養其性安其身. On the other hand, military treatises are inauspicious (65:228 ff.). Although this is not specifically stated, the *t'ien-ching* is very much like a *tung-chi ching*. The prince composes it by the same method as that employed first by the Celestial Master and then by the *chen-jen*. That ideas (the Tao) should circulate from the people to the capital and, after decantation, from the capital to the people, is one of the principal theories of the *TPC*.

Government and Hierarchies

The ideal government is naturally that which allows the "Breath of T'ai-p'ing" to spread in the world. The book revealed by the Celestial Master

---

17. Cf. 91:360: "Henceforth the virtuous prince examines carefully the instruction and the texts of Heaven and obtains the writings of the three Tao, which have been presented by the minor officials and the people who first selected and assembled them. Then the prince has them collated in the eighth month. Three commissions are formed which have separate quarters. The one that first examines the writings shall be situated to the east of the prince, and this shall be the first test. Then they are transmitted for examination to the south of the prince, which shall be the second test. Then they are transmitted for examination to the west of the prince, which shall be the third test. The books transmitted and examined shall be deposited to the north of the prince [in a dark chamber]." 自是之後, 德君詳察思天教天文爲得下吏民三道所共集上書文, 到八月拘校之, 分處爲三部, 始校書者於君之東, 已一通, 傳校於君之南, 已再通, 傳校於君之西, 已三通, 傳校者棄去於君之北 . . . . [幽室而置之]. This procedure is designed to prevent any deceit on the part of the commissions charged with examination. Those guilty of errors or omissions shall be punished by the bastinado. The collection thus created seems to be essentially a sort of repertory of types of conduct 行狀, so that the local officials 長吏 will no longer have to make judgments about them, and the prince can stay quiet and perceive, without having to stir, the state of mind of the whole empire 悉坐知天下之心.

18. 此所謂畢得天地人及四夷之心, 大樂日至, 并合爲一家, 其成一治者也 (88:333).

brings to the "prince endowed with virtue" the method that allows him to establish such a government and to eliminate the evil that has accumulated since the origin of the world through the inheritance of sins (41:84 and 50:168). Yet the prince is not alone responsible for order: it results from collaboration within the various tripartite domains and, above all, on the level of government among the Prince, the Minister, and the People (pp. 18 ff.). It is necessary that concord prevail among these three members of the political family, so that the three Breaths 太陰太陽 中和 can form the Great Harmony 太和, out of which will come the "Breath of T'ai-p'ing."

The prince must civilize and transform 化 all beings by means of Tao and Te and must do it in such a manner that each of them is in the place that suits him 令各得其所. He himself has to be joyous, because the seasons and the elements get out of order and become harmful to living beings when he is sad. The perfect government is one in which the people do not know of the existence of the Son of Heaven and govern themselves by means of *wu-wei*, of *tzu-jan* 自然, and of Tao (p. 25, *TPC ch'ao, i*). One can recognize ideas here which are directly borrowed from Lao-tzu.

A good prince is, of course, careful not to resort to punishments, because this is to act the part of a robber and to terrorize the people. The best princes 上君, who reigned in antiquity, made the people submit to them by means of Tao, the middling princes 中君 by means of Te, the inferior princes 下君 by means of Jen, the princes of disorder 亂君 by means of *wen* 文 (in the sense of "ceremonial," "decorum"), the princes of ruin 凶敗之君 by means of punishments (35:32). Punishments cause resentments which, without the knowledge of the rulers, collect among the people, who do not dare to express themselves but give robbers titles like General (*chiang-chün* 將軍) or Eminence (*shang-chün* 上君, 47:144). Yet it is necessary, as we have seen, that the prince know the thoughts of the people, because the latter represent Heaven (as in the *Shu-ching* 書經).

Nevertheless, we are told in another connection (40:80) that there are degrees in the art of complying with the will of Heaven. If the prince is obliged to institute laws, he will do so only with fear. If an offense is committed, he should recall the guilty person to order without indicting him; if the offense is so serious that it is necessary to indict him, there must be no desire to harm him. If a man becomes guilty of a crime which deserves death and if one cannot do otherwise than punish him, it is necessary to avoid having the punishment reach the family and the friends of the convict; if there are guilty persons in the family, it is necessary to take care not to destroy the whole line. But the ideal is expressed in a kind of proverb: "When the Saint governs, he constantly thinks of *t'ai-p'ing*; he has penal laws made, but he does not use them" 聖人治, 常思太平, 令刑格而不用也.

One of the rules on which the authors of the *TPC* place considerable value is not to demand from the people what is beyond their capacity (54:202, 210; 48:149). This is another application of the idea that harmony should prevail among the three domains and that the tasks and the responsibilities should be well distributed. This last theory is well set forth in 42:88 ff., where nine human categories are distinguished:

1. The divine men who are without shape and who are endowed (?) with *ch'i* 無形委氣之神人;[19] it is their task to govern the Primordial Breath 理元氣, to which they are similar in nature.
2. The great divine men 大神人; they govern Heaven. They have a shape and are great; their spiritual strength is similar to that of Heaven.
3. The *chen-jen* 眞人; it is their task to govern Earth. They are massive and reliable like Earth 專又信.
4. The *hsien-jen* 仙人; it is their task to govern the four seasons. They go through transformations like the seasons.
5. The men of the great Tao 大道人 govern the Five Elements. They are good at divination, in which they are similar to the five elements 五行.
6. The *sheng-jen* 聖人 govern the Yin and the Yang. They preside over the harmonization of *ch'i*, in which they are similar to Yin-Yang.
7. The *hsien-jen* 賢人 govern the writings 文書. They are specialists in written and oral expression.
8. The people in general 凡民 govern the cultivated plants 草木五穀. They are without intelligence and are similar to the "ten thousand beings."
9. The slaves 奴婢 govern merchandise 財貨. They obtain material goods and are similar to the goods exchanged, which they cause to circulate.[20]

19. This category of divine men is found again in 112:563, where it is stated that the divine men of old, who were without shape, sought the art of life (*sheng-tao* 生道) through study and thus had the same aspiration as the *wei-ch'i* 委氣. The exact sense of this last expression is uncertain, but it certainly refers to a way of designating the *yüan-ch'i* 元氣 "Primordial Breath." Cf. 72:282, which states that the supreme method is the one that consists in being without action like the Primordial Breath 元氣無爲, and in visualizing one's own body all white, similar to the 委氣 and without shape 若委氣而無形, which makes it possible to succeed in everything and to know everything 無不爲無不知.

20. *TPC ch'ao, ting* 丁 (p. 222) contains a similar passage on these categories, but it differs regarding the slaves, of whom it is said that they are the progeny of a decadent generation

Each of the nine human categories has the mission of putting its category of *ch'i* into harmony. It is necessary that the nine *ch'i* be in harmonious agreement and that the nine human species work with one accord 九氣合和九人共心 in order to make *t'ai-p'ing* come.

The three principal elements of political order, the Prince, the Minister, and the People, are equally, each in his sphere, in charge of the three *ch'i* mentioned above: "The Prince conducts the Breath of Heaven and has it communicate with what is below; the Minister conducts the Breath of Earth and has it communicate with what is above; the People conduct the Breath of the Central Harmony and have it communicate with what is above" (48:152).[21] Here again it can be seen what the *san-tao* consist of. It is necessary that the three *ch'i* love one another and mutually communicate in order that there may be no more evil 三氣相愛相通無復有害. That is what *t'ai-p'ing* consists of (48:148).

If the ideal for the ruler is not to resort to punishments, it is nonetheless true that in practice it is necessary to prevent the wicked from doing harm. The Celestial Master does not fear any inconsistency in personally prescribing the bastinado for people who are addicted to alcohol and for its manufacturers (69:268 ff.): they will be condemned to repair walls, roads, and official buildings (pp. 214 ff., *TPC ch'ao, ting* 丁). There is even to be a procedure for detecting criminals (35:39 ff.). Although the text is not very explicit, it nonetheless deserves attention.

When a case of brigandage or other crime has occurred, the head of the local district (*chang-li* 長吏) summons its inhabitants and has them sit down according to their rank and social quality:[22]

> Former officials, great and small 故大臣故吏, are seated facing east;
> the people who know the classics and those who have Tao-te 明經道德人 are seated facing north;
> the good sons and younger brothers 孝悌 are seated facing west;
> the diligent farmers and laborers 佃家謹 (勤) 子 are seated in the southeast corner facing northwest;
> the bad young men 惡子少年 are seated in the southwest, facing northeast;
> the head 君 takes his seat facing south.

衰世所生 and resemble vegetables, which are weak and submissive. But the most intelligent can become good (free) people 善人 and then ascend the steps of the hierarchy to reach the condition of gods 入神 and be like august Heaven 與皇天同形. They can go to live in the Purple Palace of the celestial North Pole 北極紫宮 and resemble the Celestial Sovereign 與天上帝同象. If they mount still higher, they become those *sheng-jen* without shape, who are pure *ch'i* and are no longer occupied with anything but the affairs of Heaven.

21. 君導天氣而下通, 臣導地氣而上通, 民導和氣而上通.

22. This takes place at the *fa-so* 發所: is it the yamen or the place of the crime?

This arrangement, as the text affirms, is consistent with the correspondence of categories: the former officials are in the place of Justice (*i* 義); the wise and virtuous people are in the place of Light (*ming* 明); the sons and younger brothers are in their proper domain (*pen-hsiang* 本鄉) because the east is the direction of dawn and of court ceremonies (*ch'ao* 朝), where one has to behave respectfully; the zealous laborers are in the southeast, because this is the direction of growth and of nourishment; the bad young men are in the southwest, which is the direction of Yang decreasing and Yin increasing.

The head (representing the prince) takes his place in the north behind a closed door. The persons present are summoned one by one according to their rank; note is taken of what they say as well as of their names. Later on their testimonies will be compared: contradictions between their statements will reveal the hypocrites and the liars. The bad young men will be sent together with the beadles (*li* 吏) to arrest brigands. This method should be presented to the "Prince of High Virtue" by the *chen-jen* and should also be shown to the people in general because the whole world should know it. Thus, good will triumph and evil will decline; brigands, thieves, and other troublemakers will be arrested—an expectation which, like the inquest procedure, seems somewhat utopian and sophistical.

The statements made by the different categories of people have to remain secret; that is the reason given for the fact that the magistrate (*chün* 君) must be concealed behind a door, whereas the person who speaks is in front of that same door. The details here may be difficult to understand but the principle is still clear: the procedure is public but the statements have to be secret so as to protect those who have something to reveal.

Morals and Religion

Just as the prince must promote the circulation of texts and ideas, everyone else has the duty, each in his own sphere, to circulate the things of value he possesses. That becomes evident, among other passages of the *TPC*, in 67:241 ff., where six particularly heavy sins are enumerated, which produce their bad effects upon the perpetrators and their descendants:

1. To accumulate Tao (*chi-tao* 積道), to keep it for oneself, and to refuse to teach it to others for their salvation. Those who commit this fault interrupt the Celestial Tao of life 斷天生道 and bring the wrath of Heaven upon them.
2. To accumulate Te (*chi-te* 積德) and to refuse to teach it to others so

that they may nourish their vital principle. This is to interrupt the nourishing Te of Earth 斷地養德 and to arouse her wrath.

3. To accumulate riches (*chi-tsai* 積財) and refuse to help the poor, letting them die of starvation and cold. These goods belong to the Central Harmony (*chung-ho* 中和), that is to say to mankind, and they are the means through which Heaven and Earth lavish their blessings of *jen* 天地所以行仁也. They must circulate so that everyone has what he needs. Those who interrupt this circulation and who hoard what does not belong to them are enemies of the Harmonious Breath (*ho-ch'i* 和氣) of Heaven and Earth.

4. To know that Heaven has a Tao and nevertheless to despise that Tao, to refuse to study it in order to prepare for one's own salvation and obtain long life. This comes to treating with contempt the body which was bequeathed by the ancestors, that is, to be a man without Tao 無道之人 and to be fated to die.

5. To know that it is good to practice Te but to make no effort toward the good, to do evil in contempt of oneself. This is to revolt against Earth, which loves Te.

6. The person whom Heaven has provided with muscles and physical strength so that he may nourish and clothe himself and who lives in idleness and becomes the parasite of the rich, commits a deadly sin because Heaven and Earth produce the riches necessary for man, who has to draw from them according to his strength and within the limits of his needs. If he does not make any effort and if he cannot obtain from others what he lacks, he will go so far as to seize the goods of others. Then he will be an enemy of the Central Harmony.

After enumerating these six sins, the Celestial Master gives other explanations of how abominable it is to interrupt the circulation of T'ien Tao 天道 and of Ti Te 地德 and then goes on to expound the conduct of people with Jen 仁. In the triad Tao—Te—Jen, Jen corresponds to the people and their products. That is why goods (here called *wu* 物) are the property of the Central Harmony 中和之有. It is necessary to let them circulate, easily go and come 推行浮而往來. The rich, whose accumulated wealth deteriorates, have the obligation to help the poor. Their Te 德 will then be in accord with Heaven; their fame will spread far and wide; it will be possible for them always to obtain new goods and throw away those that have gone bad 尚可常得新物而腐塗者除去也. Yet there are people who hoard and want to lend only for usurious interest, who give only to the rich and let the poor perish. These people are detested by Heaven, by Earth, by mankind, and by the gods, for these goods are the property of Heaven, of Earth, and of the Central Harmony, which together make use of them in order to nourish mankind 天地中和所有以共養人也.

Riches then belong to all men, food in the first place, but also other things of value, since our text states (67:247): "The money and the other riches that are in the treasury are not destined to provide for the needs of a single man; all those who do not have enough should be authorized to draw on them" 少 [小] 內之錢財, 本非獨以給一人也; 其有不足者, 悉當從其取也.

There follows a description of the misfortune that awaits those misers who go so far as to bury their riches in the earth, which is an abomination because everything should be between Heaven and Earth in order to provide for the needs of all. To shut riches up underground is to withdraw them from circulation and to impoverish the State (*kuo-chia* 國家) which should be the sole proprietor of the goods produced by the efforts of men (67:248).

Thus on all levels—spiritual, material, economic, and, it must be added, physiological—things have to circulate: this is what Tao and life consist of. The idea is not peculiar to the *TPC*, but it is there expressed with particular vigor.

In addition to the six sins denounced in chapter 67, the authors of the *TPC* attack "four pernicious kinds of conduct" 四毀之行, which are: (1) lack of filial piety 不孝; (2) not to procreate 不而 (＝能) 性眞, 生無後世類; (3) to eat manure and urine 食糞飲小便; (4) to beg 行爲乞. These acts constitute an insult to the true Celestial Tao 汙辱天正道. There can hardly be any doubt that this section is an allusion to Buddhist practices (or supposedly Buddhist practices, 117:654 ff.).[23]

Filial piety is an important virtue. It even extends to Heaven and Earth, as well as to the king, who is "father and mother" of his subjects. The latter have the duty to procure for him the tranquility that will allow him to govern without doing anything 垂拱而治 and to live long. In the same way, the perfect son, keeping in mind that his parents are growing old, has to seek methods of immortality for them. That is even his principal duty, because he may not go in for enriching the family since it would only give trouble to his parents by obliging them to keep the goods accumulated (47:134). Similarly, the souls of the dead have no use for too sumptuous offerings. They ask only to stay underground without anything to worry about and without thinking of the tablet 可毋自苦念主者也 (47:134). "It is not fitting to treat the dead more lavishly than the

---

23. See Yoshioka (n. 1), pp. 136 ff.; Ōfuchi (n. 1), pp. 152 ff.

living" 事死不得過生 (this is the title of one paragraph of chapter 36). This idea is justified in the following way. The dead are in the domain of Yin, which should not be superior to Yang. If Yin prevails, demonic beings (*kuei-wu* 鬼物) will cause harm. In the case of mourning, it is necessary to act like the ancients, give it total sincerity and nothing more 心至而已.

If the quantity of offerings to the deceased is exaggerated, they will be unable to eat all of it, and it will be the demons who come to eat the surplus and loiter afterwards in order to trouble the living and make them ill.

The *TPC*'s concept of life beyond the grave remains very archaic. The souls of the dead live below the earth in the family soil, whose fertility they assure.[24] They must lead a life that is without worry and joyful. But for them to be joyful, they must have known how to live joyfully in their lifetimes. It is also necessary that their descendants behave well, in which case life is transmitted. If, on the contrary, the descendants become bad and maltreat their own bodies, which is composed of cosmic *ch'i* and is a heritage from the ancestors 先人之統體, the fertility of the race will be exhausted.

The same is true for the prince: if he likes to think about *t'ai-p'ing*, his spirits are joyful and in accord with the good *ch'i* of Heaven and of Earth; but if he does not know how to make his government a just one 平其治, his souls at his death will be condemned below the earth, where they will dwell together with the various bad *ch'i*.

When the subterranean genies or souls (the text simply reads *ti-hsia* 地下) see someone newly deceased arrive, they question him about his activities and about the times he has repented (*so keng* 所更), and determine by this examination which register (*ming-chi* 名籍) he is in (40:73). Elsewhere (114:602) it is specified that Heaven keeps the register of life (*sheng-chi* 生籍) and that Earth keeps the register of death (*szu-chi* 死籍).

---

24. Cf. 50:182, which states that the souls of the ancestors must return to provide nourishment for their descendants. If the soil (where they are buried) is good, these souls return to provide nourishment; if the soil is bad, they return to cause harm 魂神復當得還, 養其子孫, 善地則魂神還養也. 惡地則魂神還爲害也. The text adds that with five ancestors the *ch'i* is exhausted and (the forefather in the fifth generation) becomes human again; then the several *ch'i*, conforming to the Tao of Heaven, return to their point of departure after having accomplished a complete circuit 周復反其始也. This may be compared with the system of the four and one ancestral tablets of kings according to the *Li-chi* 禮記, *Sang-fu hsiao-chi* 喪服小記 (trans. S. Couvreur I, 745) and the last part on the taboo of names (*ming* 名), ibid. *Ch'ü-li* 曲體 (S. Couvreur I, 59). What we have here is the traditional concept of reincarnation—which, however, is not one of a personal soul. The *TPC* affirms elsewhere that death is something definitive, without any hope of return (72:298).

Still elsewhere the supreme judge is said to be the Lord of Heaven (T'ien-chün 天君); the spirits under his authority report good and evil, which are written down in the registers of good and bad actions 善惡之籍 (110: 524 ff.; 111:540 ff.). The Lord of Heaven appears to be identical with the spirit of the heart (*hsin-shen* 心神), which is present in the interior of the human body (111:545, and cf. 114:600 where the Director of Destiny, the *ssu-ming* 司命, is in the heart).

Besides the duties of filial piety with regard to ancestors and parents, man has analogous duties with regard to the cosmic parents who are Heaven and Earth. Heaven is a father, Earth is a mother, Man is their child. In the same way as a father punishes a defiant son, Heaven sends disasters and diseases when it is dissatisfied (a very traditional concept).

As for the duties due to Mother Earth, the Master says: "Father and mother are equally human beings, and Heaven and Earth are both 'celestial'" 天亦天地亦天, which signifies that they are two aspects of Nature and have similar feelings. If, therefore, anyone commits the crime of piercing the Earth, she complains to Heaven, who gets angry, while she for her part no longer produces anything. Actually, to dig into the earth is a sin as great as wounding one's mother. Above all, one must avoid hitting subterranean waters, because that would mean touching the veins of Mother Earth and causing her loss of blood. It is therefore not allowed to dig wells: rather, one has to be content with the water of natural springs, which are like the nipples of Earth (45:112 ff.). The whole text on the prohibition of digging up the soil is very interesting, because it shows how the religious sentiments in regard to Mother Earth had remained alive side by side with the ideology of male soil gods.

Other moral prescriptions peculiar to the *TPC* deserve to be mentioned:

1. The prohibition of alcohol, which we have already referred to (p. 214, *TPC ch'ao, ting*).[25] The reason for this prohibition was not the dangers of drunkenness but the fact that Water (alcoholic liquids are similar to the element Water) is the enemy of Fire. Now Fire is the dominant element in the *TPC* and the symbol of the prince. Let us note again that the T'ai-p'ing Tao of Chang Chüeh 張角 announces the advent of Yellow, whereas here the dynastic color still seems to be Red—as certainly was the case in the *T'ien-kuan li pao-yüan t'ai-p'ing ching*, the book revealed by Ch'ih-ching tzu 赤精子 ("Master of the Essence of Red") in the days of Emperor Ch'eng.

25. On the prohibition of alcohol, cf. R. A. Stein (n. 4), pp. 12 and 58.

2. The prohibition of despising and killing daughters (35:34 ff.). "Now, ever since the world lost the Tao, there are many people who, not content with despising their daughters, kill them, so that there are fewer women than men, which leads to the fact that Yin is diminished and does not correspond any more to the norms of Heaven and Earth." By behaving thus, society as a whole shows its scorn for the original Mother 天下共賤其眞母 and exterminates the terrestrial *ch'i*. This results in disasters and the king's government does not find its equilibrium 王治不得平. This is not only the fault of the king; it is the people as a whole who behave badly 共爲非. The text states clearly that infanticide of daughters was frequent and that it was committed in all families, occasionally involving more than ten girls in one family, without counting miscarriages.

3. The murder of daughters is most of all condemned because it leads to a shortage of women, and each man should have two wives, inasmuch as Yang is odd and Yin is even (35:37 ff.). When the disciples object that the ruler has many more than two wives, the Master explains that if woman is the "spirit of Earth" 土地之精神, the king is the "spirit of Heaven." This spirit has to spread universally and that is why he has to take a wife in each *chou* 州 in order to let his Breath communicate there 以通其氣. In that way there will be rain at the desired time and the earth will be fertile.

4. For the same reason chastity is rejected (ibid.). It was prescribed by masters who had jealous wives. If men and women live in continence, they interrupt the vital process of the universe—merely in order to obtain empty fame. Nevertheless, ordinary people should not succumb to excess either, and that is why they have a right to only two wives.

The "Declaration of the (Celestial) Master"

Now we come to the problem of the *Shih-ts'e wen* 師策文 (38:62 *TPC ch'ao, ping* 丙), a text so enigmatic (perhaps intentionally so) that I will not attempt a translation. It deserves our attention, however, because the authors of the *TPC* considered it important enough to provide a commentary on it; and because, as we shall see, it seems to be very old and to antedate both the Five Pecks of Rice sect and the T'ai-p'ing Tao. It is composed of thirteen verses of seven feet. Cited under the title *T'ien-ts'e shu* 天策書 in 119:679, it is explained in 39:63 ff. 解師策書訣. Although this "explanation" is not necessarily contemporaneous with the text itself and seems to strain it, it nevertheless contains data that merit attention. Its glosses are paraphrased below and should be read in conjunction with the text of the *Shih-ts'e wen*, given in note 26.[26]

a. "I", *wu* 吾, refers to the *shen-jen* 神人 sent by Heaven to save the world of *ch'eng-fu* 承負 (39:64).

b. It is sufficient to recite the characters of this text in order to eliminate the disasters resulting from *ch'eng-fu* (39:64).

c. The salvation that comes from being taught the T'ai-p'ing Tao must begin with practice in the concentration called "retaining the One" (*shou-i* 守一), which makes man every day more enlightened inside (39:64; cf. "retain the light of the One," *shou i-ming* 守一明 in 34:15–16, and *T'ai-p'ing ching sheng chün mi chih* 太平經聖君秘旨, cited on pp. 739–40).

d. Thanks to the revelation, the red Breath will again become flourishing and bright (39:64).

e. In practicing this Tao it is necessary to go back to the ideal of the San-huang 三皇 (39:64).

f. In practicing the teaching of the *TPC* one is in accord with the will of Heaven (*t'ien-hsin* 天心) and procures for each of the ten thousand beings its proper place so that they are no longer in anarchical disorder 亂 (39:65).

g. The verse 子巾用角治其右 is interpreted as referring to the character *sung* 誦, to recite; the continuous reciting of this book assures the correctness (*cheng* 正) of all undertakings. One is tempted to see here an allusion to the Yellow Turbans 黃巾 and to Chang Chüeh 張角 (who was, however, rejected by the Celestial Masters; 39:65).

h. In the verse 潛龍勿用坎爲紀, the hidden dragon (*ch'ien-lung* 潛龍, cf. *I-ching* 易經, hexagram I) represents the Celestial Breath which returns to the point of its departure (*ch'u chiu* 初九). The year *chia-tzu* 甲子 is [corresponds to] the day of the winter solstice (cf. *Shang-shu* 尚書, *Chung-hou* 中候: 天地開闢甲子冬至). The true beginning of Heaven-Earth starts from there 天地正始, 起於是. The dragon is the small Yang 少陽 of the east, the spirit of Wood 木之精神. The celestial way starts out with Wood so that it causes the element Fire to rise 興火行. Later on it is stated that the book of salvation has to be revealed in the year *hsüan-chia* 玄甲,[27] but that the prince will not be capable of understanding it well and of using it (39:65).

26. *Shih-ts'e wen* (38:62): (*a*) 吾字十一明爲止；(*b*) 丙午丁己爲祖始；(*c*) 四口治事萬物理；(*d*) 子巾用角治其右；(*e*) 潛龍勿用坎爲紀；(*f*) 人得見之壽長久；(*g*) 居天地間活而已；(*h*) 治百萬人仙可待，(*i*) 善治病者勿欺紿；(*j*) 樂莫樂乎長安市；(*k*) 使人壽若西王母；(*l*) 比若四時周反始；(*m*) 九十字策傳方士.

27. In 102:459 we find that the text is to be revealed in *hsüan-chia* 玄甲, which is the first of all the *hsün* 旬 cycles and which starts with the *yüan-ch'i* 與元氣爲初.

i. In 人得見之壽長久, man 人 indicates the sovereign, the Unique Man 帝王一人, who will know how to use the books of Tao; who, thanks to auspicious prodigies, will not have any doubt in regard to T'ien Tao 天道; who will enjoy long life and will even be able to reach the state of *hsien* 仙. But it is necessary to beware of deceptive texts 邪偽之文 and superficial and brilliant texts 浮華文, which do not permit curing diseases and which cause *ch'eng-fu* (39:66).

j. 樂莫樂乎長安市; there is no greater joy than that afforded by the arrival of 上皇太平氣. Chang-an 長安 is explained as being not the town, but the peace and the tranquility whose benefits accrue to those who practice the Tao (39:68).

k. 使人壽若西王母; here again "Hsi-wang mu" is not the Immortal. The name is glossed character by character. *Hsi* 西 evokes the idea that each man lodges and preserves the Tao in his chest owing to a play of the words *hsi* 西 = west and *hsi* 棲 = to perch. Wang 王 is the sovereign who, in practicing the Tao, emerges as true king. *Mu* 母 evokes the idea of long life and denotes the head of the spirits 神之長, an epithet that should also be applied to the sovereign (39: 68). Since the meaning of the text here is not in doubt, we can clearly see the procedure for explanation, which claims to unveil an esoteric meaning. Other examples in the *TPC* could be cited.

l. 比若四時周反始: "this is like the four seasons, which follow one another in giving birth to one another 傳相生 and which do not hurt one another" (39:68). This implies that the government does not use any punishments.

m. 九十字策傳方士: *chiu* 九 is *chiu* 究; the Te of him who obtains this Tao shall be in perfect accord with the will of Heaven, of Earth, of Yin, of Yang, and of the ten thousand beings 得行此道, 其德究洽天地陰陽萬物之心也. As to *fang-shih* 方士, this term represents the prince devoted to Tao-Te, to whom this Tao should be revealed (39–68).

The text here seems to go back to the times of the "Red Han," before there were Celestial Masters who, like the Yellow Turbans, announced the advent of Yellow and not of Red. Great importance was attached to the beginning of cycles marked by the cyclical characters *chia-tzu* (which signal a renewal of life, like the renascence of Yang in the winter solstice). This should be kept in mind for dating the text, especially when one recalls that the revolt of the Yellow Turbans was planned for the year *chia-tzu* (and did occur that year, in 184).

The ideas expressed in this declaration (or program) of the Celestial Master are probably those which the authors of the *TPC* prized the most. They are in good accord with what is stated in the *TPC*: the prince has to reign without acting; he will live long thanks to the revelations; the latter make it possible to cure diseases. This explanation seems to make an allusion to Emperor Shun 順帝, who did not use the *T'ai-p'ing ch'ing-ling shu*.

Long Life

The *TPC* would not be a Taoist book if the ideal of long life were not present to an important degree, closely connected with the ideal of Great Justice. Men do not live to an old age except in times of T'ai-p'ing. But a normal individual cannot live forever, and life is all the more precious as death is something definitive (72:298). All living creatures come to an end, but Heaven has provided special methods 真道奇方 thanks to which it is possible to avoid dying too soon (90:340 ff.). One must gaily live out one's allotment of life and become a happy spirit beyond the grave (40:73). The allotment of life differs, moreover, from man to man. There is a celestial longevity 天壽 of 120 years, a terrestrial longevity of 100 years, and a human longevity of 80 years (102:465). Elsewhere a distinction is made between a superior longevity of 120 years, a medium one of 80 years, and an inferior one of 60 years (p. 723).

The *TPC* admits, however, that certain exceptional men can transcend the normal human condition (*tu-shih* 度世) and become immortals. It even mentions *shih-chieh* 尸解, but understands that expression a little differently than other Taoist texts (where it refers to the fact that a Taoist who reaches immortality, leaves behind a semblance of his "corpse"). Here *shih* 尸 indicates the vital spirits (*ching-shen* 精神) which are liberated from the body 尸解分形, 骨體以分 (111:553). We can give only a brief summary of the "recipes" for long life which are treated in the *TPC*—a subject that deserves more detailed treatment.

a. To live long it is in the first place necessary to *live morally*. Meager feasts and prohibitions (*chai chieh* 齋戒) must be part of the therapy, and they receive much attention throughout the *TPC*.

b. Among the positive recipes the most important (as with the Taoists of the Shang-ch'ing 上清 School who accepted this text) is the *meditation upon the One* ("to retain the One" *shou-i* 守一), or rather, upon the Light of the One (*shou i-ming*, cf. 34:15–16 and pp. 739 ff.; see above under the *Shih-ts'e wen* [c]). Therein lies the "root of long life" 長壽之根. What this means is a technique for visualizing colored lights, first red, then white, finally green. One must become totally illuminated internally and thus eliminate all diseases. That is doubtless the technique to which *Pao-p'u tzu* 18 alludes when it states, citing a "Book of the Immortals" (*hsien-ching* 仙經): "If you want to live long, you must become illuminated in retaining the One" 守一當明 (variant in the *Ling-pao wu-fu hsü* 靈寶五符序 *TT* 183, C:22b: 三一當明). As diseases are a result of sin, reflection upon one's faults tends eventually to accompany concentration: 守一思過 (122:566). Another procedure for meditation consists in concentrating upon the images of the spirits of internal organs, represented in human shape, dressed in clothes of colors that correspond to the respective elements and seasons. A man pictures the spirits to himself as male, a woman as female (pp. 21 and 27; 71:283; 72:291 ff.).

c. *Hygienic practices*: the book recommends that one eat moderately, which is not only a way of attaining long life but also a method of keeping the state prosperous and the people at peace. One should reach the point where one consumes only things noncorporeal 無形之物. Yet not to eat at all would cause a stoppage of the bowels 腸胃不通 (it is not explained why). It seems (but the text is not very clear) that a single meal a day is recommended (pp. 684 ff.). This diet eliminates diseases and avoids stoppage of the bowels 通腸. Elsewhere (p. 717, citing from the *San-tung chu-nang* 三洞珠囊 4) it is said that the first and best method for obtaining the Tao is to live on air (*feng-ch'i* 風氣), the second best is to take medicinal drugs, the third is to eat little. One should also take nourishment in accord with the seasons, but it is best of all to be satiated without eating (102:466)—which certainly means without eating *ordinary* foods. There are allusions, more often than not rather indirect, to breathing techniques that are generally connected with methods of meditation. Expressions can be found like *shou ch'i* 守氣, to retain the Breath as is done by Heaven and Earth. Or: "With regard to breathing, one must be in the position of the Mysterious Female 宜與氣爲 玄牝 (since the *Ho-shang-kung* 河上公 commentary, the *hsüan-p'in* 玄牝 of the *Lao-tzu* 6 has been connected with respiration). If one does not succeed at once in mastering respiration, one has to make a "dark chamber" (*yu-shih* 幽室, that is, a chamber of meditation) in order to meditate there upon the Tao. In this seclusion one does not eat because one is united with the *ch'i* (98:450).

Many of the formulas in the *TPC* are current in the Taoism of all times, as, for example: "The method (*tao*) of nourishing the vital principle consists in assuring the tranquility of one's person and in nourishing one's breath; one should not too often experience anger or joy" (p. 727). "If a man wants to live long, he must preserve his breath, respect his spirits, be sparing of his essence" 人欲壽者當愛氣專神重精 (p. 728). Finally, there is an allusion to something which, if it is not yet embryonic respiration (*t'ai-hsi* 胎息) proper, is at least a respiration of the embryo that one should imitate: the great saints of old taught a profound meditation in which one had to shut the nine apertures, relax one's body, and become similar to Chaos (*hun-t'un* 渾沌), inside which the circulation of the breaths makes a closed circuit as with the embryo in the womb (68:259). The embryo lives only on natural breath 自然之氣 or internal breath 內氣: after birth it inhales the Breaths of Yin and Yang or the breaths of ordinary respiration 消息之氣. In nourishing one's vital principle, thanks to the internal breath, one can return to the state of childhood (*ying-erh* 嬰兒, pp. 699–700).

d. *Medicinal substances*: medicinal plants are innumerable in Heaven. If the prince has virtue, they descend to earth. These plants have Tao-Te and are hierarchical. Some are sovereigns 帝王草; some are ministers 臣草; the most humble are the "common people" 人民草. Their efficacy varies according to their rank (50:172–73). Among the recipes utilizing plants there is also a distinction between those which act on the disease in one day by bringing about the intervention of celestial genies (*t'ien-shen* 天神); those that act in two days by summoning the terrestrial spirits; and those that act in three days through the agency of the dead (*jen-kuei* 人鬼, ibid.). Certain animals, particularly birds, have "sacred celestial medicine" 天上神藥 in their bodies. Others have only essences which are terrestrial or mixed, that is, made from human essences and from the Central Harmony. The *TPC* states in this connection that the Tao of Heaven hates killing and loves life; it requests us not to kill or to injure living creatures carelessly.

e. For curing diseases one can use *talismans* (*fu* 符), here called 重複之字 (92:380), which are consumed and directed toward the sick parts. Chapters 104 to 107 of the *TPC* consist of texts printed with characters that have the shape of Taoist talismans and are called *fu-wen* 複文. They make it possible to eliminate calamities, to secure the protection of the spirits, etc. We may suppose that the 重複之字 were characters similar to these. There are also *magic formulas* for healing, which are utterances revealed by Heaven and which are called "sacred invocations" (*shen-chou* 神祝). These formulas make it possible to summon the spirits and to command them. To make sure of their efficacy, they are tested on a sick person: those that are genuine show an immediate efficacy, and this efficacy should stay the same whoever is experimenting (50:181 ff.).

f. *Moxa, acupuncture, pulse*: these methods permit one to harmonize the 360 veins of man and to assure the circulation of the Yin and Yang Breaths, and thus to eliminate ills. These veins correspond to the days of the year in such a way that on each day a certain vein is active. Their network leads to the top of the head; in the interior parts of the body they are connected with the internal organs. Their pulsations are in accord with the seasons except when there is disease. In this case, one resorts to needles (Yin) and to moxa (Yang). As with magic formulas, the efficacy of methods is verified on sick persons who are collectively treated. The cases of recovery are noted and are used to make up a compendium of case references, a *ching-shu* 經書 (50:179–80). Analogous experimentation is indicated for the art of the pulse. The sages of antiquity seated themselves in a quiet place to feel one another's pulse, observing the rate of their pulsations. Thus they could perceive regular or abnormal states of the four seasons, the five elements, as well as the condition of their own health.

g. This account of longevity practices in the *TPC* would be incomplete if there was no reference to the therapeutic value of *music*, which generally creates harmony in nature and among the people. Each of the five notes is in tune with a spatial direction and each of them acts on one of the five internal organs. Thus the note *chüeh* 角 delights the genies of the east and assures the good health of the liver. It evokes the arrival of Jade Maidens dressed in green, who bring excellent medical recipes. It is the same for the other notes. The *TPC* recommends against prohibiting musical instruments (113: 586 ff.; cf. pp. 631 ff.).

Conclusion

It would be impossible in the format of an article to give an exhaustive account of the questions raised by the *TPC* and the ideas contained in it. I have limited myself to those points which appeared to me the most interesting for our purpose. Do they permit us to get an idea of the milieu from which the book came?

Whatever may have been the later vicissitudes of the *TPC*, our text does seem to go back to a text transmitted through the Celestial Masters, and they themselves had clearly preserved elements of an initial *TPC* (the one revealed by Kan Chung-k'o), although these elements did not agree with the ideas they were propagating.

The obvious contradictions between ideas that were democratic (even communist) on the one hand and the importance accorded to the sovereign and to hierarchies on the other, will surprise only those who cannot think outside of modern conceptions of democracy, state, and law.

The idea of T'ai-p'ing is an ideal of equity, and equity is constantly defined as the duty to give everyone the place that suits him in the hierarchy of beings. In this system the king remains the principal person responsible for universal order. But we can observe the appearance of a notion that is to remain important in Taoism, that is, the moral responsibility of each individual. It is not only the king who does expiation but all sinners. And it is up to the subjects to act in such a way that the king can govern by *wu-wei*.

It also has to be remembered that the *fang-shih* 方士 who presented the *TPC* at the Han court hoped to obtain reforms from the rulers, and that the revolt took place when this hope proved vain. Yet at the same time it is almost certain that the leaders of the revolt did not think in terms of installing a government of the "peasant masses" but rather of changing the dynasty and the cosmic cycle. The Celestial Masters of the Five Pecks of Rice sect were the ones who inaugurated an original system of society about which little is actually known, at least of its initial stage. The point is that our *TPC* does not reflect this organization—a fact that cannot be explained unless the text is anterior to it. We have in the *TPC* an ideology that is really closer to classical ideas (which are extremely systematized) than to later Taoism. On the other hand, the latter is foreshadowed by the theories concerning long life, which still retain great originality—another fact that is difficult to explain if one accepts a late date of composition.

Discussion of Kaltenmark Paper

*[The editors have slightly emended and abridged
this transcript of the discussion.]*

Introductory Remarks by Kaltenmark

The foundation of the empire [in 221 B.C.] marked a decisive turning point in the religious history of China. At this time, when the desire for unity in all domains was being fulfilled, a new official religion was created, although not in a coherent manner. In the creation of imperial cults, the influence of the *fang-shih* 方士 [magicians, specialists in the occult] seems important, if we are to believe the historical texts (such as *Feng-shan shu* 封禪書, chapter 28 in the *Shih-chi* 史記).* It is a pity, especially in the case of the *T'ai-p'ing ching*, which interests us today, that in the records no attention is paid to the social origins of these *fang-shih*. They are the ones who edited the *TPC* after it was "revealed." We do know that they were active in the eastern part of China and that the authors of the *TPC* came precisely from the region south of Shantung.

In my article (which is not an exhaustive study but only a very incomplete sketch), I give a brief reminder of what the historical texts say about the existence of books with the title of *TPC* under the emperors Ch'eng-ti [32–36 B.C.] and Shun-ti [A.D. 126–145], as well as the existence of a *TPC* used by the Celestial Master of the Way of the Five Pecks of Rice. I also mention that the ideal of *t'ai-p'ing* was already to be found in the philosophy of the Warring States period.

According to our text of the *TPC*, the state of *t'ai-p'ing* had already existed in high antiquity (which seems to mean the period of the Three Emperors 三皇), and had been characterized by simplicity in government and social customs and by the fact that not a single being suffered. The

---

*Ed. Note: Notable *fang-shih* were Li Shao-chün 李少君 and Miao Chi 謬忌. See E. Chavannes, *Memoires Historiques* 3: 463, 466, 485, et passim (reprinted Paris, 1967).

result was that the society was *p'ing* 平, that is, in a condition of perfect equilibrium without injustice. All this was because each individual occupied his proper place.

Government had become more and more decadent through successive ages; therefore it was necessary to return to primitive purity so that the "breath" of *t'ai-p'ing* 太平氣 could be restored. The teaching of the Celestial Master, who was an emissary from Heaven and who was not destined to stay here on earth, was designed precisely to help achieve these aims. This cannot be called messianism because it was not a question of awaiting a personal savior.

Next [pp. 19 and 24] I take up the complicated question of the revelation of the texts. I have not been able to determine clearly which was the text—or texts—revealed to the Celestial Master. Not only was it a revelation of Heaven, but it was at the same time a synthesis of wisdom of all ages and places. This is what is meant by *tung-chi* 洞極, which occurs in certain expressions I have noted and which is used in the title of one *TPC*. Our present text does not contain a single citation of texts anterior to it (except allusions to the *Tao-te ching*).

According to the *TPC*, the prince was to collect the wisdom of his people and encourage the circulation of their wise ideas throughout his empire. This could be accomplished by setting up *t'ai-p'ing chai* 太平宅 (similar to letter-boxes), through which the ideas and recipes of the people could reach the prince. The prince would then give them to scholars, who after having studied them, would extract the best. This created a source of wisdom to be redistributed among the people. Thus a kind of communication between prince and people, people and prince, was set up that was never to be interrupted.

Then [pp. 29–33] I talk about governments and hierarchies. Government was the result of a harmonious collaboration between the Prince, the Minister, and the People. The latter were equivalent to the three *ch'i* 氣 (*t'ai-yang* 太陽, *t'ai-yin* 太陰, *chung-ho* 中和). Later the three would unite to form the Great Harmony (*t'ai-ho* 太和), which would result in *t'ai-p'ing*. Just as in the *Lao-tzu*, the perfect government was one where the people were unaware of the existence of the ruler. Justice, which was essential, implied that the people had to have a hierarchy in which each category completely fulfilled its own responsibilities. There were nine categories of human beings, from those made of "breath" (*ch'i*) down to the common people and to slaves. In note 20 I point out a text where it is specified that these categories were not rigid and that it was possible for a slave to reach the highest degree of the hierarchy. One must suppose that even under a *t'ai-p'ing* regime there were expected to be bandits, since appropriate legal procedures were provided for them.

In the following section [pp. 33–38] I bring up certain points about morality. The basic idea in morality is that it is necessary to have free circulation of all values, including physiological values (of which I do not speak in this paper). *TPC* 67:241 ff. enumerates six sins. Other proscriptions are concerned with the prohibition of alcohol, the sale of girls, and the loss of chastity.

As for religion, I have only taken up ideas concerning death and life beyond the grave, which seem to be archaic in the *TPC*. Frankly speaking, the entire book seems to be impregnated with a religious aura.

Questions by Mather, the Discussant

1. If, as Professor Kaltenmark believes, the present T'ai-p'ing texts (*TT* fasc. 748–55, 746–47; Tun-huang Stein ms. 4226) all more or less agree with a Han original, does he also believe that Chang Tao-ling or Chang Chüeh were influenced by essentially the same text? What was the basic relation between T'ai-p'ing Tao and T'ien-shih Tao?

2. It appears from Professor Kaltenmark's paper that after Kung Ch'ung 宮崇 presented the text to the Emperor Shun (126–145) and it was rejected, some forty or fifty years passed before the Yellow Turbans Revolt took place—as a desperate countermove to replace the dynasty that refused to renew itself according to the T'ai-p'ing ideology. Was this long delay caused merely by the fact that they were waiting for a *chia-tzu* 甲子 year, or were there other causes for the rebellion than the rejection of the T'ai-p'ing ideal?

3. Since the social organization represented in this text seems to be closer to Confucian models and to antedate the more radical organization of the Five-Pecks-of-Rice sect, what were the sources for the latter's organization?

Answers from Kaltenmark

We have no idea whether our *TPC* is the *T'ai-p'ing tung-chi ching* used by the Celestial Masters, but we do have the expression *tung-chi* 洞極, in our *TPC*, where it is applied not only to the text but to the doctrine and to the Celestial Master as well. It is significant that our text speaks about a "Celestial Master," which is the same title as that used by the leader of the Five-Pecks-of-Rice sect. Therefore it must have had some connection with the latter. As for the basic relationship between the two Taoist rebel movements, it has been exhaustively studied by Fu Ch'in-chia 傅勤家 [see p. 2, n. 4] and by a number of other scholars.

With regard to your second question, it has been very satisfactorily studied by W. Eichhorn [cf. p. 8, n. 11]. Initially the text was presented to the emperor in the hope that the dynasty would reform, but after the refusal a period of time elapsed during which we do not know what happened, and finally the revolt took place.

As for dating, one of the reasons why I think the *TPC* antedates the Five-Pecks-of-Rice sect is that the social organization advocated in the former is so different from that of the latter. However, I do not think that the social organization of the *TPC* reflects a Confucian model. For instance, the highest category in the nine categories described in the *TPC* is that of the "divine men without form" 無形委氣之神人 [see p. 31] which has indeed nothing Confucian about it.

General Discussion

Stein: First, I would like to speak about this question of a Confucian model. Of course there is no doubt that the examples you have quoted are Taoist. There is no doubt that the *TPC* contains a Taoist vocabulary, atmosphere, and inspiration; but still there are some elements of Confucian ideas in it. With so much interchange between Confucianism and religious Taoism, we can even say that religious Taoism is intermixed with Confucian religion.

Second, I would like to mention the connection between the Yellow Turbans movement and that of the Five Pecks of Rice. According to you, since the organization of the two sects was different, the *TPC* must antedate the Five Pecks of Rice. But the title "Celestial Master" was not the same for the two sects. For the Five-Pecks-of-Rice the Celestial Master was a human being with religious and social sanctions, whereas for the T'ai-p'ing sect he was an emissary from Heaven.

Kaltenmark: In my view the *TPC* just represents an earlier stage of the Five-Pecks-of-Rice sect.

Stein: What, then, became of the movements of Chang Chüeh 張角, Yü Chi 于吉, and so on?

Kaltenmark: The evidence that Chang Chüeh used the *TPC* is very slight. I must point out two things. First, although the present *TPC* antedates the Five-Pecks-of-Rice sect, it represents at the same time a theoretical elaboration of what was later to become this sect. Unfortunately, most of the process of transformation still remains a mystery.

Second, the evidence pointing to a relationship between the Yellow

Turbans (Chang Chüeh) and the *TPC* is very slight. After all, only once in the *Hou-han shu* (ch. 30B) is it mentioned that Chang Chüeh made use of the *TPC*.

Stein: Just one more question: a *TPC* text or some *TPC* texts existed during the time of Chang Chüeh and Hsiang Chieh 襄楷. Do you think it was this text or texts that was adopted by the Five-Pecks-of-Rice movement? The Yellow Turbans movement seems to have enjoyed no continuance except in the Five-Pecks-of-Rice movement.

Kaltenmark: I ask Prof. Ōfuchi to correct me if I am wrong, but I think that the *Tao-chiao i-shu* 道教義樞 [see p. 255, n. 5] mentions that the text adopted by the Way of the Celestial Master is the *T'ai-p'ing tung-chi ching* (*TPTCC*).

Ōfuchi Ninji 大淵忍爾: The quotation you refer to says: "the *Cheng-i ching* states . . ." 正一經曰 . . . . However, we do not know what kind of a book this *Cheng-i ching* was. From such fragmentary quotations we cannot conclude whether the *TPC* was a book of the Way of the Celestial Master or not, nor do we know when it was written. Perhaps it was written during the Six Dynasties period. It is simply difficult to say whether it existed at the time of Chang Tao-ling.

Fukui Kōjun 福井康順: What edition of the *TPC* are you referring to?

Kaltenmark: The Wang Ming edition.

Fukui Kōjun: Then it is different from the *T'ai-p'ing tung-chi ching*.

Kaltenmark: Exactly.

Fukui Kōjun: I differ from Ōfuchi slightly. The Han *TPC* is not extant. The *TPTCC* antedates the *TPC*. Since the present *TPC* is posterior to the Han dynasty, I doubt whether it has anything to do with the *TPTCC*. I still have a question. Does the utopia described in the *TPC* contain elements of the Five-Pecks-of-Rice sect?

Kaltenmark: Yes.

Ōfuchi: I do not agree. Actually the Five-Pecks-of-Rice sect had a much smaller sphere of influence than the Yellow Turbans. It is said by some that the *TPC* was disseminated by Yü Chi, but I think it was spread by the Yellow Turbans. That is why the Five-Pecks-of-Rice sect must have been influenced by the *TPC*, but not the other way around.

Kaltenmark: This might indeed be a good possibility, but the fact remains that the *TPC* is after all a nonviolent book.

Ōfuchi: Furthermore, after Ts'ao Ts'ao 曹操 [founder of the dynasty of] Wei took over Han-chung 漢中, there must have been some sort of interchange between the followers of the two sects.

Fukui Kōjun: I thank Professor Kaltenmark for making us aware of our own limitations in this field of studies.

Needham: Although this is a digression, it might help us to date the text in a quasi-philosophical way. On page 34 of the paper [see p. 37] interdiction of alcohol is mentioned. The reason given is that alcohol is the enemy of water. Now for alcohol to burn, it must be strongly distilled. So far as my knowledge goes, the first mention of strong distilled alcohol is around 400, when China received tributes from Central Asian countries. Strong alcohol was not known in China earlier than the fifth century. Before this time only a weak wine was known in China, obtained through the "freezing out" process. If the *TPC* speaks of alcohol as opposed to water, it cannot be a Han text.

Kaltenmark: There has been a slight misunderstanding. Red and fire were emblems of the Han dynasty. Wine was compared to water and prohibited because of its opposition to fire.

Needham: How, then, could they drink water or anything else?

Kaltenmark: The text is not too coherent in many ways. As to fire being the reigning virtue, there is a passage found in the Tun-huang fragments of the *TPC*, published by Yoshioka, which is not extant in our present work and which reads 人腹各有天子文歸赤, and this, according to me, is one more indication that the *TPC* dates back to the Han.

Ōfuchi: Was there any relationship between the *fang-shih* and the *TPC*?

Kaltenmark: Of course. There was a relationship with the *fang-shih* since it was they who presented the *TPC* at the Han court, but *their* relationship with the Yellow Turbans still remains a problem.

Ōfuchi: You mean that in terms of ideology and religion there was a relationship but you are not sure of the persons involved?

Kaltenmark: Yes. I suggest looking at the *Shih-ts'e wen* 師策文, the Chinese text of which is in note 26. This Chinese text comes from chapter 38 of the Wang Ming edition and in the following chapter there is a commentary on it. Because of its method of annotation and because of expressions that can be understood in two ways, its style is similar to Han commentaries. Then the words 赤漢 also indicate that it is a Han text.

Fukui Kōjun: It is dangerous to date a text because of its ancient style, since the Chinese are experts in copying old masters.

Dull: I do not know anything about the *TPC*, yet the four things denounced (not to practice filial piety, not to have children, to eat excrement, and to beg) [p. 35] seem to be in the spirit of the Six Dynasties. It sounds very anti-Buddhist in character.

Kaltenmark: It is because the *TPC* has so many problems that I have brought it before specialists. I myself have not come to any definite conclusions as yet.

Ōfuchi: According to the article by T'ang Yung-t'ung 湯用彤 [and

T'ang I-chieh 湯一介, "K'ou Ch'ien-chih ti chu-tso yü ssu-hsiang"
寇謙之的著作與思想, *Li-shih yen-chiu* 歷史研究 8.5 : 64–77 (1961)] the
four interdictions have nothing anti-Buddhist about them.

Sakai: I think that Western scholars' translation of *mi* 米 as rice is wrong
because in Chinese *mi* does not only mean rice. Therefore I think that the
"Five Pecks of Rice" should be translated as "Five Pecks of Grain." One
should pay special attention to the areas where the "Five Pecks of Grain"
spread. These areas were rice-producing areas during the Han dynasty:
for example, Szechwan (Han-chung) and Shensi. Also, the followers of
the T'ai-p'ing sect were different from those of the Five-Pecks sect. The
former was composed of Yellow Turbans, vagrant farmers, vagabonds,
and bandits—that is, the very dregs of society; whereas the followers of
the latter were bona fide farmers who were quite well off.

As for the prohibition of wine and the four interdictions mentioned in
the *TPC*, these were traditional ideas held by Chinese peasants.

Schipper: It is well known from many different sources in Taoist books
that the first Celestial Master was called 正一平氣三天之師 ["the Master
of the Three Heavens of the P'ing Breath of Orthodox Unity"]. This
title was given to the first Celestial Master by Lao-tzu. The expression
平氣 ["*p'ing* breath"] is important because later when other priests were
given the title 後天師都功 ["Inspector of Merits, Master of the Posterior
Heaven"], 平氣 occurred in the title as 左平氣 ["left *p'ing* breath"], used
for males, and 右平氣 ["right *p'ing* breath"], used for females. It corresponds to 上平氣 ["supreme *p'ing* breath"] in the case of the first Celestial
Master. Does this represent T'ai-p'ing ideology?

Kaltenmark: Yes.

Ōfuchi: Farmers in Szechwan were rice-producing but the big farmers
emigrated to Kansu during the Han dynasty. Therefore the Five-Pecks
sect was not necessarily any better off than the T'ai-p'ing sect.

Miyakawa: This can be discussed in private.

Sivin: Talking about the Confucian elements in the *TPC*, what do we
mean by "Confucian"? In some cases we mean a system of ideas, in others
we mean the political realities of the Chinese imperial state. My sugges-
tion is that any attempt to accommodate to the authoritarian structure of
the Chinese empire was bound to contain Confucian elements, and the
TPC is no exception.

Kaltenmark: "Confucian" ideas have a concrete meaning. Even by the
end of the Han dynasty, any attempt to think about the organization of
political power had to contain Confucian concepts to some extent.

2 Religious Taoism and Popular Religion from the Second to Seventh Centuries

Rolf A. Stein

THROUGHOUT THE WORLD we are confronted with the problem of the relationship between official religion, organized into a church, and popular religion, which is unorganized and diffuse. It is often said of Christianity in Europe and of Buddhism in Tibet, China, and Japan that the national forms of these great religions owe their special characteristics to their incorporation of popular, indigenous elements. Sometimes, when two great religions have been rivals for the favor of rulers or of the people, scholars have had a tendency to subsume all kinds of "popular" elements under the rubric of the religion that lost out. This is the case with Tibetan Bon and Chinese Taoism. Everything that did not seem orthodox or purely Buddhist in Tibet has been described as "Bon" and everything that did not seem purely Buddhist or Confucian in China has been called "Taoist."[1]

A priori one can doubtless suppose a dialectical relationship between the two realms, based on the familiar and secure model of folklore. We know the process: folktales are first transmitted orally; next they are collected, published, and diffused by those who represent literary culture; then this written model prevails and is adopted, in turn, by the popular milieu.

It is the same for religions. In many specific cases popular customs and/ or beliefs have been borrowed from or adopted by a great religion. Rather than posing the chronological question of which happened first (a question that usually cannot be solved), it is better to envisage a ceaseless dialectical movement of coming and going. The priests of the great

1. Lamaist scholars went in for the same derogatory simplification. When they spoke of Chinese Taoism, they called it Bon.

religions willingly adopt popular elements and adapt them to their system and nomenclature. Inversely, when popular milieux are confronted with one or more of the great religions, they easily fall subject to the prestige of the latter, and they too proceed to assimilate, make identifications, and become syncretic; or they may even replace old traditional forms with new ones borrowed from a great religion because these have more prestige. We shall see some examples of this process.

The historical documents that bear on the various movements of religious Taoism from the end of the second to the start of the seventh centuries, contain several items of information on the relationship between these organized movements and various aspects of popular religion. Needless to say, the term "popular religion" here designates everything that does not belong specifically to an institutionalized religion (the state religion, Taoism, Buddhism). Sociologically speaking, this "popular religion" is not confined to the people but is common to all strata of society, including the imperial court.

Early in the sixth century the Taoist adept Chou Tzu-liang 周子良 had a series of revelations before dying young. He was the disciple of T'ao Hung-ching 陶弘景 (456–536), who published his papers.[2] There we are told that in A.D. 515 certain dreams of his raised doubts in the mind of his aunt. The Chou family had originally adhered to a cult of popular divinities 周家本事俗神, and it was feared that the young man had been visited by such a divinity (and not by an authentic member of the Taoist pantheon).[3] Further on, we find a Taoist divinity reproaching the young man for having earlier adhered to the cult of the adepts of Po 卿俗履帛家之事.[4] T'ao Hung-ching explains this passage by saying:

> Formerly the Chou family had been devout followers of a cult of popular divinities to whom they prayed. This cult was commonly known as the "Religion of the adepts of Po" 帛家之道, to which the master Hsü [Mai] 許[邁] had already referred at the moment when he was tested (*shih* 試) [by the divinities].[5] The grandmother of Chou Tzu-

2. *Chou-shih ming-t'ung chi* 周氏冥通記 (*Hsüeh-ching t'ao-yüan* 學津討源 edition; cf. also the edition in *Tao-tsang* (*TT*) 道藏 152).

3. Ibid., 1:2a.

4. Ibid., 1:11a. We do not know which Po is referred to here. It certainly cannot be the famous Po Ho 帛和 or Po-chün 帛君 in *Shen-hsien chuan* 神仙傳 7 and *Pao-p'u-tzu* 抱朴子, *nei* 內 19:97.16, 20:101.15 (Pai Ho 白和) (*Chu-tzu chi-ch'eng* 諸子集成 edition). Po Ho is sometimes associated with Yü Chi 于吉 and the *T'ai-p'ing ching* 太平經, see *T'ai-shang lao-chün ching-lü* 太上老君經律 (*TT* 562). Ko Hung 葛洪 cites schools (*chia* 家) in which a role is played by Yü Chi and Kuei (and?) Po 桂帛, see *Pao-p'u-tzu, nei* 14:62.20.

5. *Chen-kao* 眞誥 4:10b8 (*TT* 637). This testing consisted in being able to recognize real masters and real divinities in the disguises that they assumed to meet the adept, and in not being taken in by heterodox demons and spirits who tried to fool the adept by assuming similar disguises.

liang, who was born Tu 杜, had been a great sorceress [or female medium, *ta shih-wu* 大師巫] and this had contaminated the family of the mother of Chou Tzu-liang, that is, the Hsüs 徐. This family, however, had long been Taoist, with the rank of *chi-chiu* 祭酒, and it was Chou Tzu-liang's maternal aunt who had converted his father to Taoism. It was also she who raised the young man; but she was always afraid that he might be taken over by popular divinities.

T'ao Hung-ching's explanation is not entirely clear. Yet we might keep in mind the relations between certain families who belonged to a regular Taoist church and others who were devoted to popular cults. Doubtless the distinction was not always easy to draw, inasmuch as Taoist titles could be arrogated by mediums and sorceresses.[6] T'ao Hung-ching's identification of popular cults with "the adepts of Po" is repeated in his *Chen-kao* 眞誥 again, in connection with the Taoist Hsü Mai who was a friend of the calligrapher Wang Hsi-chih 王羲之 (ca. A.D. 300–348)[7] and the older brother (or father) of the famous Taoist Hsü Mi 謐. Hsü Mai is reproached for "having belonged to the religion of the adepts of Po" 汝本屬事帛家之道, which is here described in terms of the blood sacrifices practiced among the people.[8] We shall see that this was characteristic of the prohibited popular cults, the *yin-ssu* 淫祀. Mai's younger brother (or son) Hsü Mi (or Mu 穆 305–373) was also censured by a Taoist divinity for having permitted his servant to steal six dogs and then having eaten them with the servant in his own home. In this connection the *Chen-kao* notes that some laymen had sacrificed a white dog when they prayed to the soil gods 禱土地鬼神, and did so on the instructions of Hsü Mi.[9]

It is clear that the Hsüs, despite their belonging to orthodox Taoist movements, continued to be tempted by popular cults. T'ao Hung-ching points out that in his day the Hsü family had spread through the southeast and always practiced "the religion of the adepts of Po."[10] In this region

6. A master Hsü, who bore the same surname as the mother and aunt of Chou Tzu-liang, was the author of the *San-t'ien nei-chieh ching* 三天內解經 (*TT* 876), which is ascribed to the fifth century. In B:2b he complained that the "ordinary *chi-chiu*" of his time wore too many charms (doubtless meaning without having the right to them) 余每見今世俗祭酒佩符籙極多.

7. The family of Wang Hsi-chih had long belonged to the movement of the Five Pecks of Rice, see *Chin-shu* 80:5a (*T'u-shu chi-ch'eng*, 1739 ed.). Pills of cinnabar have been found in the tomb of a woman of that family, see *Wen-wu* 文物 10:38 (1965).

8. 血食生民. The sentence may be corrupt: cf. *Pao-p'u-tzu, nei* 9:39.6: "In all the demon religions (or cults) . . . animals are killed, and [the divinities] eat their fresh blood" 諸妖道 . . . 皆煞生血食. In 4:20.14–18 a contrast is drawn between obligatory sacrifice to the great divinities (e.g. T'ai-i 太一), offered on officially classified sacred mountains, and the sacrifices offered on minor mountains to the spirits of trees and stones (minor divinities) feeding on blood 血食之鬼. Divinities of the first kind are "correct" (orthodox 正神), while the second are "excessive" (heterodox 邪氣).

9. *Chen-kao* 7:11b10–12a5.

10. *Chen-kao* 20:4b–5b.

the Hsüs were linked by marriage to the important Hua 華 family of Ching-ling 晉陵. The latter, however, had been faithful followers of popular cults for generations 世事俗禱.[11] A certain Hua Ch'iao 華僑 (fourth century) who belonged to this family seems to have been converted to regular Taoism, but his adherence cannot have been very firm. He had been charged with transmitting revelations to Hsü Mi, but betrayed the secret. He was then punished by a divinity and replaced by the medium Yang Hsi 楊羲, whose family was also related by marriage to the Hsüs.

The circumstances of Hua's conversion to orthodox Taoism are significant. Brought up in the popular cults that his family practiced, he had had many communications with divinities 頗通鬼神. He often dreamt that he feasted with them, to the point where he used to vomit from still being drunk when he awoke. These "popular divinities" 俗神 also constantly obliged him to point out other persons (more than ten in all)—for what purpose is unclear.[12] Worn out, Hua Ch'iao joined a Taoist movement 入道. The spirits' manifestations 鬼事 then ceased, along with the troublesome dreams, and Taoist immortals came to visit him.[13]

It can be seen that adherence to organized and sublimated Taoism allowed the followers of popular religions to free themselves from the grip and the demands of their gods (partly revealed to them by mediums or sorceresses like the lady Tu, grandmother of Chou Tzu-liang). Among these demands must have been festivals with offerings of meat. Earlier in the same fourth century, Ko Hung 葛洪 shows[14] that there was a linkage and osmosis between the cults criticized by orthodox Taoists and certain Taoist movements considered to be heterodox. Ko Hung contrasts the "religions [or cults] of demons" 妖道, which involved the sacrifice of animals to gods who enjoyed their blood, with the "religion of the adepts of Li" 李家道.[15] As to the latter, he criticizes its communal meals, the

---

11. *Chen-kao* 20:12b 華僑者晉陵冠族, 世事俗禱, 僑被通神鬼.

12. Probably to serve as officials in the other world; Mr. Strickmann tells me rightly that this meant death for them.

13. *Chen-kao* 20:12b.

14. As can be seen in the *Pao-p'u tzu*.

15. *Pao-p'u-tzu, nei* 9:39. Compare the parallel expression "religion of the adepts of Po," which denotes popular cults. In the case of Li, too, it is not clear who is referred to. There is talk of a certain Li A 李阿 who must have been living in Szechwan about A.D. 250. Later one Li K'uan 寛, who came from the region of southeast China referred to in the text, pretended to be Li A. He practiced healing. Another Taoist, Li T'o 脫 (died in 324) practiced healing with the help of a "demon cult" (*kuei-tao* 鬼道). Finally, there is talk of Li Hung 弘, who is presented as a kind of savior, and of a certain Li Wei 微, a contemporary of Yü Chi. See *San-t'ien nei-chieh ching* (*TT* 876), *Lao-chün yin-sung chieh-ching* 老君音誦戒經 (*TT* 562), and A. Seidel, "The Image of the Perfect Ruler in Early Taoist Messianism," *History of Religions* 9.2–3:231–233 (1969/70).

"kitchens" (ch'u 廚) of several dozen people, with an excessive number of fancy dishes that entailed considerable expense. Yet while condemning them, he finds them preferable in that they involved no animal sacrifice. The "kitchens" or "merit meals" 福食 were nonetheless a regular institution of organized Taoism, although we do not know from what date they were introduced into its ritual. The first dated instance is contemporaneous with Ko Hung (mid-fourth century).[16] All this underlines the closeness of the cults he condemns to the regular cults of Taoism. We shall also see that Taoist "kitchen" festivals had a precedent in the communal meals which had been part of the practice of popular religion.

Popular cults with blood sacrifices and the cult of the "religion of the adepts of Li," which was closer to the Taoists but earned equal condemnation, are both included by Ko Hung in a list that has still other significant examples.[17] He makes his own the criticisms leveled against the popular cults by Confucian officials and literati, who made an effort to suppress these cults and destroy their temples. Of this he gives historical instances. A little further on he voices approval of the ostensibly rationalist reasoning of the literati when he cites cases of popular cults (of a fish, a tree, a tomb) which are borrowed word for word from the *Feng-su t'ung-i* 風俗通義 (second century).[18] The cults under criticism belong to the type of "excessive cults" (*yin-ssu* 淫祀), about which we have yet to speak. All have the following characteristics:

1. Excessive and ruinous expenditures
2. Prayers, animal sacrifices, songs, and dances
3. Use of mediums ("sorcerers" and "sorceresses") who give oracles
4. Rites of expiation to cure illnesses
5. A pantheon of minor uncodified local gods.

A certain hesitation is constantly visible in the attitude of Ko Hung, who was no less an official and literatus than a Taoist author. The demarcation between cults accepted by Taoism and "popular" or heterodox cults that it rejected was often difficult for him to establish. Initially he explains that, in order to achieve success in the great task of producing the elixir that enables one to make gold, one must offer a great sacrifice addressed not only to the major divinities (Heaven, Sun and Moon, the

16. Hsü Mi offered a "kitchen" meal to five persons (*Chen-kao* 18:8b3).

17. *Pao-p'u-tzu, nei* 9:37–39.

18. Ed. *Index du centre franco-chinois d'études sinologiques* (Peking, 1943), p. 70. Another case of popular worship addressed to a sacred tree and criticized by a literatus is described in *San-kuo-chih* 三國志, *Wei* 魏 11:8b (*T'u-shu chi-ch'eng*, 1739 ed.). For other borrowings by Ko Hung from Han Confucian works (*Lun-heng* 論衡, *Ch'ien-fu lun* 潛夫論), cf. Ōfuchi Ninji 大淵忍爾, *Dōkyōshi no kenkyū* 道教史の研究 (Okayama, 1964), pp. 136–83.

Great Bear, and the Great One, T'ai-i 太一) who were part of the official state cult, but also to lesser divinities, and above all to the tutelary gods (of the well, stove, doors, soil; the god of the Yellow River, Ho-po 河伯).[19] However, although here he accepts cults that were identical with the official cults, he criticizes the latter in chapter 14. There he attacks first the great Ch'in and Han cults of longevity, which were addressed to T'ai-i and other major gods and entailed enormous expenditures and animal sacrifices. Then, without making any distinction, he goes on to make the same criticism of the popular cults that claimed to cure illnesses and prolong life and also involved animal sacrifices and ruinous expenditures.[20]

We see that Ko Hung confirms what T'ao Hung-ching has to say about fluctuation between popular cults and Taoist cults. Besides the cases already cited, T'ao Hung-ching presents another that is equally characteristic. A certain Fan Po-tz'u 范伯慈, like his whole family, was a faithful follower of popular cults 家本事俗. He fell ill, became mad, and stayed in bed for an entire year. Then he approached a sorcerer, asking to be delivered and healed 迎師解事, which entailed such large expenditures that it slowly exhausted his family's fortune 費用家資漸盡. Still not healed, he heard talk of Taoism, which was "pure and moderate" 大道清約[21] and did not involve sacrifices 無所用. He then renounced popular religion, became a Taoist, and got well.[22] Cases of this kind were common. In his *Teng-chen yin-chüeh* 登眞隱訣 T'ao Hung-ching prescribes exorcisms for use after "the destruction of the temples where [mediums], seated on a mat, pray to improper gods" 破房廟坐席禱鬼邪物者. He adds the following commentary: "This refers to persons who formerly adhered to popular, excessive cults, but who were then converted to Taoism" 謂人先事妖俗, 今禀正化.[23]

A Taoist work of the fifth century takes such cases as typical: "Some devotees, before they entered the Tao, were laymen obsessed by 'demons' [minor gods], to whom they made sacrifices."[24] Afterwards they com-

19. *Pao-p'u-tzu, nei* 4:16. *Shih-chi* 史記 28:6b–7 (*T'u-shu chi-ch'eng*, 1739 ed.), in describing the great sacrifice of *chiao* 郊, characterizes the major divinities (Heaven, Sun, Moon, etc.) by the fact that they "feed on the blood [of animals sacrificed]" 血食. Yet this is exactly the same thing as in the prohibited "popular" cults (cf. n. 10).

20. *Pao-p'u-tzu, nei* 14:63.

21. In the *San-t'ien nei-chieh ching* A:3a4–5 (*TT* 876), this expression is used to refer to one of the Taoist movements that must have been typical of the region of Ch'u and Yüeh 楚越 (cf. below p. 63).

22. *Chen-kao* 14:11b10–12a4.

23. *Teng-chen yin-chüeh* C:21b3–6 (*TT* 193).

24. *Lu hsien-sheng tao-men k'o-lüeh* 陸先生道門科略 7a7–8 (*TT* 761) 或先是俗身, 負鬼祭饌, 越入道法.

mitted excesses. The organized Taoist religion acted as a catharsis and made possible the sublimation of obsessional contents. But it did not lie beyond the range of contamination. Between its own practices and those of the prohibited popular cults there was not a difference of nature, but only of degree; not of quality, but only of quantity. *Chen-kao* 15 contains an intriguing passage that illustrates well the difficulty encountered by "correct" authors when they tried to find a clear line of demarcation between themselves and the "excessive cults" that were so much criticized. In this passage T'ao Hung-ching gives a list of divinities, all historical personages who had died a violent death. We shall see that divinities of this type were characteristic of the "excessive cults" which were sometimes encouraged but more often prohibited by both court and literati officials. T'ao Hung-ching does not speak of their cult, but accepts them as supernatural officials occupying fixed positions in the hierarchy, and associates them with the "Six Heavens" 六天. The latter are looked upon as a principle of Evil (as opposed to the Good of the "Three Heavens" 三天) and are connected with the "excessive cults."

One group of divinities is particularly significant. They preside "over the blood sacrifices offered to the 'demons' [minor gods] of the world in small temples" 主天下房廟鬼之血食. The author is obviously aware of the contradiction between admitting these divinities into the pantheon and the principles that were generally adopted by orthodox Taoism. In his commentary T'ao Hung-ching is obliged to make a distinction: "blood sacrifices in small temples" must be taken to refer to the divinities who have received an official appointment to a position [in the celestial administration] and *not* to refer to "the harmful sprites who insidiously attach themselves [= obsess the faithful]" 房廟血食是受命居職者, 非謂精邪假附也.[25]

The foregoing documents attest to the fact that from the fourth to the sixth centuries followers of popular religion became adepts of a Taoist church because they found elements there to which they were accustomed, but which were sublimated and enclosed in a firmer and better-organized framework. The religious phenomena they found were not totally different from what they had known. Yet in absorbing these followers, the movements of organized Taoism had to be constantly on guard against excesses. The limitations they imposed could vary from one movement or author to another. The connection between the two religions was obvious enough for authors to be aware of it. Presumably it was due to the

25. *Chen-kao* 15:4b4–6a7.

absorption of popular elements by Taoism (even if this cannot be proven) and in return it facilitated the adoption of Taoist elements by popular religion.

There are some indications that the situation we have just seen obtaining from the fourth to the sixth centuries went back to the second, that is, to the very beginning of the organized movements of religious Taoism. Li T'o 李脫 (died in 324) is said to have been a Taoist master (tao-shih 道士) who cured diseases by means of "sorcery" (kuei-tao 鬼道, literally, "the religion of demons") or the art of communicating with minor gods, doubtless through "sorcerers" or mediums.[26] Convicted of practicing "diabolical arts" (yao-shu 妖術), he was decapitated.[27] Another heterodox Taoist, Ch'en Jui 陳瑞, was executed in 277 for the same reason. Coming himself from among the people, he disturbed them with "sorcery" (kuei-tao), and yet he had assumed Taoist titles (chi-chiu 祭酒, t'ien-shih 天師).[28]

Finally, of course, the very person who founded the first great Taoist movement, the Wu-tou-mi 五斗米 in the second century—Chang Lu 張魯—was noted for the same cult of kuei-tao, which he got from his mother.[29] We cannot review here the many documents that bear on this kind of "demon" cult, which entailed the evocation and apparition of such gods, followed by oracles from the mouth of a medium.[30] We need only emphasize that these techniques had already been the specialty of certain Taoists or magicians (fang-shih 方士) well before religious Taoism

---

26. Kuei-tao is the term used in the San-kuo-chih, Wei 30:11b for the Japanese mediums in the land of Yamato.

27. Chin-shu 58:3b and 61:3a.

28. Hua-yang kuo-chih 華陽國志 8:2b (Szu-pu pei-yao ed.).

29. Hou Han-shu 後漢書 105:1b (T'u-shu chi-ch'eng ed.); San-kuo chih, Wei 8:9b; Pien-huo lun 辯惑論 (Taishō [T] LII, 2102) and Erh-chiao lun 二教論 (T LII, 2103).

30. Cf. n. 26. Shortly after A.D. 222 a certain Yung K'ai gave oracles by means of the "religion of demons" 假鬼教 (San-kuo-chih, Shu 蜀 11:2b). A nineteenth-century author thought that this expression referred to oracles obtained with the spiritualist's planchette (fu-chi 扶乩): see Tu Wen-lan 杜文瀾, Ku yao-yen 古謠言 (reprinted Peking, 1958), p. 7. It is known that this method goes back to a popular custom attested to in the sixth century. It has also been thought that this same method is comparable to that used to obtain the fourth-century revelations recorded in the Chen-kao (beginning of the sixth-century). But the two are only linked by certain themes. However, the term kuei-tao is actually used of a style of writing in one of the revelations of the fourth century (Chen-kao 1:8b–9a). There a contrast is drawn between completely pure primordial writing and the ordinary writing of our world, which is impure 濁文, 濁書, but it is admitted that "true" writing 眞書 (that is, originating with a god who holds the hand of the adept) resembles kuei-tao, with only a small difference in the characters 鬼道亦然, 但書字有小乖違耳. Cf. R. A. Stein, "Un example de relations entre taoïsme et religion populaire," in Fukui hakase shōju kinen Tōyō bunka ronshū 福井博士頌壽記念東洋文化論集 (Tokyo, 1969), pp. 79–90.

as such came into being. The best known example is that of Li Shao-chün 李少君 (second century B.C.), who invoked the "demon" (that is, the god) of the stove in order to conjure up for the emperor the spirit of a dead woman.[31]

This case illustrates well the difficulty of reconstructing a historical frame. The *kuei-tao* of Chang Lu's mother seems to designate popular practices, whereas the case of Li Shao-chün seems to prove that these practices had long since been adopted by specialists in Taoism. The excessive vagueness of the terminology can obviously lead us astray, since the term *kuei-tao* can refer to a whole group of practices. It is possible that Confucian historians and Buddhist pamphleteers may have wished to denigrate Taoist movements by linking them to popular cults. Yet it is equally possible that they saw the undeniable affinity and the real link between the two religions.[32] We have already noted the difficulty experienced by Taoist authors from the fourth to sixth centuries in delineating the demarcation between their two domains. This difficulty is behind their attitude toward the "excessive cults" that were to be proscribed. The remarkable thing is that the condemnation of these cults by the Taoists, and their perplexity about how to draw the line between what should be tolerated and what should be rejected—this whole attitude of the Taoists is strictly the same as that of Confucian literati and officials, who were also constantly oscillating between condemnation and toleration.

Here are some examples of this. Historians claim that Chang Lu, like his mother, had recourse to "sorcery" (*kuei-tao*), which certainly involved blood sacrifices. However, a Taoist work attributed to Chang Lu—the *Lao-tzu hsiang-erh chu* 老子相爾注[33]—condemns certain sacrifices accompanied by prayers which it sees as part of communication with spirits 邪通.[34] As Jao Tsung-i has shown, it is not a question of *all* sacrifices, but only of those that were continuous (hence excessive) and involved assigning left-overs from food to minor or alien gods. During the last two

---

31. *Shih-chi* 28:10a.

32. According to the *Chen-cheng lun* 甄正論 (*T* LII, 2112, p. 571b), which was written at the end of the seventh century, Chang Ling invented nothing new. He simply followed the tradition of prayer and sacrifices. The functions of the *chi-chiu* in particular originated in the techniques of lay specialists which the Taoists borrowed. All this goes back to sorcerers, diviners, and mediums 尸祝, and involved the divinities of the *kuei-tao*.

33. See Jao Tsung-i 饒宗頤, *Lao-tzu hsiang-erh chu chiao-chien* 老子想爾注校牋 (Hongkong, 1956), p. 34 (and the commentary on pp. 75–76).

34. Cf. the *Tung-chen t'ai-shang pa-tao ming-chi ching* 洞眞太上八道命籍經 11b, 12a (*TT* 1029). In the list of faults there is "possession by demons" 爲鬼所著 and "communication with spirits" 爲邪所用. These are the result of "excessive cults" (*yin-ssu*) and end up in the coming of demons, in unions of men with women, etc.

centuries B.C. such sacrifices are attested to have been part of the imperial cult and of funeral rites.[35] Jao has drawn attention to the fact that an analogous disapproval of sacrifices is to be found not only in *Pao-p'u tzu* 抱朴子 (see above) but also in the *T'ai-p'ing ching* 太平經 (Wang Ming's edition, p. 52), which criticizes sacrifices to the divinities (*kuei-shen* 鬼神) who caused illnesses and took possession of people, notably the sacrifices to "other" divinities (*t'a kuei* 他鬼), whose status was irregular and not officially accepted and who were precisely characteristic of the "excessive cults."[36] For his part, Ōfuchi has pointed out that this negative attitude toward certain cults was reiterated in various Taoist prohibitions (*chieh* 戒) that are linked to the *Hsiang-erh chu*.[37] These prohibitions are still quite simple. They underwent long developments in later Taoist codes (*k'o* 科), in which the criticism of "excessive cults" comes into the schema of the present downfall and future salvation of humanity. In these codes the "excessive cults" are characteristic of the age of decadence governed by the "Six Heavens" 六天.

At the end of the Han the new religion of the "Lao-chün who has newly appeared" 新出老君 forbade such cults and intended to reestablish the golden age governed by the "Three Heavens" 三天, in which the followers of a revived Taoism would be the elect (*chung-min* 種民). The term "new Law" is generally used in the codes to designate the teaching of K'ou Ch'ien-chih 寇謙之 (died 448). Yet the relationship between the various Taoist currents or movements in the north (K'ou Ch'ien-chih) and south (Ko Hung, T'ao Hung-ching) during the Six Dynasties is a very complex historical question. Concerning the criticisms of abuses, these are everywhere attributed to the "Three Changs," or sometimes to Chang Chüeh 張角, in distinction to Chang Lu, who is exalted.[38] I shall not discuss this historical aspect of the matter, but shall confine myself to an analysis of the typical attitude.

35. Cf. *Shih-chi* 28:12b; *Chi-chiu pien* 急就篇, quoted by Jao Tsung-i (n. 33), p. 75.

36. Cf. *San-t'ien nei-chieh ching* 6a: 淫祀他鬼神.

37. "Gotobei dō no kyōhō ni tsuite" 五斗米道の教法について, *Tōhō-gakuhō* 東方學報 49.3: 333(55)–34(56) (1966) and "Rōshi Sōjichū no seiritsu" 老子想爾注の成立, *Okayama shigaku* 岡山史學 19:13–15 (1967). He cites the *T'ai-shang Lao-chün ching-lü* 太上老君經律 (*TT* 562), which forbids making sacrifices and prayers to the divinities 戒勿禱祀鬼神 (a sentence that is found in the *Hsiang-erh chu*).

38. This is found in the *Cheng-i fa-wen t'ien-shih chiao-chieh-k'o ching* 正一法文天師教戒科經 (*TT* 563), which M. Kaltenmark dates as third century (*Annuaire de l'Ecole Pratique des Hautes Etudes, 5ème section* [Paris, 1966–67], p. 74). For an attempt to clarify the historical relationships, see Fukui Kōjun 福井康順, *Tōyō shisō no kenkyū* 東洋思想の研究 (Tokyo, 1956), pp. 1–28, who contrasts the currents of the north and the south. But criticism of excessive cults comes up everywhere, in K'ou Ch'ien-chih (see n. 42), but also in Lu Hsiu-ching 陸修靜 (406–477), in Ko Hung, and in the *Chen-kao*.

The earliest work of this type of code (if it really dates from the third century), the *Cheng-i fa-wen t'ien-shih chiao-chieh-k'o ching* 正一法文天師教戒科經 (*TT* 563), draws a clear contrast between the age of decadence and the revival but gives no specific characteristics of the prohibited cults. We do find them given in the *San-t'ien nei-chieh ching* 三天內解經 (*TT* 876), which may date from the fifth century. The system there is complex. It does not consist in contrasting a single new religion with the practices of decadence. Rather, there is a set of three religions (*tao*): the first is "correct," purely *yang* 陽, and good for "China" in general; the second is *yin* 陰 and appropriate for the barbarians (Buddhism); and the third, half-*yin* and half-*yang*, prevails in the lands of Ch'u and Yüeh 楚越.[39] In an initial section, Good is contrasted with Evil and "correct" 正 with "improper" 邪, under three aspects: (*a*) the observance of kinship rules in marriage versus the nonobservance of rules and disorderly and "dirty" sexual union; (*b*) the worship of the supreme Tao and the practice of meditation versus the worship of improper divinities 信邪, 禱祀鬼神, which consists in the sacrifice of domestic animals, dances and singing, meals and drinking 烹殺六畜, 謠歌鼓舞, 酒肉是求; (*c*) the absence of intermingling, on the one hand, versus intermingling, on the other, of men with demons 人鬼交錯,[40] of the Three Religions, and of populations (Chinese with foreigners).[41]

A new section repeats this kind of opposition. After an initial intervention by Lao-tzu, Yin Hsi 尹喜, and Li Hung 李弘, comes the era of "low antiquity" (*hsia-ku* 下古), marked by decadence and characterized by sacrifices, sorcerers, and "demons" (minor divinities) 酹祭巫鬼 and by the intermingling of the True and the False. Then Yü Chi 于吉 and Li Wei 李微 receive the *T'ai-p'ing ching* to save the situation, but they are incapable of combatting the "Six Heavens" and of setting right what has gone wrong. Quite to the contrary, it gets worse under the Han: the Three Religions (see above) intermingle and the "Six Heavens" prosper.

The symptoms of this are as follows. In order to free themselves from the illnesses that are rampant, the people have recourse to doctor-sorcerers 醫巫 who come forward in great numbers and practice (*a*) religious songs[42] and dances 絃歌鼓舞; (*b*) the sacrifice of domestic animals to minor

---

39. *San-'tien nei-chieh ching* A:3a2–5; cf. n. 21.
40. The same theme is found in the *Ch'ih Sung-tzu chang-li* 赤松子章歷 1:1a (*TT* 335); this rule, like the code *T'ai-chen k'o* 太眞科, may have been promulgated by Celestial Master Chang under the Han, for at that time "men and demons (divinities) intermingled, spirits and sprites were spreading everywhere" 人鬼交雜, 精邪遍行.
41. *San-t'ien nei-chieh ching* A:1b–2a.
42. Ibid., A:4b9. The themes of these songs were minor divinities (of trees, rocks, etc.).

divinities 烹殺六畜, 酌祭邪鬼. It is then that T'ai-shang Lao-chün, "newly appeared" 新出, reveals the "Religion of the Correct One [resting on] the authority of the oath 正一盟威之道"[43] to Chang Tao-ling 張道陵, who becomes the Master of the "Three Heavens" 三天之師 and will abolish the Three Religions and the "Six Heavens" (? the Three Religions that depend on the "Six Heavens"?). The result is Good as characterized by the institutions of the Five Pecks of Rice 五斗米 (the Three Changs, Celestial Masters, the twenty-four parishes, the *chi-chiu* officials). These are opposed to Evil, which consists of the following practices: (*a*) promiscuous cults involving offerings of food and drink to "other" minor divinities 妄淫 祀他鬼; (*b*) banquets of alcohol and meat (doubtless at the end of these sacrifices).[44]

The divinities thus proscribed are called "other" because they are *alien* to the closed local group and its cult. What is remarkable is that, whereas these cults are rejected and forbidden, others equally popular are tolerated here (and elsewhere are even obligatory): worship of ancestors, the god of the stove, and the god of the soil (divinities that are *familiar* and opposed to the "others"). I shall have more to say about this below. Here I shall conclude my account of the *San-t'ien nei-chieh ching* by summarizing yet a third section, which takes up the contrast of Good with Evil for the last time but in quite a confused way. After the New Law of the Three Changs, the succession of Masters was disturbed and a new sect appeared. A final historical review contrasts again the Three Changs and the Three Mao 茅 brothers on the side of Good with the divinities on the side of Evil, who feed on the offerings in the little temples (of the popular cults) 食房廟之祇 which were being destroyed in this period of the Liu Sung 劉宋 dynasty (420–479).[45]

Some are known: see Wang Yün-hsi 王運熙, *Liu-ch'ao yüeh-fu yü min-ko* 六朝樂府與民歌 (Peking, 1957), pp. 167–81.

43. *San-t'ien nei-chieh ching* A:6a2: *Cheng-i meng-wei chih tao* 正一明 (= 盟) 威之道. The expression "newly appeared" is found in a tomb purchase contract dated A.D. 485, which begins with the words 新出老鬼太上老君符勑, see *K'ao-ku* 考古 4:182 (1965), and in a work on the 24 parishes (*Chang t'ien-shih erh-shih szu chih t'u* 張天師二十四治圖, cited in *San-tung chu-nang* 三洞珠囊 7:6b [*TT* 781] and *Yün-chi ch'i-ch'ien* 雲笈七籤 28:1b [*TT* 683]), which speaks of 新出太上老君. In the *Hsüan-tu lü-wen* 玄都律文 19a (*TT* 78), it is the doctrine of Cheng-i which is described as "newly appeared." In the *Lao-chün yin-sung chieh ching* 3b (*TT* 562), a text linked with K'ou Ch'ien-chih, the doctrine of Cheng-i is the new correct Law 新法, 更出新正. K'ou Ch'ien-chih received it in A.D. 415 (according to *Wei-shu* 魏書 114: 11b, 12b [*T'u-shu chi-ch'eng* ed.] 新科, 新法, 新經之制). According to the *Wei-shu*, K'ou Ch'ien-chih has eliminated the *false* Law of the Three Chang 除三張偽法, whereas in the *San-t'ien nei-chieh ching* the Three Chang are part of the *new* Law.

44. *San-t'ien nei-chieh ching* A:4b–6a.

45. Ibid., A:6b–9a.

The *Lao-chün yin-sung chieh-ching* 老君音誦戒經 (see n. 43) repeats the same statements and even the same schema of contrast between Good and Evil, but the abuses criticized are different: falsification of titles and functions, exactions by the masters of payments and contributions, the sexual techniques of Chang Ling,[46] and hereditary transmission of offices. The same criticisms are also to be found in the *San-t'ien nei-chieh ching*, but what is missing here are those concerning the cults.

On the other hand, these cults are criticized anew in the work of another fifth-century master, the *Lu hsien-sheng tao-men k'o-lüeh* 陸先生道門科畧 of Lu Hsiu-ching 陸修靜 (406–477). There the perfection (of, implicitly, High Antiquity, *shang-ku* 上古) is contrasted with the depravity of Low Antiquity 下古 during which reigned "the stale emanations of the Six Heavens" (*liu-t'ien ku-ch'i* 六天古氣). There too T'ai-shang Lao-chün reveals the Religion of the Correct One (Cheng-i 正一) to provide a remedy. As we shall see, these "stale emanations" imply excessive cults. This fact is explained in a description found in our text: generals and soldiers who have died in wars assume pompous titles; the men are called "generals" (*chiang-chün* 將軍), the women "ladies" (*fu-jen* 夫人). They go everywhere demanding worship and ruin the people by the sacrifices demanded in temples 責人廟舍, 求人饗祠.[47] This is exactly what had been characteristic of Chinese, Vietnamese, and Korean popular cults even very recently. In order to be appeased, the souls of those who had died a violent death demanded sacrifices and worship; and sought a recognized place in the pantheon.[48]

The text then notes that the followers of the Correct Religion of Cheng-i were violating its established prescriptions in being *seduced* by the

46. The sexual technique of the Three Chang is also alleged to have been attacked by K'ou Ch'ien-chih (*Wei-shu* and *Lao-chün yin-sung chieh ching*). This attitude is found also in the *Chen-kao* (2:1a, 5:2a, and 6:1a). On the other hand, the sexual practices under criticism are also attributed to the Yellow Turbans by Buddhist pamphleteers: see H. Maspero, "Procédés de nourrir le souffle vital," *Journal Asiatique* 401–02, 405–06 (1937). The Three Chang of the Five Pecks of Rice (Chang Ling, Heng 衡, and Lu) have sometimes, perhaps, been confused with the Three Chang whom Maspero considered the chiefs of the Yellow Turbans (Chang Chüeh 角 and his two brothers). In reality, the object of criticism was only the abuses, whereas the technique was sometimes accepted—and even recommended to a certain degree—in order to assure descendants. Cf. Yang Lien-sheng 楊聯陞, "*Lao-chün yin-sung chieh-ching hsin chiao-shih*" 老君音誦戒經新校釋, *Academia Sinica Bull. H.-Phil.* 28A:21 (1956).

47. *Lu hsien-sheng tao-men k'o-lüeh* 1a (*TT* 761).

48. The facts in the case of China are well known. In the case of Vietnamese medium cults (*ba-dong*), the divinities have pompous titles: General, Prince, Lady, Queen. The same is true of Korean road gods, which are columns 長柱 terminating in a "demonic" head and bearing the titles: 天下大將軍, 地下女將軍.

deviant ways of sorcerers 向邪僻妖巫之倒法. Whether they are expressed positively (prescribing abstinence) or negatively (seductions suffered), the following traits characterize the popular cults criticized in this Taoist book: (*a*) sacrifices (food offered) to demon divinities; (*b*) the revelation of the future through getting these divinities to speak, whether to ask for a "blessing" (*fu* 福) or to learn what action to take in the construction of houses or tombs, with regard to travel, and so on; or what taboos to observe.[49]

In the works that have just been analyzed, the abuses under criticism are mentioned as the symptoms of a period of decadence. They occupy a logical place in a coherent account of the drama of humanity. In other works this legendary framework is absent and all that remains are lists of abuses which can be inserted in the rules that prohibit them.

In the *T'ai-shang tung-yüan shen-chou ching* 太上洞淵神咒經, which dates from about A.D. 420, the theme of Evil reigning in the world is still implicitly present. But the opposition seen between antiquity and the new era has disappeared, and only isolated passages remain that bear on divinities to be avoided and cults to be eliminated. This revealed book itself is said to serve as a talisman against all ills and in it we see that minor divinities, who have been accepted, incorporated into the hierarchy of the Taoist pantheon, and placed under the orders of T'ai-shang Lao-chün, serve to keep away other divinities who have not been accepted (but who are basically of the same nature). The latter are, for example, "demons" 鬼 with improper pretensions to the title of "Great God" 妄稱大神; "demons who are not included in the registers" 脫籍之鬼; generals of defeated armies who hold sway in the temples "of the world" (= non-Taoist temples) or who are worshipped in the forests and mountains or as soil gods 山林, 社祀, 廟主.[50] Only the divinities affiliated with a given family (the god of the soil or god of the stove of *that* family and not of another) are eligible. The others, who come from outside and are alien to the group, who are trouble-makers and malefactors (notably tomb spirits) are kept at a distance 自非家祀之鬼 . . . ; 自非生人所事家親鬼 . . . .[51] The "generals of defeated armies" are persons who have died a violent

49. *Lu hsien-sheng tao-men k'o-lüeh* 8a–b.

50. *T'ai-shang tung-yüan shen-chou ching* 1:9a (*TT* 170). Cf. Ōfuchi Ninji, "Dōen shinjukyō shōkō" 洞淵神咒經小考, in *Wada Hakase koki kinen Tōyōshi ronsō* 和田博士古稀記念東洋史論叢 (Tokyo, 1951), pp. 235-46; and *Dōkyōshi no kenkyū*, chap. 4; Yoshioka Yoshitoyo 吉岡義豊, *Dōkyō kyōten shiron* 道教經典史論 (Tokyo, 1955), pp. 231-63.

51. *T'ai-shang tung-yüan shen-chou ching* 2:3b, 5a .Regarding the dual meaning of the word *kuei* 鬼, see note 83.

death, whose head and body are buried in different places,[52] whose spirits have been dispersed so that they settle on mountains or trees, troubling men and causing illnesses, and look for bloody food (cult offerings) 求其血食, their demand for which is discovered through divination by "masters" (sorcerers) with a popular following 俗師所占.[53]

As I stated above, lists of the characteristics of popular cults were retained in Taoist codes and rules until the T'ang and even the Sung. By their occasional mention of "stale emanations" (ku-ch'i 古氣), we are reminded of the conceptual framework involving the diachronic opposition of Evil and Good. The Tao-tien lun 道典論, a T'ang collection that cites earlier works including three codes 科, devotes a special paragraph to the "excessive cults."[54] First it gives a definition of "excessive cults" that is drawn from the Confucian classics (see pp. 77–78): "sacrificing to divinities ["demons"] other than one's own" 祭非其鬼. They are called "stale emanations" 故氣. Their cults entail animal sacrifices 殺生, dances 鼓舞, liturgical singing 祠祀歌吟, substantial expenditures, and unorthodox divinities 禱祀邪神 who arrogate to themselves the title "Lady" or "Sir" (unless this is being done by the mediums who incarnate them) 自稱姑郎.

Another T'ang collection, the Yao-hsiu k'o-i chieh-lü ch'ao 要修科儀戒律鈔, which quotes extracts from the codes and rules, gives a list of the days that are favorable and unfavorable for this and that measure to eliminate all sorts of ills (arising from tombs, spirits, and sprites of the house, from the soil god, and so on). Among these measures are the destruction of temples 破廟 (it will be seen below that what is involved here are temples dedicated to popular divinities),[55] and the extermination or punishment of "stale emanations" 收除故氣, of minor temples 誅房廟[56] and of their numerous sorcerer-mediums 千師萬巫.[57]

The same preoccupation recurs in a Sung collection, the T'ai-shang chu-kuo chiu-min tsung-chen pi-yao 太上助國救民總眞秘要: "to destroy the

---

52. Cf. n. 48. Separate burial of the head and body was the fate of the famous Kuan Yü 關羽 (Kuan-ti chih 關帝志 1:36a, 37a). He appeared as a snake in a tree and received the worship of a Buddhist monk: see Fo-tsu t'ung-chi 佛祖通記 (T XLIX, 2035, p. 183b). The prototype of the general whose head and body were interred at a distance from one another was Man-tzu 蔓子: see Hua-yang kuo-chih 1:2b. Regarding the worship of dead heroes, of which I have yet to speak, see Uchida Michio 內田道夫, "Kō U shin monogatari" 項羽神物語, Tōhō-gaku 東方學 12 (1956).

53. T'ai-shang tung-yüan shen-chou ching 4:1a (TT 170).

54. Tao-tien lun 3:15b–16a (TT 764).

55. Yao-hsiu k'o-i chieh-lü ch'ao 要修科儀戒律鈔 10:10a (TT 205).

56. Ibid., 10:11a4; cf. 14a1.

57. Ibid., 10:11b.

temples of divinities not [officially classified as] correct, that is, divinities who have not been included in the liturgical canon of the reigning dynasty" 破不正符廟, 破諸不正神廟, 謂非國朝祀典之神, who stay in plants and trees 依草附木 or in springs, etc., and who make excessive demands for bloody sacrifices and cause disease [if they do not receive them] 橫求血食, 興作疾病.[58] The same information about the destruction of temples and cults is already to be found in a sixth-century work (see n. 23). As we shall see once more, by destroying temples in this manner, the Taoists were acting exactly like the literati officials.

But before going on to this, we should take note of the fact that the Taoists' attitude toward popular cults contained not only the negative element of prohibition but the positive element of adoption. We have seen above (p. 64) that certain cult practices of popular religion were not merely permitted but recommended.

In the historical schema of the *San-t'ien nei-chieh ching*, the new religion that was to bring salvation after the errors of the past—the religious Taoism of the Five Pecks of Rice—condemns the popular cults but allows the following exceptions for the great mass of the faithful (*wei-t'ing* 唯聽).

1. The worship of ancestors belonging to one's own family (that is, excluding any *other* ancestor or deceased person who belongs to *other* groups), and this worship to be performed not at any time whatsoever, but solely during the five festivals fixed on the five propitious days of the year called *la* 五臘吉日祠家親宗祖父母.

2. The worship of the soil god and the god of the stove, also not at any time whatever, but solely in the second and eighth months 二月八月 祠祀社竈.

Other texts are less strict, toleration being replaced by obligation. Thus, according to the *Chai-chieh lu* 齋戒錄, "on the five *la* days one should always observe a fast and sacrifice to the ancestors" 五臘日並宜修齋并祭 祀先祖,[59] and "on the five *la* days one should always worship and make offerings to the dead; this is called 'being a filial son'; one derives blessings without end; but [if one worships] on another day, it is [considered] an excessive cult" 五臘日常當祠獻先亡, 名爲孝子, 得福無量, 餘日皆是淫 祀.[60]

58. *T'ai-shang chu-kuo chiu-min tsung-chen pi-yao* 1:6a–8b (*TT* 986).

59. *Chai-chieh lu* 9a3 (*TT* 207). This work dates from the end of the seventh century. See Yoshioka Yoshitoyo, "Saikairoku to shigensō" 齋戒錄と至言總, *Taishō daigaku kenkyū kiyō* 大正大學研究紀要 52:18 [= 300] (1967).

60. *Chai-chieh lu* 16b, repeated in *Yao-hsiu k'o-i chieh-lü ch'ao* 8:3b, which adds: "It is a sin" 有罪. The passage also occurs verbatim in the *Tung-hsüan ling-pao t'ai-shang liu-chai*

Let us at once take note of the fact that the formulation and contents of these Taoist prescriptions are purely Confucian (filial piety, ancestor worship, "blessings" derived from worship). I shall return to this. But let me first add another example of the identity of attitudes. We read in the Taoist "code," the *Lu hsien-sheng tao-men k'o-lüeh*: "The Son of Heaven sacrifices to Heaven, the Three Dukes to the five sacred mountains, the feudal lords to the mountains and rivers, and the people . . . worship their ancestors [and the gods of the soil and stove, as above]." The passage concludes by saying that "aside from these there should be no other sacrifices" and that, if these were performed on other dates, "it would violate [the prohibition] of excessive cults" 皆犯淫祠.[61] These sentences are borrowed almost word for word from the ritual prescriptions of the *Han-shu* 漢書, where it presents the official religion of the Chou (also from the *Li-chi*, see below p. 78).

We know that in the popular and official religions, *la* denoted the last month of the year and, above all, the 8th of the twelfth month, a day marked by feasting (on which meat and salted fish were eaten) and by sacrifices to the ancestors and tutelary gods. It was related to and sometimes confused with the *cha* 蜡 festival,[62] which was also set apart by feasting and by worship of "all the gods," who then held a meeting. *La* signified the end of the year and preparation for the New Year. It was also related to the soil god (*she* 社), before whose image meat was distributed. Since the Han, a midsummer counterpart of the *la*, namely the *tsu* 祖 (ancestor) had been provided, and a third term, the day of *she*, the soil god, had become associated with it. The dates varied according to the theory of the "Five Emperors" 五帝.[63] The religious Taoist movements during the Six Dynasties elaborated these concepts and ended up with a

---

shih-chih sheng-chi ching 2b (*TT* 875). The prescription is often repeated, as in *Ch'ih Sung-tzu chang-li* 2:17b (*TT* 335) (on sacrifices to ancestors). *Yao-hsiu k'o-i chieh-lü ch'ao* 10:21b (*TT* 205) has the following passage: "On the auspicious days of the five *la*, the Taoist faithful sacrifice to their dead ancestors. First a supplication (*chang*) has to be submitted to invite their presence, after which the sacrifice is offered. This conforms to the principle of filial piety" 此五臘吉日，奉道之家則依此祭先人，先須上章啟請先人，然後設祭，孝子之道也. Another such passage may be found in the *Yu-lung chuan* 猶龍傳 5:5a (*TT* 555). This is a Sung work from the end of the eleventh century, which adds that "blessings without end" are derived from this sacrifice. Finally, ancestor worship on the *la* day of the 5th of the fifth month is prescribed in the *Sui-shih kuang-chi* 歲時廣記 21:20 (undated Ch'ing Dynasty xylograph ed.), which cites the *Cheng-i chih yao* 正一旨要, a Taoist epitome.

61. 1b (*TT* 761).

62. The word *la* 臘 is also written 腊 (*la* or *hsi*, dried and salted meat) because of confusion with *cha* 蜡.

63. *Hou Han-shu* 15:4a–b; *Tu-tuan* 獨斷 A:14a (*Han-wei ts'ung-shu* 漢魏叢書 ed.).

list of five *la*, days on which the Five Emperors held a reunion in the celestial capital of Hsüan-tu 玄都. These were:

1. The *la* of Heaven on the 1st of the first month
2. The *la* of Earth on the 5th (or 1st) of the fifth month
3. The *la* of the Way and its Power (*tao-te* 道德) on the 7th of the seventh month
4. The *la* of the popular New Year (*min-sui* 民歲) on the 1st of the tenth month
5. The *la* of the kings and feudal lords (*wang-hou* 王侯) in the twelfth month.[64]

It is not possible here to make a detailed study of the annual festivals, but certain significant relationships must be mentioned. Three of the five *la* coincide more or less with the Three Great Festivals of the Taoists (*san-hui* 三會): the 5th or 7th of the first month (*shang-hui* 上會): the 7th of the seventh month (*chung-hui* 中會); and the 1st and 5th or the 5th or the 15th of the tenth month (*hsia-hui* 下會). All these were assemblies both of the parish and of the gods. These dates and festivals are in turn inseparable from three other Taoist festivals, the *san-yüan* 三元, which have become "popular": the 15th of the first month (*shang-yüan* 上元); the 15th of the seventh month; and the 15th of the tenth month. These two series are linked by their common association with the Three Officials (*san-kuan* 三官) of Heaven, Earth, and Water, who inspect man's doings on the dates in question.[65] Furthermore, the five *la* and three *yüan* make up a group of festivals called "the eight dates of deliverance" 八解日, in the course of which Taoists were permitted to sacrifice to their ancestors and "seek for blessings" (*ch'iu-fu* 求福)—blessings typical of such cults. This list should be compared to another list of eight dates, the "eight feast-days (*pa chieh-jih* 八節日 or *pa wang-jih* 八王日), which were, like the rest, marked by maigre-feasts (ritual communal meals, *chai* 齋) and by reunions of gods. This last list included the two equinoxes, the two solstices, and

64. Ch'en Kuo-fu 陳國符, *Tao-tsang yüan-liu k'ao* 道藏源流考, 2d ed. (Peking, 1963), p. 319, citing *Ch'ih Sung-tzu chang-li* 2:17a–b (*TT* 335). Cf. *Yao-hsiu k'o-i chieh-lü ch'ao* 8:2a, 3b (*TT* 205) which cites the *Sheng-chi ching* 聖紀經 2a–b (*TT* 875); and cf. also the *T'ai-shang tung-hsüan ling-pao ching-kung miao-ching* 太上洞玄靈寶淨供妙經 4b (*TT* 181). The names of the last two *la* are the same as those used in Tibet for two dates of the New Year: the "farmers' New Year" (*so-nam lo-gsar*) at about the winter solstice (end of the tenth, beginning of the eleventh month) and the "king's New Year" (*rgyal-po lo-gsar*) on the 1st of the first month.

65. The second festival (*chung-yüan*) of the 15th of the seventh month has become grafted with the Buddhist festival of Ullambana. See Yoshioka Yoshitoyo, *Dōkyō to Bukkyō* II 道教と佛教 (Tokyo, 1970), pp. 232–35 and 250–68.

Month	Day	The five *la*	The three *yüan*	The three great festivals	The eight dates of deliverance
		五臘	三元	三大會	八節日
First	1	天臘			No. 1
	5 or 7			上會	
	15		上元		No. 2
Fifth	5	地臘			No. 3
Seventh	7	道德臘		中會	No. 4
	15		中元		No. 5
Tenth	1	民歲臘		下會 (preparations)	No. 6
	5			下會 (main date)	
	15		下元	下會 (variant)	No. 7
Twelfth	8	王侯臘			No. 8

the first days of the four seasons. The equinoxes and solstices also coincided with festivals in popular worship that were accepted by the Taoists.

We have seen earlier that, according to the *San-t'ien nei-chieh ching*, the popular worships permitted to the Taoist faithful were—besides ancestor worship on the five *la* days—the worship of the soil god and the god of the stove in the spring (second month) and the autumn (eighth month). According to a Buddhist tract aimed at the Taoists, the *Erh-chiao lun* 二教論, which dates from the end of the fifth century, the Taoists "made sacrifice to the stove and worshipped the soil god at the two equinoxes of spring and autumn, and they carried on the same worship as ordinary people at the two solstices of winter and summer" 春秋二分祭竈祠社, 冬夏二至, 記祠同俗.[66]

This statement about seasonal worship follows another dealing with the "kitchen festivals," which were intended to bring about "liberation" (*chieh-ch'u* 解除, variant in *Pien-huo lun*: 解廚) from pollution and sin and which were connected with tombs (or, according to one edition of the *Pien-huo lun* 辯惑論, with sacrifice grounds bounded by cords, *tsuan* 纂). After this comes a third statement criticizing the fact that the faithful received "beforehand" (before the "kitchen festivals"? or before seasonal worship?) ranks and titles such as "parish talisman" (*chih-lu* 治籙), "soldier's charm" (*ping-fu* 兵符), or "contract of [or with?] the soil god" (*she-ch'i* 社契). These took the form of diplomas which ranked the faithful in the hierarchy of a "parish" (*chih* 治), "army" 軍, "general" 將, "official" 吏, and "soldier" 兵. It is possible, though not certain, that a logical connection links these three statements. Maspero thought so and he

66. *Kuang hung-ming chi* 8, *Erh-chiao lun*, *T* LII, 2103, p. 140c.

compared the "contracts of the soil god" with "tomb purchase contracts" (*ti-chüan* 地券, or *mu-chüan* 墓券), of which many examples are known.[67]

67. H. Maspero, *Le Taoïsme* (Paris, 1950), pp. 158–59. See n. 43 for an example of a "tomb purchase contract" that purports to be an order of the "newly appeared" T'ai-shang Lao-chün. Such a contract, dating from the fourth century, is preserved in the *Chen-kao* (10:14–16). The text is identical with that on a T'ang archaeological find: see *K'ao-ku* 8:388 (1965). The "kitchen festivals" had to be celebrated at the same times as the three major festivals of the year (*san-hui*), within the parish, and on the occasion of events that modified the civil status of the faithful (marriage, birth, etc.). In addition, there was the practice of "liberation kitchen feasts" 解廚, the purpose of which was self-purification from sins, removal of bad influences, and procurement of "blessing." Those "kitchens" were often connected with the soil god, the tombs, or various sprites and divinities of the house. Allusion has already been made to a work that gives a long list of them: see the *Yao-hsiu k'o-i chieh-lü ch'ao* 10:8a–20b and cf. n. 73. It is not certain that the *Erh-chiao lun* is really making any allusion to tombs. The same sentence about "liberation kitchen feasts" linked with tombs is found in the *Pien-huo lun* (*Kuang hung-ming chi* 8, *T* LII, 2102, p. 49a), a work of similar date; yet in one edition of the *Pien-huo lun* (indicated there) the word *tomb* is replaced by the word meaning "cords surrounding a sacrifice ground." Both variants are acceptable.

Another anti-Taoist Buddhist pamphlet of the sixth or seventh centuries (*Kuang hing-ming chi* 12, *Pien-huo p'ien* 辯惑篇, *T* LII, 2103, p. 171a) ridicules Taoists who "mark trees in order to make them into soil gods; set up bricks and stones that they call 'lords'; pile up earth to make 'sacrifice grounds' and then plait cords *tsuan* 纂 of reeds (or of straw) in order to embellish them." The purpose of all this is to beg for help in case of danger, or to pray for rain. A late work, the *T'ai-shang tsung-chen pi-yao* 太上總眞祕要 (*TT* 986–87), whose preface is dated 1116, makes it possible to get an idea of the use of these cords. They served to enclose the sacrifice ground. Gates were arranged along the perimeter of the enclosure 須安壇, 立纂, 建獄, 開門 (see ibid., 7:3a, quoted from the "Cheng-i ritual on the punishments [inflicted on erring divinities]": 正一考召儀). The same work contains the "Celestial Master's method of punishing with cords the 'demon' (divinity) of the stove" 天師考竈纂鬼法 (ibid., 7:21b). A sacrifice ground (*t'an* 壇) is prepared and enclosed by cords, with provision for the four gates of Heaven, Earth, Man, and Demons. The god of the stove is summoned, accused of having allowed "alien demons" 外鬼 to penetrate the home and cause suffering there, and then he is beaten. The rites are certainly older than this source. Already a seventh-century work that draws on earlier texts mentions the "Tribunal for Summons and Judgments" 考召院, to which anyone can turn if, for example, he wants to curb a soil god: see *Chin-so liu-chu yin* 金鎖流珠引 25:1a (*TT* 631–36).

Whether they are speaking of tombs or "cords" used in ritual, it can be seen that the reason Buddhist authors apply the term "black magic" (*tso-tao* 左道) to Taoist rituals is because the latter are concerned with summoning minor gods, assigning them tasks, or eventually punishing them in case they fail to fulfill their duties (something like Li Shao-chün's ritual, much earlier; see p. 61). The statements summarized from the *Erh-chiao lun* seem logically connected. Their relationship with "kitchen festivals" is confirmed by the grades or titles criticized in the third statement. These are found again in a detailed regulation from a code regarding the "kitchens," cited in the *Yao-hsiu k'o-i chieh-lü ch'ao* 12:1b–2a (*TT* 206). Next after *tao-shih* of a high grade, it names those who have the talisman (*lu*) of an official or a soldier and the youths who have the grade of *keng-ling* 更令童子. According to the same book (*ch.* 9–10), a first *keng-ling* title was conferred on a boy at the age of seven, a second at an unspecified age, and a third, called "talisman of a premier youth-general" 童子一將軍籙,

These contracts are a very typical product of the syncretism between popular religion and organized religious Taoism, whereas their prototype or model is to be found in real contracts for the purchase of land.[68] I am considering the publication elsewhere of a detailed study on this subject. A few adumbrations must suffice here. In the oldest specimens (49 B.C., A.D. 81, 171 and 188) the name of the purchaser, the dimensions of the plot, the price, and the witnesses are real, but very soon they become half real and half religious or mythical. Starting in A.D. 178, there appears a closing formula that guarantees the execution of the contract in accordance with the code of a divinity 如天帝律令. The pantheon involved here includes both gods of Chinese popular religion (Ho po 河伯, Hsi-wang mu 西王母, etc., and many minor soil gods) and figures who are properly Taoist (cf. nn. 43 and 67). Which were earlier is difficult to say. Here, as in other cases, there is coming and going. Minor gods of the popular religion were admitted to the Taoist pantheon, but this pantheon in turn furnished figures for popular religion.[69]

We know that the earliest movements of religious Taoism utilized other "contracts" with the great divinities of Heaven, Earth, and Water (the so-called san-kuan shou-shu 三官手書). Ōfuchi has considered that these contracts originated in popular customs of that era.[70] The Three Officials are connected with the "Code of 1,200 Officials" (cf. n. 69), which envisaged punishment for the offenses committed, not only by the faithful, but also by the minor divinities of "popular worship" who had been admitted to the Taoist pantheon.

This is not all. Still other rites were shared in common by the "popular" religion (or, in any case, non-Taoist religion) and by the organized movements of religious Taoism. The first such rites are attested to before these movements were formed. We have seen how the *Erh-chiao lun* finds a

---

was conferred on boys and girls from eight to nineteen. On this hierarchy of military ranks, cf. also Ch'en Kuo-fu, *Tao-tsang yüan-liu k'ao*, p. 341.

68. Cf. Niida Noboru 仁井田陞, *Tō-Sō hōritsu bunsho no kenkyū* 唐宋法律文書の研究 (Tokyo, 1937), pp. 13, 105–133; J. Gernet, "La vente en Chine d'après les contrats de Touen-houang," *T'oung-pao* 45:4–5 (1957); Harada Masami 原田正己, "Minzoku shiryō to shite no boken" 民俗資料としての墓券, *Philosophia* 45 (1963), and "Bokenbun ni mirareru myōkai no kami to sono saishi" 墓券文に見られる冥界の神とその祭祀, *Tōhōshūkyō* 東方宗教 29:17–35 (1967).

69. Compare the case of the "tomb contract" reproduced in *Chen-kao* 10:14–16. In it figures the god Chao Kung-ming 趙公明. T'ao Hung-ching declares in his commentary that, according to a contemporary book of ritual on the 1,200 Officials 今千二百官儀, this Chao Kung-ming was a "demon of diseases" 溫鬼. In modern popular religion, he has become a god of wealth.

70. Ōfuchi Ninji, *Dōkyōshi no kenkyū*, p. 46, n. 8.

connection between the popular rites on the equinoxes and solstices that were permitted to Taoists and, on the other hand, the Taoist practices of "liberation" from sins and faults—practices linked with tombs. However, whereas the characters used here mean to "liberate and eliminate" (*chieh-ch'u* 解除), the parallel passage in the *Pien-huo lun* uses a homophone meaning "kitchens of liberation" (*chieh-ch'u* 解廚). The two terms "liberation" and "kitchen" (the latter meaning a ritual communal meal) have non-Taoist antecedents linked to the soil gods.

Rites to "liberate and eliminate" are already attested to by the *Lun-heng* 論衡 of Wang Ch'ung 王充 (A.D. 27–97). It shows that, as with the Taoists at a later time, the negative rites to avert evil were paired with sacrifices to obtain a "blessing" 祭祀可以得福, 解除可以去凶; and furthermore, the very act of ridding oneself of a fault and its resulting evil implied a positive "blessing" such as long life 可求解除之福, 以取踰世之壽. The apology offered to the offended divinity (who has taken vengeance by causing the evil) is what "delivers" the worshipper from sin and from the evil and assures him the favor of a "blessing" that will be granted by the divinity.

Wang Ch'ung cites primarily the example of "liberation (apology and pardon) toward the [god of] the soil" 解土, a rite necessary when the soil must be disturbed to construct (a house, tomb, etc.) which involves the danger of offending the god who resides there. In order to ask for pardon and appease the god, one offers him a human figurine. One is thereby "liberated and excused by the soil god" 解謝土神 and "when the gods have given their pardon, the evils are removed from the soil" 鬼神解謝, 殃禍除土.[71] It is the soil gods and the gods of a locality who always figure in "tomb contracts," since it is from them that the land has to be "purchased." In the *Tung-kuan chi* 東觀記 we find an example of a prayer to be recited during such a rite for house construction (A.D. 60).[72] We have already seen (cf. note 67) that these rites have been adopted by the Taoists. In the list mentioned above, one can point out "the liberating apology for tombs" (*chieh meng-mu* 解塚墓, a phrase which occurs repeatedly), for the sprites of the whole house 解一宅中虛耗, for the soil god 解土公, and for the dead 解亡人.[73]

71. *Lun-heng*, para. *Chieh-ch'u p'ien*, p. 245 (*Chu-tzu chi-ch'eng* ed.).

72. *Tung-kuan chi*, cited in *Hou Han-shu* 71:6a: 爲解土, 祝曰.

73. *Yao-hsiu k'o-i chieh-lü ch'ao* 10:8a ff. (*TT* 205). All these rites necessitated petitions (*chang*) according to a fixed code. The rites are explained to Ch'ih Sung-tzu by an Elder of Heaven named P'ing-ch'ang 天老平長. This feature is found again in one of the codes, the *Ch'ih Sung-tzu chang-li* 1:1a–b (see n. 40), which refers to the Code (book of ritual) of the 1,200 Officials. Here we find all kinds of redemption of mistakes through offerings,

The Taoist communal meals called "kitchens" (see p. 57) also seem to go back to non-Taoist antecedents. They have many features in common with another Taoist ritual meal, the *chai* 齋. Frequently the two are parallel and are treated as having the same functions. For *chai* a "popular" antecedent has been suggested by a Taoist author of the seventh century: "In ancient times *chai* were called *she-hui* 社會—'festival gatherings of the soil god'. Now (or recently) [the expression] has been changed into *chai-hui* 齋會."[74] Historically speaking, this statement is doubtless invalid, but it is undoubtedly justifiable to bring together Taoist ritual feasts and the feasts celebrated in the community before the soil god. The latter are well known: there is no need to go over the whole question again here. Ōfuchi has long since highlighted the essential features.[75]

The feasts and gatherings that were the relevant traits of the ancient worship of the soil god were also characteristic of the *lou* 膢 and *la* festivals of the same era. Cheng Hsüan 鄭玄 links them with communal assemblies and drinking parties 鄉飲酒,[76] which were in turn associated with the festival of *cha* 蜡 (variant of the *la*). The *lou* are defined as sacrifices to the ancestors in the second and eighth months (like the festivals of the soil god, *she* 社, in the spring and autumn). The *she* and *la* festivals are already linked with one another by the *Han-fei-tzu* 韓非子 in connection with a critique of abuses that is in complete accord with the Confucian and Taoist prohibition of "excessive cults." Some of the common people, it says, sacrificed a bull to pray for a cure of the king's illness 殺牛塞 (read 賽) 禱. They should not have performed this sacrifice to the soil god 祠社 on an ordinary day—on a day other than that of the *she* or *la* festival 非社臘之時.[77]

In the worship of the soil god the meat of the animal sacrificed was distributed to those taking part.[78] Here, as in other forms of worship, the meat distributed (and the alcohol too) was called "a blessing" *fu* 福 and implicitly signified "the blessings" obtained by the participants, as a kind of benediction arising from the sacrifice and in compensation for the

---

among others "making one's excuses to the soil" 謝土 (1:4a), the "excuses" and "liberation" of the five tombs 謝 (and 解) 五墓 (1:5a), and the "excuses" for the dead 謝先亡 (1:5b). The texts of the "petitions" to be presented in these cases are also given (3:25a for the soil; 4:7a and 9a for the five tombs; and 4:11a for the dead).

74. *Chai-chieh lu* 7a1–2 (*TT* 207): 古來呼齋曰社會, 今改爲齋會.

75. Ōfuchi Ninji, "Chūgoku ni okeru minzokuteki shūkyō no seiritsu" 中國における民族的宗教の成立, *Rekishi gaku kenkyū* 181:24 ff. (1955).

76. See commentary of Cheng Hsüan on *Hou Han-shu* 10B:4a.

77. *Han-fei-tzu* 14:253 (*Chu-tzu chi-ch'eng* ed.); cf. above, n. 62.

78. *Shih-chi* 56:2a (= *Han-shu* 40:5b); *Ching-Ch'u sui-shih chi* 荊楚歲時記 para. *She-jih* 社日.

"merit" acquired (*kung-te* 功德).[79] We have seen above that the pursuit of such "blessings" was the essential feature of popular cults accepted by the Taoists; with regard to the condemned and "excessive" cults, the Taoists asserted (as did the literati) that they could not yield such "blessings" (cf. n. 88). The same pertinent feature also characterized the entirely Taoist rite of the "kitchen" (*ch'u*) and the "purification meal" (*chai*). The notion of *fu*, "blessings," was there confounded with that of "merit" (*kung-te*) under the influence of Buddhist notions regarding "merit" (*puṇya*, a Sanskrit word translated either by *fu* or by *kung-te*).[80] On such occasions the Taoists also utilized other Buddhist notions and terms: "field of merit" (*fu-t'ien* 福田) and the distribution of food to all the gods and all the creatures—a distribution that would result in "obtaining unlimited blessings (merit)" 得福無量.[81] But these Buddhist forms were simply superimposed on purely Chinese notions that were anterior to Buddhism and that were themselves comparable to the "merit feasts" of various indigenous peoples.[82]

Thus we can quickly see that the Taoists, in authorizing and even recommending the popular forms of worship *she* and *la*, were continuing a long tradition, which has been maintained to our own day in the face of repeated prohibitions.

The same is true of the third cult they authorized beside *she* and *la*—that of the god of the stove (*tsao*). The stove was one of the tutelary gods of the house. It replaced the "central pit" (*chung-liu* 中霤) as the locus of the soil god of the house, and from this fact comes its close association with the community's soil god (*she*). It was identified with a stellar divinity, the

---

79. See the texts cited under *fu* 福 in Morohashi 諸橋, *Daikanwajiten* 大漢和辭典 24768.

80. See the Buddhist sutra *Fo-shuo chai-fa ch'ing-ching ching* 佛說齋法清淨經, *T* LXXXV, 2900 p. 1432a, where the "*chai* assembly" 齋會 is called a "merit assembly" 福會. Cf. n. 81.

81. See *Feng-tao k'o-chieh ying-shih* 奉道科戒營始 6:6a–b (*TT* 761) for a *chai* (福田施食), and *T'ai-chi chen-jen fu ling-pao chai-chieh wei-i chu-ching yao-chüeh* 太極眞人敷靈寶齋戒威儀諸經要訣 14b–15a (*TT* 295) for a *chai* called "meal offered to worthies" 飯賢 and "meal of blessings (merit)" 福食. This last phrase is used by Ko Hung (fourth century) to characterize the "kitchen festivals" *ch'u* of the "adepts of Li" (see n. 15). The "limitless blessings" come from having participated in the "celestial or divine kitchen" 天行廚 which is characteristic of the *chai* (*Yao-hsiu k'o-i chieh-lü ch'ao* 9:12a).

82. Examples are the Chins of Burma and the Nagas of Assam: see Stevenson, "Feasting and Meat Division among the Zahan Chins of Burma," *Journal of the Royal Anthropological Institute* 67:15–32 (1937); cf. K. Birket-Smith, *Studies in Circumpacific Cultural Relations, 1. Potlatch and Feasts of Merit* (Copenhagen, 1967). Closer to China, there are some remarkable facts about the Pai-i of Yünnan, who are Buddhists, and (again with Buddhist syncretism) in the case of Laos: T'ien Yü-kang, "Pai Cults and Social Age in the Tai Tribes of the Yünnan-Burma Frontier," *American Anthropologist*, n.s. vol. 51 (1949), and Georges Condominas, "Notes sur le bouddhisme populaire en milieu rural Lao (II)," *Archives de Sociologie des Religions* 26:111–14 (1968).

Controller of Destiny, Ssu-ming 司命. In both forms it was adopted by the Taoists, who regarded the Controller of Destiny as a quite important god and the stove as a minor one (a "demon," *kuei*, as it was often put).[83] The two of them functioned separately at the same time: Ssu-ming received the reports of the Three Corpses (*san-shih* 三尸) and of the stove god.[84] Yet when it is the stove who oversees good and bad deeds and keeps watch on the house, he is again associated with the soil god.[85]

Thus the *masses* of the faithful (doubtless in contrast to the Taoist advanced in saintliness) were authorized (or recommended) to carry on the worship of ancestors, of the soil god, and the god of the stove, but *solely* on certain fixed dates that corresponded to the important festivals of the year.

I have already drawn attention to the fact that the distinction between what was permitted and what was forbidden was a delicate one and subject to variations; and I have mentioned that the kinds of criteria employed and decisions reached were common to Taoists and Confucian literati officials. I must now become more precise. We have to know whether the texts that show these attitudes on the part of Taoists are only literary recollections—citations without the sources being given—or whether they are due to a concern with real, living cults of the time. In the case of certain texts, without the slightest doubt, we are dealing with simple repetitions of famous passages from the classics that educated Taoists had surely read like all literati. Others may represent a response to a real situation. Yet even in this case, the recourse is primarily to clichés. The entire lot comes under the banner of "excessive cults" (*yin-ssu* 淫祀). The *Li-chi* 禮記 defines them as follows: "offering a sacrifice to [a divinity] to whom one has no business in sacrificing is called 'excessive worship.' This kind of excessive worship does not bring blessings" 非其所祭而祭之，名曰淫祀，

---

83. Under the Han, the word *kuei* ("demon" or "soul of a dead person") often denotes a minor god (*kuei-shen* 鬼神). Wang Mang had people take oaths in front of the soil god, *she-kuei* 社鬼 (*Han-shu* 99C:13a). Elsewhere we read of the "god of the stove," *tsao-kuei* 竈鬼, in connection with raising the spirits of the dead (*Shih-chi* 28:10a). Another popular title of these minor gods was *kung* ("seigneur," "monsieur"), as in "Monsieur soil god" 社公 (*Hou Han-shu* 112B: 6a) and *t'u-kung* 土公 (in tomb purchase contracts). The word *kuei* may even denote a major divinity in popular texts. Thus T'ai-shang Lao-chün is familiarly called "old demon," *lao-kuei* 老鬼, in a tomb purchase contract of A.D. 485 (see n. 43). This is equivalent to the "Elder of Heaven," *t'ien-lao* 天老, in another contract preserved in a Taoist book of ritual (*Yao-hsiu k'o-i chieh-lü ch'ao* 15:14a and *Ch'ih Sung-tzu chang-li* 1:1a, 2:27b).

84. *Pao-p'u-tzu, nei* 6:27.

85. "When the gods are the cause of something that brings joy to the family, the divinities of the soil and stove, indoors and outdoors, are always singled out": see *Tung-yüan shen-chou ching* 2:3b (*TT* 170). The initial section of this work dates from A.D. 420, and the rest from the sixth century.

淫祀無福.[86] The reason is that "the gods do not taste [offerings if they come from someone who is] not of the same kind; men do not render worship unless it is [to gods or ancestors] of their own family" 神不歆非類, 民不祭非族.[87]

These principles are often repeated in the writings of the literati.[88] Two other features fit in here. The first concerns the limits of competence of the different categories of worshippers. The Son of Heaven sacrifices to Heaven and Earth; the feudal princes sacrifice to the four quarters, the mountains, and the rivers; dignitaries to the five tutelary gods; and ordinary people to their ancestors. This comes from the same passage in the Li-chi and is repeated in Han-shu 25A : 2a, which adds that each category is fixed by the official books of ritual and that the "excessive cults" are forbidden 各有典禮而淫祀有禁. This second characteristic feature is often repeated.

These very principles are enunciated—sometimes verbatim—in Taoist texts. We have seen that the latter tolerate or recommend for the faithful the worship of ancestors and tutelary gods[89] and that they give the same reasons for prohibiting the "excessive cults" as are given in the classical texts (see above pp. 61–62, 77). Ko Hung repeats that "the gods shen 神 do not taste [offerings by persons] who do not belong to the same family; the gods kuei 鬼 do not eat [offerings made in] the excessive cults."[90] A Taoist code dealing with the punishments inflicted on gods who have committed offenses[91] devotes a paragraph to the State cults 國祀 that speaks of gods not inscribed in the official books of ritual who cause disturbances, mislead the people, and sometimes do evil, sometimes good. It speaks of other gods who confer "blessings" on the people although they are not inscribed in the ritual books; of still others who do evil to the people even though they are "gods [able to confer] blessings and [inscribed in] the ritual books" 祀典福神.

The Taoists, as we have said, prohibited the "excessive cults" (see above p. 67) and destroyed their temples (fang-miao 房廟, pp. 67–68), but also tolerated some of them on occasion (p. 59)—in all of which they acted exactly like the literati officials.

86. Li-chi, Chü-li 曲禮 2, trans S. Couvreur, 2:100.

87. Tso-chuan 左傳, Hsi-kung 僖公 10th year, trans. S. Couvreur, 1:279.

88. Shih-chi 39:5b, trans. E. Chavannes, 4: 275: 神不食非其宗: cf. Feng-su t'ung-i, p. 59: 淫祀無福.

89. Primarily the stove; but we have also seen above (in n. 19) that the well, stove, and the two doors may figure in a major Taoist sacrifice.

90. Pao-p'u-tzu, nei 9:37: 神不歆非族, 鬼不享淫祀.

91. Shang-ch'ing ku-sui ling-wen kuei-lü 上清骨髓靈文鬼律 A:9a (TT 203).

Imitating the "rationalism" of Wang Ch'ung, Ko Hung wrote that he did not frequent the hundreds of small temples (*fang-miao*) that lay by the roadsides, and he was none the worse for it: he did not believe in these useless popular cults.[92] The Taoist Code *Ch'ih Sung-tzu chang-li* 赤松子章歷 provides a special petition (*chang* 章) for cases where it is "desired to destroy the small temples in which [a male or female medium] sits on a mat to pray to demons or maleficent spirits."[93] Another ritual serves as exorcism to summon and enforce the submission of those spirits, sprites, or "demons" who haunt the mountains and rivers or the small temples 房廟有强鬼之處.[94] One could draw up quite a long list of historically documented cases in which we see literati and Taoists full of zeal to destroy this kind of cult, while sometimes hesitating about the limits of what could be tolerated. (Many of these cases will be found in Miyakawa, *Rikuchō-shi kenkyū*.)

About A.D. 150–160, as the people were being ruined by their worship of the "demons" of the rivers and mountains, Luan Pa 欒巴 destroyed all these cults (*fang-ssu*).[95] He "loved the Tao," but not the popular cults (*su-shih* 俗事), and it was an "art of the Tao" (*tao-shu* 道術) that allowed him to exercise authority over the gods (*kuei-shen* 鬼神) and thus to destroy the temples. In 165 Emperor Huan 桓帝 first established an ancestral cult of Lao-tzu, only to destroy soon afterwards all ancestral temples (*fang-ssu*) except two.[96] About 410–420 Mao Hsiu-chih 毛脩之 was an adept under K'ou Ch'ien-chih but "did not believe in the [minor] gods 鬼神." He also destroyed some *fang-miao*, one of which was consecrated to the "most revered great hero," Chiang Tzu-wen 蔣子文.[97] In effect, the latter's worship was classified as an "excessive cult" and prohibited in 421.[98] This did not last long, for his temples were reestablished "in the mountains and rivers" in 453–456, and his cult enjoyed a great vogue,

92. *Pao-p'u-tzu, nei* 9:39.

93. *Ch'ih Sung-tzu chang-li* 2:21b (*TT* 335).

94. See *Tz'u-i yü-chien wu-lao pao-ching* 雌一玉檢五老寶經 11a, 12b (*TT* 1025). Other texts are cited by E. Chavannes, in "Le Jet des dragons," *Mémoires concernant l'Asie Orientale*, vol. 3 (Paris, 1919). On p. 191 he cites the *Yü-kuei ming-chen ta-chai yen-kung i* 玉匱明眞大齋言功儀 (*TT* 293),. a T'ang text; and on p. 214, n. 167 he cites the *Shang-ch'ing ling-pao ta-fa* 上清靈寶大法 (*TT* 942–62) and the *T'ai-shang tsung-chen pi-yao* 太上總眞秘要 (*TT* 986–87), both Sung texts. *Fang-miao* are also called *fang-ssu* 房祀, and the latter are identified with the *tz'u-t'ang* 祠堂, or temples in honor of the dead (whose worship takes place in the *fang-t'ang* 房堂 or *fang-chung t'ang-shang* 房中堂上). Cf. *Shih-chi* 28:7b, = *Han-shu* 25:6b (worship by "female sorcerers" *nü-wu* 女巫) and the commentary on *Hou Han-shu* 87:1b.

95. See *Hou Han-shu* 87:1b.

96. *Hou Han-shu* 7:6b, 106:5a.

97. *Sung-shu* 宋書 48:4a. The same passage is found in *Nan-shih* 南史 16:3b.

98. *Sung-shu* 17:13a.

with many honors, in the fifth and sixth centuries and was still alive under the T'ang, Sung, and even the Ming. This shows how difficult it was to decide which cults should be prohibited and which others should not only be tolerated but even encouraged. Between the latter and the former there was no essential difference. I cannot enlarge on this subject here, but I shall cite one more case that was especially typical and showed something very close to Taoist attitudes.

About A.D. 180 the literatus Ying Shao 應劭 criticized the worship of the hero Ch'eng-yang Ching-wang 城陽景王, whose cult had been very successful.[99] The criteria applied were in accord with those of Taoist texts (see above, pp. 57, 63): the luxuries of the faithful (clothing, carriages, etc.); animal slaughter and feasts; songs that were "popular" or inspired (yao 謠); excessive length (several days); and the intermingling of sexes and of groups with different origins. The criticism was not directed at the *principle* of worship and sacrifice, but only at their exaggeration. As a good administrator, Ying Shao decided to limit them to twice a year. The dates are not indicated in the text,[100] but it can be surmised that they were the two festivals of the soil god on the spring and autumn equinoxes 春社秋社. We can see here a forerunner of the Taoist prescriptions referred to above (pp. 67, 70), which kept the same dates.

The prohibition of popular cults by the literati officials and the emperors never had a lasting effect. Although there is frequent mention of the destruction of thousands of temples, it is clear that the cults later recovered. A list of these prohibitions, some of which were followed by official reestablishment, would run from 40–39 B.C. to A.D. 668. The problem, then, always remained irreducible. The authorities were unable to put a stop to the popular cults. If the Taoists adopted the same principles, it was because they were faced with the same problem. Yet for them the situation was even more delicate and ambiguous than for the literati. It was all the more necessary for them to protect themselves against what might be called "leftism," in that their own practices were basically, at least in large part, the same as those of the popular specialists, the mediums or sorcerers (wu 巫, shih 師). Furthermore, they were clearly the heirs of the "magicians" (fang-shih 方士) who, in the second century B.C., brought about the fusion of these practices with the cult of Huang-ti 黃帝 and Lao-tzu and with the practices of Long Life.[101]

99. Chao I 趙翼 (1727–1814), *Kai-yü ts'ung-k'ao* 陔餘叢考 (Shanghai, 1957), 35:753.
100. *Feng-su t'ung-i*, pp. 68–69.
101. See Miyakawa Hisayuki 宮川尚志, "Dōkyō no gainen" 道教の概念, *Tōhōshūkyō* 16:1–

About 39 B.C. a literatus wanted to destroy 475 temples out of 683 because they were not "in conformity with the rites." He did not succeed because the people would not agree to it. Some of these cults were carried on by the magician officials (*fang-shih shih* 方士使).[102] In the years 6–3 B.C., when the emperor was ill, he invited many "magicians" (*fang-shu shih* 方術士), whereupon all the cults were reestablished that had been prohibited in 40–39 B.C. (37,000 temples in one year: see *Han-shu* 25B:7b). In A.D. 150–160 (shortly before the appearance of the first movements of religious Taoism), the reason why Luan Pa was able to destroy the temples of popular cults without risking the vengeance of the gods he expelled, was because he already had mastered a "magic art" (*tao-shu*) that enabled him to exercise authority over the gods, just as the later Taoists did (see above, p. 79). We have seen that four centuries later a Taoist manual expressly provided methods of exorcism to avoid the same danger when temples were being destroyed by Taoists (above, pp. 58, 67–68). At the beginning of the fourth century we find a Taoist collaborating with "sorcerers." At this time the empress Chia 賈 carried on "excessive cults" with mediums (*wu* 巫). Her favorite, Sun Hsiu 孫秀, did the same, while pretending to be the famous immortal Wang Ch'iao 仙人王喬. At this time the Taoist Hu Yao 道士胡沃 was named "General of Great Peace" 太平獎軍 and ordered to "summon good fortune" 招福祐. Thus the Taoists were competing with the "sorcerers" in the matter of exorcisms (political black magic).[103]

This ancient history is the antecedent to the present situation in Taiwan, which K. M. Schipper has explained in Paris in recent years. If the *tao-shih* have a superior domain reserved to them—that of the major rituals—the "sorcerers" (*hung-t'ou* 紅頭) carry on rituals that are parallel.

Religious Taoism has absorbed many popular divinities and practices. Popular religion has in its turn adopted Taoist forms.

---

20 (1960), and his *Rikuchō shi no kenkyū*, p. 338; Anna Seidel, *La divinisation de Lao-tseu dans le taoïsme des Han* (Paris, 1969).

102. *Han-shu* 25B:5b.
103. *Chin-shu* 59:7a.

3 Local Cults around Mount Lu at the Time of Sun En's Rebellion

Hisayuki Miyakawa 宮川尚志

ONE OF THE BEST-KNOWN TAOIST REBELLIONS in Chinese history was the one that began in A.D. 399 led by Sun En 孫恩. He recruited poverty-stricken peasants from the coasts of Kiangsu and Chekiang, many of whom feared conscription into the army, and led them to believe that, if they fought for him, they would be able to accompany him, together with their children, to the Islands of the Blest. The groundwork for the rebellion had been laid by Sun T'ai 泰, the uncle of Sun En, and it broke out when he was executed. Sun T'ai came from an obscure family in Lang-yeh 琅邪, Shantung, the time-honored commandery full of Taoist sacred places which has produced many famous Taoists, historical and legendary. His family had followed the Five Pecks of Rice sect for generations, and secret arts of Taoism had been transmitted to him by his master, Tu Chiung 杜炅 (*tzu* Tzu-kung 子恭) of Ch'ien-t'ang 錢唐, Chekiang.

The purpose of this chapter is not to give the history of Sun En's rebellion[1] but to explore some of the more obscure religious ideas that lay behind it. I shall first concentrate on Sun T'ai's master Tu Chiung, and then examine the way in which Taoist masters like him dealt with some popular cults of the time.

According to the *Sung-shu*, "Tu Tzu-kung [Tu Chiung] from Ch'ien-t'ang had mastered a Taoist art that enabled him to communicate with

---

1. Cf. Hisayuki Miyakawa, "Son On, Ro Jun no ran ni tsuite" 孫恩盧循の亂につ\
(On the rebellion of Sun En and Lu Hsün), *Tōyōshi kenkyū* 東洋史研究 XXX 2, 3:1–30 (1971);\
and by the same author: "Son On, Ro Jun no ran hokō" 孫思, 盧循の亂補考 (Supplementary\
remarks on the rebellion of Sun En and Lu Hsün), in *Suzuki hakushi koki kinen Tōyōgaku\
ronsō* 鈴木博士古稀記念東洋學論叢 (Tokyo, 1972), pp. 533–48.

spirits (*t'ung-ling* 通靈). A number of powerful families in the eastern part of Chekiang and noblemen in the capital became his disciples and served him with the utmost respect."[2] Tu Chiung's biography appears in the sixth-century work *Tao-hsüeh chuan* 道學傳 by Ma Shu 馬樞, fragments of which Ch'en Kuo-fu 陳國符 has culled from the *San-tung chu-nang* 三洞珠囊 by Wang Hsien-ho 王懸河, a Taoist of the late seventh century. The following is a full translation of these fragments.

1. When he [Tu Chiung] was grown up, he was eager for wisdom and faith. As a follower of Cheng-i, he had been enrolled while young on the records of the T'ien-shih's parish 少參天師治籙. In this capacity, he was engaged in preaching and in the salvation of the people in contact with him. He lived a life of purity and diligence. Devoted to saving others, he did not solicit alms. Finally he built a Taoist center (*chih-ching* 治靜) in order to extend his relief activities, which were fast and efficacious.

2. He was a good physician by nature. He could foresee the good and evil [fate] of people. There lived two shamans who were envious of his skill; Lung Chih 龍稚 from Shang-yü 上虞 and Ssu Shen 斯神 from Ch'ien-t'ang. They egged one another on to speak ill of him. Hearing about this from a friend, he said: "They shall be judged by the subterranean tribunal (*ming-k'ao* 冥考) for their aspersions on the righteous doctrine." Soon, Lung Chih's wife suddenly died, and Ssu Shen turned out to have a chronic disease. Thereupon both repented their wrongdoings and sincerely asked forgiveness. When Tu Chiung performed a rite of confession for them, Ssu Shen recovered immediately from his illness. But afterwards Ssu Shen fell ill again. Tu Chiung told him that he had harbored an evil spirit (*kuei-wu* 鬼物) that was causing him trouble. Ssu Shen confessed that he had secretly kept a case of fine clothes for his private use. Tu Chiung took the clothes to the center, burnt them, and instantly he got well.

3. Wang Hsi-chih 王羲之 (321–379) fell ill and called for him [Tu Chiung]. He told his disciples: "Mr. Wang's illness is incurable. I can't do anything for him." After about ten days, Hsi-chih died.

4. "Lu Na 陸納 was appointed Minister of Administration (*shang-shu-ling* 尚書令) at the age of 40. He had been suffering from cankers (*ch'uang* 瘡). He told Tu Chiung: "My ancestors died at an even earlier age of the same kind of skin disease." Tu Chiung offered a memorial to Heaven (*tsou-chang* 奏章) in his behalf, gave him a powdered mercury compound (*ling-fei-san* 靈飛散), and encouraged him by saying: "You have survived your period of ill fortune. Now you will live to be 70." That was just what happened.[3]

The last two accounts tell us approximately when Tu Chiung flourished, but it is unclear whether he lived to see the outbreak of Sun En's rebellion in 399. Even if he did, he and his parish seem to have been safe from government persecution, since we know that his descendants continued to carry on their religious activities during the succeeding dynasties. He worked for the salvation of aristocrats and commoners alike. If

2. *Sung-shu* 宋書 100:7248b (*Pai-na* ed., Peking, 1958).
3. Ch'en Kuo-fu, *Tao-tsang yüan-liu k'ao* 道藏源流考 (Peking, 1962), 2:461.

he found no reason to take the side of the oppressed populace against the ruling aristocrats, it was probably because he believed that all would be decided by the power of the great Tao, as revealed in the *T'ai-shang tung-yüan shen-chou ching* 太上洞淵神呪經. He prayed to the great Tao for mercy whenever his clients asked him to cure them of diseases or to extricate them from involvement in quarrels and lawsuits, which are treated as a kind of disease in this scripture.[4]

He also understood certain magic arts, as can be seen from the following story. Once Tu Chiung borrowed a table knife, the owner of which asked him to return it in due time. He replied that he would return it right away. Its owner then went by boat to Chia-hsing 嘉興, 120 kilometers away. During the trip a fish leapt on board. He cut it open and found a knife inside, which he believed to be the very one he had lent.[5]

That Tu Chiung could use a fish in this magical feat shows that he must have had power over the deities of lakes and rivers. In local shrines many cults of gods concerned with navigation existed. Travelers used to be asked to make votive offerings to them in exchange for safe navigation. These deities were believed to have jurisdiction over the waters near their shrines, within which fishing and boating were prohibited except with their permission. They would punish the violators. The story of Tu Chiung's miracle has to be seen in the context of many others to which I shall now turn. We shall see that they involve a contest between the old shamanistic cults at the local shrines and the superior magic of Taoist masters.

The Lake Cults

The sources on the Kung-t'ing 宮亭 Shrine, the site of the deity of Mount Lu (Lu-shan-chün 廬山君), and on other similar shrines, can serve as illustrations of (a) the way these local cults operated; (b) how Taoist masters exerted their power over these deities; and (c) how Buddhist monks used these popular cults to implant their own religion. I shall first deal with these three topics one after the other and then conclude with an examination of local deities that had the shape of a python and the connected folklore concerning pythons.

Let me begin with an example of a fishing ban provided in the *I-yüan*:

4. Cf. Hisayuki Miyakawa, "Shin dai Dōkyō no ichi-kōsatsu—Daijō dōen shinju kyō o megurite"晉代道教の一考察—太上洞淵神呪經をめぐりて(A study of religious Taoism in fourth-century China—with special reference to the *T'ai-shang Tung-yüan shen-chou ching*), *Chūgoku gakushi* 中國學誌 5:95–96 (1969).

5. *Chin-shu* 晉書 100:5666b (*Pai-na* ed., Peking, 1958).

"In the time of Ch'in 秦 (249–207 B.C.), in the Tan-yang 丹陽 district, there stood a lakeside shrine dedicated to the Lady Mei-ku 梅姑 or Ma-ku 麻姑. In her lifetime she had been well versed in Taoist arts (*tao-shu* 道術). She could walk on water with her shoes. Later she broke the law of the Tao [*tao-fa* 道法], and her husband killed her in anger, casting her corpse into the lake. It drifted onto the shore in front of the shrine. A shaman custodian (*ling-hsia wu-jen* 鈴下巫人) asked to place her in a coffin without immediately erecting a tomb; a square, lacquered coffin was found in the shrine-hall. Thereafter, on the first and last days of the lunar month, people could see in the damp and the fog a human figure on the water wearing a pair of shoes. In the vicinity of the shrine, fishing and hunting were banned. Any violator would either lose his way or be drowned. The shaman told people that the lady hated to see the fish and animals killed by men and suffer in the way that she had suffered."[6]

The next example comes from the same book and involves the motif of rediscovered offerings, closely akin to Tu Chiung's miracle of the knife. In the T'ung-lu 桐廬 district, Wu-chün commandery, there stood a shrine to Hsü-chün 徐君 which had originally been built in the time of Wu of the Three Kingdoms. If robbery took place near the shrine, the evil-doer was instantly paralyzed by a magical force (*chü-fu* 拘縛) and soon discovered and arrested by the police. Worshippers, on the other hand, might have their wishes granted, as in the case of an official, Li Tao 李瑫, who was involved in a lawsuit and had been jailed during the period 405–418. His wife set out to help him with his legal problems. Passing by the shrine on her way, she prayed to the deity for mercy, taking off her silver hairpin as an offering. As she neared the end of her journey, a fish leapt up and fell in front of her. Cutting it open, she found the hairpin she had offered. The case of her husband was favorably disposed of.[7]

In this story, the offering was made to extricate someone from a lawsuit. More commonly it was made to assist navigation. The adjoining passage in the *I-yüan* reads as follows: "In the Yung-chia era [307–312], a shrine for Wu Yüan 伍員 [minister of Wu in the Spring and Autumn Period] stood by the bank of the Yangtze. A native of Wu-chün had an uncle who held office at the capital of Lo-yang. After it fell to the barbarian invaders, he wanted to go home. Since other routes were blocked by disorders, he had to cross the [Yangtze] river southward. At the bank, an adverse wind prevented a safe crossing. After he threw a memorial (*tsou* 奏) into the shrine, he was able to cross on the same day."[8]

6. *I-yüan* 異苑 5:1 (*Hsüeh-chin t'ao-yüan* 學津討原 ed., *han* 22).
7. Ibid., 5:2a–b.
8. Ibid., 5:2b.

The wind was believed to be managed by a deity of river, lake, or mountain, for whom people would build a shrine in order to appease him with offerings. There is little material on the economy of such a shrine, but it is easily supposed that fishing and hunting rights as well as ownership of the fields and mountains around it were usually allocated to its support. Such rights were reinforced by the miraculous power of the deity. When a shrine lay on a heavily traveled route or near a center of traffic, the prestige of its deity was correspondingly greater. Such was the case around Lake P'o-yang 鄱陽, then variously called Lake Kung-t'ing 宮亭 or P'eng-tse 彭澤, and its vicinity, including Mount Lu (Lu-shan 廬山), which commanded the lake region.

There were several shrines in this district, but the deities enshrined in them all performed the same function. The *Shui-ching-chu* 水經注 states: "The mountain shrine has a most miraculous power. [Its deity] can separate winds, divide watercourses, making boats pass. So officials going on a journey and travelers in general all pay homage to the shrine. After doing so they can pass through [in safety]. The writer Ts'ao P'i 曹毗 describes it as 'dividing the winds in two, splitting the streams in twain.'"[9] What is meant here is that the deity could make the wind blow and the stream flow in opposite directions at the same time, so that all the ships could go up or down without waiting their turn for a favorable wind, and traffic congestion was reduced.

Before dealing in detail with the shrine of the god of Lu-shan, I shall recount two stories from the *Sou-shen-chi* 搜神記 which are similar to the table-knife miracle mentioned above. "Somewhere on Lake Kung-t'ing there was the Ku-shih 孤石 shrine. Once a Chien-k'ang 建康 merchant, traveling to the capital, passed by the shrine and met two girls there. They asked him to have a pair of shoes made of silk for each of them, promising him a substantial present in return. When the merchant arrived in the capital, he bought some fine silk shoes which he put in a box together with a knife he had bought for his own use. When he returned to the shrine, he burned incense and placed the box on the altar in the shrine, forgetting to take out the knife. After he resumed his journey, when his boat was in midstream, a carp jumped aboard. Cutting it open, he found the very same knife inside it."[10]

Another example occurs in the same chapter: "A man of Nan-chou 南州 despatched a clerk to offer the throne an ornamental hairpin made of rhinoceros horn. As his boat passed by the shrine, he prayed for mercy

---

9. *Shui-ching chu-shu* 水經注疏 39:56a (Peking, 1955). Ts'ao P'i is given a biography in *Chin-shu* 92:5455.

10. *Sou-shen chi* 搜神記 4:5b (*Hsüeh-chin t'ao-yüan* ed., *han* 21).

to the deity, who, responding to his prayer [through the medium], ordered him to present the hairpin on the spot. The clerk was too terrified to answer, and the hairpin instantly and of its own accord moved onto the altar. The deity issued another order to the effect that the hairpin should be returned to him as soon as he arrived at the Shih-t'ou ch'eng fort 石頭城 near the capital. The clerk, at a loss to know what he should do, resumed his trip, though he was well aware that the loss of an offering to the throne would merit the death penalty. About the time of his arrival at the capital, a big carp—three feet long—jumped into his boat and the hairpin was found inside it."[11]

We can imagine how the deity of the Kung-t'ing Lake extended his influence not only over the local inhabitants, but also over traders and travelers from various parts of China, since the lake and the adjoining rivers connected central China with the southern provinces, and were vital to the economic life of the Six Dynasties. Faced with the mortal danger of shipwreck, sailors and passengers made supplication to the deity of the lake for their safety during the voyage. On such occasions, the deity often demanded precious offerings of the worshippers, who, as travelers, were less faithful than the local villagers in observing the communal religious practices. Most travelers were either cunning merchants whose principle was quid pro quo, even in their transactions with deities; or literati who carried out the established rites merely for the sake of social expediency.

In remote antiquity water deities (for example, the deity of the Yellow River) sometimes expected human sacrifices. However, in the period

11. Ibid. 4:6. Nan-chou (lit. "south province") in this context seems to be Ching-chou, and not Nan-(chou-) chin 南 (州) 津 or South Ferry in Chekiang. An early example of this usage is given in *Chin-shu* 34:5086, biography of Yang Hu 羊祜. Hu San-sheng's 胡三省 commentary on the corresponding part of the *Tzu-chih t'ung-chien* 80:12b (Yamana 山名 ed., Tokyo, 1882) supports this identification. The man of Nan-chou may have got the rhinoceros horn from a southernmost province, say Kuang-chou. The clerk started somewhere in Ching-chou, went over mountains between modern Hunan and Kiangsi provinces, and then took the route along the Kan River 贛江 northward until he reached Lake P'o-yang. This route was used from Han times, as well as another route along the Hsiang River 湘江 in Hunan (then Ching-chou) province leading to Lake Tung-t'ing 洞庭. The Yangtze was the main waterway for trading as well as military purposes. An example is in *San-kuo chih: Wu-shu* 三國志吳書 9:4839 (*Pai-na* ed., Taipei, 1967), biography of Lü Meng 呂蒙: a Wu general started from Hsün-yang 潯陽 (modern Chiu-chiang 九江) to attack Kuan Yü 關羽, at Chiang-ling 江陵 (in modern Hunan). He hid his armored soldiers in the hatch and had men in merchant attire scull the boats. For other details and maps, see Tom Chung Yee 譚宗義, *Han-tai kuo-nei lu-lu chiao-t'ung k'ao* 漢代國內陸路交通考 (A study of land communication in the Han Dynasty, Hong Kong, 1967), pp. 203 ff.

under present consideration, this was no longer an overt element in folk-lore. Instead, there are occasional allusions to sacred marriage between gods and human beings, and also to the appointment of human beings in the otherworldly officialdom. It was most probably from this that the Taoist hierarchy of the immortals and demons developed. Through the romantic atmosphere in such stories, we can see the tension and harmony between the naïve hearts of the populace and the sophisticated minds of the Confucian, Taoist, and Buddhist elites. The supernatural experiences of an official named Chang P'u 張璞, recounted in the *Sou-shen-chi* and in the *Shui-ching chu*, suggest several points worth investigation.

Chang P'u (*tzu* Kung-chih 公直), a man of unknown dates and origin, was appointed prefect of Wu-chün. The government recalled him to the capital. On the way, accompanied by his family, he passed by Lu-shan. His sons and daughters visited the shrine. A maidservant pointed to the image of a deity, and said jokingly to one of the daughters that she would be married to him. That night Chang P'u's wife dreamt that she saw Lu-chün 盧君, the Lord of Lu-shan, who said: "In spite of the unworthiness of my son, you have chosen him as a husband for your daughter. I greatly appreciate it and express my cordial acceptance." The wife awoke and worried about the dream. The maidservant finally confessed what she had done. Thereupon Chang P'u's wife grew afraid and urged her husband to start early.

Halfway across the lake, their ship was halted. Trembling with fear, they threw their valuables into the lake. But the ship would not move. Someone exclaimed, "Throw in the daughter, and the ship will go forward." Everyone chimed in and said: "The will of the deity is manifest. How can we let our whole party be exterminated for the sake of one daughter?" Chang P'u sighed, "I cannot be an eyewitness of the terrible scene to come." He withdrew to the upper cabin and lay down, leaving his wife to push the daughter into the water. She managed, however, to substitute a daughter of her husband's brother for her own, spreading a mat on the surface of the wave and putting the girl on it.

When Chang P'u found the ship safely underway and his own daughter intact, he grew angry, saying, "How can I be indifferent to the censure of the world?" Thereupon he consigned his daughter to the water too. Yet when the party arrived at the shore, they saw the two daughters standing some way off. A clerk stood on the bank and told them, "I am a secretary of the Lord of Lu, who has to apologize to you. He is now aware that humans and spirits make a poor match. Appreciating your righteousness, he wishes to return both girls to you." Questioned by their family, the girls replied that they had seen lovely palaces and officials, but they did not remember being in the water.[12]

Chang P'u's conformity to Confucian family ethics so strongly affected the water spirits that they declined human sacrifice. Another story in the *Sou-shen chi* tells of Ts'ao Chu 曹著, a petty clerk of Chien-k'ang. He was visited by a messenger of the Lord of Lu-shan, who wished to marry his daughter. He felt uneasy, both mentally and physically, and tried to break off several times. At last his daughter, Yüan 婉, parted from him in tears, composed a farewell poem, and presented him with embroidered under-clothes.[13]

A fragment of the *Po-wu chih* 博物志 by Chang Hua 張華 cited in the *Shui-ching chu* 39 states that, according to Ts'ao Chu, the deity (of Mount Lu) used the surname Hsü and was enfeoffed at the mountain. The *Chih-kuai* 志怪, cited in the *T'ai-p'ing yü-lan* 太平御覽 758, reads as follows:

> Ts'ao Chu was once invited by the Lord Prefect (*fu-chün* 府君) of Mount Lu to come to his palace, where he saw at the gate a huge jar big enough to hold over a hundred bushels (*hu* 斛), and out of it came winds and clouds.[14]

This suggests that the Lord of Mount Lu, whose shrine was named after the lake Kung-t'ing, could menace ships sailing on the lake by using the contents of his fabulous jar.

Another story in the *Sou-shen-chi* provides us with a mass of valuable information on the local cults of the lake region.

> Ou Ming 歐明, a native of Lu-ling 盧陵 (in modern Kiangsi) crossed the P'eng-tse Lake on a boat accompanied by a party of merchants. Following the established custom for travelers, he threw some articles into the water from the ship as a gift to the lake deity. A couple of years later, he again crossed the lake, and to his surprise, found a broad highway stretching from one shore to the other. He saw several officials on horseback and in chariots raising a cloud of dust and coming toward him. They greeted him and told him that they were messengers of the Lord of the Blue Flood (Ching-hung-chün 青洪君) who wished to invite him to his residence as a guest. Soon they reached a place where there stood an administration building filled with attendants and soldiers. Ou Ming was overcome with awe until an officer said to him: "Be not afraid. My Lord appreciates the gifts you have offered frequently. So he invites you today in order to present you with abundant gifts in return. But one thing: don't take too much, only ask him for '*ju-yüan*' 如願 ('as you like')." When he talked with the Lord,

---

12. *Sou-shen chi* 4:4b–5b. See also *Shui-ching chu-shu* 39:56ab.

13. *Sou-shen chi* 4:5b.

14. This fragment of the *Po-wu chih* does not figure in the extant edition, as Hsiung Hui-chen 熊會貞 remarks at the related passage in the *Sui-ching chu-shu* (39:52b). He also refers to a fragment of the *Chih-kuai* found in the extant edition of the *T'ai-p'ing yü-lan* 4:3364a (Peking, 1959).

he accordingly asked for 'ju-yüan,' which turned out to be the name of a maid-servant. After returning home with her, he got anything he wanted, and within a few years he became enormously rich.[15]

Later on, it happened that Ju-yüan got up so late one New Year's morning that Ou Ming, being a little tipsy, beat her. She ran away into the dust and dung at the back of the house, and disappeared. Nowadays, people bind a doll with rope, throw it into the dust and dung, saying, "Let everything I request be fulfilled." This practice owes its origin to the above story. The story of Ju-yüan is particularly significant because, as Minakata Kumagusu has pointed out, it may be connected with the god of the latrine, Tzu-ku-shen 紫姑神 who, in turn, is connected with the automatic writing of Taoist adepts.[16]

The local cult of the P'o-yang Lake region seems to have entered religious Taoism in the fourth century. This lake deity, called Ch'ing-hung-chün, was like the alter ego of the Lord of Lu-shan. What was the nature of the latter, and what sort of interrelation does it suggest between the local cults and the more sophisticated religion of the time?

Taoist Victories over Cults near Lu-shan

According to Yang Shou-ching, the name of Lu-shan existed in early Chou, as is shown by a reference in the *Bamboo Annals*.[17] The *Shui-ching chu*, quoting some earlier works such as *Lu-shan-chi* 廬山記 by the famous monk Hui-yüan 慧遠 (334–416), mentions a widely accepted tradition to the effect that the name of this mountain was taken from the name of its first inhabitant Lu Su 廬俗 or K'uang Su 匡俗, a Taoist hermit early in the Chou 周.[18]

The first authentic evidence of the relation between the local cults around this mountain and the more sophisticated world is presented in the

15. *Sou-shen chi* 4:6. Tsung Lin 宗懍, *Ching-Ch'u Sui-shih chi* 荆楚歲時記 pp. 5b–6, (*Pao-yen t'ang pi-chi* 寶顏堂秘笈 ed., *han* 14) citing the *Lu-i chi* 錄異記, gives the merchant's name as Ch'ü Ming 區明 and the deity's name as Ch'ing-hu Chün 青湖君.

16. Minakata Kumagusu 南方熊楠, "Shi-shin 厠神 (Latrine Deity)" in *Minakata Kumagusu Zenshū* (Tokyo, 1971), 2:144 ff. See also Nagao Ryūzō 氷尾龍造, *Shina minzokushi* 支那民俗誌 (Tokyo, 1941), 2:519–39; R. A. Stein, "Un exemple des relations entre taoïsme et religion populaire," in *Fukui hakushi shōju kinen Tōyō bunka ronshū* 福井博士頌壽記念東洋文化論集 (Oriental culture: a collection of articles in honor of the seventieth anniversary of Dr. Kōjun Fukui; Tokyo, 1969), pp. 84 ff.

17. *Chu-shu chi-nien* 竹書紀年 2:3b (*Ssu-pu pei-yao* 四部備要 ed., Taipei 1965) reads: "In the 16th year of King K'ang 康王 of Chou, the king went to the south as far as Lu-shan near Chiu-chiang 九江." Based on the citation just mentioned, the *Shui-ching chu-shu* 39:52 says that the name of Lu-shan can be traced back to Yin-Chou times.

18. *Shui-ching chu-shu* 39:51b–52b,

biography of Luan Pa 欒巴 (*Hou Han-shu*). Much earlier than Tu Chiung, he used the power of "Tao" to tame water deities.

> Luan Pa (*tzu* Shu-yüan 叔元) was a native of the Nei-huang 內黃 district, Wei-chün 魏郡 commandery (in modern Honan). He adored the Tao. During the reign of Shun Ti 順帝 (126–144), he reluctantly served in the imperial harem as a eunuch. Honest in nature and well versed in the classics, he could not stay on good terms with the corrupt and powerful agency of the Imperial Household Office. Soon he recovered his virility and asked for leave. Later he became prefect of Yü-chang 豫章 [near Lu-shan in modern Kiangsi], where a number of demons and spirits of hills and rivers were worshipped by the poor inhabitants, who spent money lavishly for prayer and sacrifice. He possessed the art of the Tao and could make demons do as he wished. He destroyed all the superstitious shrines and punished the wicked shamans. After that the evil atmosphere faded of its own accord. At first, people had misgivings, but soon got a sense of security.[19]

According to the *Shen-hsien chuan*, the deity of Lu-shan was believed to sit behind the curtain, talk, and at times eat and drink with the worshippers. By throwing a wine-cup up in the air he could make the wind on the lake separate so that boats could sail both up and down the lake at the same time. Yet starting more than ten days before Luan Pa's arrival at his post, the deity did not utter a word. There was also a demon called Yellow Father (Huang-fu 黃父) who caused epidemics and annoyed people. After Luan Pa's arrival, no one knew of the demon's whereabouts, and no more epidemics broke out in the district.[20]

Another powerful Taoist adept connected with Lu-shan was Wu Meng 吳猛. We read of him in the above-mentioned fragment of the *Po-wu-chih* cited in the *Shui-ching chu*.

> Later Wu Meng passed by the mountain and was greeted by the mountain deity, to whom he said: "You have been the king of this mountain for nearly six hundred years. According to the Mandate of Heaven shown in the talismans (*fu-ming* 符命), your term has already expired. You should no longer remain in the place where you have no right to reside." So saying Wu Meng presented him with a poem:
>
>> Looking up to the residence of the immortals,
>> Seeing below the eyes the lodging-place of a divine king,
>> Letting my subtle thoughts traverse infinite ages,
>> I turn down the canopy of my wagon to salute the three
>> revered friends.[21]

19. See biography of Luan Pa in *Hou-Han shu, lieh-chuan* 列傳 47:656b (Wang Hsien-ch'ien 王先謙, *Hou-Han shu chi-chieh* 後漢書集解, *Jen-shou t'ang erh-shih-wu shih* 仁壽堂 二十五史 ed., Taipei, 1957).
20. *Shen-hsien chuan* 神仙傳 5:7–8b (*I-men kuang-tu* 夷門廣牘 ed., *han* 6).
21. *Shui-ching chu-shu* 39:52b.

Li Tao-yüan 酈道元 then comments as follows: "According to this tale the identity of deities in the divine world changes successively in so abstruse a way that we cannot elucidate it. Wu Meng is the man who attained the Tao by hiding himself in a mountain." Then Li Tao-yüan quotes the following from the *Hsün-yang chi* 潯陽記 of Chang Seng-chien 張僧鑒:

> On Lu-shan there were three stone beams—some hundred feet in length and less than one foot wide—that spanned a deep abyss. Wu Meng, accompanied by his disciples, climbed up the mountain and crossed the beams. Sitting under a Judas tree he found an old man who filled a jade cup with sweet dew syrup and gave it to him to drink. He went on to a place where several men supplied him with some nectar (*yü-kao* 玉膏). One of his disciples stole a treasure there in the hope of showing it to non-believers. Suddenly the beams shrank and became only as wide as fingers. Wu Meng made him return the treasure, and, ordering his disciples to shut their eyes, he led them across the place.

Wu Meng is also given a biography in the *Chin-shu*:[22]

> He was a native of Yü-chang near Lu-shan. He was known for his filial piety. In summer when he was bitten by mosquitoes, he never drove them off lest they fly to his parents to find new victims. Ting I 丁義, his fellow-provincial, first conferred on him a divine art at the age of forty. Then he returned to Yü-chang. On the Yangtze River the billows were very high. He did not get on board a ship, but touched the water with a white feather fan and safely crossed over on foot. All the bystanders were astonished at this sight. Yü Liang 庾亮 (289–340), the governor of Chiang province, knew of Wu Meng by reputation and, when he fell ill, he invited him to come and give him a prognosis. Wu Meng declined to answer on the grounds that he had reached the limit of his own life-span. He asked that a coffin and shroud be prepared for him, and about ten days later he died. Yet he still looked alive. Before the formal funeral his corpse vanished. Well-informed persons regarded this as an omen of Yü Liang's death. In the end the governor did not recover.[23]

The *Sou-shen chi* gives a short account of Wu Meng that emphasizes his magical power of calming the wind:

> A native of P'u-yang 濮陽 [in modern Hopei], he served as an official at the Wu court. Then he was appointed to be magistrate of Hsi-an 西安 [near Wu-ning, Kiangsi], and hence he settled down at Fen-ning 分寧. He showed great filial piety toward his parents. He encountered a perfect man (*chih-jen* 至人) called Ting I who bestowed on him a divine prescription. He also acquired secret arts and divine talismans (*pi-fang shen-fu* 秘方神符). His art of the Tao became widely known. Once, when a strong

---

22. *Chin-shu* 95:5620b.

23. *Chin-shu* 73:5326–29 has the biography of Yü Liang who was the governor of Ching-chou in 334–340. Cf. Wu T'ing-hsieh 吳廷燮, *Tung-Chin fang-chen nien-piao* 東晉方鎮年表 3:3485 (*Erh-shih-wu shih pu-pien* 二十五史補編, Taipei, 1959).

wind was blowing, he wrote a talisman and threw it onto the roof. A blue crow took it away in its beak and the wind abated. Someone asked him to explain. He replied: "A ship was confronting this wind on the South Lake. A Taoist adept requested my help." Investigation proved that what he had said was true. Kan Ch'ing 干慶, magistrate of Hsi-an, died. After three days Wu Meng stated: "His fate is not yet settled. I must appeal to heaven." Then he lay beside the corpse for several days, at the end of which he got up again and the dead man rose with him. Afterwards he made a journey around Yü-chang commandery with his disciples. The Yangtze River ran so fast that no one could pass. He touched the water with a white feather fan in his hand, and started to cross the stream. A shoal appeared, and his party walked slowly over it. When everyone had passed, the water came back again. All the onlookers were frightened. Once when he was in charge of the Hsün-yang commandery headquarters, the house of Chou 周, his military chief of staff, was hit by a sudden storm. As soon as Wu Meng wrote a talisman and threw it onto the roof, the storm abated.[24]

Since his activities took place around the Kung-t'ing Lake, Wu Meng clearly had power over the deity who caused the wind. Together with Hsü Hsün 許遜, he was revered as one of the founders of the Ching-ming Chung-hsiao Tao 淨明忠孝道.[25] In his deeds we can see an example of the Taoist victory over popular shamanism.

Buddhist Dealings with the Lake Cults

Among various identifications of the deity of Lu-shan, the earliest and therefore most deeply rooted is in the Kao-seng chuan 高僧傳—the biography of An Ch'ing 安清, a Parthian noble better known as An Shih-kao 安世高. The following is excerpted from the part of his biography that is related to the local cult of Lu-shan:

> Soon after his arrival at Lo-yang early in 148, during the reign of Huan Ti 桓帝 of the Later Han, he mastered Chinese well enough to translate Buddhist sutras from Sanskrit into Chinese. At the end of the reign of Ling Ti 靈帝 (168–189), he sought refuge from the troubles at Ch'ang-an 長安 and Lo-yang 洛陽 by going south of the River. On this occasion he said, "I must call at Lu-shan to bring about the salvation of one who was a colleague of mine in a former life." He went to the Kung-t'ing 郏 [=宮] 亭 Lake Shrine, the deity of which had worked miracles for traders who had prayed for mercy when they passed by. In response to their prayer the deity separated the wind into breezes blowing both up and down the lake, so that it was always possible to sail where one wanted to. Once somebody had coveted the bamboos [growing in the holy precincts], and, without securing the permission [of the shrine], he had taken the liberty of cutting some of them down. As soon as he sailed off, his ship sank and the cut

24. Sou-shen chi 1:9a–b.
25. Akizuki Kan'ei 秋月觀暎 has done a series of studies on this Taoist sect. To mention only one: "Kyo Son kyōdan to Jōmei-chūkō-dō ni tsuite 許遜教團と淨明忠孝道について (La secte de Hiu Souen et le Tsing-ming tchong-hiao tao)" in Dōkyō kenkyū (Tokyo), 3:197–246 (1968).

bamboos returned to join their stumps. Thereafter all who sailed nearby were filled with awe at the power of the deity.

An Shih-kao and his party crossed the lake in more than thirty ships. From every ship offerings were made to secure a safe passage. The deity of the lake took possession of a shaman (*chiang-chu* 降祝)²⁶ and said: "There is a monk on a ship. Call him up to us." Everyone was terrified. Asking [An Shih-] kao to enter the shrine, the deity told him: "I became a monk together with you many years ago in a foreign land. Though I have studied Buddhism and practiced alms-giving, I am very irascible by nature. On account of this defect I now have the status of Kung-t'ing shrine-deity. My jurisdiction extends to a perimeter of a thousand miles. Alms are lavishly bestowed upon me and I have abundant treasures. But alas! The fruit of my anger has been to fall to my present state. Facing you, my old colleague, I have mixed feelings of joy and sorrow. My time will soon come to an end; my ugly body has grown long and thick. If I gave up my life at this moment I would pollute the [Yangtze] River and the lake. I would like to move to the marshes west of the mountain [Lu-shan]. However, after my body perishes my soul will fall into hell. Now, I have a thousand rolls of silk and various other treasures; use them to build a stupa to enable me to be reborn in a better world."

[An Shih-] kao replied, "Why don't you show yourself since I have come here to rescue you?" The deity said, "My body is so ugly and extraordinary that people would be afraid of me." The monk retorted: "Just come out! Nobody will be surprised." So the deity showed his head from behind the bed and it could be seen that he was a huge python (*mang* 蟒). His tail was too long to measure, reaching as far as the monk's knees. [To help him] the monk uttered some words in Sanskrit and recited stanzas from some hymns (*tsan-pai* 讚唄). The deity shed showers of tears and then disappeared. The monk took the silk and treasures and left the shrine. The sailors unfurled the sails when the python reappeared on the summit to see them off. People raised their hands [in response] and again it disappeared. In a short while An Shih-kao reached Yü-chang, where he built the East Monastery with the valuables donated by the deity. After his departure the deity came to the end of his life as a python. At dusk a boy got on the ship, knelt down before the monk, asked him to accept his invocation (*chou-yüan* 呪願), and soon vanished. The monk told the crew that the boy was the deity who had been freed from his former shape as a python. Thereafter no more miracles took place. Later a dead python was found in the marsh west of Lu-shan. Its length from head to tail was several miles. The place is now called Serpent Village (*She-ts'un* 蛇村) in Hsün-yang District.²⁷

26. I think the use of the word *chiang-chu* in this passage means that a deity "descended into a shaman" (text: *shen nai chiang-chu* 神乃降祝), which, however, Robert Shih has translated as "La divinité accorda sa benediction" in his *Biographies des Moines Eminents (Kao Seng Tchouan) de Houei-kiao* 慧皎 (Louvain, 1968), p. 6. The word *chu* is often compounded with *wu* 巫. As for the difference between the two words, Naba Toshisada 那波利貞, "Fu-shū kō-gen 巫祝攷源 (On the origin of Chinese shamans)" in *Shintōshi kenkyū* 神道史研究 5:2–34 (1954) has presented a less known but significant opinion that the *wu* (shaman) were of northern origin and the *chu* (shaman-priest) native to China, but in later ages the two intermingled with each other. One of the early works on Chinese shamanism to be mentioned is Kano Naoki 狩野直喜 "Shina jōdai no Fu, Fukan ni tsuite 支那上代の巫, 巫咸に就いて (On the *wu* and *wu-hsien* in ancient China)" in his *Shinagaku bunsō* 支那學文藪 (Tokyo, 1973), pp. 16 ff.

27. *Kao-seng chuan*, Taishō [= *T*] L. 2059.1:323–24.

Hui-chiao also presents in the succeeding passages different legends about An Shih-kao, which he has collected from other sources. In all of them he saves the shrine deity and builds a temple with funds furnished by the deity converted from a local cult to Buddhism. Most conspicuous in these legends is the discovery that the natural form of the deity was that of a snake. Serpent worship in China had some interesting peculiarities, to which I shall now turn.

Folklore Connected with the Python

The species of snake called *mang* 蟒 has been tentatively rendered above as "python."[28] Compared with the dragon (*lung* 龍) and the snake (*she* 蛇) in general, the stories about the *mang* are limited in number. It is evident that it was regarded as an ominous and execrable animal. The *She-shan-chi* 攝山記 states: "Chin Shang 靳商, minister of the kingdom of Ch'u during the period of Warring States, better known as *Shang-kuan ta-fu* 上官大夫, after he caused the death of Ch'ü Yüan 屈原 by a false accusation, was punished by Heaven and turned into a huge python that came to dwell in the rear of this mountain [She Shan], where a shrine was built to him in later times."[29] In the *Yü-chang chi* 豫章記 by Lei Tzu-tsung 雷次宗 (386–448) we find a serpent story involving Wu Meng. At the end of the Yung-chia era (307–312) there was a huge serpent, over a hundred feet long, which cut off the road and sucked in anyone who came within reach of its breath. By the time it had taken a hundred victims, no one dared to go that way. Wu Meng led several disciples to go and slay the python. He remarked that it was the spirit of Shu 蜀. When the python died, the rebel of Shu [namely, Tu T'ao 杜弢] perished.[30]

The next story is perhaps the oldest one that uses python folklore to explain—or explain away—the lore of Taoist immortality. It comes from the *Po-wu chih*:

> In the T'ien-men 天門 commandery [in modern Hupei] there was a steep valley deep in the mountains. Anyone going along the path at the bottom of the valley suddenly

28. In the *Erh-ya*, 9:13 *Shih-yü* 釋魚, (*Erh-ya chu-shu* 爾雅注疏, *Ssu-pu pei-yao* ed.), the *mang* is called *wang-she* 王蛇 (king-serpent). The *Tz'u-hai* 辭海 identifies it with boa constrictor, which is akin to *jan* 蚺 or Python reticularis. Giles's *Dictionary* defines both *mang* and *jan* as boa constrictor. The *jan* reaches thirty Chinese feet in length and is longer than the *mang*, which reaches twenty.

29. *Yüan-chien lei-han* 淵鑑類函 439:2b (Shanghai, 1926).

30. *Yü-chang chi* cited in the *T'ai-p'ing yü-lan* 886:3937a (Peking, 1960). See also *Chin-shu* 95 (*Wu Meng chuan*) and *Chin-shu chiao-chu* 晉書斠注 by Wu Shih-chien 吳士鑑 and Liu Ch'eng-kan 劉承幹, in *Erh-shih-wu shih* 二十五史 9:1621b–22b (Taipei, 1963).

soared out of the forest like a flying immortal, and then disappeared. Such cases occurred all year round, and the place came to be called the Valley of the Immortals. A
number of men who loved the Tao and liked marvelous things went into this valley
to bathe and wash themselves in the hope of becoming flying immortals. Occasionally
they disappeared as if they had acquired immortality. There was a certain man of
thoughtful disposition who suspected the existence of a monster. After throwing a big
stone into the valley, he entered it following his dog. The dog flew away [as if it had
become immortal]. So he went back and notified the local villagers. Scores of them
made bold to follow him with sticks to push aside the grass and axes to fell the trees.
When they reached the summit of the mountain, they saw a huge thing several dozen
feet in length and high enough to hide a standing man. Its ears were as large as a win-
nower. They attacked it with arrows and knives and finally stabbed it to death. Piled
up in mounds around it they found human bones. It proved to be a python with a
huge mouth—over a foot wide. The missing persons had been inhaled by its vaporous
breath. Thereafter no more disappearances were reported.[31]

The *T'ai-p'ing kuang-chi* 太平廣記 gives two items quoted from the
Yü-t'ang hsien-hua 玉堂閑話 by a T'ang writer that deal with similar
stories. The first is entitled "The place for selecting immortals" (*Hsüan-
hsien ch'ang* 選仙場):

In a province far to the south is located a place for selecting immortals. It lies under a
steep cliff, near the top of which is found a cave. Tradition has it that immortals (*shen-
hsien* 神仙) reside therein. Each year on the day of *chung-yüan* 中元 [the fifteenth day of
the seventh lunar month] one Taoist used to be selected to ascend to heaven. His
comrades prepared an altar at the foot of the cliff. At an appointed hour on the day
people came from far and near in their best clothes. They held a *k'o-i* 科儀 ceremony,
fasted and purified themselves (*chai-chiao* 齋醮), and burned incense as an offering.
After seven days the gathering chose from among themselves the most virtuous, pure,
and honest person. Holding a written prayer (*chien* 簡), he would stand upright on the
altar. People waved their sleeves, bade him farewell, and then retired. While they
were kneeling at a distance to watch him, auspicious clouds of the five colors came
gradually down from the portal of the cave to the altar. The elect, wearing a crown and
clad in a robe, stood motionless clasping his hands in veneration. Then stepping onto
the five-colored clouds, he ascended to heaven. All the spectators shed tears out of envy
for his acquiring immortality and bowed repeatedly toward the entrance of the cave.
One or two (*sic*) cases a year used to be reported.

One year the virtuous person elected had a cousin, a Buddhist monk who came from
Mt. Wu-tu 武都 to bid him farewell. He brought a pound of realgar (*hsiung-huang*
雄黄), to present to him saying: "This is the very thing you need for your trip. You
should hide it [under your clothes] between your waist and stomach. Be careful not to
lose it." The chosen man was delighted. With the gift in his bosom, he mounted the
altar. From its top he stepped onto the clouds and went up into the sky. After a fortnight, people smelled an awful stench coming from the rocks of the mountain. A few

---

31. *Po-wu chih* 2:9ab (*Chih-hai* 指海 ed., *han* 5).

days later a hunter climbed up to the cave and found a huge python putrefying there. The bones of those who had been selected to ascend to heaven were piled up in the cave. In actuality, the clouds had all along been the vapor of the python's breath. Ignorant Taoists fell victims to it. What a pity![32]

The second story is entitled "The Mountain of Dog Immortals" (Kou-hsien-shan 狗仙山):

Many rocks and cliffs are found in the land of the Pa 巴 and Tsung 賨 people [in modern Szechwan], who lead a hunting life. Every place is haunted by water and forest monsters. In a high steep mountain there is an unfathomable cave. Once a hunter loosed his dog, who, despite his master's calling, ran away with staring eyes and wagging tail. Looking at the mouth of the cave, the dog noticed colored clouds hanging down which came to receive him and take him in. Such cases were reported annually. Those who liked the Tao called it the mountain of dog immortals. One wise man found all this hard to believe. Taking his dog and carrying a bow, he went to the place. When he arrived at the cave, he tied the dog to a big tree with a thick rope that went round its waist. Then he withdrew to observe what would happen. The colored clouds came down; the dog circled round barking many times without knowing how to get away. Suddenly there appeared a monster whose head was like a gigantic jar and whose eyes were like a turtle's. Its scales glittered so brilliantly that the whole valley was lit up. Gradually it lowered its body out of the cave and then noticed the dog. The hunter shot a poisoned arrow which hit it in the right spot. The monster did not appear again. Ten days later the whole mountain was foul with a stench. The hunter went down by rope from the summit and found a huge python decomposed among the rocks. No more casualties were heard of at Mt. Kou-hsien.[33]

The common feature of these two stories is the aspersion cast on the lore of immortality, in one case from a Buddhist standpoint, in the other from a realistic or protoscientific standpoint. I have been unable to ascertain whether the story of flying immortals was in the original version of the *Po-wu chih* by Chang Hua, an enlightened man of great learning. An early example of the Buddhist assertion that Taoist immortals were the victims of a python is found in the apologetic treatise, *Erh-chiao-lun* 二教論 by Tao-an 道安 of Northern Chou,[34] who quotes the *Shu-chi* 蜀記 by Li Yung 李膺. The latter tells us that the cause of the death of Chang Tao-ling 張道陵 in A.D. 177 was his being bitten by a python. Chang Heng 張衡, his son and successor, who could not find his father's corpse and was afraid of public censure (*ch'ing-i* 清議), invented a miraculous story about his father ascending to heaven from the summit of a rocky cliff. In order to convince his ignorant followers, he fastened a stork to the cliff by the legs, and waited for the New Year, when he announced

32. *T'ai-p'ing kuang-chi* 458:1250 (Taipei, 1962).
33. Ibid.
34. *Kuang Hung-ming chi* 廣弘明集 *T* LII. 2103.8:140.

to the people that the Celestial Master had ascended to Hsüan-tu 玄都 on the seventh day of the first month.[35]

Conclusion

The popular cults we have discussed flourished at the time and in the region of Sun En's Taoist rebel movement. We must elucidate his relation to them and his use of Taoism as an ideology superior to the local beliefs.

The Taoist secret arts and practices of Tu Chiung were transmitted to him through his uncle Sun T'ai, who had been Tu Chiung's disciple. Tu Chiung was a rather conservative, orthodox Taoist who made many converts not only among the literati, including some eminent officials of northern origin, but also among the notable clans and the populace in the South. Among his disciples and patrons we find Wang Hsi-chih and his son Ning-chih 凝之 from Lang-yeh 琅邪 in the North, Lu Na 陸納 from Wu commandery in the South, as well as Sun T'ai, a man of low and obscure birth who (or whose ancestors) had fled from the North and found a new but unpleasant environment south of the Yangtze which was then under the rule of immigrant northerners.

When Tu Chiung propagated his Cheng-i doctrine among the populace in the South, he had to come to terms in a complex way with their shamanistic cults. There were many local shrines dedicated to the deities of mountains and rivers who were believed to control the winds and the waters in their vicinity. The inhabitants, mostly peasantry, had to support, both morally and financially, these shrines, which were managed by shaman-priests who pursued pecuniary profit at the expense of the people. We see that the Taoists eagerly denounced this abuse of shamanistic

---

35. Minakata Kumagusu is the only scholar who has offered a scientific interpretation of this legend. He cites the case of Herakleides, who kept a snake with tender care. When he was at death's door, he asked a friend to hide his body and lay the snake on his bed immediately after his death. In this way people would be convinced of his deification. After pointing out that Pliny noted the likeness of the snake's vestigial feet to that of a water-fowl, Minakata argues that Chang Heng persuaded his followers that his father, riding on a python, had come to the cliff, where he left the python's traces and ascended to the Taoist paradise. See his "Hebi ni kansuru Minzoku to Densetsu 蛇に關する民俗と傳說 (Folklore and legends concerning the snake), in *Minakata Kumagusu Zenshū* (Tokyo, 1971), 1:202–03. Minakata also says that, although according to a Chinese proverb first seen in the *Chan-kuo-ts'e* 戰國策 the legs of a snake (*she-tsu* 蛇足) were something superfluous, ancient Chinese as well as ancient Romans wanted to affirm that the snake had some kind of organ for walking. According to a story in the *Hsüan-shih chih* 宣室志, a T'ang work, the snake was believed to stretch out legs when heated with the fire of mulberry wood. Minakata (p. 161) noticed that there is no sharp demarcation between snakes and lizards, which have legs. In Japan the *mang*, usually called *uwabami*, has always been involved in legendary stories, as in China.

shrines in scriptures such as the *Lu hsien-sheng tao-men k'o-lüeh* 陸先生道門科略 and the *San-t'ien nei-chieh ching* 三天內解經. Also, other Taoists took various measures against shamanism by displaying the superiority of their Taoist secret arts and thereby defeating the small arts of "small shamans" (*hsiao-wu* 小巫).

The miraculous story of Tu Chiung, who sent back a borrowed knife, can only be understood in the light of the shamanistic practice of inducing travelers to make offerings to the deity of a nearby shrine. The case of Lu-shan-chün, who was believed to control navigation on Lake Kung-t'ing (P'o-yang), is especially noteworthy because the lake region is situated at the important crossroad connecting south China with the Yangtze valley. Lu Hsün 盧循, Sun En's successor, marched his army from Canton to Hsün-yang 潯陽, along the Kan River and Lake P'o-yang, and then along the Yangtze, to attack Chien-k'ang.

What kind of people supported and fought for Sun En and Lu Hsün? First of all, poverty-stricken peasants and fishermen in the coastal provinces, Kiangsu, Chekiang and Fukien, became the core of the rebellion. Notable clans of the South, who were less privileged and looked down upon by the aristocrats come from the North, had without doubt sympathy with their countrymen and were inclined to accept the teaching of Tu Chiung, who was a member of a southern clan. There were also some ruined nobles whose fortune and status, in spite of their northern origin, declined in the newly developed areas south of the Yangtze. Both Sun En and Lu Hsün belonged to this last group and harbored resentment against the aristocratic rule which was at this time showing signs of commotion due to the threat of the northern barbarians and the disturbances among the military cliques in both the middle and lower valleys of the Yangtze.

Under the ineffective rule of Hsiao-wu-ti, assisted by his brother Ssu-ma Tao-tzu 司馬道子, prince of Kuei-chi, sycophantic but able courtiers of lower birth made their way in the central government. Many of them were southerners who pursued commercial profit through the generous patronage of the emperor and first-rank nobility who disliked the sober business of government. Because of the difficulties of their careers in the Eastern Chin bureaucracy, these southerners tried to enrich themselves in agriculture and commerce. The internal wars among military cliques at the end of the Eastern Chin gave them a chance of earning money. It was among these southern parvenus, as well as among the best society in the capital, that Tu Chiung, law-abiding, conservative and all-embracing master of orthodox Taoism, found patrons and followers.

At that time, the Yangtze, Lake P'o-yang, and the Kan River formed the main route to be followed by merchants who brought goods to the capital. There were also some messengers from the local governors despatched to forward presents to powerful dignitaries in the capital. The route was full of danger and trouble. The merchants and travelers had to pay homage to shrines along the route. The deity of the Kung-t'ing shrine was the most powerful of all. Fortunately, they came to know the miracle of Tu Chiung, who proved to have power over the deity of the shrine. In Tu Chiung's system of teaching such miracle working was peripheral. But some disciples of his exploited this miracle in order to appeal to the less intelligent, credulous people.

Sun T'ai, a descendant of Sun Hsiu 孫秀 of Western Chin who instigated Chao-wang (Ssu-ma) Lun 司馬倫 to usurpation, was a heterogeneous element among the faithful followers of the Cheng-i Sect. Exploiting the reputation of his master, Sun T'ai lured many people, mostly the oppressed and impoverished in the eastern districts near the capital. Moreover, he established an acquaintance with the nobility, including Yüan-hsien 元顯, the son of the prince of Kuei-chi. Seizing the occasion of Wang Kung's 王恭 rebellion, he mobilized and armed his followers. But for Hsieh Yu 謝輶, a perspicacious official who accused him of treachery, Sun T'ai would have been the ring-leader of this country-wide rebellion which broke out under the leadership of his nephew and successor Sun En. Sun En did not hesitate to massacre Wang Ning-chih's family, since he was at odds with the orthodox Cheng-i doctrine faithfully followed by the Wang family.

Sun T'ai, Sun En, and his successor Lu Hsün used Tu Chiung's prestige and power over the local cults in order to gain adherence; they also used Taoism as a religion superior to the local cults, with which to impress the peasantry and instigate them to political rebellion. More peaceful Taoist adepts such as Wu Meng, as well as Buddhist monks like An Shih-kao, proselytized followers of shamanism to more civilized religions without assuming an antidynastic attitude.

4 K'ou Ch'ien-chih and the Taoist Theocracy at the Northern Wei Court, 425-451

Richard B. Mather

But this civil government is designed, as long as we live in this world, to cherish and support the external worship of God, to preserve the pure doctrine of religion, to defend the constitution of the Church, and to regulate our lives in a manner requisite for the society of men.

John Calvin,
Institutes of the Christian Religion

THE USE OF THE WORD *theocracy* may seem far-fetched in any discussion of a church-state relation which is not in the Western tradition, especially if the religion in question is not, strictly speaking, theistic. But even in that paradigm of theocracies—Geneva in the sixteenth century—there was no implication of a direct rule of God, or even an indirect one through his "viceregents," the clergy. Geneva was governed by secular magistrates who derived their sanction and power from God and who were obligated to uphold the institutions of true religion. It is in this sense that I use the term to describe the government of the Northern Wei state in the second quarter of the fifth century. The state claimed its ultimate authority from a supernatural power and maintained an external religious establishment whose hierarchy and rituals served as a kind of authentication of its faithfulness to the Heavenly Mandate, as well as providing it with direct access to the ultimate source of power.

K'ou Ch'ien-chih's 寇謙之 brief but dazzling career as Celestial Master (*t'ien-shih* 天師) in the Northern Wei capital between 425 and his death in 448 is generally acknowledged to be a unique event, unparalleled in the previous experience of the Taoist communities in relation to the state. It represented the culmination of fortuitous events within the court itself, and was in no sense the result of a popular movement, like the Taoist enclave in Han-chung (southern Shensi and northern Szechwan) following the peasant uprisings at the close of the second century. It differed radically, also, from the various Taoist rebel movements of the fourth and early fifth centuries,[1] against which it was a kind of reaction.

K'ou Ch'ien-chih happened to be in the right place at the right time. After he died and his chief supporters were supplanted by others, his personal influence quickly faded, though much of his program persisted on a purely institutional level. It will probably never be known what effect his reforms had at the grass roots. At this stage of the investigation it would appear to have been negligible, since the chief targets of his attack—popular uprisings and the expectation of messianic deliverers, rice-levies (*tsu-mi* 租米) for the support of Taoist officers, as well as their hereditary succession, and the sexual rites known as the "union of vital forces" (*ho-ch'i* 合氣)—were all evidently still flourishing at least as late as the sixth century, when Buddhist polemicists were attacking them;[2] and the expectation of the messianic figure, Li Hung 李弘, lived on well into T'ang and Sung times.[3]

If we were to trace the factors responsible for the brief ascendancy of the Northern Wei Taoist theocracy, we would find at least five interwoven strands, none of which by itself might have produced such a result, but which in combination proved to be a potent force:

1. The survival of the "Way of Great Peace" (*T'ai-p'ing tao* 太平道) in the eastern provinces even after the suppression of the Yellow Turban Rebellion in the last years of the Later Han period, and its apparent amalgamation with the Five-Pecks-of-Rice sect (*Wu-tou-mi tao* 五斗米道),

---

1. See Sunayama Minoru 砂山稔, "Ri Kō-kara Kō Kenshi-e: seireki yon-go seki ni okeru shūkyō-teki hanran to kokka shūkyō" 李弘から寇謙之へ一西歴四・五世紀における宗教的反亂と國家宗教, *Shūkan tōyōgaku* 集刊東洋學, 26:1-21 (1971). Among the Taoist-led rebellions, mostly associated with someone named Li Hung 李弘, mentioned by Sunayama are: one in the Chekiang area, suppressed in 324; one in the Shantung area between 335 and 341; one in the Hupei area between 345 and 356; one in the Szechwan area, suppressed in 370; Sun En's rebellion in the Chekiang-Kiangsu area, suppressed in 402 and carried on by Lu Hsün 盧循 until 411; a rebellion in the Ch'ang-an area between 407 and 417, which was probably directly experienced by K'ou Ch'ien-chih himself; and one in the Kansu area between 424 and 427.

2. See *Hung-ming chi (HMC)* 弘明集 8, *Pien-huo lun* 辯惑論 (sixth cent.), *Taishō (T)*, LII. 2102. 48bc; *Kuang hung-ming chi (KHMC)* 廣弘明集, 9, *Hsiao-tao lun* 笑道論 (A.D. 570), *T* LII. 2103. 152ab.

3. A. Seidel, "The Image of the Perfect Ruler in Early Taoist Messianism: Lao-tzu and Li Hung," *History of Religions* 9.2-3:224 (1969-70).

later known as the Celestial Master sect (*T'ien-shih tao* 天師道), which had originated simultaneously in the Han-chung area to the southwest.

2. The receptivity of the T'o-pa rulers themselves to an immortality- and magic-oriented form of Taoism, and of Emperor T'ai-wu 太武 (T'o-pa Tao 燾, r. 424–452) in particular, to the idea of being the "Perfect Ruler of Great Peace" (*T'ai-p'ing chen-chün* 泰平眞君).

3. The influence of K'ou Ch'ien-chih's elder brother, Tsan-chih 讚之 (363–448), who became the Northern Wei governor of the Later Ch'in refugees in "Southern Yung," stationed in Lo-yang, after 417.

4. The timeliness of converting primitive Taoism into an established church, and the attractiveness to the Wei court and to the powerful gentry families of K'ou's essentially conservative, counterrevolutionary ideology.

5. The coincidence of K'ou's dream of a "chosen people" (*chung-min* 種民) with the ambitions of the influential minister, Ts'ui Hao 崔浩 (381–450), to restore a Chinese state in north China.

The Survival of Religious Taoist Communities

The rebellion of the Yellow Turbans in the eastern provinces, led by Chang Chüeh 張角 in 184 and tirelessly suppressed by the Later Han government through the next two decades, left behind many communities which, though no longer posing a powerful political threat, continued to follow the original religious practices of the Way of Great Peace, includ- ing prayer and fasting, group confessions to obtain healing, group reci- tation of the *Tao-te-ching* and other sacred texts, and a quasi-military hierarchy of local and regional officers who became hereditary and were supported through regular contributions of rice and other commodities.[4] Because of the decentralized organization of the local communities, they could carry on their subgovernmental hierarchies and their periodic fes- tivals without maintaining any formal contact with a "mother church" or Celestial Master. From the beginning, however, there was always some communication with Taoist communities in other parts of the realm. The Five-Pecks-of-Rice sect, which originated about the same time in Han- chung under the leadership of the first Celestial Masters, Chang Tao-ling 張道陵 (d. between 157 and 178) and his son and grandson, Chang Heng 衡 and Chang Lu 魯 (fl. 190–220), practiced very similar rites and main- tained a similar form of organization. After Chang Lu's surrender to Ts'ao Ts'ao 曹操 in 215, he and his officers were all given fiefs and noble titles by

4. See Howard Levy, "Yellow Turban Religion and Rebellion at the End of Han," *Journal of the American Oriental Society* (*JAOS*) 76.4:216–19 (1956).

the Han government, but his followers managed to maintain a semi-autonomous enclave in Han-chung for the next century and a half.

After the Former Ch'in ruler, Fu Chien 苻堅 (r. 357–384), had engulfed Han-chung in 373 in his effort to unify all of China,[5] it is very probable that many of the Taoist families moved, or were moved, to the Ch'in capital in Ch'ang-an (in Shensi). Still later, in a bid to build his own image as the unifier of China, the Eastern Chin general, Liu Yü 劉裕, who claimed descent from the Han imperial family and himself once figured as a Taoist messiah,[6] and who afterwards founded the Liu-Sung Dynasty (420–479) in Nanking, conquered Ch'ang-an in 417, and once more there were mass migrations, this time to the eastern commanderies of Ho-nan, Ying-yang, and Ho-nei (Honan and Shansi) in the Northern Wei domain.

K'ou Ch'ien-chih's family was at the time living in P'ing-i 馮翊, near Ch'ang-an, and his elder brother, Tsan-chih, was a leader in this mass exodus. Because of his part in winning the allegiance of "several tens of thousands of (Later Ch'in) households" for the Northern Wei, K'ou Tsan-chih was appointed the Wei governor of "Southern Yung Province" (i.e. of the immigrants from Shensi) and was stationed in Lo-yang.[7] It is not unreasonable to assume that some of these households, like that of the K'ou's, might also have been adherents of the Celestial Master sect. In any case, in the course of time the eastern and western branches of Taoism seem more or less to have lost whatever distinctions they may originally have had, though the actual numerical strength of the Taoist community in Northern Wei would be extremely difficult to assess.[8]

The Receptivity of the T'o-pa Rulers to Taoism

The original religion of the T'o-pa, who were a branch of the Hsien-pei 鮮卑, was, like that of most nomadic and seminomadic peoples, a blend of shamanism and animism, and the T'o-pa rulers felt at home in the presence of Taoist practitioners who could control the powers of nature and predict events, and who offered prescriptions for warding off sickness and

5. *Chin-shu* 113:16a (*T'ung-wen* ed.); Michael Rogers, trans., *The Chronicle of Fu Chien* (Chinese Dynastic Histories Translations), no. 10 (Berkeley and Los Angeles, 1968), p. 136.
6. See Seidel, "Image of the Perfect Ruler," p. 238, citing *Tung-yüan shen-chou ching* 洞淵神咒經, 1:3b–4a (*Tao-tsang* [*TT*] 170).
7. *Wei-shu* (*WS*) 42:6b (*T'ung-wen* ed.).
8. See R. A. Stein, "Remarques sur les mouvements du taoïsme politico-religieux au IIe siècle ap. J.-C.," *T'oung Pao* 50:7 (1963). Professor Stein's corrections and additions to this article are carried in the Japanese translation by Kawakatsu Yoshio 川勝義雄 in *Dōkyō kenkyū* 道教研究 2:5–113 (1967).

death. Even as early as 400, over two decades before K'ou Ch'ien-chih appeared at the Wei capital, the court had established an office of Erudite of Transcendent Beings (hsien-jen po-shih 仙人博士) and had built a Laboratory for Transcendent Drugs (hsien-fang 仙坊) near the palace grounds for boiling and smelting elixirs. When K'ou himself was first given a berth at court in 424, he was filling the office of Erudite of Transcendent Beings recently vacated by the luckless incumbent, Chang Yao 張曜. Chang had been dismissed from court and set up as a recluse in the hunting preserve at the insistence of the court physician, perhaps out of professional jealousy, but ostensibly because of the latter's alarm over the number of deaths resulting from the ingestion of Chang's concoctions among unsuspecting convicts who were being used as guinea-pigs.[9]

It is also understandable that the T'o-pa Emperor T'ai-wu, who had newly mounted the throne when Ts'ui Hao introduced K'ou to him in 424, would have responded positively to Ts'ui's intimation that, since all sage-kings on receiving the Mandate received with it a "heavenly corroboration" (t'ien-ying 天應), he should likewise accept K'ou Ch'ien-chih's heaven-revealed documents: the "Articles of a New Code to be Chanted to Yün-chung Musical Notation" (Yün-chung yin-sung hsin-k'o chih chieh 雲中音誦新科之誡, corresponding to the Lao-chün yin-sung chieh-ching 老君音誦誡經 of Tao-tsang 562), and the "Perfect Book of Talismans and Designs" (Lu-t'u chen-ching 錄圖眞經, now lost).[10] According to the Shih-Lao chih 釋老志 (Wei-shu 114), K'ou had received these documents by direct revelation[11] from the deified Lao-tzu, Lao-chün 老君, and from his "great-great grandson," Li P'u-wen 李譜文, on two separate occasions, in 415 and 423, while he was living in a hermitage on the slopes of the central sacred peak, Mount Sung (in Honan). He had originally gone into a hermitage near his home in the Ch'ang-an area on the western peak, Mount Hua (in Shensi) around 410 or 411, and thence with his teacher, Ch'eng-kung Hsing 成公興 (d. 417?), to Mount Sung, where he remained until the eve of his appearance in the Northern Wei

---

9. Shih-Lao chih 釋老志 (SLC = WS 114) 66; Tsukamoto Zenryū 塚本善隆, Gisho Shakurōshi no kenkyū 魏書釋老志の研究 (Kyoto, 1961), p. 321; James R. Ware, "The Wei-shu and the Sui-shu on Taoism," JAOS 53:224 (1933). Cf. also WS 113:2b.

10. See Yang Lien-sheng 楊聯陞, "Lao-chün yin-sung chieh-ching chiao-shih" 老君音誦誡經校釋, Chung-yang yen-chiu-yüan, Li-shih yü-yen yen-chiu-so chi-k'an 中央研究院歷史言語研究所集刊 (CYYCY) 28.1:50 (1956).

11. For an account of similar direct revelation of Taoist scriptures, see Michel Strickmann's description of T'ao Hung-ching's 陶弘景 (452–536) recording of the Chen-kao 眞誥 in "The Mao Shan Revelations; Taoism and the Aristocracy," T'oung Pao 63.1 (1977).

capital in 424.[12] Now he was bringing both documents voluntarily to the Wei court and not to another, which was a clear sign that T'ai-wu's reign was in accord with Heaven.[13] Later, in 440, after the annexation of Northern Liang (in Kansu) had extended the Northern Wei domain from Manchuria to Central Asia and K'ou, in accord with a prophecy in one of these documents, suggested that Emperor T'ai-wu was now the "Perfect Ruler of Great Peace of the North" (*pei-fang T'ai-p'ing chen-chün*) and should change the reign-title accordingly, the emperor could easily see the logic in this and complied with enthusiasm.[14]

The Influence of K'ou Tsan-chih

We have already observed the important role played by K'ou Ch'ien-chih's brother, Tsan-chih, in winning over to Wei the displaced families from Later Ch'in after Liu Yü's sack of Ch'ang-an in 417. It is hardly a coincidence that the younger brother should also have found honor in Wei. The road to the Wei capital at P'ing-ch'eng from K'ou's hermitage on Mount Sung passed near Lo-yang, where Tsan-chih was stationed. A letter of introduction from him would have carried great weight. In addition, the K'ou brothers claimed descent from an important family of the northern gentry hailing originally from Shang-ku 上谷 (in Hopei), which thirteen generations earlier had produced K'ou Hsün 恂 (d. A.D. 36), a key figure in the Later Han restoration.[15] This was a favorable point in winning the support of other Chinese families of the gentry in Wei, and also explains to some extent the strong counterrevolutionary bias of K'ou's religious reforms.

From Primitive to Established Religion

The desire among conservative members of the gentry to convert the unpredictable dynamism of primitive Taoism into an established church was, two-and-a-half centuries after Chang Tao-ling, already in the air, and K'ou's program to do just that was timely. It seems that his own viewpoint was that of the ruling class. Though there is as yet no adequate basis on which to estimate the size or the social composition of the Taoist community in the Northern Wei domain, there is ample evidence that prominent gentry families of the gentry from various parts of China during the fourth and fifth centuries had been "for generations" adherents of the

---

12. *SLC* 69; Tsukamoto, *Gisho*, p. 334; Ware, pp. 231–32.
13. *SLC* 70; Tsukamoto, *Gisho*, p. 340; Ware, pp. 235–36.
14. *Tzu-chih t'ung chien* 資治通鑒 (*TCTC*) 123:3885 (Peking ed. of 1956).
15. *Hou-Han shu* 46:17b–23b.

Celestial Master Sect—the Wangs 王 of Lang-yeh (Shantung), the T'aos 陶 of Chiu-chiang (Kiangsi), the Hsüs 許, the Shens 沈, and the Kos 葛 of the Chekiang area, to name only a few. But how numerous they were in relation to peasant adherents or those from other social groups, or what actual relation existed between the higher and lower levels during religious celebrations, would be hard to reconstruct.

It seems likely, however, that the audience to whom K'ou Ch'ien-chih's "New Code" was addressed was largely composed of families with little or no wealth or status, though some evidently possessed slaves (article 24; Yang, p. 47), and some could afford to hold "feasts" (ch'u-hui 厨會: articles 11–13; Yang, p. 44). It is also clear from his reiterated complaints against inherited offices (articles 4, 14, 25; Yang, pp. 39, 44, 48) and against levies of rice or silk (article 7; Yang, p. 43) that he was aiming at existing practices which tended to make the Taoist communities into a sort of subgovernment, potentially dangerous as pockets of rebellion. Only two decades earlier, in the Chekiang-Kiangsu area, under the leadership of Sun En 孫恩 (d. 402), whose own motives may well have been mixed, local Taoists (as distinct from Taoists who had migrated thither from the north) erupted spontaneously in protest against certain conscription measures of the governor of Yang Province (Chekiang-Kiangsu), and after overrunning most of the province, causing enormous loss of life and property, threatened the tenuous existence of the Eastern Chin capital in Chien-k'ang (Nanking) itself.[16]

No official or landowner could afford to look on these threats to order and security with equanimity. Nor was anyone so deluded as to think that a religion so firmly entrenched in the hearts of the common people could be eliminated by mere repressive action from without. The answer obviously was to reform the religion from within. Even as early as 320 Ko Hung 葛洪 (284–363) had already complained about the disregard for propriety (li 禮) among some Taoists, and their insubordination to authority.[17] And numerous Buddhist polemics had been leveled against Taoist "abuses," which were later included in the sixth-century collection *Hung-ming chi* 弘明集 (*Taishō* #2102), and its seventh-century sequel, *Kuang hung-ming chi* 廣弘明集 (*Taishō* #2103).[18] Typical of these is the

16. See W. Eichhorn, "Description of the Rebellion of Sun En," *Mitteilungen des Instituts für Orientforschung* 2.1:338 (1954); also Miyakawa Hisayuki 宮川尚志, "Son On, Ro Shun no ran ni tsuite" 孫恩盧循の亂について, *Tōyōshi kenkyū* 東洋史研究, 30.2–3:1–30 (1971).

17. *Pao P'u-tzu* 抱朴子 (*Wai-p'ien*) 31:156 and 7:119 (*Chu-tzu chi-ch'eng* ed.); T'ang Yung-t'ung 湯用彤 and T'ang I-chieh 湯一介, "K'ou Ch'ien-chih ti chu-tso yü ssu-hsiang" 寇謙之的著作與思想, *Li-shih yen-chiu* 歷史研究 5:70 (1961).

18. E.g. the *Pien-huo lun* of Hsüan-kuang 玄光 (sixth cent.), *Hthe siao-tao lun* of Chen

"Discourse against Delusion" (*Pien-huo lun* 辯惑論) by the sixth-century monk, Hsüan-kuang 玄光, in which he wrote:

> The "Yellow Writings" [*Huang-shu* 黃書, corresponding to the *Tung-chen huang-shu* 洞眞黃書 of *Tao-tsang* 1031, a ritual manual for certain sexual rites] says, "Open the Gate of Life [*ming-men* 命門, i.e. the right kidney, thought to be the repository of semen], and embrace the embryo of the Realized Man (*chen-jen* 眞人). Play in rotation the game of Dragons (*yang*) and Tigers (*yin*) (*hui lung-hu hsi* 廻龍虎戲)." Is it permissible to do this kind of thing to ward off misfortune and dispel disaster? Is it permissible? During the Han the rebel leader [*i-chün* 蟻君, literally, "lord of the ants," i.e. Chang Tao-ling] practiced this as the Way, and his demonic confusion of morals reached all the way to Tuu-huang [in the extreme northwest]. Later in the time of Sun En this moral laxity became even more pronounced. Men and women mingled indecently, no different from birds or beasts. It is easy to be infected by world contamination, but difficult to dispel the bonds of erotic attachment. How much more so when there is "union of the vital forces" (*ho-ch'i*) in the "cinnabar field" (*tan tien* 丹田, i.e. the lower abdomen) and "prolongation of life" through the "cave of transcendent beings" (*hsien-hsüeh* 仙穴), or when the troops are indulged beyond the forbidden confines of the "Jade Gate" (*yü-men* 玉門), and aberrant practices have exhausted the powers of the "Dragons and Tigers"! Such practices in life lack the restraint of loyalty and chastity, and after death produce suffering in the Blue Court [of hell]. . . .
>
> People like the Yellow Turbans and the rest gazed like vultures on the Han royal house. Since they opposed and sought to alter the clear decree of Heaven, their crimes were all suppressed and they were executed. Next there was [Chang Heng's] son, Lu, who also claimed to follow the Way of Demons [*kuei-tao* 鬼道, i.e. sorcery]. Since the gods of heaven and earth (*shen-chih* 神祇) did not come to his aid, he was gored (? *t'u* 突) by a wild deer. Last of all, Sun En in his turn claimed to follow the Purple Way (*tzu-tao* 紫道). Not caring for the ignominy of the common people's lowly estate, he wished to make a bid for the dignity of an emperor's nobility. He raised cloud-echoes from the secluded water-courses [of Chekiang], and released vain imaginings in the empty darkness. As the "Transcendent Being of the Waters" (*shui-hsien* 水仙) he deluded others, and recklessly slaughtered both old and young, destroying the state and ruining the people. Was he not a cruel and rapacious rebel?[19]

Aimed as they are against the sexual rites (a threat to social stability) and the excesses of rebels like Chang Chüeh and Sun En, these complaints are perhaps more a reflection of their authors' social status than of their religion. In any case, they suggest why a religious leader like K'ou Ch'ien-chih, whose credentials showed that he intended to "purify and reform the Taoist religion (*Tao-chiao* 道教), to eradicate the counterfeit methods of the 'Three Changs,'[20] the rice-levies and the cash taxes (*ch'ien-shui*

Luan 甄鸞 (A.D. 570), the *Erh-chiao lun* 二教論 of Tao-an 道安 (sixth cent.), and the *Mieh-huo lun* 滅惑論 of Liu Hsieh 劉勰 (sixth cent.).

19. *T.* LII. 2102:48bc; see also H. Maspero, "Les procédés de 'nourrir le principe vital' dans la religion taoïste ancienne," *Journal asiatique* 229:403–13 (1937).

20. Though the term "Three Changs" is usually understood as referring to Chang Tao-

錢稅), and the techniques of the 'union of the vital forces' "[21] would be sure to endear himself to worried rulers and nervous landlords. Furthermore, his program for a theocratic state in which the head of the church had the title Celestial Master, and the head of the state the title Perfect Ruler of Great Peace, would greatly comfort those who feared the subversive potentialities of a popular movement devoid of responsible direction.

K'ou's brand of religion combined a Confucian love of ritual and order with Buddhist models for ethical behavior, and a "Neo-Taoist" compromise between conformity with the demands of society (*ming-chiao* 名教) and a modified kind of naturalness (*tzu-jan* 自然). The Confucian-Buddhist ethos appears in the "New Code" itself, which, though somewhat redundant and unsystematic as it appears in the *Tao-tsang*, is nevertheless in the form of brief statutes, each ending with a formula, somewhat similar to contemporary legal codes and to parts of the Buddhist Vinaya. The "Neo-Taoist" compromise is best exemplified in K'ou's own life, which was spent half as hermit in the solitary quest for immortality and half as public figure. At the same time, K'ou was offering lay disciples like Ts'ui Hao improved techniques for the nurture and preservation of life which he had brought with him from Buddhist missionaries in Ch'ang-an.[22] His appeal to the upper levels of Wei society was assured, although it will probably never be known how much support he actually had among the common people.

The "Chosen People" and the Restoration of Chinese Rule

But by far the most crucial factor in K'ou Ch'ien-chih's rise was the role played by his disciple and chief collaborator, Ts'ui Hao 崔浩 (381–450). So crucial, in fact, was Ts'ui's role, that K'ou could almost be considered the figurehead behind whose religious reforms Ts'ui operated his own grand plan for the revival of Chinese rule in north China. Ts'ui Hao is sometimes described as a "reactionary Confucian,"[23] but this does scant justice to another side of his character which counterbalanced his Confucian orthodoxy. He appears to have been obsessed with the occult sciences

---

ling, his son Heng, and his grandson Lu, some historians (e.g., T'ang, p. 65) prefer to understand it here as referring to Chang Chüeh 角 and his brothers Pao 寶 and Liang 梁, the leaders of the Yellow Turbans, since K'ou himself professed to be restoring the broken tradition of Chang Lu.

21. *SLC* 68; Tsukamoto, *Gisho*, p. 331; Ware, pp. 229–30.

22. T'ang (n. 17), pp. 74–77; see also n. 29.

23. See Holmes Welch, *The Parting of the Way: Lao-tzu and the Taoist Movement* (Boston, 1957), p. 151; Kenneth Ch'en, *Buddhism in China* (Princeton, 1964), p. 147; W. Eichhorn, *Chinese Civilization* (English ed. New York, 1969), p. 184.

of his day: the "mysterious symbols" (*hsüan-hsiang* 玄象) of the "Book of Changes," the interplay of Yin and Yang forces, astrology, mathematics,[24] and Taoist techniques for longevity through diet and nurture of life (*fu-shih yang-hsing* [= *yang-sheng*] *chih shu* 服食養性[養生]之術).[25] Though it is true he had no use for the books attributed to Lao-tzu and Chuang-tzu, and could not believe that the "misleading and deceitful sayings" of the former were written by the Chou archivist whom Confucius once consulted about ritual,[26] he did, nevertheless, like to compare himself to the Taoist recluse-adviser, Chang Liang 張良 (d. 187 B.C.), whose inside track to the powers of the universe aided the founding of the Han Dynasty.[27]

So when K'ou Ch'ien-chih appeared in P'ing-ch'eng in 423, fresh from the caves of Mount Sung, with his revealed books—the "Articles of a New Code to be Chanted to Yün-chung Musical Notation" and the "Perfect Book of Talismans and Designs," written in a startlingly new style of calligraphy[28]—Ts'ui Hao, who also prided himself on being something of a calligrapher, was immediately drawn to him. And since Ts'ui was looking for a master who might improve his own longevity techniques, he could not fail to be impressed by the superior mathematical and medical skills which K'ou had learned from his Buddhist mentors in Ch'ang-an. There many Indian and Central Asian missionaries, including the great Kumārajīva (350–409), had been working, and K'ou had sharpened these skills for seven years on Mount Sung with his special guru, Ch'eng-kung Hsing 成公興, a disciple of the Buddhist mathematician-monk, Shih T'an-ying 釋曇影 (d. between 405 and 418), one of Kumārajīva's collaborators.[29]

But what drew the two together most intimately was a common dream of a "purified" society, which Ts'ui envisioned as a return to the golden age of Chou feudalism, with the original five orders of nobility at the top and the subject people knowing their place beneath,[30] and which K'ou envisioned as a return, through the "chosen people" (*chung-min*) of the Taoist church, to the primitive simplicity associated with the utopian

---

24. *WS* 35:1ab; *SLC* 68, 69.

25. *WS* 35:9a.

26. Ibid. 6b.

27. Ibid. 9b.

28. For the relation of calligraphy to Taoism, see Ch'en Yin-k'o 陳寅恪, "Ts'ui Hao yü K'ou Ch'ien-chih" 崔浩與寇謙之, *Ling-nan hsüeh-pao* 嶺南學報 11.1:123–24 (1950).

29. Tsukamoto, *Gisho*, pp. 326–27, citing the biography of Yin Shao 殷紹 (*WS* 91:12b) and *Kao-seng chuan* 高僧傳 (*KSC*) T L. 2059. 6:364a.

30. *WS* 35:9b and 47:1a.

kingdom of Ta Ch'in 大秦, rumors of which had circulated in China since Han times, and which is described in the *Wei-lüeh* 魏略 (quoted in P'ei Sung-chih's 裴松之 commentary to the *San-kuo chih, Wei-chih* 30). Although K'ou did not specifically use the term "Ta Ch'in," it is at least plain that this idealized state, which is vaguely identified in the *Wei-lüeh* (and later in *Hou-Han shu* 118 and *Wei-shu* 102) with the Roman Orient, or possibly India, is the model on which the organization of both Chang Chüeh's "Way of Great Peace" and Chang Tao-ling's Han-chung community were based, as Rolf Stein has convincingly demonstrated.[31]

Basically, this utopia could be described as a land of perfect government where peace and justice prevailed; but for K'ou Ch'ien-chih in particular it was a place where everyone was also restrained by rules of ritual behavior (*li-tu* 禮度).[32] In their early association in 423, Ts'ui and K'ou used to have long discussions lasting far into the night on "the course of order and rebellion in antiquity,"[33] and it appeared that Ts'ui's preoccupation with "rules for control and codes of law" (*chih-tu k'o-lü* 制度科律)[34] coincided with K'ou's own interest, especially as it was embodied in his "New Code," which in its turn was possibly influenced by the new translations of the Buddhist Vinaya emanating from Ch'ang-an.[35] For example, article 32 of the "New Code" states:

> The method of cultivation for Taoist officers and libationers (*chi-chiu* 祭酒) as they visit the people east, west, south, and north, coming or going, exiting or entering, is as follows: With straight body and straight face, going straight in a single direction, they may not turn to look either to the left or to the right. And when they arrive at the homes of the people they may not be unjustifiably angry or make scolding accusations, or miscellaneous comments on whether the food or drink is good or bad, or on the rightness or wrongness of the bed, the mat, or the house. Nor may they first go to the homes of the noble, the powerful, or the wealthy, and look with distaste on the practice of visiting the people. Rather they should first go to the homes of the lowly and poor (*han-p'in* 寒貧) and instruct them on how to seek blessings, enabling them to be thorough in abiding by the code. Let this be clearly and carefully carried out like a statute or order.[36]

The similarity to the following item in the fifty-ninth chapter of the *Smṛtyupasthāna-sūtra* (*Cheng-fa nien-ch'u ching* 正法念處經), translated by Prajñāruci in the mid-sixth century, though later in date and not actually

31. See Stein, "Remarques," pp. 8–21.
32. *SLC* 68; Tsukamoto, *Gisho*, p. 331; Ware, pp. 230–31.
33. *WS* 35:9a.
34. Ibid. 9b.
35. Ch'en Yin-k'o, "Ts'ui Hao," p. 47.
36. Yang (n. 10), p. 47.

part of the Vinaya, has already been pointed out by Yang Lien-sheng (see n. 10):

> On entering a village or town, or traveling along the road . . . a monk should walk straight ahead, neither turning the body nor casting sideward glances, but looking straight in a single direction, with a bearing which is orderly and proper. . . . When he comes to a donor's home, he may not shout and burst in, without first snapping the fingers. And when occupying the superior seat he may not speak endless and unprofitable words, unaware of what he is saying, nor make a great noise in a place where people are seated in silence, nor stare at all the women, nor be unjustifiably angry, nor look about to left and right, nor front nor back, nor treat the members of the household with arrogant contempt, nor break into other people's homes like a robber. . . .[37]

K'ou once confided to Ts'ui, "I had been practicing the Way in retirement and had never involved myself in worldly responsibilities, when suddenly I received these secret bequests (chüeh 訣) from the gods, stating that I should simultaneously cultivate the moral teachings of the Confucians (Ju-chiao 儒教) and come to the aid of the Perfect Ruler of Great Peace in carrying on the thousand-year rule that has been interrupted. But in my studies I have never delved into antiquity, and in the presence of worldly affairs I am dull and benighted. Would you compile for me the canons of rule for all the ancient kings, and add to them a discussion of their general essentials?"[38] K'ou's mention of the "thousand-year rule that has been interrupted" seems to imply a nostalgia for the golden years of the Han, which characterizes most of the utopian ideologies of Six Dynasties Taoists.[39]

In any event, Ts'ui Hao, who was temporarily out of favor at court and had a great deal of leisure, gladly acceded to K'ou's request, and produced a work in over twenty sections, beginning at the Grand Beginning (t'ai-ch'u 太初) and coming down to his own times, tracing in outline all the "changes and failures" of Ch'in and Han. He was actually writing the preamble for the constitution of a new state, in which K'ou Ch'ien-chih, as Celestial Master, would serve as the transcendent link with Heaven and give noumenal support to the dynasty, whereas the T'o-pa emperors and generals would provide the temporary military power needed to subdue the numerous barbarian states of the north and to create the era of "Great Peace" necessary for the establishment of a universal state. Ts'ui himself, as chancellor, would then be able to implement his policy of "regulating and correcting the social relationships and separating and clarifying the sur-

37. T XVII. 721:348c.
38. WS 35.9b.
39. See Seidel (n. 3), pp. 244, 246.

names and clans" (ch'i-cheng jen-lun, fen-ming hsing-tsu 齊整人倫, 分明姓族).[40]

Everything worked out with amazing precision. In 424 Ts'ui easily persuaded Emperor T'ai-wu to accept the spiritual services of this "retired transcendent being of pure virtue" who had shown Heaven's approval by coming unsummoned to the court.[41] The following year K'ou was officially declared Celestial Master, restoring the broken tradition of Chang Lu, and his "New Code" was promulgated throughout the realm.[42] As evidence of his sincerity, the emperor proceeded, with K'ou's instructions, to build an elaborate five-tiered altar (t'an 壇) for Taoist ceremonies southeast of the capital, and to invite 120 Taoist practitioners (tao-shih 道士), some of whom had been K'ou's personal disciples on Mount Sung, to live on the premises and perform rites and prayers at the prescribed hours every day. He also subsidized large monthly feasts (ch'u-hui) at which "several thousand persons" were fed.[43] In 431, altars and officiating priests were also set up in every provincial seat (chou 州) to supervise local practices.[44] With all this impressive superstructure of state religion imposed from the center, however, even with representatives in every chou, there is still no indication of a mass following at the local level. The ease with which the theocracy was superseded after 450 would suggest that it was largely a court phenomenon.

Meanwhile, however, Ts'ui himself, as K'ou's sponsor, was back in favor at court. His rank was raised to duke and he was appointed Grand Ordinary (t'ai-ch'ang 太常) in charge of court ceremonials. Then, with his own uncanny genius as an armchair strategist and the supernatural aid of K'ou Ch'ien-chih's prognostications, he proceeded to mastermind a series of military successes for Northern Wei (always, according to his biographer, against the seasoned judgment of generals in the field). In 427 the Wei armies defeated Ho-lien Ch'ang 赫連昌 (r. 424–427), ruler of the Tai state in the Ordos region.[45] In 429 they crushed the Juan-juan 蠕蠕 in the Peking area, and again in 430 thwarted an attempted comeback by Ho-lien Ting 定 (r. 427–430).[46] Finally, in 439, they annihilated the Northern

40. WS 47.1a.
41. See above, note 13.
42. Ibid.
43. TCTC 119:3762; Li Tao-yüan 麗道元 (d. 526), Shui-ching chu 水經注 (SCC) 13:8ab (Ssu-pu ts'ung-k'an ed.).
44. Fei Ch'ang-fang 費長房 (A.D. 479), Li-tai san-pao chi 歷代三寶記 T XLIX. 2034.41; Tsukamoto Zenryū, Shina Bukkyōshi kenkyū: Hoku-Gi hen 支那佛教史研究, 北魏篇 (Tokyo, 1942), pp. 116.
45. TCTC 120:3795.
46. Ibid. 121:3810 and 3826.

Liang state in Kansu,[47] adding thousands of square miles to the territory of the Northern Wei empire.

Earlier, in 429, Ts'ui had joined the staff of historians compiling the Wei annals, and from then until his death in 450 he dominated the editing of what went into them.[48] In the same year he became Personal Attendant (*shih-chung* 侍中) to Emperor T'ai-wu, and the latter's confidence in him knew no bounds. Drawing Ts'ui into his inner apartment, the emperor once said to him: "Never keep anything back from Us. Even though from time to time We may be angry or resentful and do not follow your advice, nevertheless We always ponder long and seriously over what you have said."

Later, leading Ts'ui into a conference with his civil and military advisers, the emperor announced to them: "Do you gentlemen see this man— emaciated, puny, soft and weak, unable even to draw a bow or hold a spear? Ah, but what he holds in his bosom far surpasses weapons or armor! We may have the will to go on expeditions and campaigns, yet We are incapable of making decisions. Early or late, if there have been any successes, they have all been due to this man's instructions. . . . In all cases where major plans for army or state are involved, whatever you gentlemen cannot decide yourselves, always consult first with Ts'ui Hao before acting."[49]

In 431 Ts'ui had been appointed Director of Instruction (*ssu-t'u* 司徒), a post equivalent to chancellor.[50] For the next two decades he dominated all the decision-making at court, but except for his personal participation in the military campaign against Northern Liang in 439 he was content to remain behind the scenes, busily writing his Wei history and his new commentaries to the Classics, working tirelessly to rid the realm of alien and subversive influences. In 444, for example, with the reluctant cooperation of K'ou Ch'ien-chih, who owed a great deal to his Buddhist teachers and basically had no quarrel with Buddhism, he initiated the well-known purge of the Buddhist clergy, which culminated in the devastating proscription of 446. The decree of 444 was directed, not only against "privately supported monks," but also against "mediums and sorcerers" (*wu-hsi* 巫覡),[51] an obvious attack on the local "heterodox cults" (*yin-ssu* 淫祀), which K'ou was attempting to supplant. Later in the same year

47. Ibid. 123:3874.
48. *WS* 35:10b and 21a; W. Eberhard, *Das Toba-reich Nordchinas* (Leiden, 1949), p. 189, observes that Ts'ui also brought partisans of his own clique into the Historian's Office.
49. *WS* 35:14b.
50. *TCTC* 122:3833.
51. Ibid. 124:3903.

Ts'ui memorialized that all the numberless shrines to the "little gods" (*hsiao-shen* 小神) of these same local cults scattered along the waysides be reduced to only fifty-seven specified places of worship, and that all the rest be abolished.[52]

Though these attacks on Buddhism and the "little gods" were both part of Ts'ui's efforts to rid the land of the baneful effects of competing or uncontrolled religion, they did not by any means signify that he was himself antireligious, or that he was merely a Confucian rationalist opposed to all worship not specifically enjoined in the "Record of Rites" (*Li-chi* 禮記). As we have already observed, he was interested in the occult and in longevity techniques, and he had no difficulty accepting the supernatural credentials of K'ou Ch'ien-chih. We read in his biography that during the last illness of his father, Ts'ui Hsüan-po 玄伯,[53] for more than a year prior to 418 when the old man died, Ts'ui had "trimmed his fingernails and cut off his hair, and every night looked up from the courtyard and prayed to the Dipper and Pole Star on his father's behalf, pleading for his life and asking to die in his place, striking his head on the ground till the blood ran."[54] Although in itself this is not direct evidence that he was, even in those days, a Taoist, but only that he acknowledged the divine powers of the Pole Star, Ts'ui's actions were nevertheless somewhat reminiscent of the observances prescribed in the case of sickness in the family to be found in K'ou's "New Code" itself. Article 31 of that code reads in part:

> If among the people of the Way there is sickness or illness, let it be announced to every home. The Master (*shih* 師) shall first command the people to light the incense fire. Then the Master from inside the Calm Chamber (*ching* 靖), and the people on the outside, facing toward the west with their hair unbound, striking their heads on the ground, shall confess and unburden their sins and transgressions. The Master shall command them to tell all—nothing is to be hidden or concealed—and to beg for clemency and pardon. . . . Members of the sick man's family by day shall face the Calm Chamber, and by night, facing north, shall strike their heads on the ground toward Heaven and Earth, confessing their transgressions, not allowing even a moment's omission. . . ."[55]

K'ou's prescription appears to be a toned-down version of the Fast of Smearing Soot (*t'u-t'an chai* 塗炭齋), so graphically reconstructed by

52. Ibid. 3906. For illuminating discussions of local cults in relation to "orthodox" Taoism, the reader is referred to the articles by Miyakawa Hisayuki and R. A. Stein elsewhere in this volume.
53. For his biography, see *WS* 24:14b–15a.
54. *WS* 35:6b.
55. Yang (n. 10), p. 50.

Maspero,[56] but purged of its "revivalist" excesses. Since it was meant for group participation, it is not quite comparable to Ts'ui's solitary observance, yet the underlying principle on which the two are based seems the same. Beside this, we know Ts'ui's mother was the grand-daughter of Lu Chan 盧諶, great-grandfather of Lu Hsün 循, the brother-in-law and successor of Sun En. With this connection it may well be that Ts'ui Hao's early upbringing was in the Celestial Master tradition.[57]

All this helps to explain why, though boggling at the "redundancy" and trifling expense created by the thousands of wayside shrines to the "little gods," Ts'ui not only did not shrink from but actively supported, the astronomical outlays required to build the five-tiered Taoist altar in 425 and the sky-scraping Palace of the Calm Wheel (Ching-lun kung 靜輪宮) northeast of the altar in 438, where K'ou wished to mount "to commune with the gods of heaven."[58] That it was Ts'ui's influence with which the latter building was associated in the popular mind is proved by the fact that it was torn down immediately after his death in 450.[59]

The Perfect Ruler of Great Peace

Though the pinnacle of Ts'ui's career had already been reached by 431, the year he became Director of Instruction, and the emperor's confidence in him was merely confirmed by the success of the Northern Liang campaign in 439, the latter date signaled the high point of the Taoist theocracy at the Northern Wei court, for it was on the strength of the Wei's hegemony over all of north China that K'ou was able to persuade the emperor to accept the role of "Perfect Ruler of Great Peace," and to adopt that title for the reign-period of 440–451.

In the first month of 442, in a grand ceremony of investiture, the emperor, arriving in "full ceremonial equipage" (pei fa-chia 備法駕) at the Taoist altar southeast of the capital, mounted to receive talismans (fu-lu 符錄) from K'ou's hand, in corroboration of his "sage virtue."[60] This was the first of a series of Taoistically solemnized enthronements in Northern Wei. Talismans were received even by the pro-Buddhist emperors, Wen-ch'eng (r. 452–465) and Hsien-wen (r. 466–471), after whom the custom was discontinued.[61] The other state Taoist rites, however, per-

56. H. Maspero, Le Taoïsme (Paris, 1950), pp. 159–66.
57. Tsukamoto, Shina Bukkyōshi kenkyū, p. 103.
58. SLC 71; Tsukamoto, Gisho, p. 343; Ware, pp. 237–38; SCC 13:8b.
59. Ibid.
60. WS 4B:2a; SLC 71; Tsukamoto, Gisho, p. 343; Ware, p. 231. See also Miyakawa Hisayuki, Rikuchōshi kenkyū: shūkyō hen 六朝史研究宗教篇 (Kyoto, 1964), p. 153.
61. WS 5:3a and 6:2b.

sisted, and were even transferred with the capital to Lo-yang in 493, where a new altar was constructed south of the city.

When Kao Huan 高歡 (496–547), the Chinese chancellor of Wei whose son later mounted the throne as the first emperor of Northern Ch'i (550–577), revolted and moved the capital to Yeh, north of the Yellow River, in 534, *all* Taoist ceremonies, apparently associated in his mind with the old regime, were permanently dropped. On the other hand, the Northern Chou emperors, who tried consciously to preserve the old T'o-pa traditions in their new capital at Ch'ang-an, reinstated the original Taoist investiture ceremony, which then persisted until 574, when both Taoism and Buddhism suffered temporary reverses.[62] It is a measure of the success of K'ou Ch'ien-chih's identification of Taoism with the T'o-pa state that whereas the Chinese minister, Ts'ui Hao, wishing to eliminate the alien religion of Buddhism, had given his support to the indigenous Chinese Taoism, the T'o-pa rulers of Northern Chou, on the other hand, wishing precisely to assert their non-Chinese identity, should have chosen this same Taoism for their national ideology.

I have been unable to discover if any other northern states beside the T'o-pa Wei and Northern Chou utilized a Taoist investiture ceremony. It may very well have been unique to them, but there is an intriguing notice in the *Sung-shu* that in 420, twenty-two years earlier than Emperor T'ai-wu's investiture in P'ing-ch'eng, when Liu Yü mounted the Sung throne in Chien-k'ang, he also built an altar (*t'an*) in the south suburb, where a "ceremony" (*li* 禮) was performed, and afterward returned in "full ceremonial equipage" to the palace.[63] Nothing is said of this being a Taoist altar, or of the giving or receiving of talismans, and it was probably only the traditional sacrifice on the Altar of Heaven by the Son of Heaven.

There are, however, other indications of Liu Yü's connection with Taoism. As noted earlier, his name appears in the *Tung-yüan shen-chou ching* 洞淵神呪經 (*Tao-tsang* 170) as a messianic figure.[64] And in the year of his campaign against Later Ch'in, 417, Liu heard an indirect report from a Buddhist monk of a prophecy by "the god of Mount Sung" (*Sung-kao shen* 嵩高神) that he, Liu Yü, would found a new dynasty, and that there were jade and gold tokens hidden in the mountain to prove it. Naturally intrigued, Liu sent the monk, whose name was Shih Hui-i 釋慧義 (372–444), to the sacred mountain to verify the report. Directed in a dream by

62. *Sui-shu* 35: 30b; Ware, p. 249. See also Miyakawa, *Rikuchōshi*, p. 155.
63. *Sung-shu* 3:1a–2a; *TCTC* 119:3734.
64. See above, n. 6.

the god of the mountain, Hui-i discovered thirty-two pieces of jade and a gold disc in the vicinity of the god's temple, substantiating the prophecy.[65] While it is clear that Mount Sung, being the central sacred peak, serves in this account as a symbol for the reunification of a divided China and is not necessarily a Taoist deity, it is nevertheless noteworthy that it was also a god of Mount Sung, with the slightly different title, "Lord of the Spirit-assembled Transcendent Beings Stationed on Mount Sung" (*Sung-yüeh chen-t'u ling-chi-hsien kung-chu* 嵩岳鎮土靈集仙宮主) who, according to the *Shih-Lao chih*, in 411 petitioned the officials of heaven to have K'ou Ch'ien-chih occupy the position of Celestial Master.[66]

In any case, at the same time that Liu Yü was getting his own confirmations from Mount Sung, one of his subordinates, Mao Hsiu-chih 毛脩之, whose name reveals his family's adherence to the Celestial Master Sect,[67] had been stationed by Liu in the Lo-yang area, and "paid his respects to the Taoist practitioner K'ou (*K'ou tao-shih*)," who was then still in hermitage on Mount Sung. Later, when Mao fell into the hands of the T'o-pa Wei, this connection saved his life.[68] Though these fragmentary, and plainly indirect, contacts between K'ou Ch'ien-chih and Liu Yü may have no significance, there remains the intriguing possibility that they belonged to a common tradition. The fact that Liu was the primary agent in the suppression of Sun En's rebellion in 402 would not necessarily prove him to be anti-Taoist. K'ou also was against Sun En.

The End of the Theocracy

At the height of his influence at court, in the year 448, K'ou Ch'ien-chih was "released" from his mortal body. No successor was named, and nothing is said of a son inheriting the title.[69] Two years later Ts'ui Hao, having outraged the T'o-pa nobility and even some members of his own faction by the arbitrary dismissal of "several tens" of local commandery wardens and prefectural magistrates in five provinces and replacement of them with members of important families allied to himself,[70] proceeded

65. *Sung-shu* 27:29a; *KSC* 7, T L. 2059.7:368c. See also Tsukamoto, *Shina Bukkyōshi kenkyū*, p. 109.

66. *SLC* 68; Tsukamoto, *Gisho*, p. 331; Ware, p. 229; *Lao-chün yin-sung chieh-ching* 5 (Yang [n. 10], p. 40).

67. On the use of the taboo-sheltered syllable, *chih* 之, which also appears in K'ou's name, in the personal names of Taoists of the Celestial Master sect, see Ch'en Yin-k'o, "T'ien-shih tao yü pin-hai ti-yü chih kuan-hsi" 天師道與濱海地域之關係, *CYYCY* 3.4:444 (1934).

68. *Sung-shu* 48:9ab; Tsukamoto, *Shina Bukkyōshi kenkyū*, p. 109.

69. *SLC* 72; Tsukamoto, *Gisho*, p. 347; Ware, p. 238.

70. *WS* 48:3b.

to have the national history, which he had edited and which contained an unflattering exposé of the founders of the dynasty, carved in stone and paraded through the streets of the capital where all could read it. This was too great a provocation even for the emperor who had hitherto trusted him so implicitly. He was promptly executed, together with 127 other members of his immediate and collateral families and all his retainers.[71] A curious tale, doubtless of Buddhist provenance, records the circumstances of his death. His wife, Lady Kuo 郭, had been a devout Buddhist and often chanted sutras at home. Whenever Ts'ui caught her at it he would angrily seize and burn them, dumping the ashes into the privy. Poetic justice therefore demanded that for that sin, and for his persecution of Buddhism in 444 and 446, after he was arrested and was being led in the van to the place of execution, "several tens" of guards urinated on him as they shouted obscenities.[72]

A former member of his faction, Kao Yün 高允, who had at one time been a Buddhist monk and whose relatives later founded the Northern Ch'i Dynasty, gave the following testimony after Ts'ui's arrest:

> With only the ability of tumbleweed and artemisia Ts'ui Hao was entrusted with a weight fit only for pillars and beams. In the court he lacked the integrity of an outspoken counselor, and in private life he earned no reputation for flexibility. His personal desires submerged his public spirit and modesty, while love and loathing obscured his honesty and reason.[73]

Early in 452 Emperor T'ai-wu was murdered by a palace eunuch. When the new emperor, Wen-ch'eng (r. 452–465), ascended the throne, one of his first acts was to rescind the anti-Buddhist laws and to declare Buddhism the state religion.[74] The Taoist theocracy was over.

Long-term Effects of K'ou's Reforms

In spite of certain fortuitous and temporary aspects of K'ou Ch'ien-chih's influence, however, the quarter-century he spent at the Northern Wei court does mark a kind of watershed in the history of religious Taoism in China. It was the only recorded instance in Chinese history in which a "legitimate" reign-period received a specifically Taoist title—namely, "Perfect Ruler of Great Peace" (*T'ai-p'ing chen-chün*, 440–451)—and the

---

71. *WS* 35:22a.
72. Ibid. 22b.
73. *WS* 48:5b.
74. *SLC* 38; Tsukamoto, *Gisho*, p. 318; Leon Hurvitz, trans., "Wei Shu, Treatise on Buddhism and Taoism," in Mizuno and Nagahiro, *Yün-kang, the Buddhist Cave-temples of the Fifth Century*, vol. 16, Supplement (Kyoto, 1956), p. 70.

only case on record in which a Taoist Celestial Master had the dignity of being a court minister, and when a specifically Taoist code, the *Lao-chün yin-sung chieh-ching*, was officially promulgated by the throne. Before this the Celestial Master sect had been the matrix out of which subversive movements had arisen. Sun En's rebellion a few years earlier was one of the last of such uprisings within the Celestial Master tradition. After K'ou's time the sect became more and more willing to submit to establishment control, while popular risings tended to become less and less orthodox and only marginally religious.[75] It is K'ou Ch'ien-chih who is credited with changing the titles of the leaders of Taoist communities from "libationer" (*chi-chiu*), which originally had political overtones, to "practitioner of the Way" (*tao-shih*),[76] the term already in use for Buddhist monks. With a purely religious connotation, however, the title *chi-chiu* has survived to modern times, applied to the officer directly below a *tao-shih*.

After K'ou Ch'ien-chih, Taoist adherents were no longer to think of their religious hierarchy even in *pseudo*-political terms. K'ou seems also to have been the first to use the term *Tao-chiao* 道教 to describe the tradition of the Celestial Masters,[77] placing it in the eminently respectable category of the Confucian teaching, *Ju-chiao*, and the at least acceptable category of Buddhism, *Fo-chiao*. It was, I suppose, an inevitable transition, comparable to the shift from primitive Christianity to established church under the Emperor Constantine in the fourth century, and taking about the same length of time. In his monumental history of Taoism, *Dōkyō kiso-tekt kenkyū* 道教基礎的研究, Fukui Kōjun 福井康順 does, in fact, mark the end of what he calls "Primitive Taoism" (*genshi Dōkyō*) with the rise of K'ou Ch'ien-chih.[78] Thus we have the ultimate irony that the primitive utopian community K'ou set out to recover became in fact an established church whose primitiveness had come to an end.

75. T'ang (n. 17), pp. 70–71.

76. Ibid., p. 70; see also Stein, "Remarques," pp. 43–59. Also *Erh-chiao lun* (*KHMC*, in *T* LII. 2103.8:140c).

77. Miyakawa, *Rikuchōshi*, p. 152.

78. Fukui Kōjun, *Dōkyō kiso-teki kenkyū* (Tokyo, 1952), preface, p. 1.

5 On the Alchemy of T'ao Hung-ching

Michel Strickmann

Contents

Acknowledgment

In an earlier form, this essay was suggested by Nathan Sivin, discussed with Joseph Needham, and much improved by Holmes Welch. I would also like to acknowledge the valuable assistance given by my teacher, R. A. Stein, of the Collège de France.

Abbreviations Used in Footnotes

CK   *Chen-kao* 眞誥, "Declarations of the Perfected" (*HY* 1010, *TT* 637–40)

HY   Reference to a work in the Taoist Canon by its consecutive number in the table of contents, Harvard-Yenching Index to the Canon (*Tao-tsang tzu-mu yin-te* 道藏子目引得, Peking, 1936; reprinted Taipei, 1966, pp. 1–37). On the problems raised by the current, often imprecise, and cumbersome method of referring to texts in the Taoist Canon by fascicle numbers of the 1925–27 or 1962 reprint editions (as *TT* 000), and the advantages of referring to them instead by the consecutive numbers in the Harvard-Yenching list (as *HY* 000), cf. my article in the *Newsletter of the Society for the Study of Chinese Religions* 3:15–19 (February 1977). To minimize confusion, the present article provides both numbers.

MTC   (*Chou-shih*) *Ming-t'ung chi* 周氏冥通記, "A Record of Master Chou's Communications with the Unseen World" (*HY* 302/*TT* 152)

NC   (*Hua-yang T'ao yin-chü*) *nei-chuan* 華陽陶隱居內傳, "Detailed Life of Hermit T'ao of Hua-yang" (*HY* 300/*TT* 151)

T   *Taishō Daizōkyō* 大正大藏經, the Chinese Buddhist Canon (Tokyo, 1924–35)

TCYC   *Teng-chen yin-chüeh* 登眞隱訣, "Concealed Instructions for Ascent to Perfection" (*HY* 421/*TT* 193, and fragmentary passages elsewhere)

TPYL   *T'ai-p'ing yü-lan* 太平御覽

TT   *Tao-tsang* 道藏, reference to a work in the Taoist Canon by fascicle numbers of the 1925–27 Shanghai or 1962 Taipei reprint editions

YCCC   *Yün-chi ch'i-ch'ien* 雲笈七籤, "Seven Slips from the Bookbag of the Clouds" (*HY* 1026/*TT* 677–702)

1 Alchemy in the Mao Shan Revelations

Introduction

THE PROMINENT PLACE occupied by T'ao Hung-ching 陶弘景 (456–536) in the intellectual, scientific, and religious history of China appears never to have been put in doubt. Known to Western scholars above all as the virtual founder of critical pharmacology, he ought soon to receive his due as the presiding genius of the Mao Shan 茅山 school of Taoism as well. Indeed, T'ao might seem to be a typical representative of the mingling of faith and technology which we are accustomed to think of as Taoist, and in Western writings he is with special frequency described as "the great alchemist."[1] Yet as long ago as 1930, Arthur Waley contended that alchemy receives no more than passing mention in T'ao's own writings, and from this it might have been inferred that the portrait of T'ao as a past master of the arcane art was a later, legendary development.[2]

No historian of either Taoism or Chinese science has taken up Waley's challenge to our received ideas. This is not for lack of source material, however. T'ao's surviving writings are voluminous, though all are couched in a scholastic form—as textual commentaries—that renders them at first somewhat forbidding. Still, once we begin to read through them, we soon find that, in addition to very detailed explanations of Taoist lore and practice, these works also contain much circumstantial information about T'ao's own activities. There is, of course, very good reason for trying to learn as much as possible about the life of a figure as important as T'ao. Yet we shall see that there are even greater rewards in store for those who are willing to undertake the systematic study of his neglected writings.

1. E.g. by Nathan Sivin in his *Chinese Alchemy; Preliminary Studies* (Cambridge, Mass., 1968), p. 103; cf. p. 252. Early notices in English are T. L. Davis and L. C. Wu, "T'ao Hung Ching," *Journal of Chemical Education* 9:859–62 (1932), and W. H. Barnes and H. S. Yuen, "T'ao the Recluse (A.D. 452–536); Chinese Alchemist," *Ambix* 1:138–47 (1937–38). In Chinese, the latest biographical account is that of Sun K'o-k'uan 孫克寬, in his *Yüan-tai tao-chiao chih fa-chan* 元代道教之發展 (Taichung, 1968), pp. 92–115, who adds little if anything to the work of his predecessors. Much more auspicious is the conscientious research of Mugitani Kunio 麥谷邦夫 (Tokyo University), who has published a chronological study of T'ao's life, carefully correlated with the cultural history of his time: "Tō Kōkei nempo kōryaku" 陶弘景年譜考略, *Tōhō shūkyō* 47:30–61, 48:56–83 (1976).

2. A. Waley, "Notes on Chinese Alchemy," *Bulletin of the School of Oriental Studies* 6:14 (1930).

In the course of sifting the evidence for T'ao's alchemy, we shall be able to identify, date, and localize a new corpus of early alchemical literature, one that has so far received little or no attention from historians of Chinese science. Moreover, the particular circumstances under which these documents came into being may cause us to reflect on a problem which, though fundamental, has yet to be satisfactorily formulated: that of the true relationship of Chinese alchemy to the Taoist religion, with which it is invariably, and perhaps somewhat uncritically, associated in the writings of modern scholars.

The Hsü Family's Manuscript Legacy

The keys to this hidden realm of new material are all to be found in the texts which T'ao annotated with such care. T'ao's religious aspirations crystallized around a revelation that had taken place during the Eastern Chin dynasty, some ninety years before his birth. During the years 364–370, a young man named Yang Hsi 楊羲 (330–?) underwent a succession of visionary experiences, in the course of which he was visited by some dozen perfected-immortals (*chen* 眞, *chen-jen* 眞人) from the heaven of Shang-ch'ing 上清. They presented him, over those seven-odd years, with certain of the sacred texts current in their own dominions. They also dictated quantities of oral instructions (*chüeh* 訣), both in elucidation of the practices enjoined in these scriptures and in answer to Yang's queries concerning various aspects of the unseen world.

Besides the visionary himself, these texts were directed to one Hsü Mi 許謐 (303–373), an official at the imperial court in Chien-k'ang (the modern Nanking), and his youngest son, Hsü Hui 翽 (341–ca. 370). Both these men were members of a respectable family of the governing class, who had intermarried during several generations with the family of the famous Ko Hung 葛洪 (Pao-p'u tzu 抱樸子), and with the T'aos, ancestors of T'ao Hung-ching himself.[3] Although Hsü Mi appears never to have relinquished his post at the capital and to have continued to be active in affairs despite repeated celestial admonitions, the younger Hsü, after returning his wife to her parents, moved out to Mao Shan, a chain of hills some fifteen miles southeast of the family home in Chü-jung 句容. There, until his premature death, he dwelt in the retreat his father had built on the mountain.

3. The only attempt at a historical account of the Mao Shan revelations is that of Miyakawa, in his history of Six Dynasties religion: Miyakawa Hisayuki 宮川尚志, *Rikuchō shi kenkyū, shūkyō hen* 六朝史研究, 宗教篇 (Kyoto, 1964), pp. 127–52. A comprehensive genealogical table of the Hsü family's relationships appears as appendix 1 of my article, "The Mao Shan Revelations; Taoism and the Aristocracy," *T'oung Pao* 63, 1:40 (1977).

It may well have been precisely this physical separation of the principal parties—the elder Hsü chiefly at the capital or at home in Chü-jung, his son at the mountain, and the visionary Yang seemingly now at one, now at another of these places—that in part accounts for the great mass of writings produced in those seven years: the Shang-ch'ing scriptures, the biographies (chuan 傳) of some five of the bestowing perfected-immortals, elaborately drawn talismans (fu 符), and finally, the voluminous "orally transmitted instructions" that now make up the bulk of the Chen-kao 眞誥, compiled later by T'ao. So much, at least, of the manuscript legacy of Yang and the Hsüs survived, often in more than one copy, and had reached T'ao by 492, when he himself retired to Mao Shan to edit and annotate it all. T'ao accomplished the work with characteristic thoroughness, indeed with scientific precision.[4] Yet perhaps as much as to T'ao's competence as a textual critic, we owe the preservation of these documents to the enormous subsequent influence of the organization he founded at Mao Shan. The Mao Shan school was the most powerful Taoist order during the T'ang, when its primacy was virtually unchallenged, and it maintained its great prestige and importance down to modern times.[5]

It must be hardly comprehensible to those unfamiliar with the present state of Chinese religious studies that this abundant material, which has all been easily accessible since 1927 in the current reprint of the Taoist Canon, and which constitutes the most extensive dossier on any early Taoist movement—as well as an invaluable source of information on fourth-century society—has never been made the object of systematic investigation. The Chen-kao itself has indeed aroused a good deal of curi-

4. On the Chen-kao, see R. A. Stein, in Annuaire de l'Ecole pratique des Hautes Etudes, Section des Sciences Religieuses, pp. 51–52 (Paris, 1963–64); pp. 62–64 (1964–65). Ishii Masako 石井昌子 has undertaken the study of the documents of Mao Shan Taoism from a purely textual point of view and has prepared an edition of the Chen-kao that includes a selection of variant readings drawn from other sources: Kōhon Shinkō 稿本眞誥 (Tokyo, 1966–68), 4 vols. Unfortunately, the text she has produced is more corrupt than either of those on which it is based, her choice of variants is open to serious criticism, and her tentative conclusions subject to caution.

5. Miyakawa has studied the role of Mao Shan masters in the founding and legitimation of the T'ang; see his Rikuchō shi kenkyū, shūkyō hen, pp. 176–87. The Records of Mao Shan (Mao-shan chih 茅山志), in its several editions, provides a splendid conspectus of the mountain's history. The Taoist Canon contains the Yüan edition, on which all others are based (HY 304, TT 153–158). The various versions are described by Ch'en Kuo-fu 陳國符, Tao-tsang yüan-liu k'ao 道藏源流考 (2d ed., Peking, 1963), 2:247–50. Giuliano Bertuccioli visited Mao Shan in 1947, and has written an account of his experiences: "Reminiscences of the Mao-shan," East and West 24:3–16 (Rome, 1974). Tokiwa Daijō 常盤大定 was an earlier visitor, in 1922: Shina bukkyō shiseki tōsa ki 支那佛教史蹟踏査記 (Tokyo, 1938; reprinted 1972) pp. 396–99; see also Tokiwa Daijō and Sekino Tei 關野貞, Shina bunka shiseki 支那文化史蹟 (Tokyo, 1940–41), 4:8–12.

osity, but its subsidiary nature, as a collection of often fragmentary glosses on the revealed scriptures of Shang-ch'ing, seems never to have been understood. This is perhaps not surprising, as these scriptures are now to be found scattered throughout the huge Canon. It is only after extensive preliminary reconnaissance, followed by careful collation with the relevant passages of the *Chen-kao* and T'ao's scholia on them, that their authenticity can be definitely established. Once this has been done, however, the entire corpus of the Mao Shan revelations can be read as a comprehensible whole, and the true purport of the often cryptic fragments collected into the *Chen-kao* can be grasped in relation to the celestial literature that inspired them.

To the extent, then, that elements of the original Mao Shan revelations—notably the *Chen-kao*—have come within the periphery of studies centered elsewhere, the hypothesis has been put forward that the Mao Shan school was rather given to interiorized, subtilized procedures (generally subsumed under the term *ts'un* 存, "visualization," or *ts'un-ssu* 存思, "visualization and concentration") than engaged in the gross physical acts of conventional Taoist practice, whether liturgical, dietetic, or alchemical.[6]

The directives of the perfected to the elder Hsü, in particular, do frequently suggest that such a line of least resistance was being proffered to that sixty-year-old town-and-country Taoist. In their communications to him we detect, for example, a certain emphasis on beneficial operations which might be performed inwardly, while in the company of others, taking care that they should not become aware of them.[7] Hsü Mi was also told that regular morning and evening worship, normally carried out in the oratory with numerous prostrations, might be as efficaciously accomplished when merely envisioned within his own heart. To this extent, the Perfected were ready to accommodate their teaching to the worldly circumstances and bodily infirmities of their mortal disciple. Yet such is far from being the total picture presented by the documents—whether scriptures, biographies, or the texts collected into the *Chen-kao*. Allusions to tangible drugs abound, together with the remains of letters and memoranda indicating that they were in use. Then, too, the younger Hsü

6. This view was first put forward by Ch'en Kuo-fu in the second edition of his *Tao-tsang yüan-liu k'ao*, 2:390, line 7. Miyakawa considered that the Mao Shan school contrasted forcibly with the alchemical tradition represented by Ko Hung: *Rikuchō shi kenkyū, shūkyō hen*, pp. 137–38. K. M. Schipper, too, declares that operative alchemy is never favorably mentioned in the *Chen-kao-L'Empereur Wou des Han dans la légende taoïste* (Paris, 1965), p. 24.

7. E.g. *CK* 9:6b.

certainly did not share his father's obtrusive social commitments, and it is his case that will most interest us here.

The Case of Hsü Hui (365–370)

Book Six of the *Chen-kao* (*ch.* 17–18) comprises records of dreams, letters, and practical memoranda of Yang and the Hsüs themselves (in contrast to the first five books, which contain matter dictated by the Perfected). Included here in a note concerning a dream experienced by Yang Hsi in the fourth month of 365, that is, two months before our earliest record of his full-scale waking visions in the sixth month of that year.[8] This note was in the possession of the younger Hsü, who had evidently written it down from what Yang had told him.

> In the third year of the Hsing-ning reign-period [365], on the 27th of the fourth month, Master Yang dreamt he saw a man dressed in a vermilion robe and basket cap, holding two tablets in his hands. Projecting from his robe were two other tablets. He summoned Hsü Yü-fu [玉斧 "Jade Axe," Hsü Hui's intimate name 小名] to appear. On all the tablets were written characters in green, which said, "Summoned to serve as chamberlain." A moment later I [i.e. Hsü himself] appeared. Yang pointed to me and said, "This is young Master Hsü." I myself said, "I am supposed to have thirteen more years. If you summon me just now, I will not yet have acquired an understanding of the proper forms of procedure [as required by the post]." The other answered, "If such is the case, you may submit a protest," and I composed one, stating that I had not yet come to understand the procedural norms, but that I was just then diligently working at it and required an additional thirteen years. He then bowed to me and departed.[9]

This is nothing less than the "untimely summons" familiar to us from Six Dynasties fiction. As this passage illustrates, it was a concrete fact of Six Dynasties life as well. Elsewhere in the *Chen-kao*, we find the Perfected offering encouragement to Hsü Hui as he labored to assimilate the practices of perfection—those "procedural norms"—in isolation at Mao Shan, and they reassured him that the post of chamberlain (*shih ti-ch'en* 侍帝晨) was to be his in the celestial courts when his program of studies on earth was completed. Yet it is clear that he was not granted the prolonged deferment he had requested: by 370 the younger Hsü was dead. The only account of his passing, however, is one quoted by T'ao from local tradition:

He burnt incense and did obeisance on the stone altar at the entrance to the north

---

8. The earliest dated transcript of a vision by Yang seems to be one from the 21st of the sixth month, 365 (*CK* 1:4b–5a). The transmission of scriptures to him by the Perfected had already begun on the 1st and 4th days of the first month, 364 (*CK* 19:2b).
9. *CK* 17:5b10–6a6.

cavern [of Mao Shan]. Then he prostrated himself and did not arise. When, the following morning, they discovered his body, it was as if he were still alive.[10]

Thus it would seem that Hsü Hui was, in the end, obliged to respond betimes to a summons which might be deferred but not abrogated. It remains for us to find clues to the conceptual vehicle that effected his translation to the unseen world.

Some Formidable Potions

For their conception of the crucial moment in which the Taoist adept finally attained immortality, scholars have until now relied mainly on hagiography. A rather hazy picture has been produced by this means. We have become accustomed to the term *shih-chieh* 尸解, by which the process of transformation is often described, whether we translate it as "liberation from the corpse," "liberation by means of a corpse," or "corpse-free."[11] We know, too, that some cases of immortality were described as *chien-chieh* 劍解, "sword-liberated," and others as *chang-chieh* 杖解, "staff-liberated." Here the adept's sword or staff served as a temporary stand-in for his real body, which was transformed and vanished away to the realm of the immortals.

Yet we can hardly claim even to know what was supposed to have happened, let alone what Taoists actually did to prepare for this event. In hagiography it is usually suggested that the successful immortal somehow managed to bypass death entirely. He would either ascend under his own power or be conveyed heavenward by an airborne equipage. There are some hagiographic accounts, however, that make willingness to follow a master in apparent suicide the crucial test of a disciple's resolution. The means of death in the most famous of these narratives is, significantly, an alchemical elixir.[12]

It is possible that the imprecision of the sources is no accident, and that the secret of ultimate transformation was a mystery in the religious sense. Communication of precise knowledge of the process would then have been one of the sacraments of medieval Taoism, conveyed, like other

10. *CK* 20:10a–10b. T'ao composed a famous inscription on this altar (*HY* 304/*TT* 156, 20:7a–11b).

11. Joseph Needham's *Science and Civilisation in China*: vol. 5, *Chemistry and Chemical Technology*, pt. 2, *Spagyrical Discovery and Invention: Magistries of Gold and Immortality* (Cambridge, 1974), furnishes an enormous quantity of information on this and related subjects. It will all be set in historical order in part 3 of the fifth volume of Needham's magnificent work.

12. Needham, vol. 5, pt. 2, p. 295. The story of Wei Po-yang 魏伯陽, his dog, and his disciples, comes from the early fourth-century *Shen-hsien chuan* 神仙傳 (*YCCC* 109:5a–6a).

arcana, in a formal rite of transmission or empowerment. If such was indeed the case, attempts to elucidate the question by the means at our disposal, which are merely textual, are not likely to be very satisfactory.[13] Still, we have not yet studied all of the relevant texts, even on the limited subject of Taoist attitudes toward death. In the *Chen-kao*, for example, a striking series of mortuary vignettes occurs:

> Those who feigned construction of a tomb after swallowing Efflorescence of Lang-kan 琅玕之華 are Yen Men-tzu 衍門子, Kao Ch'iu-tzu 高丘子, and Master Hung-yai 洪涯先生. . . .[14] The residents of the three counties [in which their graves are found] all call them vacant tumuli of the dead of highest antiquity. They are unaware, though, that on one occasion Kao Ch'iu-tzu entered Mt. Liu-ching 六景山 through liberation by means of a corpse. He afterwards consumed a powder of Liquefied Gold (*chin-i* 金液), then ingested Efflorescence of Lang-kan at Chung Shan 中山 and feigned the appearance of still another death, whereupon he at last entered Hsüan-chou 玄州.[15]

> Those who died directly they had rinsed their mouths with Dragon Foetus (*lung-t'ai* 龍胎), or else drank Jade Essence (*ch'iung-ching* 瓊精) and then knocked together their coffins are my old teacher, Lord Wang of the Western Citadel 王西城, Chao Po-hsüan 趙伯玄, and Liu Tzu-hsien 劉子先.[16]

> Those who declared their end was nigh when they had taken the Gold Elixir (*chin-tan* 金丹) are Tsang Yen-fu 藏延甫, Chang Tzu-fang 張子房, and Mo Ti-tzu 墨狄子.[17] Those whose corpses stank when they had quaffed the Nine-times Cycled (*chiu-chuan* 九轉), from whose bodies the maggots streamed when they had swallowed [no more than] a spatulaful (*tao-kuei* 刀圭) are Ssu-ma Chi-chu 司馬季主, Ning Chung-chün 寧仲君, King Chao of Yen 燕昭王, and Wang Tzu-chin 王子晉.[18]

13. The reader may compare the pertinent remarks of E. Conze on the study of Tantrism and the mystery religions of classical antiquity in *Buddhist Thought in India* (London, 1962), pp. 271–73.

14. Yen Men-tzu is identical with Hsien-men (Tzu-)kao 羨門子高; see *Shih-chi* 史記 28:23 (Takigawa 瀧川 ed.). The other two immortals are more obscure.

15. In the sixth-century *Record of the Ten Continents* (*Hai-nei shih-chou chi* 海內十洲記), Hsüan-chou is described as being an island of the immortals in the northern ocean (pp. 2b–3a, *HY* 598/*TT* 330). Earlier Taoist references, however, suggest that the name also designated the heavens, or a particular region of the heavens: "the Sublime (or Celestial) Continent."

16. The author of these vignettes was the perfected-immortal Mao Ying 茅盈. Here he refers to his master, Wang Yüan 王遠, "Lord of the Western Citadel." The two other personages seem to be unknown.

17. Tsang Yen-fu seems not to appear in other sources. Chang Tzu-fang is Chang Liang 良, counsellor of the founder of the Han, patron of occult military arts, and putative ancestor of the first Celestial Master, Chang Tao-ling 張道陵. Mo Ti-tzu, *recte* Mo Ti 翟, is the Warring States philosopher of universal love, better known in later times as a military engineer. His works are included in the Taoist Canon (*HY* 1168/*TT* 843–45).

18. *CK* 14:16a–17a. A biography of the Han diviner Ssu-ma Chi-chu, who died ca. 170 B.C., is found in *Shih-chi* 127:1–12. He is prominent in anecdotes recounted to Yang Hsi by the Perfected, and we know that Hsü Mi intended to place him at the head of a *Lives of the*

Here there is no attempt to play down death and its grisly concomitants. On the contrary, the transfiguration of the destined immortal appears all the more wondrous for being set against the bleak facts of death, decay, and putrescence.[19]

This entire passage is described by T'ao as an extract taken by the younger Hsü from the *Sword Scripture* (*Chien-ching* 劍經), one of the Shang-ch'ing corpus revealed to Yang Hsi. The scripture itself unfortunately no longer survives intact, though lengthy quotations from it are found in later compendia.[20] From these fragments it would appear that the *Sword Scripture* dealt quite explicitly with the ultimate stage in the attainment of immortality. The liberating agents mentioned in the passage just quoted all seem to be intended as alchemical elixirs. We may list them:

1. Efflorescence of Lang-kan
2. Powder of Liquefied Gold

Immortals that he was compiling (*CK* 17:16b9–10). This work was probably meant for presentation to Hsü's patron, Ssu-ma Yü 司馬昱, king of Lang-yeh; the Chin ruling house belonged to the Ssu-ma clan. Ning Chung-chün is probably identical with Ning Feng-tzu 寧封子; see M. Kaltenmark, *Le Lie-sien tchouan; Biographies légendaires des immortels taoïstes de l'antiquité* (Peking, 1953), pp. 43 ff. King Chao of Yen (r. 311–278 B.C.) is said to have sent an expedition in search of the isles of the immortals. Wang Tzu-chin is the famous Wang-tzu Ch'iao 王子喬, see Kaltenmark, *Biographies légendaires*, pp. 109–14. He was Lord of the Golden Court at Tung-po Shan 桐栢山 in Chekiang, and appeared to Yang Hsi as a sword-girt adolescent (*CK* 2:3a; this apparition is illustrated in *HY* 612/*TT* 334, pp. 18a–19a).

19. The *Chen-kao* contains another passage remarkably like this one. Describing the variety of means by which immortality could be attained, the Lady of the Southern Peak declared: "Some took two swallows of Jade Essence and knocked together their coffins, or had their corpses putrefy after consuming a single spatulaful. Lu-p'i Kung 鹿皮公 swallowed Blossoms of Jade, and the maggots streamed out under the door. Ch'ou Chi-tzu 仇季子 gulped down Liquefied Gold, and the stench was perceptible a hundred *li* away. The Yellow Emperor fired his nine crucibles at Ching Shan 荊山, and his grave is still to be seen. Ssu-ma Chi-chu ingested cloud powder in order to vanish away and mount on high, yet his head and his feet ended up in different places. Mo Ti gulped down a Rainbow Elixir and threw himself into a river. Master Ning ingested Eaglestone ("stone-brain") and leapt into the fire. Wu Kuang 務光 cut shallots and entered the abyss of Ch'ing-leng 清泠之淵 [cf. the "outer" *Book of the Yellow Court, Shang-ch'ing Houang-t'ing wai-ching ching* 上清黃庭外景經, verse 3.42, in K. M. Schipper's critical edition (cited in n. 146, below), pp. 1*–7**]. Po Ch'eng 栢成 held in his vital-breaths, and his entrails rotted three times over . . ." (*CK* 4:15a–15b). Wu Kuang's shallots are possibly connected with the preparation of quartz-pellets to preserve the five viscera after death; see p. 183, below. This passage is quoted in the ninth-century *Yu-yang tsa-tsu* 酉陽雜俎 2:8b (*Chi-ku ko* 汲古閣 ed.), with some omissions, and the intrusion of Lord Wang from the other, parallel series of vignettes which I have quoted in the text.

20. Its full title was *Wondrous Scripture of the Perfected Immortal of the Grand Bourne, Essence of Stone and Radiance of Metal, on Storing the Effulgent-spirits and Preserving the Body* 太極眞人石精金光藏景錄形神經. *TPYL* 665, in its entirety, is an extract from this work, with annotations by T'ao Hung-ching (see p. 156, below).

3. Dragon Foetus
4. Jade Essence
5. Gold Elixir
6. The Nine-times Cycled

Our surest source prior to the Mao Shan texts, the inner chapters of the *Pao-p'u tzu* (抱樸子內篇 written ca. 320, by Ko Hung, a kinsman of the Hsüs), mentions both Liquefied Gold and the Gold Elixir with great frequency and describes their preparation in some detail.[21] By the middle of the fourth century, then, these two elixirs should have been familiar to most cultivated seekers after immortality south of the Yangtze, in the dominions of the Eastern Chin. Indeed, Hsü Mi writes of his having at one time planned to prepare Liquefied Gold, and T'ao Hung-ching records the existence of a *Book of Liquefied Gold* (*Chin-i ching* 金液經), written on yellow silk in the hand of Hsü Mi's official colleague, Ch'ih Hsin 郗愔 (313–384), to whom the Perfected occasionally condescended to address advice through Yang Hsi. This copy, according to T'ao, included "the commentary composed by Ko Hung."[22] But the Hsüs and their circle were soon to learn that the Perfected held these renowned elixirs in comparatively low esteem. Their consumption led only to the more humble ranks in the otherworldly hierarchy. Of the mere immortals (*hsien* 仙) it was said that "their Liquefied Gold and nine elixirs are truly minor arts; none of them has been enabled thereby to fly up to Shang-ch'ing."[23] The compounding of such elixirs as these was thus no proper work for those who aspired to perfection.

The remaining names on our list, however, seem to belong more especially to the Mao Shan revelations and to have given access to the palaces and chanceries in the loftier heaven of Shang-ch'ing. The Elixir of Nine Cycles will occupy me at some length below, but I may note here that the transmission of a Nine-times Cycled Wondrous Elixir (*chiu-chuan shen-tan* 九轉神丹) figured prominently in the *Life of Lord Mao* (*Mao-chün chuan* 茅君傳), the eponymous patron of Mao Shan as revealed to Yang Hsi.[24] Dragon Foetus, too, is mentioned elsewhere in the revealed texts,

21. The inner chapters are available in an English translation by J. R. Ware, *Alchemy, Medicine, and Religion in the China of 320 A.D.* (Cambridge, Mass., 1966).

22. *TCYC* in *TPYL* 672:2a–2b. For Hsü Mi's one-time plan to prepare Liquefied Gold, see *CK* 11:1929–10.

23. *YCCC* 105:21b; *Life of Lord P'ei, Perfected Immortal of Ch'ing-ling, Ch'ing-ling chen-jen P'ei-chün chuan* 清靈眞人裴君傳.

24. Cf. *CK* 5:4a: "His Lordship said: 'Among the formulae of immortality is the Wondrous Elixir of Nine Cycles. When consumed it is transformed into a white crane.'" On this, T'ao's note reads, "The foregoing is in the *Life* of Director of Destinies Mao (*Mao ssu-*

both in the *Chen-kao* and in the only one of the original biographies of the Perfected to survive intact, the *Life of Lord P'ei*.[25] In a note on the present passage, T'ao identifies "Jade Essence" with a certain Elixir of Ch'ü-ch'en 曲晨 ("the winding constellation," that is, the Northern Dipper), to which reference is frequently made in the texts collected into the *Chen-kao*. That the nature of this elixir was pragmatic and operational (rather than the formula being intended as a guide to contemplation) seems confirmed by its mention, in T'ao's pharmacological scholia, as containing amber among its ingredients.[26] There is good reason, too, for believing that its formula originally formed part of the lost *Sword Scripture*; a number of passages in the surviving fragments of that work allude to its use in the process of liberation by means of a sword.[27]

The Lang-kan Elixir

We are left with the first-mentioned of these sublime substances, Efflorescence of Lang-kan. Though *lang-kan* came to signify, among other things, a variety of coral, it originally belonged to the legendary mineralogy of Mount K'un-lun 崑崙山, and was one of the enigmatic geological components of that cosmic mountain standing in the northwest, at the gate of heaven. T'ao also mentions the elixir in his annotations to the pharmacopeia: "[Lang-kan] is, furthermore, the name of a major elixir in the scriptures of the Perfected."[28] But the most intriguing evidence is a curious series of metamorphoses listed in the *Chen-kao*:

> His Lordship said: Among the formulae of immortality is Lunar Efflorescence of Sulphureous Solution (*huang-shui yüeh-hua* 黃水月華). When consumed it is transformed into a moon.[29]

---

ming 茅司命)." Mao Ying is in fact said to have ascended to heaven on a white crane. For the Elixir of Nine Cycles, see pp. 146–50, below.

25. *CK* 3:15b, 6:2b; *YCCC* 105:8b.

26. *Honzōkyō shūchū* 本草經集註 (Osaka, 1972), p. 37D (references are to quarters of each page, as p. 37A, B, C, or D). This is a facsimile reproduction of T'ao Hung-ching's annotated edition of the Shen-nung pharmacopeia, as reconstructed by Mori Risshi 森立之 and his collaborators between 1849 and 1852. The reference may also be found in the *Cheng-lei pen-ts'ao* 正類本草 of 1249, and in the *Pen-ts'ao kang-mu* 本草綱目, in the entries on amber (*hu-p'o* 虎珀).

27. E.g. *TPYL* 665:4a–b, 6b. Cf. also *CK* 5:4b8: "His lordship said, 'The Tao of the immortals includes the airborne covered-carriage of the Winding Constellation. The body of him who rides in it will fly up by itself.' " T'ao comments; "This is in the *Sword Scripture*."

28. *Honzōkyō shūchū*, p. 30B (s.v. *ch'ing lang-kan* 青琅玕). The reading 九眞經中 should doubtless be simply 眞經中. A scribe seems to have had at this point a confused recollection of the *Chiu-chen chung-ching* 九眞中經 (*HY* 1365/*TT* 1042), one of the texts of the Shang-ch'ing corpus. It does not, however, contain the formula for the Lang-kan elixir.

29. T'ao supposes the dictating immortal to have been Lord P'ei (*CK* 5:1a).

His Lordship said: Among the formulae of immortality is Jade Essence of Swirling Solution (*hui-shui yü-ching* 徊水玉精). When consumed it is transformed into a sun.

His Lordship said: Among the formulae of immortality are Seeds of the Tree of Ringed Orbs (*huan-kang shu-tzu* 環剛樹子).[30] When consumed they are transformed into a cloud.

His Lordship said: Among the formulae of immortality is Virid Iridescence of Aquaeous Yang (*shui-yang ch'ing-ying* 水陽青映). When consumed it is transformed into stone.[31]

His Lordship said: Among the formulae of immortality are White Seeds of the Red Tree (*ch'ih-shu po-tzu* 赤樹白子). When consumed they are transformed into jade.

His Lordship said: Among the formulae of immortality are Virid Fruits of the Crimson Tree (*chiang-shu ch'ing-shih* 絳樹青實). When consumed they are transformed into gold.

His Lordship said: Among the formulae of immortality is the Elixir of Lang-kan Efflorescence (*lang-kan hua-tan* 琅玕華丹). When consumed it is transformed into a flying dragon.[32]

On this passage (preserved in two manuscript copies, one in the hand of Hsü Mi, one in that of his son) T'ao comments, "The foregoing seven items are in the *Purple Writ in Transcendent Script* (*Ling-shu tzu-wen* 靈書紫文); they are all transformation of the Lang-kan Elixir."[33]

The Taoist Canon contains several works with the component "Purple Writ" in their titles. In the present context, by far the most promising is the *Purple Writ in the Transcendent Script of T'ai-wei, Supreme Scripture of the Wondrous Perfected on the Elixir of Lang-kan Efflorescence*.[34] This treatise of eight folios describes the preparation of a fourteen-ingredient mineral compound through three distinct and protracted stages of firing, ultimately producing a highly concentrated, pearl-like elixir. Planted in an irrigated field, this arcane seed grows after three years into a tree with ringlike fruit. When this is, in turn, further matured through three additional replantings, a fruit resembling the jujube is at length produced, ingestion of which brings about assumption into the high, circumpolar

---

30. The character 剛 is used interchangeably with 綱, in the sense of "orb," or else "circular, or curving, path of transit." In this latter meaning it is applied to those asterisms which Edward H. Schafer has designated as "the Mainstays of Heaven" (in his book, *Pacing the Void: T'ang Approaches to the Star* [Berkeley, 1977], pp. 241–42).

31. "Aquaeous Yang" is a vivid oxymoron.

32. *CK* 5:3b.

33. The "seventeen" of the text, an early corruption shared by both the Taoist Canon and *Ts'ung-shu chi-ch'eng* 叢書集成 (p. 60.2) editions, should be amended to read "seven."

34. *T'ai-wei ling-shu tzu-wen lang-kan-hua tan shen-chen shang-ching* 太微靈書紫文琅玕華丹神眞上經 (*HY* 255/*TT* 120).

heaven of Tzu-wei 紫微. But the product of each stage of the compounding is effectively an elixir in itself, which will translate its consumer into
the heavens. Each step in the remarkably elaborate procedure is to be
accompanied by incantations, given in the text. Particular attention is
devoted to the construction of the laboratory and, above all, to the
precisely phased firing of the furnace. The entire operation is an extraordinary amalgam of vegetable and mineral processes, reminiscent of
the instructions for producing, by chemical insemination of the earth, the
five marvelous mushrooms of immortality.[35]

When we come to consider the relationship between this independent
treatise and the extract from the *Chen-kao* quoted above, it is immediately evident that the seven items listed among the "formulae of immortality" are in fact the names of the successive products given in the scriptural text. "Lunar Efflorescence of Sulphureous Solution" is one of the
section-headings in the formula (p. 5a), as are Jade Essence of Swirling
Solution (p. 5b) and Virid Irridescence of Aquaeous Yang (p. 6b). The
three trees named in the *Chen-kao* are cited in the text as the results of the
successive replantings (pp. 6a and 6b). The seventh item in the *Chen-kao*
list, the Elixir of Lang-kan Efflorescence, is the first and fundamental
product of firing, which serves as the point of departure for all subsequent
developments (p. 4b). Thus, the pearl-like Lang-kan Elixir itself might be
produced without undertaking the long horticultural sequel.

Somewhat less conspicuous in the scripture are the transformations
attributed to each of the substances, but they are all there in the body of
the text, and are correlated precisely as in the *Chen-kao*: moon (p. 5b),
sun (p. 5b), cloud (p. 6a), stone (p. 7a), jade (p. 6b), gold (p. 6b), and flying
dragon (p. 5a). If a further indication of authenticity be required, the text
of the elixir formula still contains certain graphic anomalies which,
thanks to T'ao, we know to have been peculiar to the Yang-Hsü manuscript corpus, such as the use of the character *sheng* 盛 for *ching* 淨—,
"clean," "pure," as in the *Chen-kao* itself.[36]

Ritual Suicide

There is no more doubt, then, that this particular *Purple Writ* was one of
the texts revealed to Yang Hsi and by him transmitted to his patrons, the

35. As in *HY* 932/*TT* 597. Perhaps it was by similar means that Lord Mao planted his
famous five mushrooms at Mao Shan (see p. 150, below).

36. See *CK* 19:7a3. T'ao enumerates a number of such graphic peculiarities, study of
which, and comparison with contemporary archaeological documents, would probably
repay the efforts of a competent palaeographer.

Hsüs. It is clear, too, that the operations it describes, for all their extravagance, were intended as practicable alchemical procedures. Moreover, this was the Lang-kan Elixir that was supposed to have been responsible for the death and transfiguration of more than one eminent immortal of antiquity, as we have seen. Thus, though the Perfected of Shang-ch'ing may have disdained the imperfect forms of alchemy that were then current among mortals, operative alchemy was by no means absent from the Mao Shan revelations. The denizens of Shang-ch'ing had formulae of their own, which they bestowed upon their chosen mortal disciples. Through preparation and ingestion of an elixir of the Perfected, the favored adept might gain direct access to their otherworldly sphere. Yet there was no belying the death that he first had to die.

The Lang-kan Elixir and the other preparations referred to above are not the only deadly drugs mentioned in the *Chen-kao*. A text contained therein describes the effects of a "White Powder of the Perfected of the Grand Bourne (*T'ai-chi chen-jen* 太極眞人) for abandoning the waistband":[37]

> When you have taken a spatulaful of it, you will feel an intense pain in your heart, as if you had been stabbed there with a knife. After three days you will want to drink, and when you have drunk a full *hu* 斛 your breath will be cut off. When that happens, it will mean that you are dead.[38] When your body has been laid out, it will suddenly disappear, and only your clothing will remain. Thus you will be an immortal released in broad daylight by means of his waistband. If one knows the name of the drug [or, perhaps, the secret names of its ingredients] he will not feel the pain in his heart, but after he has drunk a full *hu* he will still die. When he is dead, he will become aware that he has left his corpse below him on the ground. At the proper time, jade youths and maidens will come with an azure carriage to take it away. If one wishes to linger on in the world, he should strictly regulate his drinking during the three days when he feels the pain in his heart. This formula may be used by the whole family. It begins with the words, "Take nine *liang* of 'Garb of Cloudy Radiance' (*yün-hsia i* 雲霞衣).[39]

Anyone undertaking the preparation of this powder, or of any of the elixirs mentioned earlier, must certainly have known what lay in store for him when the work was completed. Within this context, the prospective alchemist must have been strongly motivated by faith and sustained by a

37. *I-tai* 遺帶—that is, casting aside the constraining girdle of proper social *tenue* (*cheng-tai* 正帶: metaphorically, the restrictive coil of formal social relationships). This text is also quoted in HY 1130/*TT* 777, 87:6a(*Wu-shang pi-yao* 人無上祕要 from the 570s).

38. *Ch'i-chüeh* 氣絶, "arrestation of breath," is a common expression for death, but also for fainting.

39. *CK* 10:5a. "Garb of Cloudy Radiance" is a cover-name for an unidentified substance. T'ao Hung-ching had not succeeded in finding the formula for this preparation.

firm confidence in his posthumous destiny. In effect, he would be committing suicide by consecrated means.

Hsü Hui seems to have taken a special interest in the *Sword Scripture* and its gruesome catalogue of alchemical fatalities, as we have seen. Though this text has not been preserved, we must remember that, according to the *Chen-kao* passage quoted earlier, the Jade Essence (or Winding Constellation) Elixir of which it contained the formula was as deadly a preparation as any of the others in the repertoire of the Perfected. It is possible that Hui may have made use of it in concluding his stay in the world of men—and have done so in a ritual fashion quite like that attributed to him by local tradition. It is licit for us to imagine how, guided by an initial summons and sustained by further intelligence and encouragement transmitted through Yang Hsi from his celestial mentors, he oriented himself toward the hidden caverns beneath Mao Shan (into which he hoped to be taken for preliminary instruction), then burnt incense, and consumed an elixir concerning the toxicity of which the communications of the Perfected could have left him in no doubt.

2 Alchemy in the Life of T'ao Hung-ching

T'ao's Secular Career (456–492)

T'ao Hung-ching was born in 456, by his own testimony, on the 30th day of the fourth month.[40] His forebears were notable landowners, whose entrenched status in the area around the capital as well as much farther south, in present-day coastal Fukien, had been recognized by successive southern dynasties since the third century. T'ao's ancestor in the seventh degree (inclusive) had been made marquis of Chü-jung, with an income of two thousand households, under the Wu. His grandfather, T'ao Lung 隆, was enfeoffed as marquis of Chin-an (in modern Fukien) by the Liu Sung.[41] T'ao's grandfather and father both had profound knowledge of

40. *TCYC* 3:23b9. In demonstrating how to calculate from one's destiny-day (*pen-ming iih* 本命日), which had an important ritual function, T'ao naturally had recourse to the set of vital statistics with which he was most familiar: his own. In Western works, the year of T'ao's birth is often erroneously given as 452. This is based on the statement, in the *History of the South, Nan-shih* 南史 76:12b (Palace edition), that he was eighty-five when he died in 536. All the contemporary sources, including two commemorative tomb inscriptions, agree that he was born in 456 and was eighty-one when he died in 536 (the inscriptions may be found in *NC* 3:1b–5b and 7a–8a, and in the *Records of Mao Shan*, 21:5b–11a) (*HY* 304/*TT* 156).

41. *YCCC* 107:2a4, 2b8 (T'ao I's 陶翊 account of his uncle's ancestry and activities, *Hua-yang yin-chü hsien-sheng pen-ch'i lu* 華陽隱居先生本起錄). T'ao I is mentioned by Hung-ching in his correspondence with Liang Wu Ti 梁武帝 on the subject of calligraphy; see T'ao's

medicinal drugs and were accomplished calligraphers, thus prefiguring two of T'ao's own principal interests. His grandfather was a pious Buddhist, and so, we are told, was his mother.[42]

T'ao pursued an official career under the Sung dynasty and its successor, the Ch'i, and served as reader-in-attendance (*shih-tu* 侍讀), with secretarial functions, to several of the young Ch'i imperial princes. When he came out of mourning for his father in 483, aged twenty-eight, he was appointed commander of the left detachment of palace guards. He was beginning to cut a figure in the literary world of the court when the death of his mother in the year after his appointment obliged him to retire from official life once again.[43]

It was during this second three-year mourning period, extending over 484–486, that T'ao received his formal Taoist training and had his first sight of the Mao Shan manuscripts that were to occupy him for the rest of his life. He was instructed by Sun Yu-yüeh 孫遊嶽, head of the Hsing-shih Kuan 興世館, in the capital. Sun had been a leading disciple of the most prominent Taoist master of the Sung, Lu Hsiu-ching 陸修靜 (406–477), and we may assume that T'ao learnt from him the essentials of ritual practice, particularly the Ling-pao 靈寶 rites, of which Lu had been the principal codifier.[44] But Sun had also inherited from Lu Hsiu-ching a number of texts belonging to the Mao Shan revelations. Most of these were later copies, but there were among them a few fragmentary manuscripts in the handwriting of Yang Hsi and the two Hsüs, father and son.[45]

T'ao seems to have been immediately struck by the remarkable qualities of the calligraphy of Yang and the younger Hsü, and it was probably at this time that he formed the resolution to recover as many as possible of their autograph manuscripts. In 488, two years after his return to official life, he was able to acquire a number of texts from Taoists living at Mao Shan.[46] It was not until 490, however, that he found the occasion to undertake a major expedition to the eastern region (modern Chekiang), in the course of which he traced nearly every surviving possessor of auto-

---

reconstructed literary collection, *Hua-yang T'ao yin-chü chi* 華陽陶隱居集 1:16b8–9, *HY* 1044/ *TT* 726.

42. *YCCC* 107:2b9, 3b2.

43. *YCCC* 107:6a8.

44. Fragments of a biography of Lu Hsiu-ching included in the *Lives of Taoist Scholars* (*Tao-hsüeh chuan* 道學傳 by Ma Shu 馬樞, 522–581) have been assembled by Ch'en Kuo-fu in *Tao-tsang yüan-liu k'ao*, 2:466–68. Ch'en has also recovered a brief notice on Sun Yu-yüeh from the same source (p. 478).

45. *YCCC* 107:8a2–4.

46. *YCCC* 107:8a5–6. See also *CK* 20:2b–3a, where T'ao lists Yang-Hsü autograph texts recovered from Taoists at Mao Shan and residents of nearby Chü-jung 句容.

graph texts of Yang and the Hsüs, and managed (presumably with official assistance) to acquire, or at least to copy, a great quantity of manuscripts.[47]

Retirement to Mao Shan (492)

In the course of his secular career, T'ao had written or compiled several learned works, including a number of the short commentaries on the classics that were in those days produced by every young man of breeding. T'ao's ambitions as a polymath could already be discerned in the immense, incomplete draft of his *Garden of Learning* (*Hsüeh-yüan* 學苑), a classified encyclopedia in one hundred *chüan*.[48] When in 492 T'ao finally retired to Mao Shan at the early age of thirty-six, he had three major textual projects in hand. Two of them concerned the Mao Shan materials he had assembled. He planned a collection of all the practical directives contained in the biographies of the Perfected, as well as other ritual instructions revealed to Yang Hsi and by him transmitted to the Hsüs. To the texts he would add a massive commentary covering every detail of ritual action. He entitled this work *Concealed Instructions for Ascent to Perfection* (*Teng-chen yin-chüeh* 登眞隱訣). Owing to the esoteric nature of much of its contents, it was not intended for general diffusion. Much of it has been lost, but three *chüan* remain under that title in the Canon; in one of them the date 493 is mentioned.[49]

The second project involved collecting all the loose Yang-Hsü manuscript remains, exclusive of the scriptures of Shang-ch'ing and the biographies of the Perfected, into a single book. This had been attempted earlier by Ku Huan 顧歡, who produced a compilation of traced facsimiles called *Chen-chi* 眞迹, *Traces of the Perfected*.[50] Though he greatly admired Ku Huan and his efforts, T'ao did not find his compilation satisfactory. He therefore attempted to make his own *Chen-kao, Declarations of the*

---

47. *YCCC* 107:8a6–8b1. T'ao himself refers to this trip in his notes to the *Chen-kao* (*CK* 20:1b1). I have given an annotated translation of T'ao's history of the Yang-Hsü manuscript corpus, from the beginning of the fifth century down to his own day (*CK* 19:9b–20:4b), as appendix II of my article, "The Mao Shan Revelations; Taoism and the Aristocracy," *T'oung Pao* 63, 1:41–62 (1977).

48. *YCCC* 107:8b–9a. After settling at the mountain, T'ao turned the manuscript over to his nephew, T'ao I, and the work seems never to have been finished.

49. *TCYC* 3:25a2.

50. T'ao notes several differences between Ku's compilation and his own (e.g. *CK* 19:2a–9b) which help us to form some idea of Ku's work. Unlike the *Chen-kao*, it was composed of traced facsimile copies of the original texts (and so its circulation must in any case have been rather limited). It also included extraneous matter, such as the biographical notes on Hsü Mi's elder brother, Hsü Mai 邁 (300–348), written by Wang Hsi-chih 王羲之 and Wang Hsien-chih 王獻之.

Perfected, a definitive corpus of the fragmentary Yang-Hsü manuscripts, and in this he succeeded: Ku's *Traces* have vanished. The *Chen-kao* was intended for unlimited circulation, seemingly with the aim of bringing both the literary brilliance and the saving message of the Perfected to the attention of a wider cultivated public. T'ao's commentary was therefore much more restricted in scope here, in view of the stringent rules of secrecy which hedged round the revealed texts, and he refers readers desirous of more detailed information to his *Teng-chen yin-chüeh*.[51] He also notes the date 499 in his commentary several times, and thus it seems that he completed the *Chen-kao* after most of his work on the *Teng-chen yin-chüeh* was done.[52]

T'ao's third textual project fulfilled what he felt to be an obligation inherited from his forebears: a critical commentary to the standard work on pharmacology, the *Shen-nung Pharmacopeia* (*Shen-nung pen-ts'ao ching* 神農本草經). T'ao seems to have completed his *Collected Commentaries* (*chi-chu* 集註) which, like the two earlier works, was arranged in seven books, shortly after the *Chen-kao*, which he mentions there.[53] In this valuable compendium, T'ao often cites the writings of his predecessors and makes frequent allusions to his personal observations as well. The Mao Shan revelations are several times referred to, as are the flora, fauna, and mineralia of Mao Shan.[54]

Thus, for evidence of T'ao's activities on the mountain during the first seven or eight years of his reclusion we have, not only the considerable bulk of these three exegetical works, but also many explicit statements by T'ao in his commentaries to them. In none of these texts is there any indication that T'ao was engaged in alchemical operations at that time, though we do have valuable first hand testimony that he was occupied with imperially sponsored experiments in sword-foundry at Mao Shan from 497 on.[55] In the *Chen-kao*, however, there is an interesting foreshadowing of T'ao's alchemy. In describing the esoteric topography of Mao Shan,

51. *CK* 19:7a6; cf. 19:1b8–9.
52. *CK* 13:8b, 15:5a. T'ao also writes of its being "seven or eight years since I came to live at this mountain" (*CK* 11:12a6–7, i.e. 498 or 499). Though the bulk of the *Teng-chen yin-chüeh* may already have been done (the present, incomplete text contains the date 493, cf. 3:25a2b), it seems certain that T'ao continued to add to it as his experience broadened. This is suggested by the numerous passages of the work, either cited by T'ao's biographer or found independently elsewhere, which bear on T'ao's activities during the first decade of the Liang dynasty (502–512).
53. *Honzōkyō shūchū* p. 4A7–9.
54. *Honzōkyō shūchū* pp. 25D, 28A, 40A, 60A, 115A. References to two mentions of the Shang-ch'ing scriptures in the pharmacopeia have been given in notes 26 and 28, above.
55. See pp. 156–57, below.

a revealed text notes several spots as being suitable for compounding an elixir (*k'o ho tan* 可合丹). One of these, on the ridge leading northward from Great to Middle Mao Shan, excited T'ao's special interest. It was close to his own Hua-yang Kuan 華陽館, and he describes the terrain in loving detail.[56] The ideal location seemed to be on the west side of the ridge, hard by his hermitage. A stream bubbled forth there throughout the year. The only problem was that it flowed away to the west, not to the east, as required in alchemy. Nonetheless, T'ao remarks that by channeling it could be brought round to flow eastward.

All this was as yet only theoretical; most of T'ao's energy at the time was still going into scholarship. T'ao's practical alchemy began about four years after the completion of his three great books. There was to be no other major work from T'ao's own hand until 516, however, and so it is in the light of what his biographers have to tell us that we may best consider the few fragmentary notes of his own which refer to his activities in the intervening years.

The fullest biographical source is the *Detailed Life of Hermit T'ao of Hua-yang*, written during the T'ang dynasty by a certain Chia Sung 賈嵩.[57] In addition to T'ao's own works, Chia drew upon two chronological accounts of the master, both recorded during T'ao's lifetime. The

56. *CK* 11:10b.

57. *Hua-yang T'ao yin-chü nei-chuan* 華陽陶隱居內傳, HY 300/*TT* 151. Chia was known as the author of a collection of rhapsodies (*fu* 賦). In the *Wen-yüan ying-hua* 文苑英華 he is represented by a work of this genre, on the theme of summer heat (5:9a–10a, 1567 ed.; reprinted Peking, 1966). In the *Complete T'ang Prose, Chüan T'ang wen* 全唐文, this is joined by an extract from the preface to his biography of T'ao (762:19a–b, 1814 ed.; reprinted Taipei, 1974). Chia Sung draws on a considerably fuller version of the Biography of T'ao by T'ao I than is found in *YCCC* 107 (nearly all the biographical notices in *YCCC*, when alternative texts are available for comparison, prove to have been drastically abridged). He also claims to make use of *TCYC* and the original version of T'ao's literary collection, both of which seem to have been lost in large part by the Sung. As we shall see, there is very good reason to consider these claimed citations as being in entire accord with T'ao's other pronouncements, independently available, on the subjects discussed.

The third *chüan* of the *Detailed Life* is occupied by various documents, and opens with the text of Sung Hui Tsung's 宋徽宗 decree of 1124, augmenting T'ao's posthumous title (cf. *Records of Mao Shan* 4:9a–11b, HY 304/*TT* 153). This is followed by two commemorative inscriptions composed shortly after T'ao's death in 536, together with a text inscribed on the back of one of the stelae by Ssu-ma Ch'eng-chen 司馬承禎 in 724 (*NC* 3:6a–7a).

There is every likelihood that Chia Sung's work did not originally comprise more than two *chüan* (in which case the T'ang inscription would be equally irrelevant for dating). The "three" *chüan* mentioned in the preface may well represent a later alteration, the more so in that the author makes no mention of inscriptions among his sources for facts about T'ao, and that the *Detailed Life* itself is complete in two *chüan*: the first devoted to T'ao's antecedents and secular career, the second to his doings after retirement to Mao Shan.

first, by a nephew, T'ao I 陶翊, did not go beyond 499. As we have seen, 499 is the latest date mentioned in T'ao's notes to the *Chen-kao*, and it was that year in which T'ao moved into a tower he had recently added to his Hua-yang hermitage at Mao Shan, with the intention of abstracting himself still farther from all mundane relations.[58] Thereafter Chia Sung relied upon a continuation of T'ao I's narrative by one of the master's disciples, P'an Yüan-wen 潘淵文, who carried the tale down to 507–508 and was a participant in the events he describes.[59]

A Choice of Formulae

The story of T'ao's alchemical operations as told by Chia Sung begins in 504 with dreams granted simultaneously to T'ao and to Emperor Wu of the Liang, concerning favorable auspices for the achievement of an elixir. Hard on these dreams come the emperor's proposal of sponsorship and the suitable demur of the recluse. When at last convinced, we are told, by the substance of the emperor's dream, T'ao had P'an Yüan-wen and another disciple clear a space on the east side of the ridge, to the west of which he had in 492 established his Hua-yang Kuan. It was on this spot, already foretold in the Mao Shan revelations, that the elixir was to be compounded. As he had envisioned when writing his commentary on

---

58. The text of T'ao I's narrative (see n. 41, above) is preserved in *YCCC* 107:1b–11b. We may suppose that it was called into being by Hung-ching's decision to sever all superfluous human contact, which also inspired Shen Yüeh's 沈約 poem, "Master T'ao's Gone up into his Tower and Won't Come Down Again," *Hua-yang hsien-sheng teng-lou pu fu hsia* 華陽先生登樓不復下, in *Shen Yin-hou chi* 沈隱侯集 2:77a–b (*Han Wei Liu-ch'ao pai-san chia chi* 漢魏六朝百三家集 ed.). This might explain the confusion in chronology with which the imperfect *YCCC* text opens. The numerical date given for T'ao's initial retirement to Mao Shan is 492, but this is equated with the *cyclical* designation of 499, the year of his withdrawal into the tower. This is probably the result of overly hasty editorial compression on the part of the *YCCC*'s compiler. A different kind of error is the incorrect cyclical designation that T'ao I gives to the day of his uncle's birth: *chia-hsü* 甲戌 rather than *chia-yin* 甲寅 (*YCCC* 107:3b10). This seems to be a pious falsification, since *chia-yin* was one of the two worst-omened days of the cycle, together with the more notorious *keng-shen* 庚申 day (*CK* 10:21b; on the history and rites of the *keng-shen* day there are several studies by Kubo Noritada 窪德忠, including his monumental *Kōshin shinkō no kenkyū* 庚申信仰の研究, Tokyo, 1961). As we have seen, T'ao Hung-ching did not tamper with his own birthdate, and apparently faced its inauspicious implications with equanimity.

T'ao Hung-ching's purpose in seeking increased isolation may have been understood by his nephew and others as being preparatory to a still more definitive departure from the world of men. It would then not be accidental that T'ao I's narrative has so much the look of a "report on conduct" for submission to the court historiographers; its bland emphasis on T'ao family history and Hung-ching's own secular eminence lends credence to this view.

59. P'an is mentioned by T'ao in his notes to the *Ming-t'ung chi* (3:4a9). His account of T'ao's life has not otherwise been preserved.

the *Chen-kao*, T'ao solved the problem of the "eastward-flowing stream" by an engineering feat. He had the intervening rock bored through and so diverted eastward the brook that flowed to the west of the ridge.[60]

T'ao is next depicted as pondering the choice of a formula, and his biographer cites the *Teng-chen yin-chüeh* as evidence for the substance of the master's musings. This review of possible preparations is an inventory of the alchemical formulae known to a very well-informed adept dwelling near the Liang capital at the beginning of the sixth century. The list also serves as a positive indication of the value of Chia Sung's biography; his information on the elixirs mentioned tallies perfectly with what we know from other, earlier sources.

The first possibility was the Nine Crucibles Elixir, which was attributed to the legendary Yellow Emperor. T'ao stated that the formula was found among the scriptures of *T'ai-ch'ing* (*T'ai-ch'ing chung ching* 太清中經), but he noted that the text was so confused that no one in latter days had been capable of understanding it.[61]

Next he mentioned two elixirs of which the formulae were apparently unknown in the world of men. One was the Rainbow Elixir of Lord Wang (*Wang chün hung-tan* 王君虹丹), Perfected Immortal of the Hsiao-yu 小有 heaven of Pure Vacuity, beneath Mount Wang-wu 王屋山 (Shansi).[62] The other was the Nine Blossoms (*chiu-hua* 九華) Elixir of the famous thaumaturge, Tso Tz'u 左慈, supposed to have been an early frequenter of Mao Shan.[63] These elixirs were known by name alone, having been mentioned in the texts that constitute the *Chen-kao*.[64]

T'ao goes on to remark that there were some thirty-odd other possibilities. Of these he names four: the elixirs of the Five Transcendent Powers (*wu-ling* 五靈),[65] Seven Transformations (*ch'i-pien* 七變), Wondrous Essence (*shen-ching* 神精), and the Soul-summoner (*chao-hun* 召魂).[66]

---

60. *NC* 2:5a–6a.

61. *HY* 884/*TT* 584–85 is a *Huang-ti chiu-ting shen-tan ching-chüeh* 黃帝九鼎神丹經訣 in 20 chüan, of which the first agrees with quotations in the *Pao-p'u tzu* 抱朴子 (4:5a–7a [*P'ing-chin-kuan ts'ung-shu* 平津館叢書 ed.]; see Nathan Sivin, *Chinese Alchemy; Preliminary Studies*, p. 155, n. 23), and thus may well be the work in question.

62. *CK* 14:8b3. Wang Pao 王褒 was the teacher of the Lady Wei of the Southern Peak. There is a résumé of his life in *YCCC* 106:1a–8a.

63. *CK* 12:3b5. There is an account of Tso Ssu in the *History of the Later Han, Hou Han shu* 後漢書, 112B.

64. *NC* 2:6a.

65. This term usually refers to the five emblematic animals of the four directions and the center.

66. "The lesser elixirs for recalling *hun* souls" (*chao-hun hsiao-tan* 召魂小丹) are placed among the "common, everyday drugs" by the *Pao-p'u tzu* 5:3b (see Needham, *Science and Civilisation in China* vol. 5, pt. 2, p. 89).

According to T'ao, the formulae of these various preparations were so cryptic in places that they were hard to translate into reality. What is more, the virtue of such elixirs as these was merely to confer eternal youth, at the very most enabling their consumer to become an earth-bound immortal (*ti-hsien* 地仙). Even the formulae of this group that had celestial pretentions would under no circumstances give one access to the upper echelons of the invisible world. They were only the methods of T'ai-ch'ing, that lowlier heaven to which no disciple of the Perfected of Shang-ch'ing would conceivably deign to aspire.

There remained two formulae, both of which were more famous and apparently more practicable than the others. T'ao calls them the two elixirs of Liquefied Gold. The first was that of T'ai-i 太乙, on which Ko Hung had allegedly composed a commentary.[67] This could have been attempted, save for the difficulty of obtaining nitre now that the north was in foreign hands. The absence of a transcript of the formula written by one of the Perfected (i.e. Yang Hsi and the two Hsüs) was still another cause for hesitation. Secondly, there was the Liquefied Gold of T'ai-ch'ing, the method which had been transmitted by An Ch'i 安期.[68] But it demanded lake-salt, or "salt of the tribes" (*lu-hsien* 鹵鹹 or *lu-yen* 虜擔), likewise difficult to obtain under current conditions. And it also required blood sacrifice—a most repugnant feature.[69]

Finally, T'ao considered what he termed the four supreme methods of the Exalted Perfected (*kao-chen shang-fa* 高眞上法). These were the four principal elixirs that had been directly associated with the Mao Shan revelations. The first of these mentioned by T'ao is one we have not yet encountered: the Fourfold Floreate (*ssu-jui* 四蕤). A formula for this elixir existed in T'ao's day, and we still have it. T'ao seems to have doubted its authenticity, however, and so declined to consider preparing it.[70]

He next refers to the profundities of the Lang-kan Elixir and the marvels of the Elixir of Ch'ü-ch'en ("the winding constellation"), both of

---

67. See page 133, above.

68. A most celebrated legendary immortal; cf. Kaltenmark, *Biographies légendaires*, pp. 115-18.

69. The Way of the Celestial Master insisted with particular force upon its missionary role in abolishing the practice of animal sacrifice. Such sacrifices were current among the exorcistic priesthood of what Taoists termed the "gods of the profane" (*su-shen* 俗神)—local cults outside the Taoist institutional framework. In its condemnation of the practices of popular religion, the Way of the Celestial Master was entirely in accord with both Buddhism and the secular administration. On the relationship of Taoism to "inorganic" popular religion, see R. A. Stein, "Les religions de la Chine" in *Encyclopédie Française*, vol. 19 (Paris, 1957), and his article in the present volume.

70. *NC* 2:7a. This formula will be studied at length below, pp. 171 ff.

which we have already met with above. The problem here, according to the passage of the *Teng-chen yin-chüeh* adduced by his biographer, was that T'ao questioned whether a mere mortal such as himself had the right to attempt them. T'ao had received no call from the invisible world, no firm assurance of his posthumous deserts, and so did not have the authorization to prepare either of these major elixirs of the Perfected. And besides, both formulae required the bothersome nitre and lake-salt.

After the enumeration of these various elixirs and the several factors militating against their preparation, it was natural that T'ao's choice should have fallen upon the last of the four "supreme methods of the Exalted Perfected." All the necessary ingredients were said to have been obtainable, there were apparently no undue restrictions upon its preparation, and T'ao had a text of the formula in the hand of one of the three Perfected. It was the Elixir of Nine Cycles, which had been bestowed upon Mao Ying, Director of Destinies and Minister of the East (Tung-ch'ing Ssu-min g東卿司命), eldest of the three brothers Mao for whom the mountain had been named. The *Life of Lord Mao* had been revealed to Yang Hsi, and the elixir formula was one of a set of technical instructions appended to the narrative. In the spring of 505, then, T'ao moved to the spot he had chosen on the eastern slope of the ridge connecting Great and Middle Mao Shan, taking with him three prominent disciples, and there began his preparations.[71]

The Elixir of Nine Cycles

The text of the *Life of Lord Mao* has not proved durable, and the auricular instructions it once contained have been dispersed.[72] There is a short text in the Canon entitled *Essential Instructions of the Perfected Immortal of the Grand Bourne on the Elixir of Nine Cycles.*[73] It concludes with Lord Mao's remarks on the five sacred mushrooms of Mao Shan, a subject we know to have been treated in the original biography. Before considering this text, however, I shall examine yet another fragment of the *Teng-chen yin-chüeh*, cited in the tenth-century encyclopedia, *T'ai-p'ing yü-lan.*[74] Here we find T'ao himself discussing precisely the Elixir of Nine

71. NC 2:7b.

72. A résumé of the historical narrative is found in *YCCC* 104:10b–20a; also at much greater length in the *Records of Mao Shan* 5:1b–18b (*HY* 304/*TT* 154). The first part of *HY* 424/*TT* 194 is a set of orally transmitted instructions taken from the *Life of Lord Mao.*

73. *HY* 888/*TT 586*, *T'ai-chi chen-jen chiu-chuan huan-tan ching yao-chüeh* 太極眞人九轉還丹經要訣.

74. *TPYL* 671:1a–2a. The Taoist section of this work (*ch.* 659–79) is invaluable for the study of the subject, and is particularly rich in early Mao Shan literature and writings of T'ao

Cycles and its preparation. He first studies the line of transmission, from a Perfected Immortal of the Grand Bourne (*T'ai-chi chen-jen*) down to Mao Ying, who is supposed to have received it in 98 B.C. Although the usual typographic distinction between text and commentary is not made here, T'ao is clearly quoting and annotating the formula for the elixir and comparing it with similar references occurring in the *Sword Scripture*.

T'ao then traces the transmission of the formula from that time on. Mao Ying apparently showed it to his two younger brothers, and it was the elder of these, the Certifier of Registers (*ting-lu chün* 定錄君), a frequent guest in Yang's visions, who gave it to Yang for revelation to the two Hsüs. This, we may note, is entirely in accord with the information, found in the *Chen-kao*, that it was the Certifier of Registers who was responsible for making known the text of his brother's biography to Yang Hsi.[75]

The question of transmission was, as we have seen, exceedingly important for T'ao. Here he had a formula that was totally of the Perfected in that it had descended through a whole series of them to Mao Ying, eponymous patron of Mao Shan. By his agency it had come to be bestowed upon those latter-day Perfected, Yang and the Hsüs, in the very hand of one or more of whom it was extant.

T'ao also emphasizes the exalted standing of the formula when he notes that, apart from Mao Ying, none of those who worked to achieve the Tao during the Han or Chin dynasties, celebrated though they may have been as alchemists or thaumaturges, had ever made this elixir. In fact, the only accomplishment of any of them actually recorded was the concoction and ingestion of liquefied gold, followed by mere immortality *tout court* (*hsien* 仙). After some additional remarks on the protocols for transmission of the formula (gold and silk to be provided as pledges of secrecy, in accordance with the frequently repeated instructions in the Shang-ch'ing scriptures), T'ao begins to tell us just how to set about the preparations:

The vessels are to be earthenware pots made of clay from Jung-yang 榮陽, Ch'ang-

---

Hung-ching. It includes many extended quotations from works now lost. Caution is required, however, as the titles of books drawn on in this section have sometimes been strangely scrambled. Many passages attributed to the *T'ai-p'ing ching* 太平經 or the *Chen-kao*, for example, really come from the *Lives of Taoist Scholars* referred to in note 44, above. The uniqueness of the Taoist section of the encyclopedia was recognized by the compilers of one of the Taoist canons, as the Ming Canon contains a work in three *chüan*, entitled *T'ai-p'ing yü-lan* (*HY* 1220/*TT* 988); it simply consists of *ch.* 674, 675, and 676, from the encyclopedia —perhaps the entire Taoist section was reprinted in an earlier Canon.

75. *CK* 11:12a.

sha 長沙, or Yü-chang 豫章: this is what is meant by the term "pottery vessels" in the formula.

For fuel, chaff of grain is to be employed.

The operations are to be carried out in a secluded spot on a holy mountain, in proximity to a stream. There the laboratory ("furnace house," *tsao-wu* 竈屋) is to be constructed, four *chang* 丈 long by two wide, with three doors, one each to the south, east, and west.[76]

The preliminary luting of the vessels should be preceded by a hundred-day fast. This done, the luting ingredients are to be pounded. These preliminaries should have been so calculated that the firing may begin at dawn on the ninth day of the ninth month ("Double Yang").

Here T'ao digresses to observe that, in compounding elixirs, there is no particular prohibition with regard to the years of the sexagesimal cycle. It is only the day and month that are prescribed, and only with reference to them that the portentous cyclical associations are to be considered. In making the Lang-kan Elixir, he continues, the fire must be ignited during the middle decade of the fourth, seventh, or twelfth month,[77] while for the Elixir of Ch'ü-ch'en this is to be done during the fifth month. As for the nine elixirs of T'ai-ch'ing, although no precise month is enjoined for lighting the furnace, preparation of the six-one lute is said to be best done in the fifth, seventh, or ninth month.

The text, whether at this point it is T'ao's own note or the work on which he is commenting in the *T'ai-p'ing yü-lan* fragment, goes on to remind us that the aspirant must desist from all normal activities, from the beginning of his fast to the completion of the elixir. He may, however, have the company of no more than four or five reliable persons of like purpose, all of whom must share his reclusion.

On the day when the long term of abstinence is begun, one should first pour five *hu* 斛 of clear spirit (*ch'ing-chiu* 清酒) into the adjacent stream. In the absence of a stream, a well may be dug instead and the spirits poured therein. This is done to repress influences (*ch'i* 氣) coming up from the earth.[78] All those engaging in the fast are to partake of the stream- or well-water so treated. T'ao also remarks that ten *chin* 斤 of fine-quality dragon's bones (fossil bones? *lung-ku* 龍骨) may be enclosed in an envelope of bluestone (or blue clay? *ch'ing-shih* 青石) and placed in the eastward-flowing stream. The stream's waters are then styled

76. *TPYL* 671:1b7-8.

77. This is in accord with the text of the formula, p. 4b (*HY* 255/*TT* 120).

78. Correcting *hsüan-chiu* 玄酒 (a ritual term for water) to *ch'ing-chiu* 清酒, as in *HY* 888/*TT* 586, p. 5a4. The Lang-kan formula, too, specifies "clear spirit" p. 2a8-9 (*HY* 255/ *TT* 120). A text in the *Chen-kao* states that all demonic influences (*kuei-ch'i* 鬼氣) attack from the earth upward (*CK* 10:7b10-8a1).

"fluid of the blue dragon" and are likewise to be consumed by all participants, to promote communion with the water spirits (shui-ling 水靈).

Next, one is to take left-oriented male oyster shells from Tung-hai 東海, white clay of Wu 吳 county, mica powder, soil turned by earthworms, talc, and alum—a total of six ingredients—in equal quantities . . . and here unfortunately, with the directions for preparing the six-one lute, the T'ai-p'ing yü-lan citation breaks off to merge into another, unrelated passage from the Teng-chen yin-chüeh. Enough has been glimpsed, however, to show the essential congruity of Chia Sung's account with what T'ao himself has to tell us. What is more, we now have sufficient information to identify this formula for the Elixir of Nine Cycles with the text preserved in the Taoist Canon (see n. 73).

These *Essential Instructions of the Perfected Immortal of the Grand Bourne on the Elixir of Nine Cycles* not only record the same data on preliminaries that we have found in the quotation from the Teng-chen yin-chüeh cited in T'ai-p'ing yü-lan, as well as the same genealogy for the formula, beginning with the Perfected Immortal of the Grand Bourne; they also give us the seven ingredients of the elixir and instructions for their firing.[79] As in the preparation of the Lang-kan Elixir, the firing is very precisely phased. The vessels are gradually brought closer to the flame during six successive nine-day stages. They are then kept at half an inch from the fire for a final thirty-six days, making a total of ninety days of firing, or nine ten-day cycles. After carrying us through the completion of the elixir, the text brings on several curious sequels. First we are told that the projection of a dram of the elixir on a large quantity of lead will turn it all to gold, and that a similar projection on one *chin* of mercury and seven of tin will turn those substances to silver. Yet this procedure is not to be followed with the aim of producing silver or gold; its only end is to test the elixir's state of completion.[80]

Next we are instructed on how to compound pills using the residue in the vessels. Two of these pellets placed in the mouth of a corpse not more

79. The ingredients are alum, verditer, quartz, cinnabar, realgar, orpiment, and mercury (p. 2a, HY 888/TT 586). It should be noted that these *Essential Instructions of the Prefected Immortal of the Grand Bourne on the Elixir of Nine Cycles* were already recorded as a separate work in the bibliographical section of the *Sui History, Sui-shu* 隋書, 34:34b (Palace ed.).

80. Despite the difference of materials, this account of projection must have inspired the analogous operations which are described by Ho Wei 何薳 at the end of the eleventh century as the "Tan-yang transmutation of copper" (Tan-yang hua-t'ung 丹陽化銅), or as "projecting [into] Mallow" (= Mao Shan/Lord Mao; tien-mao 點茆—in the thirteenth and fourteenth centuries, Mao Shan was often written with the homophonous character for mallow; see Needham, vol. 5, pt. 2, pp. 233–35.)

than three days dead will bring it back to life. Crushed to a powder and externally applied, they will heal blindness, deafness, and all manner of lesions. Swallowing two pellets will cure internal ailments. One pill taken at dawn will confer endless longevity. Objects on which a pill is rubbed will come back to you if you lose them.

Directions are then given for preparing two powders, one under the patronage of the Yellow Emperor, the other under that of the Queen Mother of the West (Hsi Wang Mu). Both composed of vegetable substances, these powders are to be taken to cleanse the body of mundane impurities before work on the elixir is begun. Finally, the text lists the five species of marvelous mushrooms that were sown by Lord Mao at Mao Shan. The pure-hearted devotee who searches for them there in the third or ninth month may be allowed to find one.

We may now permit T'ao's biographer to proceed, our confidence in him considerably reinforced. Chia Sung next cites the master's literary collection—perhaps a report to the emperor on his progress—to the effect that when the vessels were opened, on New Year's Day 506, it was found that the elixir had not been achieved.[81] On the following double ninth (and it is P'an Yüan-wen's account that is now being quoted), operations recommenced. But something appears to have gone wrong from the start. Just after firing, a great many fine cracks appeared in the lute. This was considered a result of the ingredients' indwelling spirits (*ching* 精) having been upset by recent thunderstorms in the mountains: in their fright they were driven from the crucible. Fresh ingredients were added; but as the proper moment for combustion had passed, T'ao did not dare light the fire anew. He continued with the old fire, and when the time was up, at year's end, the result was found to be as inconclusive as before.

T'ao is said to have blamed these failures on the lack of genuine isolation. Indeed, as the fame of the mountain grew, Mao Shan became the object of many a pilgrimage of both the pious and the curious. The mountain was only some thirty miles from the imperial capital; writing in 499, T'ao describes the multitudes that annually flocked there on one of the two days of the year sacred to the brothers Mao.[82] The community of permanent residents was constantly growing too, and we have good evidence of the daily tumult at Mao Shan a little later, in 515. In the

81. *NC* 2:7b.
82. *CK* 11:13a. The two days, which in the ritual calendar are still sacred to the Director of Destinies Mao and his two brothers, are the 2d of the twelfth month and the 18th of the third month. The latter day was far more popular, owing to the more clement weather; in the twelfth month, Mao Shan was usually covered with snow.

visionary narrative recorded then by Chou Tzu-liang 周子良, the mountain is described as being peopled not only with grave Taoist recluses, but by whole households of the faithful, their children scampering about everywhere, often as not in a state of nature. "While you still dwell among all this mundane bustle," as one of Chou's transcendent guests tellingly phrased it, "we find it distasteful to come and visit you more often." In 508, then, according to his biographer, T'ao departed incognito on a trip to the eastern region (now Chekiang and Fukien), there to accomplish in the mountain solitude what he had not been able to effect among the crowds at Mao Shan.

An Eschatological Pilgrimage (508–512)

It happens that we have full confirmation of this romantic-sounding expedition from T'ao's own pen. It was during the course of this journey that T'ao met Chou Tzu-liang, who was to become his disciple and to furnish, in the form of posthumous visionary manuscripts, a splendid occasion for T'ao once more to display his text-critical powers as editor and annotator of the *Chou-shih ming-t'ung chi* 周氏冥通記.[83] In the prefatory essay that relates Chou's brief life, T'ao describes his itinerary in the southeast from his setting-out in 508 until his return in 512. The geographical facts agree with what we are told in Chia Sung's biography, except that the latter goes into more detail with regard to intermediate points along the way. The congruence is all the more convincing in that Chia Sung gives no indication of knowing the *Ming-t'ung chi*. Also, whereas T'ao's brief account of the trip makes no mention of alchemy— or, for that matter, of any other spiritual activity—his biographer describes his purposes as being all but exclusively alchemical. Drawing on the master's lost literary collection as well as on parts of the *Teng-chen yin-chüeh* that no longer survive elsewhere, Chia recounts how T'ao went from one site to another, guided by a prophetic dream but harassed, now by the absence of chaff for firing (here people only pounded enough grain for each day's use and thus had no stockpiles of chaff), now by the constant menace of brigands or pirates. For one reason or another, according to his biographer, the elixir was not achieved in the southeastern wilds either.

Although we have no explicit statement from T'ao concerning the real object of this journey, we do know that his original destination, ultimately attained after many adventures on land and sea, was Great Huo Shan of

83. "A Record of Master Chou's Communications with the Unseen World" (*MTC*), *HY* 302/*TT* 152.

the South (*Nan Ta-huo shan* 南大霍山).[84] This mountain was located within the bailiwick of Chin-an 晉安 (near present-day Nan-an 南安 *hsien*, Fukien), but its exact location has until now remained uncertain.[85] It was here, though, that both the Lady Wei ("of the Southern Peak"), who had been Yang Hsi's otherworldly preceptress, and Mao Ying himself, Minister of the East, had their supernatural headquarters. From this mountain they presided over the destinies of dwellers in Wu and Yüeh—the entire seaboard area from the capital southward—in their capacity of Directors of Destinies.[86] It was, then, toward this focal-point of interest for all

84. *MTC* 1:1b6.

85. Down to the Liang (502), and both in the texts of the *Chen-kao* and in T'ao's annotations on them, it is referred to as Huo Shan of Lo-chiang 羅江. Lo-chiang *hsien* is one of the four recorded early settlements in what is now Fukien to which no definite site has been assigned by Chinese geographers; see H. Bielenstein, "The Chinese Colonisation of Fukien to the End of the T'ang," in *Studia Serica Bernhard Karlgren Dedicata* (Copenhagen, 1959). In the *Ming-t'ung chi* of 516, T'ao refers to the mountain as Huo Shan of Chin-an 晉安, suggesting (as the documents studied by Bielenstein confirm) that Lo-chiang had fallen out of administrative currency since the advent of the Liang, and that the mountain had subsequently been reassigned to the long-established port of Chin-an, which survived.

An interesting tale in the *Lives of Eminent Monks* (*Kao-seng chuan* 高僧傳, *T* L. 2059. 404a), compiled ca. 530, both gives the older assignment to Lo-chiang (as it doubtless stood in its source) and shows the mountain's proximity to Chin-an. Huo Shan, it informs us, stands alone in the sea. At its peak is a great stone basin, ever full of sweet water. According to local tradition, the immortals drink of that water and so never know hunger or thirst. The prefect of Chin-an, one T'ao K'uei 陶夔, learned of it and sent for a sample of the water, but by the time it reached him it had turned putrid. After the experiment had been several times repeated, he at last set out himself for the mountain island. But though the day was bright and clear when he sailed, as he approached his goal, it clouded over and rained, becoming in the end so dark and stormy that his attempt was foiled. We may note the probable place of the disappointed prefect among the ancestors of T'ao Hung-ching (the story is set sometime during the Chin dynasty).

Though not all their personal names are known, it is recorded that several of T'ao's forebears held office in the area around Chin-an and, as we have seen, T'ao's grandfather, T'ao Lung, was created marquis of that very district. Knowledge of this particular "Sacred Peak of the South" may well have been a tradition of that same group of families whose mutual cohesion and Taoist proclivities are so strikingly attested by the texts of the Mao Shan corpus. As for the mountain itself, Tai-yün Shan 戴雲山 to the north of Nan-an 南安 (the Chin-an of old), the dominant peak in the district with an altitude of 1,849 meters, would not only correspond to the dimensions of the range as given by T'ao's biographer ("some six or seven hundred *li* in length," *NC* 2:10b–11a), but is also said to have at its peak a striking basinlike formation. Its being described as an "island" (mentioned only in the *Lives of Eminent Monks*) is easily explained; access by sea and the Ta-chang ch'i 大樟溪 must have been far more practical than the tortuous, bandit-infested mountain trails of inland Fukien. Older sources, such as the *Shan-hai ching* 山海經, regularly refer to points on the mainland of Fukien as being "in the sea" (*yü hai-chung* 於海中)—see Ichimura Sanjirō 市村瓚次郎, "Tō izen no Fukken oyobi Taiwan ni tsuite" 唐以前の福建及び 臺灣に就いて, in his *Shina-shi kenkyū* 支那史研究 (Tokyo, 1939), p. 320.

86. There were thirty-six directors of destinies, of whom all but four were stationed on

devotees of the Perfected that T'ao was heading. It is perhaps possible, too, to obtain some notion of his object in making this pilgrimage.

Central to the conceptions of Yang and the Hsüs had been the expectation of a savior who, after a preliminary time of trials during which the wicked were to be exterminated, would descend from heaven and summon the elect to join him in the reign of Great Peace (*t'ai-p'ing* 太平). His advent was imminent, the signs of the times were already upon them, and Yang and the Hsüs were promised high offices in the new imperium. The basic textual authority for these eschatological prospects was the *Annals of the Sage Who is to Come, Lord of the Tao of Shang-ch'ing*, which had been revealed to Yang Hsi and by him transmitted to the Hsüs.[87] It is there that the teachings were specified (all of them having originally been practiced by the savior-sage himself) whereby one might, even then, prepare for the advent: ingestion of solar, lunar, and astral essences; propitiation of celestial spirits who would assure a satisfactory transformation when the moment arrived; and preliminary exercises in the art of walking the stars of the Dipper. For each of these operations a scripture was also revealed.

When, then, was the great event to come about? The *Annals* contain a prophecy designating the time when the eschatological process would be set in motion as the forty-sixth *ting-hai* 丁亥 year from that occurring in the reign of the legendary emperor Yao.[88] Now although the texts gathered into the *Chen-kao* leave no doubt that Yang and the Hsüs expected the advent in their own lifetimes, T'ao could not help considering the sage's kingdom as still to come. Furthermore, T'ao was a renowned expert in matters of chronology and accordingly had his own definite opinion on the dates of Yao's reign.[89] Its initial year, he states, was a cyclical *wu-hsü* 戊戌, "just 2,803 years prior to this cyclical year *chi-mao* 己卯 of our Ch'i dynasty" (=499).[90] Thus, *ting-hai* would correspond to the fiftieth year in Yao's century of rule (and such a calculation would also ensure that there would have been only a single *ting-hai* year in that long reign). We can see that, according to this interpretation, the crucial forty-sixth

---

the isle of Fang-chu 方諸, in the Eastern Sea. They were under the supervision of the Lord Blue Youth (Ch'ing-t'ung chün 青童君), Grand Director of Destinies and Chief Minister to the Sage Who is to Come (*CK* 9:21b–22a).

87. *Shang-ch'ing hou-sheng tao-chün lieh-chi* 上清後聖道君列紀, *HY* 442/*TT* 198.

88. *Annals*, p. 3b6 (*HY* 442/*TT* 198).

89. Among his works was a chronographic account of ancient Chinese history, to which later Buddhist authors often had recourse, entitled *A Chronography of Rulers* (*Ti-wang nien-li* 帝王年曆; *YCCC* 107:9a10–9b2). It has not been preserved.

90. *CK* 13:8b.

ting-hai year was to fall in 507. The terms of the prophecy specified that after the purifying scourges of plague, war, and flood had done their work, the sage would descend on the 6th of the third month in the year *jen-ch'en* 壬辰. This by the present calculation, would be 512. So it is that we find T'ao at that time, by his own testimony as well as that of his biographer, standing before the towering walls of the Red Citadel of the Directors of Destinies.

Perhaps he was hoping for admission to the security of the cavern-palace within. Other living men were said to have been so favored before, even at less crucial junctures—as, for example, Tso Tz'u, at Mao Shan itself.[91] Yet even though T'ao does not tell us how he occupied himself as the promised day approached, he had, as do we, a revealed text in which precise reference is made to the alchemy that was to be practiced at the time of the sage's advent.

The text is found in the *Chen-kao* and is entitled *Prolegomena on the Ingestion of Atractylis (Fu-chu hsü* 服朮敘). T'ao owned a transcript in the hand of Hsü Hui.[92] It is a prolonged literary excursus dictated by the Lady Wang of Tzu-wei 紫微王夫人, an elegant colleague of the Lady of the Southern Peak, in which her poetic virtuosity adorns the wide selection of topics treated, and of which T'ao has recorded his great admiration.[93] The Lady Wang told how the last days would soon be at hand, in all their catastrophic fury. The elements would be released from their orderly cycle of interdependence and turned loose toward destruction, the seasons unseated and opposites violently conjoined, with calamitous effect. Deluge, thunder, and lightning would rage from above, while over the surface of the earth a host of apocalyptic beasts would range, wreaking havoc. At that time only those who had practiced the Tao in solitude would be secure.

In those days, singular practices and supreme arts will be expounded in the most secret recesses of the cavern-heaven of Pure Vacuity, whilst the names of the elect will be chosen in the subterranean pavilions of Mount Wei-yü.[94] There will be those who

91. *CK* 12:8b.
92. *CK* 6:1a–5b.
93. *CK* 6:1a.
94. The cavern-heaven of Pure Vacuity 清虚, known as the Cavern-terrace 洞臺, is the first in the series of ten major cavern-heavens (*tung-t'ien* 洞天) beneath sacred mountains. It is the Hsiao-yu 小有 heaven at Wang-wu Shan 王屋山 (Honan), presided over by Wang Pao (see note 62, above). Complementing it is the Ta-yu 大有 heaven of Vacant Luminosity 虚明, the second of the series, beneath Mount Wei-yü 委羽山, under the rule of the Han diviner, Ssu-ma Chi-chu (note 18, above). Like several other particularly sacred mountains, Mount Wei-yü's location was not known to mortals; cf. E. Chavannes, "Le Jet des dragons," *Mémoires concernant l'Asie Orientale* (Paris, 1919), 3 : 131 ff.

produce by transformation in their furnaces the sublime essence of cinnabar, or who powder jade and smelt gold to purplish ichor. Lang-kan will send forth its thick-billowing emanations and the eight gems, in a radiant cloud, will fly aloft. Crimson fluid eddies and ripples, Dragon Foetus cries out from its secret place. Tiger Spittle, Phoenix Brain, Cloud Lang-kan, Jade Frost, Lunar Liquor of the Grand Bourne, and the Triple-ringed Transcendent Orbs:[95] let but a single spatulaful [of one of these] be brought forth and wondrous wings will spread their supporting pinions. You will peruse the figured pattern upon the vault of space and glow forth in the chamber of primordial commencement . . . [96]

T'ao and his companions remained at the Southern Peak until the sixth month of 512, when they returned to Yung-chia by sea. Continuing their northward voyage, they arrived at Mu-liu Island 木溜嶼 in the eighth month. Extensive and deserted, with the remains of abandoned grainfields, this (the modern island of Yü-huan 玉環嶼 off the southeast coast of Chekiang) seemed ideal for their purpose, and the party settled in. But in the tenth month, we are told, the idyll ended with the sudden arrival of an emissary from the emperor who ordered them to return. After several days of arguing to no avail, the captive adept and his disciples accompanied the emissary back north. T'ao has left no record of his feelings about this peremptory conclusion to his four years of wandering.[97]

The Question of Imperial Sponsorship

T'ao's travels in the south were thus cut short by the emperor's personal

95. We have already come across certain of these substances above.

96. *CK* 6:2a10–2b8.

97. *NC* 2:11a–11b. A seeming relic of T'ao's return trip is one of the most famous and enigmatic monuments of Chinese calligraphy, the "Inscription on the Burial of a Crane" (*I-ho ming* 瘞鶴銘). It was discovered during the Northern Sung dynasty on a broken stele submerged beneath the waters of the Yangtze at the little islet of Chiao Shan 焦山 (Kiangsu), and immediately attracted great attention. Its author styles himself "The Perfected Recluse of Hua-yang" (i.e. Mao Shan), Hua-yang chen-i 華陽眞逸, and after being attributed—on no evidence—to Wang Hsi-chih and several other luminaries of calligraphic history, the inscription was at length ascribed to T'ao Hung-ching. Two cyclical years, *jen-ch'en* and *chia-wu*, are mentioned in the text, and once T'ao's authorship had been suggested, they were equated with 512 and 514, respectively.

Some scholars have contested the attribution to T'ao, yet no one seems to have remarked how well this inscription ties in with T'ao's chronology. In the *jen-ch'en* year, the author writes, he acquired the crane in Hua-t'ing 華亭 (in Tung-yang 東陽 commandery, northern Chekiang, a great center for crane breeding); in the *chia-wu* year, it died at "the Vermilion Locus (*chu-fang* 朱方—the capital of the fire-endowed Liang dynasty). In 512, T'ao was northward bound and almost certainly passed through Tung-yang. If he himself did not compose the inscription, it was probably written by one of the disciples who had accompanied him on his southern wanderings. The history of the stele and reproductions of several rubbings will be found in *Shodō zenshū* 書道全集 (Tokyo, 1966), 5: 19–23, and plates 22–23. The rubbing reproduced as no. 54 of the series *Shoseki meihin sōkan* 書跡名品叢刊 (Tokyo, 1961) is also worthy of attention.

intervention. We have already seen that, according to his biographer, T'ao's experiments in alchemy began at Emperor Wu's behest, in 504. This might seem strange, as 504 was also the year of Emperor Wu's formal renunciation of Taoism, which had for generations been the religion of his family, in favor of Buddhism. This act was followed by official measures against Taoists, the effectiveness of which is vouched for by a reference in T'ao's own writings.[98] As we shall see, even the secular sources all agree that T'ao's alchemy was carried out for Emperor Wu's benefit. The question of T'ao's relations with the supreme secular power is important to understanding the background of his alchemy. It also invites speculation about the status of the Taoist community over which he presided at Mao Shan.

The posts T'ao held during his secular career under the preceding dynasty, the Ch'i, were not ordinary administrative positions. All were court appointments, and the highest of them, commander of a wing of the palace guard, was directly the emperor's gift.[99] T'ao's first journey to the southeast in 490, during the course of which he assembled most of his collection of Yang-Hsü autograph texts, must have been undertaken with the imperial consent. Indeed, the trip was probably officially sponsored, with the aim of discovering valuable spiritual relics.[100] On his retirement from the court, T'ao settled in at Mao Shan with an imperial bestowal of silk and wax tapers, as well as a monthly allowance of five *chin* of *pachyma cocos* (*fu-ling* 茯苓) and two *tou* of honey toward his new dietary requirements.[101]

The most interesting evidence of imperial patronage of T'ao's technological projects is found in still another fragment of his writings preserved in the *T'ai-p'ing yü-lan*. The whole of *chüan* 665 of the *Yü-lan* is taken from a commentary by T'ao on the lost *Sword Scripture*, the canonical Shang-ch'ing text on liberation by means of a sword (*and* an elixir). Here he records that in 497 an artisan from the imperial atelier (*shang-fang* 尚方), during the Ch'i, was sent to Mao Shan to assist him in his

98. *MTC* 3:8b9, discussed in my article, "A Taoist Confirmation of Liang Wu Ti's Suppression of Taoism," to be published in the *Journal of the American Oriental Society*, 1978.

99. *NC* 1:7a.

100. A mission of this sort was assigned to a court specialist in auspicious signs and portents, Tung Chung-min 董仲民, in 481. He was sent to Lu Shan to "accumulate merit"— that is, to present imperial offerings to the temples there in return for their spiritual interest. He was also to look out for auspicious tokens, and the calligraphic remains of saintly persons fell within this category; Tung acquired a text in the hand of Yang Hsi (*CK* 19:15b; cf. my article "The Mao Shan Revelations; Taoism and the Aristocracy," *T'oung Pao* 63, 1:53, note 118 [1977]).

101. *YCCC* 107:7a.

efforts to forge swords conforming to the specifications laid down by the Perfected Immortals of the Grand Bourne. Such a sword was required for the operations enjoined in the *Sword Scripture*. The sword-founder, Huang Wen-ch'ing 黃文慶, remained active at Mao Shan after the change of dynasty in 502. T'ao states that in 505 he was commanded to present swords for the emperor's own use. The results were so fine that Huang was granted permission to become a *tao-shih*. His name was accordingly removed from the civil registers and placed on those of Mao Shan.[102]

Meanwhile, T'ao had made a contribution to the debates on the relative merits of Buddhism and Taoism which occupied the court during the early months of 504.[103] On the Buddha's birthday in that year, the 8th of the fourth month, the emperor publicly announced his repudiation of Taoism and embarked on his historic role as the greatest patron of Buddhism in Chinese history. Soon after this came measures against Taoists, including the obligatory return to lay life of many unmarried female Taoist practitioners.[104] There is no evidence that the effects of this were felt at Mao Shan, however. Indeed, the imperial proposal of an alchemical project so soon after the anti-Taoist decrees could be seen as an intentional reaffirmation of support for the eminent Taoist master. Viewed from the court, T'ao's alchemy would have been a continuation of the technological researches he had been conducting at Mao Shan, with official approval and assistance, starting in the previous dynasty. Even from the official standpoint, of course, such work was of more than material significance. The craft of making fine talismans was an essential component of dynastic prestige. Similarly, certain elixirs might prove to be beneficial to the imperial health. This is probably why T'ao chose the one elixir formula of the Perfected which, deadly as it was, also made provision for relatively modest therapeutic applications of the elixir's byproducts.[105]

102. *TPYL* 665:5a. This shows that Mao Shan continued to function as an officially recognized center of Taoist ordination even after the proscriptive measures of 504.

103. Shen Yüeh's 沈約 "Essay on the Equivalence of the Sages" (*Chün-sheng lun* 均聖論), together with T'ao's rebuttals, is found in the *Kuang-Hung ming chi* 廣弘明集 *T* LII. 2103. 121b–123a. We can date their efforts to 504, thanks to T'ao's use, in referring to Shen, of an official title that Shen held only in that year (*T* LII. 2103. 122a11; *Liang-shu* 梁書 13:7a1, Palace ed.).

104. The emperor's decree is contained in the *Kuang Hung-ming chi*, *T* LII. 2103. 112a ff.

105. We should also mention at this point, as evidence of T'ao's intimacy with the emperor, their exchange of correspondence on the subject of calligraphy which is preserved in the 2d *chüan* of the mid-ninth-century compilation, *Fa-shu yao-lu* 法書要錄, and reprinted in the various editions of T'ao's literary collection (e.g. 1:10b–18a, *HY* 1044/*TT* 726; see also *T'ao Chen-po chi* 陶貞白集, ed. with text-critical notes by Wang Chen-chih 汪振之 in *Chin-ling ts'ung-shu* 金陵叢書).

Confirmation of T'ao's close relationship with the emperor should not surprise us. A substantial proportion of the texts in the Taoist Canon owe their genesis and preservation to imperial patronage, and the successive Taoist canons were of course compiled, copied, and in time printed, all by imperial command.[106] Whatever winds of doctrine might be blowing at court, a commitment to the national higher religion, at least as represented by certain recognized institutions and reputable masters, was a durable feature of every native Chinese dynasty. For T'ao, however, the most considerable token of Emperor Wu's favor was still to come. In 514, the emperor ordered that the site of the Hsü family's old retreat at Mao Shan be purchased with a view toward establishing a state-sponsored hermitage (*kung-kuan* 公館) there for T'ao. The location was ten *li* to the north of T'ao's old Hua-yang Kuan, and had been occupied since the 420s by a small Taoist community.[107] Construction work on a grand scale was begun at once, and on the 19th of the tenth month, 515, T'ao installed himself in the new Chu-yang Kuan 朱陽館.[108] He had now truly become the master of all Mao Shan.

However, renewed disappointment concerning the Elixir of Nine Cycles followed close upon this worldly success. It was only four months later that T'ao's disciple, Chou Tzu-liang, received a revelation on that very subject. According to Book 4 of the *Ming-t'ung chi*, he was visited on the 25th of the second month, 516, by the two secretaries of Mao Shan's inner chanceries, with whom "the Elixir of Nine Cycles was much discussed."[109] Nothing more is said. In his note on this passage, T'ao bitterly laments that no fuller record of their remarks on the elixir survived among Chou's posthumous papers. T'ao was no visionary; otherworldly intimations seem to have come to him only in dreams. Chou had been secretive about his own visions while he was alive, and only now that he was dead did T'ao discover the opportunity for inquiry that he had let slip.

We should remember that the whole of the *Ming-t'ung chi*, as assembled and annotated by T'ao, was addressed to the emperor.[110] The series of

---

106. The relevant documents are reproduced in Ch'en Kuo-fu, *Tao-tsang yüan-liu k'ao* 1: 112–203. The first printing of the Canon was carried out ca. 1117–20, under Sung Hui Tsung, who had taken a great personal interest in its compilation and in the arrangement of its contents. Many of the basic anomalies in the organization of the present Ming Canon can be traced to this first printing and Hui Tsung's intervention (described in my article, "The Longest Taoist Scripture," *History of Religions* 17, nos. 3–4 [Feb.–May, 1978]: 331–54).

107. *CK* 11:15a–15b.

108. *MTC* 3:15b.

109. *MTC* 4:16b.

110. T'ao's letter of presentation and Wu Ti's response have been inserted in the text of the *Ming-t'ung chi* 1:7b–8a.

visitations by the Perfected to T'ao's disciple at Mao Shan, where at that very moment the finishing touches were being put to a new, officially sponsored temple, could be seen as a most favorable response by the unseen world to His Majesty's enlightened reign, and a fitting recompense for his munificent patronage of T'ao's projects. Yet, so far, the results of T'ao's alchemy had been meager, and now there had been this additional disappointment—a chance missed to elucidate the formula in which he had placed the greatest hopes.

The Case of Chou Tzu-liang (515–516)

One formula that does find elucidation in the *Ming-t'ung chi* appears to have been the means by which Chou Tzu-liang effected his translation into the caverns of Mao Shan: the Ninefold Perfected Jade-liquor Elixir (*chiu-chen yü-li tan* 九眞玉瀝丹), as transmitted by the Perfected Immortal Chou Tzu-yang 周紫陽. As the adolescent visionary noted himself, "He said that it is simpler than the Elixir of Nine Cycles."

> One *chin* of Lang-ko mushroom 琅葛芝, the nine-stalked purple fungus. [T'ao comments: Its place of origin is southern Fukien; it is also to be found north of Mao Shan.] Two *tou* of jade-infusion of vermilion. [T'ao: Also from southern Fukien, but found here at Mao Shan as well.][111]

The powdered mushrooms were to be steeped overnight in half the liquid and buried on the south side of the northern boundary-wall of one's living-compound, three inches from the wall and one foot beneath the earth. They were to be put there in an earthenware vessel of a minimal capacity of four pecks (*tou* 斗) and covered with another earthenware bowl, the vessels then being tightly sealed together with wax, to a thickness of two inches. The burial was to be carried out at noon of the same

---

111. *MTC* 4:19a–19b. It should be recalled that in the original text of this work (as indeed in all his other annotated textual editions) T'ao used ink of different colors and characters of different sizes to distinguish among the text itself, any original annotations, alterations, or superscriptions, and his own commentary. In the *Chen-kao* as it left his hands, large purple characters indicated that the passage so written was extracted by T'ao from Yang and the Hsüs' copies of the revealed scriptures of Shang-ch'ing. T'ao's own notes were written in small vermilion characters; small black characters were used for passages that figured as annotations in the original manuscripts—all this in addition to the large black characters that represented the original texts (*CK* 19:9a–9b).

These important distinctions have often been blurred or effaced in the process of transmission, and of course the present texts of all T'ao's works are monochromatic. We must remember, too, that in T'ao's day commentary was written in single, not double, columns of smaller characters within the body of the text. All this is a potential source of confusion, and careful scrutiny is often necessary to distinguish text from commentary. In the present passage of the *Ming-t'ung chi*, we must separate the note by Chou Tzu-liang, in the original manuscript which T'ao was editing, from the note added by T'ao just below it (which would originally have been written in vermilion) (*MTC* 1:8b).

day and the exhumation to be at noon on the morrow, after which the containers were to be carried back southward, in twelve strides, to one's dwelling and installed at the head of the bed. The next day, again at noon, the residuum was to be heated in a copper vessel, the fire being kept even under the bottom of the pot and not allowed to flame up along its sides. When it had fully come to a third boil, the remaining liquor was to be added and the whole mixture then boiled until there was a residuum of one peck. This was to be left sealed for three days. When at length the vessel was opened, it should give forth a dazzling purple radiance, such as might effectively replace a lamp for nighttime reading. This would be the sign that the elixir had been achieved.

The contents of the vessel were to be put in a wooden mortar and pounded with three hundred and twenty strokes of the pestle. If then wrapped tightly in paper and thrown into a stream, the current would at once come to a halt. A door sealed with the elixir would not open, though ten thousand men should tug at it. A throng of brigands would stand transfixed before it. A mountain on which it was pressed would open, while a man, given the same treatment, would fall prostrate. Should one desire to ascend to heaven with all due speed, he should swallow the potion at once: death would immediately follow. But if one wished to prolong his stay among men, he should consume it little by little, and when at last it had all been taken, he too would then find himself to be an immortal. It was not to be shared with others, nor was anyone else to be told of it or see it.[112]

It was probably this rudimentary vegetomineral compound of mushrooms and cinnabar that Chou had just swallowed when his mother and aunt rushed into his little house on Mao Shan and found him gasping out his life.[113] We are back once more in the world of decisive, suicidal alchemy, which was also, I believe, the atmosphere in which Hsü Hui passed his last days. That would not be the only resemblance between his case and that of Chou Tzu-liang. Through his alchemical suicide, Chou responded

---

112. *MTC* 4:19b–20a.

113. *MTC* 1:3b–4a. Tzu-liang had told his younger brother that he was not feeling well and intended to take some medicine. This news, when reported to Chou's aunt, roused her latent fears for the young visionary, and she sent the brother back to Tzu-liang at once—but from the doorway he saw Tzu-liang lying on the floor and did not dare to enter. The mother and aunt arrived soon after, crying out when they saw him, "What have you done, what have you done?" But Tzu-liang only closed his eyes, raised his hand, and snapped his finger three times, saying, "Don't cry out, don't cry out—you'll ruin everything!" His mother tried to lift his head, and in doing so happened to kick aside his cap. He raised his hand once more to straighten his cap, and a moment later he died.

to the summons he had received at the summer solstice of the preceding year, 515. This summons inaugurated the course of his brief career as a visionary. His visions did not begin until the pronouncement, in a strange waking dream, that he had been chosen for an administrative post in the hidden chanceries of Mao Shan.[114] The summons was "untimely" (like Hsü Hui's in 365) for, as his transcendent informant admitted, the rolls still allotted him forty-six years of life. "But why should you continue to linger on among men, sowing sins?"[115] Once again, the call of the Perfected proved irresistible.

The young were, of course, not the only ones subject to inopportune decrees of destiny. The examples of Chou Tzu-liang and Hsü Hui are the more poignant, though, because of their youth and unquestioning faith. T'ao at this time, aged sixty, had just completed a full cycle of years and was at the height of his eminence. It is therefore somewhat surprising to discover that he too, just at this point, was threatened with a call from the beyond. At one place in his commentary to the *Ming-t'ung chi* we read:

> In the fourth month of this year (515) I dreamt I was to receive a summons. It was said that all arrangements for the position had been made, only the seal of office had not yet been fashioned. I was extremely anxious, and straightaway informed Chou about it. He immediately mentioned it to his aunt who, without telling me, prepared offerings (*hui-hsin* 賵信) and instructed P'an Yüan-wen to write out the text of a statement (*tz'u* 辭).[116]

Here, then, at last was otherworldly notification, for lack of which T'ao had earlier declined to start work on either of the two most potent Shang-ch'ing elixirs. Now that the time had finally come, T'ao seems to have been less than elated by the prospect. In the event, Chou Tzu-liang obtained assurance from his contacts in the invisible world that T'ao's prospective summons would be postponed, information which he hastened to report to his master.[117] T'ao therefore still refrained from following

---

114. *MTC* 1:11a. The communicating spirit, a secretary in the Mao Shan cavern-palace administration, told him: "At present there is a vacant post in our chancery, and we should like you to fill it. The title and functions will be specified later, and there is no need for overmuch discussion now. You will be summoned in the tenth month of next year, and so should make all necessary preparations. That is why I have come to make this announcement to you. If you do not obey our orders, however, the lictors of the Three Offices will come for you—beware!" Later the same day, when another cavern-official appeared, Chou begged for a deferment of the summons (like Hsü Hui before him), but the spirit refused it and proceeded to give him instructions concerning his eventual place and manner of interment (*MTC* 1:14a–14b).

115. *MTC* 1:11a5.

116. *MTC* 3:4a.

117. *MTC* 4:3b.

the example of Hsü Hui—at any rate, he did not yet complete an elixir and he did not die.

T'ao's Alchemy in the Official Histories

After the *Ming-t'ung chi* of 516 there is no other major work of T'ao's against which to test the statements of his biographer.[118] It may be as well to turn now to the accounts of T'ao's life in the dynastic histories, which have so far been the principal sources from which modern scholars have drawn information about him, although the earliest one dates from nearly a century after his death. Here is the relevant passage from the *History of the Liang* (compilation ordered in 629), in the standard palace edition:

> At the beginning of the Ta-tung reign period [527–529] T'ao presented two elixirs to Emperor Wu. One was named Good Victory (*shan-sheng* 善勝), the other Accomplished Victory (*ch'eng-sheng* 成勝). Both were fine treasures.[119]

The text is corrupt and has caused some confusion. The latest critical edition of the *History of the Liang* simply gives the correct reading, *tao* 刀 "swords" for *tan* 丹 "elixirs," without comment.[120]

The garrulous *History of the South* (compiled in the following reign) repeats the same tale and, in the palace edition, the same corruption. It specifies a different year (528) for the swords' presentation, however, and states that T'ao had already given swords to the throne during the T'ien-chien reign-period (502–519). This latter claim is substantiated by the passage quoted earlier, in which T'ao declares that he submitted swords to Emperor Wu in 505. But the *History of the South* brings the swords on the scene only after having given what is clearly an account of alchemical activity:

> Hung-ching had obtained supernatural talismans and secret instructions. He considered that he might succeed in achieving an elixir, but was hindered by the lack of ingredients. The emperor supplied him with gold, cinnabar, malachite, realgar, and the rest, and he subsequently compounded a Sublimated Elixir (*fei-tan* 飛丹). It was the color of frost or snow, and when ingested made the body weightless. When the emperor had consumed this elixir, there were confirmatory effects, and he honored T'ao all the more.[121]

118. From the last two decades of T'ao's life, there remain only the texts of his inscriptions "At the Altar by the Old Hermitage of Senior-Officer Hsü" (518), and the memorial inscription on Ko Hsüan 葛玄, the "Duke-immortal" (522), both included in all editions of T'ao's literary collection, e.g. 2:1a–8b, *HY* 1044/*TT* 726 (see also n. 105, above).

119. *Liang-shu* 梁書 51:13b.

120. *Liang-shu* 51:743 (Peking, 1973 ed.). The correct reading is also found in Li Po's 李渤 *Chen-hsi* 真系 of 805 (*YCCC* 5:10b1).

121. *Nan-shih* 南史 76:15a.

For this historian, T'ao was a successful alchemist, and success in alchemy contributed to his good relations with Emperor Wu. Chia Sung's biography concludes on the same note of fulfillment; after several further inconclusive attempts, T'ao is there depicted as having achieved the Elixir of Nine Cycles in 525.[122] Yet in neither account is the product of all this labor described as functioning as a deadly catalyst of supreme transformation. It was, rather, a tonic iatro-alchemical compound—and both alchemist and emperor lived on.

In its concise résumé of developments in Taoism during the Six Dynasties, the bibliographical section of the *History of the Sui Dynasty* (apparently completed by 656) gives a contrasting version of these events:

> (T'ao Hung-ching) also maintained that a marvelous elixir (*shen-tan* 神丹) might be achieved, which upon ingestion would prolong one's life so as to be coterminous with heaven and earth. The emperor commanded Hung-ching to attempt to compound the marvelous elixir, but he was in the end unable to accomplish it. Thereupon he said that it was on account of the poor quality of the ingredients, now that communications with the central plain had been interrupted. The emperor believed this, and honored him all the more.[123]

In the same treatise T'ao is credited with a number of relevant works:

> *Assorted Arts of Refining and Transformation* (*Lien-hua tsa-shu* 練化雜術), one *chüan*.
> *Collected Essentials on the Elixirs of T'ai-ch'ing* (*T'ai-ch'ing chu-tan chi-yao* 太清諸丹集要), four *chüan*.
> *Rules for Timing in the Compounding of Elixirs* (*Ho-tan chieh-tu* 合丹節度), four *chüan*.
> To Sun Wen-t'ao 孫文韜, known to have been T'ao's disciple and an accomplished calligrapher, is attributed a *Prolegomena to a Résumé of Essentials for the Compounding of Elixirs* (*Ho-tan yao-lüeh hsü* 合丹要略序), one *chüan*.[124]

Thus, from texts preserved in the Taoist Canon we have been able to verify T'ao Hung-ching's practice of alchemy. Alchemy has also proved to be a useful theme around which to assemble some of the ample information about T'ao's life which is contained in his works. Moreover, we have discovered the presence of alchemical formulae among the Mao Shan

---

122. *NC* 2:15a.

123. *Sui-shu* 隋書 35:29b–30a.

124. *Sui-shu* 34:34a. Sun Wen-t'ao merited a notice in the *Records of Mao Shan*; he was the calligrapher of two of T'ao's major lapidary inscriptions (15:3a–3b, *HY* 304/*TT* 155).

revelations, and have been able to recover the greater part of the original texts. I shall now proceed to a more comprehensive analysis of the facts.

3 Alchemy in a Taoist Context

History and Taoist Definitions: The Way of the Celestial Master

Operative alchemy has for so long been a component of our preconceptions about Taoism that it is difficult at first to see that the grounds for the association are rather vaguely documented. If we are to assess the evidence, the first requirement is a satisfactory definition of Taoism itself. Despite the confusion apparent in so many English-language secondary sources, I do not think the problem of definition is nearly so difficult as has been presumed. We tend to forget, in this case, that we have the supreme advantage of hindsight, on which—for good or ill—all historical definitions are ultimately based.

At the present time, Taoism flourishes in Taiwan and Hong Kong. Taiwan has also provided a refuge for the Celestial Masters (*t'ien-shih* 天師), who claim descent from the first Celestial Master, Chang Tao-ling 張道陵 (second century A.D.). The sixty-third of the line came to Taiwan in 1949, and his successor lives there today. The *tao-shih* 道士 of Taiwan, who are married priests and live at home, seem generally to acknowledge the nominal authority of the present Celestial Master, and recognize in his distant ancestor the founder of their diverse, hierarchical orders.[125]

To my knowledge, all the Taoist priests of Hong Kong belong to a quite distinct tradition, the Lung-men 龍門 lineage of the Ch'üan-chen 全眞 order. Ch'üan-chen Taoism was founded with the support of the Mongol ruling house during the Yüan dynasty.[126] Its priests (and priestesses) are supposed to be celibate and to dwell in convents. The present representatives of the sect seem to have no interest in the current Celestial Master, but they do venerate the first Celestial Master as the founder of their religion.[127]

125. This emerges from the various writings on Taiwanese Taoism by K. M. Schipper, the outstanding authority, e.g. "The Written Memorial in Taoist Ceremonies," in A. P. Wolf, ed., *Religion and Ritual in Chinese Society* (Stanford, Calif., 1974), pp. 311 and 316, and still more clearly from his unpublished essays.

126. In addition to Waley's *Travels of an Alchemist* (London, 1931), the reader is referred to the standard work of Ch'en Yüan 陳垣, *Nan-sung ch'u ho-pei hsin tao-chiao k'ao* 南宋初河北新道教考 (Peking, 1941), and the more recent studies by Kubo Noritada, among them *Chūgoku no shūkyō kaikaku* 中國の宗教改革 (Kyoto, 1967).

127. Information obtained from Mr. You Che Joy 游自在, president of the Hsüan Tsung Taoist Society of Hong Kong 道教玄宗協會 and his associates, Hong Kong, August 1972.

If we were to proceed with this comparative method of reconstructing a kind of original language of Taoist belief and practice from the common elements found in these two separate traditions, as well as in the older texts of the canon, we could, of course, go very much further. For our present purpose, we have only to note that the high evaluation of Chang Tao-ling was shared by the original recipients of the Mao Shan revelations, as well as by T'ao Hung-ching.[128] Indeed, as we read more of the texts in the Taoist Canon, we come increasingly to realize that every new Taoist group which came into being over the centuries recognized the fundamental position of the first Celestial Master in the history of the religion—though they may well have had no relations at all with the "Celestial Masters" of their own day. Even many of the most truly original of latter-day Taoist movements represented themselves as restoring practices of the first Celestial Master which had been hidden or misconstrued by his disciples.

Chang Tao-ling and his immediate followers clearly effected a religious revolution. They inaugurated a new dispensation that defined itself, then as now, not in relation to Buddhism or "Confucianism," but rather in antithesis to the false gods whom the benighted populace worshipped with blood offerings. Though the early Taoists spoke of high antiquity, of the Yellow Emperor Yü the Great and the famous immortals of the Chou dynasty, and though they used the *Lao-tzu* for their own purposes, the social history of Taoism begins with the founding of the Way of the Celestial Master in the second century A.D.

Thus, I am proposing to use the word *Taoist* only in referring to those who recognize the historical position of Chang Tao-ling, who worship the pure emanations of the Tao rather than the vulgar gods of the people at large, and—I may add—who safeguard and perpetuate their own lore and practices through esoteric rites of transmission. In other words, I should like to restrict the term to the Way of the Celestial Master and the organizations that grew out of it. To me, this definition seems to emerge naturally from study of the texts in the Taoist Canon. Yet I recognize that for many others in the English-speaking world—which has a profusion of translations of the *Lao-tzu* and *Chuang-tzu* but, so far, none of

---

128. In the Mao Shan revelations a careful distinction is made between the integrity of the Celestial Master, Chang Tao-ling, and the degenerate practices of his latter-day followers. The sexual rites of the Way of the Celestial Master, for example, were said to have been used by Chang as an alluring means of converting the multitudes, but he never practiced them himself (*CK* 2:1a5, 9). His grandson, Chang Lu 張魯, is also mentioned with respect, but no reference is made to later successors. A fifth-century text from Chiang-nan 江南 is explicit on the subsequent falling-off of the line (1:7a6–8, *HY* 1196/*TT* 876).

any major Taoist religious text—such a view may be difficult to comprehend.

Still, whether or not my own criteria are accepted, I maintain that utter and disgraceful confusion will flourish in Sinology as long as scholars try to define Taoism without reference to the contents of the Taoist Canon, and without taking into account the complexities of Chinese social history. Lacking a solid documentary and historical framework of this kind, efforts toward discussion are commonly based upon what is assumed to be Taoist doctrine—and such assumptions, often as not, are founded on unalloyed hagiography. One might as well attempt, as an outsider, so to define Buddhism or Christianity. Such definitions are inevitably founded upon a priori notions, or else on the obiter dicta of a tiny elite, rather than upon observed facts. *Taoist* is potentially a clear, unambiguous technical term denoting China's indigenous higher religion, and should not be debased by being made to serve as a denomination for everything Chinese that does not fit our own notions of what is Buddhist or (still worse) "Confucian."

As for all the technology, I see no reason to call it "Taoist" except where it occurs in an indubitably Taoist social context. The history of Taoism would obviously gain enormously in precision if we were to see it as a succession of social groups developing out of the Way of the Celestial Master, with considerable local incidence of assimilation and syncretism (as we find in the Mao Shan revelations from fourth-century Chiang-nan). Surely the various technologies would also emerge more clearly against the backdrop of Chinese society if visualized as separate entities, weaving in and out of Taoist (and other) contexts in the course of history, rather than as somehow being integral parts of a "Taoism" that depends on them for its definition yet lacks any social dimension.

Finally, what is to become of "philosophical Taoism"? I earnestly hope that this term will be allowed to revert to the original restricted usage of its Chinese model, *tao-chia* 道家, as a bibliographic classification. It seems to me that the two opposing faces of Taoism, philosophical and religious, which have been posited by modern scholars, in reality represent two such disparate phenomena that they do not admit of meaningful comparison. Still less do they invite a factitious union under a single descriptive term. The classics of "philosophical Taoism" are anonymous compilations of the Warring States period; in later times they were indiscriminately read and quoted by the whole scholar-official class. Did one become a "Taoist" by citing the *Chuang-tzu* in one sentence, and a "Confucian" by referring to the *Analects* in the next? It is to the Warring States and early empire that "philosophical Taoism" belongs—in short, to the prehistory of Taoism.[129]

Who, for example, can name a "philosophical Taoist" from the Six Dynasties period? The unwary may reply with an array of "neo-Taoists" of the third and fourth centuries; they should be referred to E. Zürcher's lucid demonstration of the inaccuracy of this term and the inanity of its implications.[130] The Taoists of medieval China were men and women who ultimately owed their authority and their corporate identity to the revelation received by Chang Tao-ling, and of these Taoists, T'ao Hung-ching was one of the most "philosophical."

After the founding of the Taoist religion in west China (the traditional date for the Most High's revelation to Chang Tao-ling is A.D. 142), the next significant date in Taoist history is 215, when Chang's grandson, Chang Lu 魯, submitted to the Han general Ts'ao Ts'ao and went to live in Yeh 鄴 (Hopei). During the following hundred years, many great families of the north were converted to the religion. It was the fall of the Lo-yang in 311 that spread the Way of the Celestial Master to all of China. At that time the imperial house (by then of the Chin dynasty) and nearly the whole official class moved south of the Yangtze, establishing their capital in present-day Nanking. Their religion went south with them.

There is no evidence that Chang Tao-ling or his immediate successors ever practiced alchemy.[131] It is hard to see how operative alchemy could

129. It is important to note that the term *tao-chia* 道家, after the Han, came to be yet another way of referring to Taoist priests. This does not, of course, indicate any necessary identity between pre-Han "Taoist" speculations and post-Han religious developments; rather, it suggests that we rely too heavily upon nominal distinctions, as we conceive them, without taking adequate account of the real extent of Chinese semantic boundaries as revealed in centuries of usage. Concerning the terminology applicable to pre-Han thought, I feel that the *Lao-tzu* should simply be referred to as the *Lao-tzu*, and the *Chuang-tzu* as the *Chuang-tzu*—each is clearly the product of a distinct milieu, and the considerable differences between them have often been remarked by later Chinese authors; there is no intrinsic justification for creating a "Taoism" on the basis of these two texts. Now that nearly everything from their period has been translated at least once, surely specialists in pre-Han thought could afford to be just a bit more precise.

130. E. Zürcher, *The Buddhist Conquest of China* (Leiden, 1959), p. 87.

131. The earliest extant hagiographical account of Chang is from the *Shen-hsien chuan* 神仙傳, composed in early fourth-century Chiang-nan. This collection was an important source of the hagiography contained in the Mao Shan revelations, as T'ao's notes to the *Chen-kao* make clear. In his account of the Celestial Master, the unknown author of the *Shen-hsien chuan* was already attempting a fusion of this seminal figure, patron saint of the newly arrived northern Taoists, with southern tradition. He credits Chang with alchemical practice, and the high point of the narrative is the arrival of Chang's destined disciple, Chao

have been accommodated to their strict parish administration and round of ritual. The primary concern of the priests of the Way of the Celestial Master is said to have been the curing of disease. No drugs were to be used for this purpose, however. Sickness was the result of transgression—whether one's own or that of one's ancestors. Their therapeutic methods were therefore supposed to have consisted of confession and prayer, and this description of the early Way of the Celestial Master is confirmed by the oldest of its liturgical texts to have been preserved. It speaks of forgiveness, health, and limitless material abundance.[132] Yet in the course of the third century, many of the upper-class members of the Way of the Celestial Master became addicted to the fashionable mineral drugs then currently in use in Lo-yang, particularly the redoubtable "cold-food powder" (han-shih san 寒食散).[133] Already the strict rules of the organization had been breached by new ideas and practices of a pharmacochemical nature. This process of infiltration was to be greatly accelerated by the movement's extension to the region south of the Yangtze.

The Southern Occult Tradition

When members of the Way of the Celestial Master arrived in Chiang-nan after the fall of Lo-yang, they found a flourishing drug-culture. To understand how central a place pharmaka occupied in the spiritual traditions of third- and fourth-century Chiang-nan, one need only read through the most representative texts: the inner chapters of the Pao-p'u tzu, and the Five Ling-pao Talismans, both of which bristle with names of drugs.[134] Ko Hung, author of the Pao-p'u tzu, was related to both the Hsüs and the T'aos. All belonged to a group of families who had been in the south since the end of the second century A.D. and had served as officials of the Wu dynasty. These families spoke their own dialect and proudly preserved Han traditions of scholarship which their ancestors had brought with them

Sheng 趙昇 of Wu. Significantly, a bogus suicide figures importantly in the story: T'ai-p'ing kuang-chi 太平廣記 (Peking, 1959), 8:55–58.

132. TCYC 3:10b–11a. This text is certainly as early as the beginning of the fourth century. In my opinion, it may go back earlier still, close to the origins of the movement.

133. On which the basic study remains that of Yü Chia-hsi 余嘉錫, "Han-shih san k'ao" 寒食散考, in Fu-jen hsüeh-chih 輔仁學誌 7:29–63 (1938). See also Rudolph G. Wagner, "Lebensstil und Drogen im chinesischen Mittelalter," T'oung Pao 59:79–178 (1973).

134. T'ai-shang ling-pao wu-fu hsü 太上靈寶五符序, HY 388/TT 183. It has been assumed that the first of this work's three chüan dates from the third century; the following two chüan are supposed to be later, or at least contain later interpolations; see Max Kaltenmark, "Ling-pao, note sur un terme du taoïsme religieux," in Mélanges publiés par l'Institut des Hautes Etudes Chinoises (Paris, 1960), 2: 559–588, and Ch'en Kuo-fu, Tao-tsang yüan-liu k'ao, pp. 62–66. The text was known in its present form to T'ao Hung-ching, writing at the end of the fifth century (Honzōkyō shūchū, p. 78D).

to Chiang-nan.[135] They also maintained a spiritual legacy that included a cult of the immortals based on Han beliefs. To judge by the *Five Ling-pao Talismans* and the *Pao-p'u tzu*, pharmacology and alchemy formed an important part of their heritage.

By the 320s these families had all found it expedient to pledge their loyalty to the Way of the Celestial Master, the religion of many of their new overlords, refugees from the north. The question then arose of what to do with their own spiritual traditions. Synthesis was the inevitable answer, and it came in the form of revelation. The Mao Shan texts provide the most comprehensive testimony to the integration of old southern beliefs and practices within the social and liturgical framework provided by the Way of the Celestial Master. Out of this mingling was born a new Taoism of the intelligentsia which, by the end of the Six Dynasties period, had in its turn spread to all of China.

The recipients of the Mao Shan revelations continued to perform morning and evening obeisance to the celestial lords, emanations of the Tao, as revealed to Chang Tao-ling. A version of the standard liturgical text was included in the matter revealed to Yang Hsi.[136] But these southerners, having broader spiritual interests, were conscious of an additional metaphoric dimension as they knelt before the smoking incense-burners that would speed their prayers heavenward. At the conclusion of the office they added a phrase that had not been present in the older liturgy: "Thurifer-emissary, Lords Dragon and Tiger of Left and Right, may there suddenly be in this oratory the Mushroom, Liquefied Gold, Essence of Cinnabar, and all transcendent powers intermingling before the flame of this incense-burner."[137] The incense-burner was thus assimilated to the alchemist's furnace. The officials of the Celestial Master's heavenly hierarchy were pressed into service to procure the old obsessions of the south, including the elixirs and the mushrooms of immortality about which Ko Hung had so eloquently written.

Structure: Toward an Astroalchemy

The liturgical metaphor was to prove extremely fecund. The alchemy of

135. See my article, "The Mao Shan Revelations; Taoism and the Aristocracy," *T'oung Pao* 63, 1: passim (1977).

136. *TCYC* 3:5b–10b. This text was originally appended to the *Life of the Lady Wei, Wei fu-jen chuan* 魏夫人傳 (now lost). Wei Hua-ts'un 魏華存 was said to have been a libationer (*chi-chiu* 祭酒) in the Way of the Celestial Master, and to have received this liturgy directly from the Celestial Master himself in the course of a midnight vision (*TCYC* 3:5b6).

137. *TCYC* 3:10b3–4. A modified version of this phrase continued to figure in liturgy and is still intoned at the present day; see Needham, vol. 5, pt. 2, pp. 130–31.

the oratory (*ching-shih* 靜室: essentially a closely sealed meditation chamber, an athanor in itself) seems already to announce the "internal alchemy" (*nei-tan* 內丹) of later times. Meanwhile the texts we have been studying clearly show that some adepts, at least, did not confine their alchemical efforts to forming an idealized, vaporous elixir in the smoke of their incense-burners. Still, Ko Hung's alchemy, his earthbound immortals, and his optimal heaven of T'ai-ch'ing were by now all outmoded. It remained for the Perfected of Shang-ch'ing to provide newer, more suitable instructions and a worthier goal.

Now that we have unearthed the Shang-ch'ing alchemical literature, we must try to put some order into it. We have found the names of four major elixirs and the formulae for three of them. We must now see if we can discover something about their relationship to one another, and sketch a line of development among them.

Surprisingly enough, this is quite easily done. We can set the three texts in their relative positions by the simple criterion of complexity. The Elixir of Nine Cycles which T'ao eventually selected for his imperially sponsored project is by far the most conservative of the three formulae. It is also the simplest, being purely mineral and having the least number of ingredients—only seven, compared to the Lang-kan's fourteen and the twenty-four of the Fourfold Floreate (see below, p. 171ff.). The Elixir of Nine Cycles seems to come directly from the old traditions represented in the *Pao-p'u tzu*, and the straightforward presentation of its formula is reminiscent of Ko Hung's descriptions of laboratory procedure. Its language is unexalted and it makes provision for a therapeutic application of the elixir's byproducts. Also suggestive of an uncertainty of direction is the curious and sudden shift, at the climax, to the making of gold and silver by projection—as though the author still wondered if he should depart as an immortal or linger on and make a heap of gold. All the evidence combines to place this work at a very early stage in the Mao Shan literature, before the glowing vegetomineral structures of the Perfected had fully taken shape in the upper air. The *Life of Lord Mao* which contained the elixir formula was one of the first texts transmitted by Yang Hsi to the Hsüs in 364, when they were still just coming to learn of the tremendous spiritual resources of Mao Shan.

We have seen that the elixir formula was followed in the *Life of Lord Mao* by a description of the five mushrooms which Lord Mao himself is said to have sown at Mao Shan. The juxtaposition of alchemy and occult horticulture is very suggestive. When we proceed to the second text of the three, the Lang-kan formula, we must suspect that it came into being through a conscious fusion of the two types of instructions, originally discretely mineral and vegetable, in the *Life of Lord Mao*.

With the Lang-kan formula, we are in a world grown more luxuriant in every way. It doubles the number of ingredients to fourteen and increases the complexity of the operations. After describing the preparation of a basic mineral elixir, it proceeds to narrate its strange vegetable transformations. The language of the formula is elaborate and diffuse, and includes rhymed incantations. What is more, the Lang-kan Elixir's standing is appreciably higher than that of the Nine Cycles. It was compounded by the Lord of the Golden Porte himself, the Sage Who Is to Come, and its revelation formed part of the lofty announcement of the imminent otherworldly imperium over which that ruler of the heaven of Shang-ch'ing would preside. The *Purple Script* containing the elixir formula was probably transmitted to Hsü Mi by Yang early in 365, by which time both the central message and the literary form of the Mao Shan revelations had become more clearly defined.[138]

For a fuller view of developments in Taoist alchemy, we must now consider the last of what T'ao termed the "supreme methods of the Exalted Perfected," one we have not yet studied. With the instructions for preparing the Fourfold Floreate Elixir, we pass beyond the original Mao Shan revelations into the burgeoning Taoist literature of the early fifth century.[139]

At least that is what I think we can infer from T'ao's suspicions concerning this formula's "authenticity." The twenty-four-ingredient Fourfold Floreate Elixir is certainly later than the Lang-kan, which is mentioned in the preface to the formula; and though the text contains elements of the characteristic Mao Shan vocabulary, the coherence is gone. It is a patchwork, a pastiche. And as if in anticipation of doubts about its orthodoxy, authorship of the formula is attributed to Chang Tao-ling himself.[140]

Fourteen of the elixir's ingredients are identical with those required by the Lang-kan formula and are designated by the same cover-names, with one variant.[141] The remaining ten ingredients include amber, pearls,

138. See p. 135, above.

139. On the imitation and elaboration of Mao Shan scriptures, a lucrative activity which developed mightily at that time, see part 2 of my article "The Mao Shan Revelations; Taoism and the Aristocracy," *T'oung Pao* 63, 1:19–30 (1977).

140. The Fourfold Floreate formula has been preserved in two texts. The ascription to the Celestial Master is found in the older of these, 2:8b10–18a3, *HY* 1365/*TT* 1042. It has prudently been expunged from the later, eleventh-century edition, *YCCC* 68:1a–9b.

141. Alum (*shih-tai* 石黛) in the Lang-kan formula bears the sobriquet "Volatile Efflores-

"dragon bones," lodestone, haematite, and five vegetable substances, among them three potent aromatics.[142] In this opulent formula, plants and minerals are mingled from the outset.

After preliminary fasting and purification, the ingredients are to be separately pounded and placed in a retort according to their sequence in the formula, with the last ingredient, haematite ("surplus rations of T'ai-i" 太乙餘粮), on top of all the others. Five *chin* of quicksilver are then to be poured over the mixture, and the vessels firmly luted together.

As in the earlier formulae, firing is to be precisely phased. Starting with the fire one foot from the bottom of the retort, the distance is gradually diminished until the flame reaches the rim of the lower vessel, in stages of 18, 9, 7, 5, 27, 30, and 24 days—a total of 120 days of firing. The elixir is then complete.

The luminous finished elixir is described as improving its consumer's appearance, as well as giving him access to the secret resorts of the Perfected. What is more, it could be regularly taken in a mixture of hemp juice. A daily dosage allowed one to divide his body and become ten thousand men, and to ride through the air. In other words, we may infer that it produced sensations of pluricorporality and levitation.[143]

These last instructions seem to reflect their hallucinatory aura back on the preparation of the elixir itself. We shall perhaps never be able to make a clear distinction between cause and effect in the narratives written by the enthusiastic theoreticians of alchemy, who, even as they wrote, were subjecting themselves to pharmaceutical regimens that we cannot hope to

cence of the Emerald Citadel" (*pi-ch'eng fei-hua* 碧城飛華, 2b7, *HY* 255/*TT* 120). The Fourfold Floreate text dubs it "Cultured Marquess of the Emerald Hill" (*pi-ling wen-hou* 碧陵文侯, 2:10b7, *HY* 1365/*TT* 1042; *YCCC* 68:2b7).

142. *Hsün-lu hsiang* 薰陸香, *ch'ing-mu hsiang* 青木香, and *chi-she hsiang* 雞舌香.

143. The formula for the hemp-juice potion was older than the Fourfold Floreate formula itself, and a copy existed, in Hsü Mi's handwriting, lacking one ingredient mentioned in the later text (*CK* 10:4b–5a). It is thanks to T'ao's note on this fragment that we are able to identify the Fourfold Floreate formula. It should be remarked that another preparation, the *Ch'u-shen wan* 初神丸 ("Bolus of Incipient Marvels"), also contained a substantial proportion of hemp. The formula is given in a text from the very end of the fourth century, the *Life of Chou Tzu-yang, Tzu-yang chen-jen nei-chuan* 紫陽眞人內傳 (pp. 4a–4b, *HY* 303/ *TT* 152). But it was already in use among the first Mao Shan adepts. In a letter to Hsü Mi, Yang Hsi inquired if he had begun to take the pills. Of his own experience, Yang writes: "I have been taking them regularly every day, from the lot which I obtained earlier. I have not really noticed any special signs, except, at the very beginning, for six or seven days, I felt a sensation of heat in my brain, and my stomach was rather bubbly. Since then there have been no other signs, and I imagine that they must gradually be dealing with the problem" (*CK* 17:15a2–4). The stated purpose of these pills was to improve health by eliminating the Three Worms (*san-ch'ung* 三蟲, or corpse-spectres, *san-shih* 三尸) from the body—but their incidental contribution to visionary susceptibility may have been considerable.

reconstruct in full. "Theory" comes to mind more readily here, in that the Fourfold Floreate text in some ways seems further removed than our other formulae from actual laboratory practice. Despite its derivation from Mao Shan materials, its affinities do not appear to lie with the suicidal alchemy that we have considered in the cases of Hsü Hui, Chou Tzu-liang, and T'ao Hung-ching himself.

The most promising line of approach in this instance seems to be a symbolic one. This is indeed already suggested by the numerical emphases of the elixir's full title: Wondrous Elixir of the Five Pearls and Crimson Life, Fourfold Floreate Purple Liquor of the Eight Effulgences of the Most High.[144] The word *ching* 景, which I am translating as "effulgence," is a key term in the Mao Shan revelations and their derivative literature. The visionary Yang Hsi realized a union with a celestial maiden, and a similar match was promised to Hsü Mi. The expression used in both cases is *ou-ching* 偶景, "pairing effulgences." It seems intended to mark a clear contrast to the "mingling of [sexual] breaths" (*ho-ch'i* 合氣) that designated the ritual union of mere mortals practiced within the Way of the Celestial Master. The "effulgences" here are the luminous spirits of the two partners, one airborne, one terrestrial. They meet and mingle in a pure atmosphere free from carnal passion.[145]

The *ching* are essentially bodies of light, and it is thus that they are visualized in the celebrated *Book of the Yellow Court*. The version of this text revealed to Yang Hsi was appropriately designated "of the inner effulgences" (*Huang-t'ing nei-ching ching* 黃庭內景經).[146] This work in later times became the most famous of all the Mao Shan texts and gave rise to a considerable literature of its own. It provides a comprehensive review of the indwelling spirits that people and regulate the three divisions of the body. The "inner effulgences" correspond to the thrice-eight spirits, the "twenty-four gods" described in earlier Taoist texts.[147] Thus,

144. *T'ai-shang pa-ching ssu-jui tzu-chiang wu-chu chiang-sheng shen-tan* 太上八景四蘂紫漿五珠絳生神丹, *YCCC* 68:1a4.

145. The expression *ou-ching* seems to embody a deliberate pun on the common term *ou-ying* 偶影—the hermit-ascetic who withdraws to the mountains "with only his own shadow for company." The characters *ching* and *ying* are interchangeable in medieval texts.

146. K. M. Schipper has published a valuable concordance to both this Mao Shan text and the older "outer" *Book of the Yellow Court* on which it was freely based, including critical editions of the two scriptures: *Concordance du Houang-t'ing king* (Publications de l'Ecole française d'Extrême-Orient, vol. 104, Paris, 1975).

147. A Mao Shan manual of the 24 spirits is copiously annotated by T'ao Hung-ching in *TCYC* 1:3a–11b. His commentary elsewhere in the same work reveals the essential fact that a 25th spirit exists, ruling over all the others (*TCYC* 3:22b7). This is also reflected in our elixir formula (n. 148). The first part of *HY* 405/*TT* 191 is a Mao Shan text that reproduces a rather earlier, simpler schema of 24 spirits.

the eight effulgences of our elixir's title appear to be related to at least one of the three vertically staged sets of inner spirit-officers and so, by extension, to the whole array of twenty-four. This is no haphazard speculation based on numerical accident: the elixir formula explicitly states that its twenty-four ingredients correspond to the twenty-four gods within the body.[148]

The term "eight effulgences" puzzled Maspero and has recently been studied anew by Max Kaltenmark.[149] The problem lay in the expression's multiple field of reference. Not only did *ching* designate luminous spirits dwelling within the body of the adept, it also referred to the brilliance of the heavenly constellations. In view of all we have been able to glean from the Mao Shan texts, however, this is less a source of bewilderment than a key to understanding. In this very plurality of levels, envisioned simultaneously, we may perhaps perceive the conceptual pivot by means of which, in this formula, mortals were turned into immortals, and the limited and contingent was perfected and made perdurable.

In the Mao Shan revelations, the stars loomed uncommonly large. The brilliant perfected-immortals who descended into Yang Hsi's midnight room were lords and ladies of the constellations. Ritual at Mao Shan was directed toward astral divinities, who were the oldest and purest manifestations of the Tao. The rising sequence of heavenly palaces unveiled by successive revelations in the course of the fourth and fifth centuries involved the incorporation into ritual of ever more precisely delimited celestial bodies and their canonical protocols. This development was a natural consequence of the fusion of the Way of the Celestial Master with the technologically well-endowed southern occult tradition.

Yang Hsi's preceptors were members of a band of twenty-four perfected-immortals, whose mission had been announced in the *Annals of the Sage Who is to Come*.[150] They were to descend into the world of men

---

148. YCCC 68:3b; 2:11b, HY 1365/TT 1042. The quicksilver poured over the 24 vertically stacked ingredients corresponds to the 25th, all-encompassing spirit mentioned in the preceding note.

149. "*Ching yü pa-ching*" 景與八景, in the Fukui Kōjun 福井康順 Festschrift, *Tōyō bunka ronshū* 東洋文化論集 (Tokyo, 1969), pp. 1147–54. Cf. Henri Maspero, *Le taoïsme et les religions chinoises* (Paris, 1971), p. 494 n. 1; p. 588.

150. P. 7b, HY 442/TT 198. The Sage declares: "And I shall delegate certain ones to descend and give instruction to those who are so destined and who devoutly maintain their zealous study to achieve immortality. I shall send Ma Ming 馬明, Chang Ling 張陵, Yin Sheng 陰生, Wang Pao 王褒, Mo Ti, Ssu-ma Chi-chu, and from the Cavern-terrace of the Heaven of Pure Vacuity [n. 94, above], seven perfected and eight elders. There will be twenty-four in all, some of whose names shall be hidden, and others manifest. When they have altered their original clan-names and by-names it will be hard indeed to determine their real identities. Yet you have only to continue zealous and devoutly resolute, and you

and instruct those mortals who were destined to participate in the new order. To a favored disciple like Yang, they manifested themselves outwardly, before his eyes. For the average practitioner of no special visionary aptitude, however, the miniature internal spirits were probably easier to visualize. These luminous objects of inward contemplation were also twenty-four in number; and what is more, they followed a course exactly parallel to that of the Perfected. The effulgences within the body were not always present there, ready to hand. They had to be brought down and incorporated into the adept through his own concentrated vision, for they too were spirits of the stars.

In this way, through contemplation, the mortal plane could be infused and animated by essences from the highest celestial spheres, where the stars and time were one. For the fifth-century adept, there would have been little need to make these correspondences explicit. Mention of *eight* effulgences would immediately conjure up the remaining two sets of eight. Groups of three naturally implied a vertical axis.[151] Thus, the very term "eight effulgences" would inevitably propel the elixir's compounder upward, the more so in that all his prior meditations would have had as their aim an incorporation of star-substance.

To complete his symbolic metamorphosis, the alchemist was instructed to bedeck his person with a product of the elixir's final transformations, five pearls.[152] Even as threes imply verticality, groups of fives are deployed upon a horizontal plane, in the four quarters and the center.[153] Hung about with these five gleaming periapts and enclosing the thrice-eight luminous spirit-substances, the mortal-immortal being would achieve his transformation and enjoy a mastery over all of space.

---

shall yourself of a certainty come to behold them. Once you have seen them, they will decline to you their full identities."

151. The number three embodies a hierarchy of degrees, as in *shang chung hsia* 上中下, and in the cosmic triad (*san-ts'ai* 三才) that places man squarely between heaven and earth. It should be noted that in addition to their associations with the stars and with man, elixirs were often assimilated to a third, intermediate stage, as the vehicle for man's ascent to the stars: a white crane (n. 24, above), the "airborne covered-carriage of the Winding Constellation" (n. 27, above, and *Annals of the Sage*, p. 2a6, HY 442/TT 198), or a "jade car of the Eight Effulgences" (*pa-ching ch'iung-yü* 八景瓊輿 in CK 5:4b3, and *Annals of the Sage*, p. 2b5).

152. The five pearls also figure prominently in the elixir's full title (n. 144, above).

153. Five planets, elements, sacred peaks, all represent a basic interchangeability of function on a single level. One is naturally drawn to compare the analogous union on the adept's person of the two prototypical texts of southern occult literature, the *Script of the Three High Lords, San-huang nei wen* 三皇內文 and the *Five Talismans, Wu fu* 五符, or the *Diagrams of the Five Peaks, Wu-yüeh chen-hsing t'u* 五嶽眞形圖, on which see K. M. Schipper, "*Gogaku-shingyozu no shinkō*" 五岳眞形圖の信仰 (*Le Wou-yue tchen-hing-t'ou et son culte*), *Dōkyō kenkyū* 道教研究 / *Etudes taoïstes* 2:114–62 (Tokyo, 1967).

Even before being enabled to make free with the cosmos, the adept was capable, in his alchemy, of overcoming the normal limitations imposed on the elements and could transcend their obstructive separateness. Not only did water and fire hold no terrors for him; using the flame of his furnace, he was able to liquefy and then amalgamate metal and wood within the baked earth of his retort. Thus all five elements lent themselves to his purpose. The fusion of plants and minerals—which we have found elaborately expressed in the list of ingredients for the Fourfold Floreate Elixir and the successive processes of the Lang-kan, and which was pathetically reflected in Chou Tzu-liang's compound of mushrooms and cinnabar—was in one sense an indication of the mortal-immortal's comprehensive power over the elements. It might also have been seen as an anticipation of the ultimate apocalyptic fusion that would, in time, fashion a new earth and populate it with a new, perfected race. Yet the elemental affinity of plants and minerals rested on a broader basis of observation and speculation.

Both shared a single theater of life and growth, the earth. The effects of mineral deposits upon the plant-life above them had long been noted, and relations presumably not observed in nature were conjectured by analogy.[154] Plants and minerals were also related by similar patterns of growth. Like the more lasting of the plants overhead, minerals slowly grew to full maturity, passing from less perfect to more perfect forms.[155] As in the case of plants, with the apogee of growth came special powers of transformation. The pines that T'ao Hung-ching planted at Mao Shan, when grown to full thousand-year maturity, would add their arboreal magic to the mountain's spiritual resources.[156] The hidden mushrooms that had been sown there by Lord Mao were already operative in T'ao's own day. Similarly, the mountain drew force from its extensive deposits of the most highly perfected minerals, including eight or nine thousand *chin* each of gold and white jade. Lord Mao had also planted there six

---

154. J. Needham, *Science and Civilisation in China* (Cambridge, 1959), 3:675–80, "Geobotanical and bio-geochemical prospecting."

155. Needham, 3:636–41, "The Theory of chhi and the growth of metals in the earth."

156. T'ao matter-of-factly mentions his afforestation of Mao Shan ("The mountain is especially well suited for pine and thuya, only no one has ever planted them here and there is no way for them to get started by themselves. Now I am planting them over the mountainside every year," *CK* 11:11a2). It also figures, suitably romanticized, in the dynastic histories ("He especially loved the wind in the pines, and so planted pines in his courtyard; he was delighted whenever he heard them rustling," *Nan-shih* 76:11a)—should they not be called "the dynastic novelettes"?

thousand *chin* of Khotanese cinnabar: a fully ripened source of immense power and light.[157]

Though their common matrix was terrestrial, the rhythms of growth of the diverse vegetable and mineral species were complex protocols of time determined by a higher power. The interlocking patterns of their development in the earth met in the heavens, in the pure sphere of the eternal stars. Indeed, this astral determination was shared by all matter, as well as by all morality. Since Han times at least, the stars had been recognized as embodying the essences of all things.[158] The heavenly bodies were the earliest crystallizations of the original Tao, and it was their primordial and pristine qualities that men found most impressive. In the words of the *I-ching*, the stars were the celestial images, or emblems, of all material forms below: "In the heavens [the Tao] made images; on earth, forms."[159] Stars and planets were pure bodies of light but nevertheless had close relationships with all the earth's varieties of tangible matter. The movements of the stars regulated all nature. Stellar bodies were portentous of events in human society, and often appeared on earth to quicken wombs destined for auspicious births.

No less did their rays and rhythms impregnate plants and minerals. Astral influence on plant and mineral growth was first recorded in the context of omen lore. It was in the Han apocrypha that the association of terrestrial matter with the stars was most elaborately propounded. In the surviving fragments of this literature, we learn of the relationship between different vegetable and mineral species and the planets, asterisms, or individual stars by which they are ruled. Jupiter and Venus (planets of earth and metal, respectively) determine the fate of the harvest; the Winnowing Basket (*Chi* 箕, Sagittarius) is the spirit of the mulberry; the seventh star of the Dipper, Waving Radiance (*Yao-kuang* 搖光), beckons mushrooms and cinnabar forth to ripeness.[160]

Thus, if plants and minerals conform to common patterns of growth,

---

157. *CK* 11:9b–10a. Cinnabar was, of course, the most fully perfected of all minerals, and synonymous with "elixir."

158. *Shuo-wen* 說文, quoted in *TPYL* 5:1a: 萬物之精, 上爲列星.

159. *I-ching* 易經, *Hsi-tz'u* 繫辭 1:359 (*Shih-san ching chu-shu* 十三經注疏 ed.): 在天成象, 在地成形.

160. Yasui Kōzan 安居香山 and Nakamura Shōhachi 中村璋八, *Isho shūsei* 緯書集成, vol. 4, pt. A (Apocrypha on the *Spring and Autumn Annals*; Tokyo, 1963), pp. 201–03, and in the revised re-edition, in progress, *Isho shūsei*, vol. 2 (Apocrypha on the *Book of Documents*; Tokyo, 1975), p. 43. On the relationship of life cycles to astronomical cycles, see Nathan Sivin, "Chinese Concepts of Time," *Earlham Review* 1 (1966): 82 ff.

it is because both derive from a single celestial rule. Joined in common allegiance to the heavenly bodies, the two classes of matter are mutually assimilable—and the noblest specimens of both classes may be interchangeable with the stars themselves. In preparing his operative or contemplative elixirs, the adept was in effect already working with materials that he knew to be veriest star-substance. The author of the Fourfold Floreate text, who does not shrink from explicit identifications, is once more at our side to spell it all out. He declares that the twenty-four ingredients, equivalent to the twenty-four gods of the body, are the solidified essences of the nine celestial and nine terrestrial regions: the entire universe.[161] The luminosity of the finished elixir was not borrowed light but the effulgence of the stars themselves.

Up until this point, we have regarded our alchemical texts as describing chemical operations within an all-encompassing symbolic system. In the formula of the Fourfold Floreate Elixir, with its sedulous numerology and far-reaching cosmic equivalences, the figures and background appear suddenly to have changed places. We seem now to perceive alchemical operations functioning as a sequence of symbolic procedures within a diffuse frame of pharmacochemical reference. All the elements that contributed to this transformation must already have been latent in the older alchemy. In the present formula, however, a careful correlation of symbolic effects appears to have become the main principle of organization. The progress of this formalistic approach should be studied in conjunction with the contemporary manuals of contemplation, notably the *Book of the Yellow Court* and its derivative literature.[162] Astrally ordained and infused, the human body is another alchemical compound, and must be worked to perfection throughout life. Like the aurifaction of liturgy, with its inspired alchemy of the incense-burner (Needham, vol. 5, pt. 2, pp. 130–31), the symbolic correlations of which the Fourfold Floreate Elixir is composed seem to light the way toward systematic internal alchemy.

Eschatology and Destiny

Through a ritual enactment of alchemical processes, the barrier separating the mortal and the eternal worlds could be breached without dying. Nevertheless, the older alchemy had posed certain fundamental questions con-

---

161. YCCC 68:3b; 2:11b, HY 1365/TT 1042.

162. The numerous references to elixirs in both texts, "inner" and "outer," of the *Book of the Yellow Court*, already suggest a comprehensive application of alchemical metaphor to physiology.

cerning both the prolongation of life by chemical means and its drastic abridgment. So long as operative alchemy survived in China, it was to be hedged about by these pervasive matters of life and death, and we can hardly claim to understand the alchemist until we have studied his conceptions of the afterlife.

This task has already been begun by Joseph Needham, whose lucid analysis of early Chinese ideas about the state of the dead and their relationship to the arts of immortality has brought us closer than ever before to comprehending the origins of alchemy in China.[163] Needham has suggested that the absence of an ethically determined otherworld was a necessary condition for the birth of alchemy. In his opinion, the art would never have come into being in Han China had not "the cosmological framework permitted of a permanent 'going-on.' " The eschatology of China in the Warring States and early Han was not ethically polarized.[164]

The fourth- and fifth-century texts we have been studying, however, come from a China which had been morally transformed out of all recognition. The religious revolution that had begun almost simultaneously (and, as I believe, independently) with the founding of the Way of the Celestial Master and the introduction of Buddhism was by this time coming to maturity. By the end of the fifth century it had radically influenced nearly all aspects of ethics and social life. We might reasonably expect a greater social and ethical complexity to find expression in the structure of the unseen world. We might also suppose that rank in the posthumous hierarchy would have come to be determined by a greater variety of means. Both these assumptions are fully borne out in the Mao Shan texts.

In one chapter of his *Concealed Instructions for Ascent to Perfection* (*Teng-chen yin-chüeh*), T'ao Hung-ching synthesized the data on the bureaucratic hierarchy of the invisible world found in the Mao Shan revelations and other Taoist and secular literature current in his day. Since the T'ang, this chapter has been transmitted as an independent work under its original title, *Ranks and Functions of the Perfected and Other Powers.*[165] In T'ao's

163. Needham, *Science and Civilisation in China*, vol. 5, pt. 2, pp. 77–85, "Ideas about the After-life in East and West."

164. Ibid., p. 82.

165. It is quoted at length in a late seventh-century text as "The Book of Ranks and Functions of the Perfected and Other Powers in the *Concealed Instructions for Ascent to Perfection*" (*Teng-chen yin-chüeh chen-ling wei-yeh ching* 登眞隱訣眞靈位業經; 2:16a, HY 1120/TT 762). Taken to the north in the course of the sixth century, perhaps by Taoists fleeing from the severity of Liang Wu Ti's repressive measures, much of this chapter of the *Concealed Instructions* was incorporated into the Taoist encyclopedia *Wu-shang pi-yao* 無上秘要, completed ca. 577, on imperial order, under the Northern Chou. The *Ranks and Functions* is also preserved independently in the canon as HY 167/TT 73, in a ninth-century edition by Lü-

synthesis, the other world is divided into seven levels—just as his editions of the *Chen-kao*, *Teng-chen yin-chüeh*, and *Shen-nung Pharmacopeia* were each divided into seven books. They are as follows:

1. Jade Purity (*Yü-ch'ing* 玉清), dwelling-place of eternal spirits who have never manifested themselves on earth.
2. Supreme Purity (*Shang-ch'ing* 上清), and
3. The Grande Bourne (*T'ai-chi* 太極), both in the north, containing the palaces of the Perfected (*chen*).
4. Great Purity (*T'ai-ch'ing* 太清), in the east, and
5. The Nine Mansions (*Chiu-kung* 九宮) in the west over Mount K'un-lun, both staffed by immortals (*hsien*).
6. The cavern-heavens (*tung-t'ien* 洞天) beneath the earth, under the rule of the celestial-perfected, but peopled by terrestrial immortals and postulants for perfection.
7. Feng-tu 酆都, or Lo-feng Shan 羅酆山. Alias the Six Heavens 六天, T'ai-yin 太陰, the Citadel of Night 夜城. An island in the far north, administrative headquarters of the unhallowed dead. It contains the dreaded Three Offices (*San-kuan* 三官), the Inquisition of the shades. Feng-tu's authority extends over the numerous other abodes of the dead beneath mountains and rivers in the Central Kingdom itself, all of which are also included on this seventh level.

It is clear that this schema in some sense corresponded to the historical development of Chinese religion and also reflected the diverse objectives of different groups of contemporary religious practitioners. Levels one through six are all Taoist and, through level five, celestial. Levels six and seven are both terrestrial and illustrate, on a single plane, the radical opposition between the practice of the pure Tao and the worship of the sanguinary gods of popular religion.[166] The Taoist knew that these "gods" were nothing more than the spirits of the dead. At their best, they were useful auxiliaries in quelling the more rowdy spectres, but at their worst they were themselves dangerous demons. They were confined to Feng-tu and the other dark homes of the shades on ethical grounds, mainly

---

ch'iu Fang-yüan 閻丘方遠. This text has been compared with the *Wu-shang pi-yao* version by Ishii Masako, in *Dōkyō kenkyū/Etudes taoïstes* 3:105–82 (Tokyo, 1968).

166. Lo-feng Shan was already mentioned as the abode of the dead and domain of the Five Emperors by Ko Hung 葛洪 (*Pao-p'u tzu* 3:7a; see also Needham, vol. 5, pt. 2, p. 112). References to it, often as Lo Shan, in Six Dynasties literature are frequent though dispersed. On the opposition between organized Taoist practice and the "inorganic" cults of the profane, the writings of R. A. Stein are most illuminating (see n. 69, above).

owing to bloody deeds performed during their lifetimes. After judgment had been pronounced on the newly dead by the Three Offices, they might be given some minor administrative post among the other shades, or assigned to retributive corvée labor; shifting rocks at the Yellow River's source is mentioned. In their obscure exile the dead were nourished by blood offerings, made either in their public temples or (for those who had not yet attained otherworldly ennoblement) by their descendants among the living.

Leaving the shades to their unenviable fate, let us look at some of the diverse means by which immortality could be attained in this complicated system. T'ao Hung-ching has listed a few of the many possibilities.[167] He notes that, even as during their lifetimes different persons perform deeds more or less meritorious and show greater or lesser devotion to the immortals, so do the posthumous means by which they attain immortality vary. Some in their own bodies become terrestrial immortals and do not die. Others leave their bodies and depart through liberation by means of a corpse. After death, some are able to enter the cavern-palaces deep within the earth and continue their studies there; others go to the Palace of Vermilion Fire (*Chu-huo kung* 朱火宮), where their bodies are smelted and remoulded.[168] Some first become agents-beneath-the-earth (*Ti-hsia chu-che* 地下主者), the lowest rank in the administration of the cavern-palaces, and advance in status from that point.[169] There are even some who are promoted to immortal office from positions among the dead. Yet another class is formed of worthy persons who are unable to become immortals themselves. The merit of their good deeds extends to their descendants, however, causing them to study the Tao and to attain immortality (and this success naturally reflects back favorably upon the ancestor who is its source). For T'ao Hung-ching, writing at the

167. *CK* 16:1b.

168. Details concerning this celestial locus formed part of the Ling-pao intelligence revealed at the end of the fourth century. In T'ao's *Ranks and Functions*, two figures, the brothers Kung Chung-yang 龔仲陽 and Kung Yu-yang 幼陽 are described as belonging to the official echelons of the Vermilion Palace (p. 8b2, *HY* 167/*TT* 73; cf. Ishii's article cited in n. 165, above, p. 143, no. 139).

169. Agents-beneath-the-earth are said to qualify for receiving minor Taoist teachings after 140 years; subsequently they advance one degree in rank, after examination, once every 140 years (*CK* 16:10a). They may qualify as terrestrial immortals after 280 years (*CK* 16:12a). The *Annals of the Sage* declares that one who has obtained the text of the *Annals*, even should he fail completely to practice its injunctions, is nonetheless assured of obtaining the posthumous office of agent-beneath-the-earth (p. 7a, *HY* 442/*TT* 198; see also my article "The Mao Shan Revelations; Taoism and the Aristocracy," *T'oung Pao* 63, 1:28, note 49 [1977]).

end of the fifth century, entry to any one of these various paths to beati-
tude was a result of faith and good works. Like death and disease, immortality was morally conditioned. But T'ao was only repeating the view
that had already been expressed in the Mao Shan revelations of 364–370.

At the end of Book I of the *Chen-kao*, T'ao placed two extracts from
the Shang-ch'ing scriptures to illustrate some of the nobler methods of
departure from the world of men.[170] These passages demonstrate that
certain of the ideas on immortality most prominent in later times go
back to fourth-century Mao Shan texts. One had been excerpted by Hsü
Mi from the *Inner Book of the Nine Perfected* (*Chiu-chen chung-ching* 九眞
中經), a work that Yang Hsi had formally transmitted to him in the spring
of 365.[171]

> Sometimes a person temporarily dies (*chan-ssu* 暫死) and goes to T'ai-yin, where he
> stays for a time in the Three Offices.[172] His flesh falls apart, his blood sinks into the
> earth, and his veins are dispersed. Yet his five viscera are still alive, and his white bones
> gleam like jade. The seven *p'o* are encamped in attendance, the three *hun* guard their
> lodging, the three primordials (*san-yüan* 三元) control his vital-breath, and the chief

170. *CK* 4:16a–17a. One of these extracts had been made by Hsü Mi, the other by Hsü
Hui, the first from the *Nine Perfections, Chiu-chen chung-ching* 九眞中經, the second from the
Sword Scripture. As we shall see, they are much-reduced memoranda taken from more
ample scriptural contexts. The scriptures were, of course, highly secret, but T'ao did not
fear to make public these abridged extracts from them.

171. The first part of this scripture, on the summoning and integration of nine celestial
spirits, is now to be found as the first *chüan* of *HY* 1365/*TT* 1042. This text does not contain
the original conclusion from which Hsü Mi's extract was taken, but it is cited in extenso in
the sixth-century *Wu-shang pi-yao* 87:6a10–12b10 (*HY* 1130/*TT* 777).

172. As already stated, the Three Offices that judged the dead were located at Mount
Feng-tu, also known as T'ai-yin. It was axiomatic that *all* the newly dead, whether destined
to be immortals or hungry ghosts, had first to undergo interrogation by the Three Offices
(*MTC* 1:15a3). From this passage, however, it appears that certain adepts were thought to
journey voluntarily to the land of the dead, to achieve their posthumous refinement in that
unlikely venue. This topos, eternal life gained at the very headquarters of death, must be
added to our collection of mortality/immortality paradoxes drawn from Mao Shan texts.
It has a prehistory; cf. the third-century "outer" *Book of the Yellow Court*, verse 3.78, "Hidden in T'ai-yin my shape is formed" 伏於太陰成吾形, and in Yang Hsi's "inner" *Book of the
Yellow Court*, verse 35.23, "Hidden in T'ai-yin my shape is seen" 伏於太陰見我形.
The theme underwent an extensive development in Taoist liturgical texts from the fifth
century on. The wide diffusion of these tales from the *Chen-kao* is attested by the presence of
this and the following passage in the ninth-century *Yu-yang tsa-tsu* 2:8a–8b; the information
they contain is frequently found repeated in Taoist manuals down to the present day (cf.
Needham, vol. 5, pt. 2, pp. 301–02, where the much-quoted directions for scrutinizing a
corpse also go back ultimately to the *Chen-kao*: if the body looks like that of a living man, if
the feet have not turned blue and the skin has not wrinkled, if the light in the eyes has not
gone dull and looks like that of a man still alive, if the hair has all fallen out and the body
and bones disappeared—all these are signs that *shih-chieh* 尸解 has taken place [*CK* 4:15b–
16a; also cf. 16:12a]).

spirit (*t'ai-shen* 太神) sits at his ease within.[173] Then he reappears whenever he wishes, whether in thirty years, in twenty, in ten, or in three. When he is about to come to life again, he collects his blood and builds up his flesh, reanimating the liquids and making them his body-fluids. Thus he restores substance to his body, and it becomes better than it was before he died. This is what is meant when we speak of a perfected-immortal remoulding his form in T'ai-yin, and changing his appearance in the Three Offices. The Emperor of Heaven has said:

> T'ai-yin's remoulding of bodily form
>> Surpasseth Elixir of Cycles Nine.
> Noble is his expression, and proud,
>> His countenance like a radiant cloud.
> He mounts on high to the Grand Bourne's portal
>> To be appointed perfected-immortal.[174]

Five or six years after Chao Tzu-ch'eng 趙子成 had died, a man was walking one evening in the mountains and saw his corpse in a cave. The flesh had rotted away, but the bones remained. He also saw the five viscera in his stomach, still alive as they had been before. The body fluids and blood were preserved within them, knotted up into purple parcels.

When one who has obtained the Tao goes to roam for a while at T'ai-yin, the Grand Unity (*T'ai-i* 太乙) watches over his corpse, his three *hun* encamp in the bones, his seven *p'o* guard the flesh, and the spirit of the embryo (*T'ai-ling* 胎靈) preserves the vital-breaths.[175]

From this it might at first seem that technology was being put on the shelf: "T'ai-yin's remoulding of bodily form surpasseth Elixir of Cycles Nine." But this passage was only Hsü Mi's résumé of a much longer original. The full text has been preserved in a late sixth-century Taoist encyclopedia. It allows us to add one more formula to the corpus of Mao Shan mineral preparations, and still another variation to the old theme of corporeal continuity. After a fast of 160 days, a special laboratory is to be constructed. Five pieces of pure white quartz are then carefully rounded and polished on a whetstone. The pellets are next cooked in a mixture of

173. The three primordials are, or have charge of, the three major divisions of the body, vertically staged: head, chest, and lower abdomen (*shang-, chung-, hsia-yüan* 上, 中, 下元). The chief spirit presumably corresponds to the 25th inner regent, referred to in notes 147 and 148, above.

174. There are several minor textual variants in the full scriptural version as quoted in the *Wu-shang pi-yao*. Also, there the "Emperor of Heaven" is the Celestial Monarch of T'ai-wei (T'ai-wei t'ien ti chün 太微天帝君), and the following verses are inserted just before the final couplet: "The five stones assemble celestial perfection / The Grand Unity wards the gateway of marvels." The significance of the five stones will become clear directly.

175. *CK* 4:16a–17a. In the scriptural text reproduced in the *Wu-shang pi-yao*, the tale of Chao Ch'eng-tzu (not Tzu-ch'eng) is told by Ch'ih Sung-tzu 赤松子, and at much greater length.

shallots ripened in the earth for five seasons, white honey, the plant *chü-sheng* 巨勝, and water. When ready, they are cooled and then ingested with invocations to the Lords of the Five Directions. Each pellet will enter one of the viscera and eternally preserve it from decay.[176]

The other passage quoted by T'ao was taken from the *Sword Scripture*. It, too, is concerned with a chemical product, though we do not in this case have the formula:

> None of those who employ drugs other than the Transcendent Bolus (*ling-wan* 靈丸) to achieve liberation by means of a corpse can ever again return to their old homes.[177] This is because they are held by the Three Offices. There are some who die and come back to life again. Others have their heads broken off and come forth from one side. The corpses of some disappear before they can be laid out. The bodies of others remain but the bones are gone. Sometimes the clothes remain and the body is gone. Sometimes the hair falls out and the body disappears. One who departs in broad daylight is said to be a superior immortal liberated by means of a corpse. If at midnight, he is called a lesser immortal liberated by means of a corpse. If toward dawn or dusk, he is called an agent-beneath-the-earth.[178]

Even by the end of the fifth century, there were undoubtedly still men who employed the minor elixirs to achieve a qualified liberation of this sort, even as there were others who made use of alchemical tonics in order, in T'ao's words, to live on in their own bodies and not die. When secularized, the old alchemy of the terrestrial immortals formed the basis of later chemotherapy. Yet even within its religious context the art had continued to develop. In an eschatological system that had become so involved and so obsessively ethical, it is no wonder that the most elaborate examples of alchemical development should have reached two extremes, becoming either suicidal or allegorical.

In defense of the suicidal alchemy of Mao Shan, we must remember the powerful wind of time that blew through the whole eschatological scaf-

---

176. *Wu-shang pi-yao* 87:6a10–12b10 (*HY* 1130/*TT* 777). Needless to say, this preparation would be pharmacologically inert. In the scripture, the man who found the corpse poked about in the entrails and discovered the five quartz pellets at their work of preservation. He divined their purpose, and proceeded to extract and swallow the lot. Ch'eng-tzu's corpse was due to come to life ten-odd years later, and at the appointed time, all the pellets flew out of the thief's mouth like a flight of cicadas and directly reentered the viscera of the corpse. Greatly distressed, the thief returned to the mountain cave, only to find Ch'eng-tzu resurrected. With him was an immortal in full regalia, who cried out to Ch'eng-tzu, "That man with the pock-marked face is the one who long ago stole the treasure-pellets from your viscera!" No sooner had he spoken than the thief's face broke out in ugly pustules. He returned home in consternation, the affliction spread to the other members of his family, they all died, and his clan became extinct (87: 11b–12b).

177. Cf. the scriptural text in the *Sword Scripture* extract, *TPYL* 665:6b.

178. *CK* 4:17a. On agents-beneath-the-earth, see note 169, above.

folding. Yang and the Hsüs were convinced of the imminent end of the old terrestrial order of things and awaited the approach of a new, celestially supervised dispensation. Their belief was shared by T'ao Hung-ching, a century and a half later. We are accustomed to think of "messianism" in medieval China only as characterizing popular movements of violent rebellion. This impression is due, not to any lack of contemporary documents, but rather to our backwardness in making use of the available sources. The expectation of a renewal of the world can be traced back, in upper-class consciousness, to Han-time cosmological speculation.[179]

It is significant, I believe, that those scholars whose forebears had migrated south of the Yangtze at the end of the Han took particular pride in maintaining their ancestral traditions of learning in *I-ching* studies and the apocryphal books. The tenor of their scholarship was strongly opposed to the "sublime learning" (*hsüan-hsüeh* 玄學) of the northern aristocrats, which found its highest expression in Wang Pi's commentary on the *I-ching*. What is more, as T'ang Chang-ju has shown, all those men whose views on cosmology are quoted in the treatises on the calendar of the Chin and Liu Sung histories were members of the same group of old southern families.[180] Their names recur again and again in the pages of *Science and Civilisation in China*.[181] They had a hereditary concern with discovering and analysing the secrets of heaven and earth. They hoped by that means to descry destiny, and their expectations were cast in the mold of the Han apocrypha. It was of course, to this group of families that our Mao Shan Taoists also belonged.

Only a brief reference can be made here to another potent source of eschatological expectation in fourth- and fifth-century Chiang-nan. Very prominent among the "efficient" (or ritual) texts of Six Dynasties Buddhism were the *dhāraṇī-sūtras*, collections of Sanskrit or pseudo-Sanskrit spells. A number of such texts were translated, or transcribed, at the third-

179. It was, of course, inextricably linked to the cyclical conception of time; see Needham, "Time and Eastern Man," in *The Grand Titration; Science and Society in China and the West* (London, 1969), pp. 219–98; James Zimmermann, "Die Zeit in der chinesischen Geschichtsschreibung," *Saeculum* 23 (1972):332–50, and Fukunaga Mitsuji 福永光司, "*Chū goku ni okeru tenchi hōkai no shisō*" 中國における天地崩壞の思想, in the Yoshikawa Kōjirō 吉川幸次郎 Festschrift, *Chūgoku bungaku ronshū* 中國文學論集 (Tokyo, 1968), pp. 169–88.

180. T'ang Ch'ang-ju 唐長孺, "*Tu Pao-p'u tzu t'ui-lun nan-pei hsüeh-feng ti i-t'ung*" 讀抱朴子推進論南北學風的異同, pp. 351–81 in his *Wei Chin Nan-pei ch'ao shih lun-ts'ung* 魏晉南北朝史論叢 (Peking, 1955), pp. 361–71.

181. For example, Ko Heng 葛衡, Lu Ch'eng 陸澄, Ch'en Cho 陳卓, in Needham, vol. 3, passim.

century court of the rulers of Wu. Many more were rendered into Chinese in the north before the fall of Lo-yang in 311, and were then brought south by the émigrés. *Dhāraṇīs* also figured conspicuously in many larger scriptures, including the *Lotus Sūtra*. In Chiang-nan, from the early fourth century on, independent *dhāraṇī-sūtras* continued to be translated, or indeed written directly, in Chinese. Each of these *sūtras* was preceded by an historical introduction (*nidāna*), narrating the circumstances under which the Buddha was supposed to have authorized the text. From these narratives it is clear that the *dhāraṇī-sūtras* were intended to be propagated toward the end of the final 500 years of the Law, during a period of irreversible decline. Thus Buddhism in fourth-century Chiang-nan was mantled in an aura of apocalyptic fatality. The presence in the Mao Shan revelations of references to the stage-properties of Indian apocalypse, the succession of kalpas, and the three ultimate calamities (*san-tsai* 三災), indicates that the message had been heeded by the old, established families of the region.[182]

It is generally assumed that the proponents of a messianic eschatology must be, in some sense, have-nots: otherwise what would be the point of their trying to transcend the world as they find it? Yet Hsü Mi belonged to the royal entourage of Ssu-ma Yü 司馬昱, King of Kuei-chi, who was soon to become regent and King of Lang-yeh, and eventually Emperor Chien-wen of the Chin.[183] We are already familiar with the facts of T'ao Hung-ching's court career, and have noted that his relations with the court continued even after his retirement to Mao Shan. On what fodder could a messianic ideology batten in such refined milieux?

The answer is to be found in the social history of the Six Dynasties. During the first few years after the great exodus from the north, in the second decade of the fourth century, the Chin rulers followed a policy of conciliation toward the great families of Chiang-nan, in whose traditional territory they now found themselves. It was at this time that many influential southerners, including Hsü Mi's father, were enfeoffed by the newly transplanted dynasty, who thus recognized their extensive proprietary claims. Yet once the Chin had firmly established themselves in the south, the clannish self-interest of the northern aristocrats and their natural arrogance toward southerners began to dictate the shape of social hierarchy. Soon there came to be a firm upper limit set upon the advance-

---

182. The *dhāraṇī-sūtras* and their relationship to the co-eval and colocal Taoist literature are studied in my monograph, *The Consecration Sūtra, A Buddhist Book of Spells*, to be published in the *Berkeley Buddhist Studies Series*.

183. *CK* 20:8a9, 11b4–5.

ment of southerners in the ranks of government. The "southern scholars" (*nan-shih* 南士) were to labor under this onus of exclusion until the time of the Ch'en.[184]

So it is that we find a number of gifted southerners in court circles rather than in the bureaucratic hierarchy or in the employ of the military dictators who came to hold the real power under the southern dynasties. In the protocol-bound courts they found an appreciative audience for their hereditary learning and technological expertise, especially in the *Rites*, calendar and portents, and the *I-ching*. It was as a member of this class that T'ao Hung-ching spoke when he exhorted all *tao-shih* to the study of astronomy and the calendar.[185] Barred from occupying the higher official ranks, members of the old southern families flourished in these recondite areas of inquiry.

They were also instrumental in the great religious movement that profoundly altered the structure of Chinese society in the course of the fifth century. First came the Mao Shan revelations of Shang-ch'ing, received by Yang Hsi and the Hsüs in 364–370; then the Ling-pao scriptures, transmitted by Ko Ch'ao-fu 葛巢甫 in 397.[186] These two great bodies of celestial literature, revealed to southern scholars, contained a consoling message for those excluded by birth from high civil office. But these texts also furnished the authority for a new class of Taoist priests that emerged in the following century. All the great fifth-century Taoist masters of whom we have record, men like Lu Hsiu-ching 陸修靜, Sun Yu-yüeh 孫遊嶽, Ku Huan 顧歡, and T'ao Hung-ching himself, belonged to old southern families. All enjoyed the patronage of emperors and aristocrats of northern origin. Through their spiritual position, these southerners attained far greater power and prestige than they could ever have done in the course of an ordinary official career.[187]

The eschatological message of the Perfected had been addressed to

---

184. See Chou I-liang 周一良, "*Nan-ch'ao ching-nei ti ko-chung jen chi cheng-fu tui-tai ti cheng-ts'e*" 南朝境內的各種人及政府對待的政策, in his *Wei Chin Nan-pei ch'ao shih lun-chi* 魏晉南北朝史論集 (Peking, 1963), pp. 30–93, which gives a clear picture of the various social groups and their status under successive southern dynasties.

185. *NC* 2:18a8.

186. Ch'en Kuo-fu, *Tao-tsang yüan-liu k'ao*, p. 67; Kaltenmark, "Ling-pao, note sur un terme du taoïsme religieux," p. 560. Ōfuchi Ninji 大淵忍爾 has undertaken a reconstruction of the original Ling-pao corpus, comparing extant works in the Canon with a Tun-huang scriptural catalogue, with other manuscripts from Tun-huang, and with quotations found in early Taoist texts: "On *Ku Ling Pao Ching* 古靈寶經," in *Acta Asiatica* 27 (Tokyo, 1974): 33–56.

187. See part 3 of my article, "The Mao Shan Revelations; Taoism and the Aristocracy," *T'oung Pao* 63, 1:35–40 (1977).

southern scholars before this compensatory development had come about in the world of men. With the advancing official status of Taoist organizations in the fifth century, the message might be read in various ways. By those eager to curry favor with the secular powers, the messianic prophecy was interpreted as having been fulfilled in their rule. This was first done under the Liu Sung dynasty, which took over from the Chin in 420.[188] Other adepts were not convinced by this identification. It is significant that K'ung Hsi-hsien 孔熙先, who attempted to overthrow the Sung "using prophecies found in the apocryphal books," had earlier come into a legacy of Mao Shan texts.[189] He was executed in 445, together with his eminent associate in the plot, Fan Yeh 范曄, author of the *History of the Later Han*.[190] Thus, messianic eschatology was by no means excluded from the thought of the upper classes. We must recall, though, that it shared a single set of metaphors with the imperial cult. In consequence, even as religious imagery was drawn from court ritual, notions essentially religious in origin might function effectively within the context of secular politics.[191]

For the Hsüs there had been no question of taking direct action to overturn the social order. They recognized its injustice but were content to await the ineluctable revolution that would be effected by destiny. Their own auspicious destinies had been mapped out long before, and their names were already inscribed upon the registers of Shang-ch'ing. They knew themselves to be firmly supported by a dual causality of ancestry and reincarnation.[192] Their only concern was to link themselves

188. This development is well documented in a sequence of fifth-century texts: *HY* 335/*TT* 170, ch. 1; *HY* 1194, 1195, and 1196/*TT* 876. Beyond the Mao Shan revelations, a text of the original Ling-pao group (*HY* 318/*TT* 165; no. 5 in Ōfuchi's reconstructed catalogue) was drawn upon for scriptural authority in this identification.

189. *CK* 19:10b–11a, translated as an appendix to "The Mao Shan Revelations; Taoism and the Aristocracy," *T'oung Pao* 63, 1: 44–45 (1977).

190. The affair is fully described in the standard histories' accounts of Fan Yeh, *Sung-shu* 宋書 69 and *Nan-shih* 33.

191. All of Taoist ritual was ideally based upon the procedures of the Han imperial court, and thus throughout the period of disunion Taoist priests mimed the overpowering nostalgia of empire. Similarly, under the menace of foreign rule, Taoist rites were later seen as expressing a specifically Chinese hegemony of the cosmos; see my article, "The Longest Taoist Scripture," in *History of Religions*, vol. 17, nos. 3–4 (Feb.–May, 1978).

192. Hsü Mi's inclination to study the Tao and the high posthumous deserts of which he was assured derived from the merit sown by his ancestor in the seventh degree (inclusive), who was said to have saved 408 people from starvation in a famine during the Han (*CK* 4:11a–11b). Yet the perfected also declared that a Chou dynasty worthy, named Hsüeh Lü 薛旅, had requested and obtained birth as Hsü Mi so as to profit from the Hsüs' stock of otherworldly merit. It was as the reincarnation of Hsüeh Lü that Hsü Mi was troubled by untoward sensual longings, for it had been an excessive fondness for women that had kept Hsüeh Lü from achieving immortality in his earlier life (*CK* 3:13b–14a).

ever more closely to the impending celestial regime. Indeed, they were informed by their otherworldly teachers that they already ranked among the Perfected, and had therefore to make their behavior conform as faithfully as possible to celestial canons.

Thus *imitatio* was the essence of the rites revealed to Yang Hsi. Dancing up to, around, and over the stars of the Dipper formed part of the daily activities of the Perfected in the heavens; their disciples on earth should comport themselves in like fashion. Even certain bedtime optical exercises, transmitted for Hsü Mi's particular benefit, were identical with practices regularly performed by the Perfected: "Only *we* do them in a seated position, as we never [sleep and so never] lie down."[193]

It was when the adept proposed to emulate perfected dietetics that he confronted the alchemy of Shang-ch'ing. In the biographies of the Perfected there are sufficient indications that the elixirs of Shang-ch'ing were their daily meat and drink. Terrestrial immortals eschewed cultivated foods and consumed the wild fungi, roots, and berries of their mountain retreats. The Perfected also drew their nourishment from their surroundings—but they dwelt among the stars. Thus they supped on Lang-kan Efflorescence, and Jade Essence, and the mysterious Dragon-Brain.[194] If the postulant wished to behave as they, he must adapt his diet to theirs; the most complete incorporation of celestial patterns was to be realized through the process of ingestion.[195]

Nor was it surprising that the sustenance of celestial beings should prove fatal to mortals. It could not be otherwise, for substances of extreme astral purity must react violently upon the perishable integument that

193. CK 9:8b5–6. Cf. 9:7b7–8: "These practices are not to be abandoned even after one has become a perfected-immortal.'"

194. E.g. *Annals of the Sage* p. 2a7, 2b6 (*HY* 442/*TT* 198).

195. The act of swallowing is equivalent to the sealing of a compact, as in the oath (*meng* 盟) of old, with its smearing the lips with the blood of a sacrificial victim, so often and meaningfully alluded to in Taoist rites of transmission. Compare Yang Hsi's "inner" *Book of the Yellow Court*, describing its own transmission (verses 36.14–18): "The bestower is termed 'master'; the recipient is thereby enlightened / Cloud-brocade and phoenix-bombast are bound with a golden lock / This stands in lieu of shearing the hair—the body is kept intact / Hand in hand they climb the mountain and sip the liquid elixir / Then golden writing in luminous letters of jade may be transmitted." *Et antiquum documentum novo cedat ritui*—before, the hair was shorn and the lips smeared with blood; now, the ingestion of blood-colored cinnabar seals a compact which has been "locked" by the transmission of pledges of gold and silk, and this ingestion is like the swallowing of a talisman, which will at once call forth and unite its consumer to its errant celestial moiety (a theme often recurring in accounts of Taoist feasts of consecration or transmission—*ch'u* 廚). See R. A. Stein, "Les fêtes de cuisine du taoïsme religieux," *L'Annuaire du Collège de France* 71 (1972):431–40, and "Spéculations mystiques et thèmes relatifs aux 'cuisines' du taoïsme," ibid. 72 (1973): 489–99.

encloses the immortal embryo in man. The stellar essences on which the Perfected delicately feasted were deadly poisons here below, in a world that openly reversed all celestial values. Yet by what better means could one effect the essential transition from corrupt mortality to luminous perfection? Thus, when the sign was finally given by the unseen world, the adept would complete his program of practice by preparing and swallowing the stellar nutriment of the Perfected. In partaking of that communion, he would at last die entirely to his mundane life, and be that much further advanced toward his ultimate goal of full participation in the harmonious movements of the stars.

Conclusion

Having recalled the passionate apocalyptic atmosphere in which the Mao Shan revelations came into being, let us return for one last look at the alchemy of T'ao Hung-ching. As far as we have been able to discover, T'ao did not make alchemy the culmination of his life. Though he had ample information and opportunity, he did not taste the deadly rations of the Perfected. T'ao's hesitations may seem rather unheroic when glimpsed in the saintly light cast by Hsü Hui and Chou Tzu-liang. After our brief glance at the development of Taoism during the fifth century, however, his reasons are comprehensible enough.

As we have remarked, T'ao was not a visionary. His work was mainly scholastic in nature, and all his practical undertakings were carried out in strict fidelity to the written word. Yet at the heart of T'ao's scholarship was no blind veneration for the texts of remote antiquity. Though he was conversant with every branch of ancient learning, T'ao's greatest reverence and his scholarly acumen were reserved for a body of literature that had come into being less than a century before his own birth.

. T'ao Hung-ching was the virtual founder of Mao Shan Taoism. Though only the ninth of the Shang-ch'ing patriarchs in the official genealogy of the school, it was with him that the line of great Mao Shan masters, confidants of emperors, really began.[196] T'ao's works leave no

---

196. The earliest formal ordering of the lineage seems to be the *Filiation of the Perfected* (*Chen-hsi* 眞系), composed in 805 by the prominent literary recluse Li P'o 李渤 (text in *YCCC*, *ch.* 5). Its point of departure is T'ao's succinct history of the Yang-Hsü manuscript corpus (*CK* 19:9b–20b4), translated as appendix II to my article, "The Mao Shan Revelations; Taoism and the Aristocracy," *T'oung Pao* 63, 1:41–62 [1977]). T'ao's sober textual history became Li P'o's hagiography, and later codifiers of the lineage also went back to T'ao's narrative—they drew from it several obscure recipients of Yang-Hsü autograph texts, to become "patriarchs" intervening between the Lady Wei, Yang Hsi, Hsü Mi, and Hsü Hui, on the one hand, and T'ao Hung-ching, on the other. The history of the patriarchs

doubt as to the sincerity of his faith. Yet it was only natural that he should hesitate before taking leave of a world which, through his scholarly and liturgical efforts, he was so actively molding to conform to the Taoist ideal. From his writings it is clear that he was fully cognizant of the alternatives, and made his choice. Whatever had happened at the Peak of the South in 512, T'ao's decision to remain in the world was reaffirmed shortly after he reached sixty, when he had intimations that an otherworldly summons was being prepared for him. We do not know if the death he eventually met in 536, at the age of 81, was of his own choosing.[197]

Still, T'ao did practice alchemy, and that brings us once again to the problem of intention: the purpose of the alchemist, the cross-purposes of the secondary sources. For it is from secondary sources that most of the stereotypes on Chinese alchemy derive. Far too much reliance has been placed upon hagiography, as well as on that rather special class of exemplary historical fiction, biographies contained in the dynastic histories. In particular, the modern notion of "accidental elixir poisoning," applied to supposedly misguided alchemists and their unwitting imperial patrons, should be reexamined. The evidence we have presented proves that the deadly toxic qualities of many elixirs were adequately, even rapturously, described in what was to become the best-known body of Taoist literature in medieval China. There is every probability, then, that some of the alchemical deaths recorded from the late Six Dynasties and the T'ang were intentional. Since death was known to result from the ingestion of certain elixirs, the class of "accidental" poisonings should be restricted to the misapplication, or false claims, of iatro-alchemy. And in the T'ang, chemotherapy was at least as much a part of secular medical practice as it was of Taoism.[198]

If by the seventh century alchemical preparations were employed in

---

given in the *Records of Mao Shan* resumes the state of tradition in the early fourteenth century (*ch.* 10–12, *HY* 304/*TT* 154–55).

197. Deaths at eighty-one invite suspicion. Nine times nine, the perfect product of ultimate Yang, is the ideal term of a man's life. Sixty-one and eighty-one are the preferred ages for the deaths of saintly recluses, and before our study of Mao Shan alchemy, we might have been tempted to infer frequent hagiographical falsification. The dates of T'ao's birth and death are both quite certain, however, and so perhaps he made a considered end of himself at the last.

198. This has been shown by Nathan Sivin, in his *Chinese Alchemy; Preliminary Studies* (Cambridge, Mass., 1968). Sun Ssu-mo 孫思邈, the seventh-century subject of that book, may or may not have been a Taoist in my proposed strict sense of the term, but it is in any case certain that chemotherapy reached a wide and various public through Sun's writings.

secular as well as in religious contexts, the Six Dynasties evidence does not allow us to infer that alchemy was that at time already split up into radically different types and schools. On the contrary, we may state that the surviving texts of Six Dynasties alchemy can all be situated at successive stages along a perceptible line of development. The filiation of the alchemists themselves is as easy to trace as that of the formulae. Like the other texts that were to compose the earliest Taoist Canon, all our fourth- and fifth-century alchemical formulae were first revealed to members of an endogamous group of families. They belonged to a larger class of "southern scholars" who preserved through hereditary transmission their legacy of Han erudition and technology. It was their efforts, through the long period of disunion, that eventually linked the learning and practical experience of the Han to the newly reunified empires of Sui and T'ang. Alchemy was included in their rich heritage and so formed part of the new Taoism, which they also created. In this way, alchemy came to be perpetuated in a Taoist context, though it was to serve wider purposes during the T'ang.

The substance of Six Dynasties alchemy was therefore relatively homogeneous, and its application largely an individual matter. We have seen that a single alchemical formula might allow ample latitude for interpretation as being suicidal, therapeutic, or symbolic and contemplative. Its implementation might be a unique, decisive event or a repeated, ritual phantasmagoria. Context and intention were everything and must be determined in each individual case. After our efforts to recover the alchemy of T'ao Hung-ching, it should be clear that there is only one way to flesh out the bare bones of the texts. The crucial social and personal factors must be rediscovered and correlated with the pronouncements of scripture. Neither religion nor technology can be adequately studied in isolation. Our efforts to elucidate both Taoism and the Taoist arts must be firmly grounded within the study of Chinese society.

6 The Chinese Belief in Baleful Stars

Ching-lang Hou 侯錦郎

Introduction

THE BELIEF IN THE INFLUENCE of the stars, as well as the sacrificial rites and astrological theories relating to them, goes back to very early times in China. The stars could be propitious as well as dangerous, but it is understandable that the notions relating to evil stars should be the more highly developed, since it was necessary that precautions be taken against them. The characteristics of these evil stars were noted by astrologers as early as the Han dynasty. For example, in an apocryphal text on the *Spring and Autumn Annals*, it is stated: "Stars that are pointed and have long tails are baleful stars (*hsiung-hsing* 凶星). Their color is white, and they emit rays. Stars that are large, with small tails, are auspicious stars (*chi-hsing* 吉星); they are bright and translucent."[1]

The belief in baleful stars appears in the daily life of the people and in popular literature even today. There is a remarkable historical continuity in these beliefs, and their psychological influence on social life is considerable. However, in the modern context, the original astral concept has become secondary, and the former "baleful stars" are now no more than a particular category of demons. These demons exist in opposition to a special class of benevolent deities, who were themselves originally "auspicious luminaries" (*chi-yao* 吉曜). A full treatment of this rich subject would require an extended series of detailed studies. Here I shall limit myself to the investigation of the belief in three of the baleful stars, Great Year (T'ai-sui 太歲), White Tiger (Pai-hu 白虎), and Dog of Heaven

---

1. See the *Ch'un-ch'iu ch'ien-t'an pa* 春秋潛潭巴, in *Isho shūsei* 緯書集成 (Tokyo, 1953), 4: 109–10.

(T'ien-kou 天狗). These three are probably the most feared in Taiwan, where they haunt the popular imagination.

In Taiwan—my own native island—I have found a promising field for research on this subject. Chinese religious tradition is especially well preserved in this area, which is relatively isolated from the mainland and peopled for the most part by the descendants of settlers who emigrated here from south China in the seventeenth century. The Taiwanese as a whole have remained all the more attached to their beliefs in that the island has been governed by a succession of foreign occupying powers that have consistently opposed the religion of the island's inhabitants. Numerous sources bear witness to the importance of the belief in baleful stars to the present-day Taiwanese: the almanacs which no family neglects to buy; the manuals of divination on which the soothsayers rely in order to identify the dangers that threaten, and to indicate the most direct means of escaping from them; the ritual books of the Taoist priest, to whom recourse is had in serious cases; the secular popular literature, plays, poems, and songs; and finally, the mediumistic texts.

The beliefs preserved in Taiwan go back, as we shall see, to Chinese classical tradition. Nearly all the dynastic histories, in their chapters devoted to astronomy and astrology, preserve documents relating to baleful stars. Throughout the course of Chinese history, soothsayers, priests, and mediums, belonging to different traditions and social groups yet all sharing the common belief, have exerted themselves either to foresee the effect of baleful stars on various levels of society, or to take measures against them. These stars play as much of a role in the Taoist religion proper as in the popular religion. Their study will perhaps help us to clarify the relationship of Taoist priests with the people, as well as with the various categories of mediums and soothsayers. Further, what we learn of present-day belief and practice may well have some relevance for the understanding of similar phenomena at an earlier period.

I have chosen the three baleful stars to be discussed because (together with the Five Spectres, *wu-kuei* 五鬼) they seem to be the most important ones. In the rite of "Sending Off the Baleful Stars" (*sung hsiung-hsing* 送凶星), which is celebrated by a Taoist priest (*tao-shih* 道士) in order to expel all such stars, only the images of these three and of the Five Spectres actually appear on the altar. It is they who are most often depicted on the paper money burned during this ceremony, as well as on that burned during the lay exorcism of "Leave-taking Outside" (*hsieh wai-fang* 謝外方). They have the longest historical tradition and yet they are still "alive" and held in awe on Taiwan, whereas others survive mainly as names mentioned in texts.

Before any exorcism is performed, it is necessary to identify the demon with whom one has "collided" (*ch'ung* 衝), whom one has "offended" (*fan* 犯), or by whom one has been "killed" (*sha-chao* 煞着)—that is, to identify the demon who has seized one's vital spiritual components, one's "primordial spirits" (*yüan-shen* 元神)[2] or souls *hun* 魂 and *p'o* 魄. In order to discover this, the believer can consult an almanac (*t'ung-shu* 通書) or go to see a soothsayer (*hsiang-ming shih* 相命師) or a medium (*t'ung-chi* 童乩). We may take the example of a child who falls ill on Wednesday, 31 May 1972 (cyclical day *jen-hsü* 壬戌). He has a fever, or perhaps a headache or stomachache. In order to find out which spirit has been offended, the parent need only turn to the 1972 almanac, where it is written, in the column of *jen-hsü* days:

> Falling ill on a *jen-hsü* day, he has collided in the north with the Divine Killer With Hair Unbound Who Flies in the Heavens, the White Tiger, and the Vermilion Bird. . . . If ill with fever, with aches in head, stomach, or four limbs, one must use money of all five colors, burning 300 notes of each, and arrange a paper horse, rice, water, fruits, and wine, and, facing north, send off [the demons].[3]

If the believer decides to consult a soothsayer who has specialized in divination by the hexagrams, and if the "oracle" should fall, for example, on *lei-shan hsiao-kuo* 雷山小過 (*I-ching* hexagram 63), he would then read in the *Ming-yün ta-kuan* 命運大觀 part 1, page 70:

> In the case of a child he has offended the Dog of Heaven. . . . It is proper to use Money for Deliverance from Danger and White Tiger paper money.[4]

In Taiwan at present, the Taoist priest does not act as soothsayer. But once our believer is seriously worried about illness in his family, he may call in a priest to perform the ceremony of "Sending Off the Baleful Stars." This is long and solemn, in contrast to the short and simple "Leavetaking Outside" carried out by the layman himself, which I shall consider

---

2. According to the Formosan tradition that is still current today, each man is the seat of twelve "primordial spirits" (*shih-erh yüan-shen* 十二元神). If they are all intact, the body and mind are healthy. Their absence, even if it is only partial, leads to illness and mental confusion. In the waking state the mind works with all its faculties and the twelve spirits are present. Dreams are explained as the adventures they have during their peregrinations outside the body during sleep. If they are stopped on the way by the kings of hell, gods, or demons, their host loses his life.

3. *T'ung-shu* 通書, ch. *Ta-fu* 大符, 5b (Chia-i 嘉義, Ling-an t'ang 靈安堂, 1971).

4. *Ming-yün ta-kuan* (Taiwan, Jui-ch'eng shu-tien 瑞成書店, 1967).

later. An altar is set up in the central hall of the house. According to a Taoist ritual text,[5] the rite then takes place in two parts. During the first part, the priest expels the "Killers";[6] during the second, he sends off the baleful stars. To start with he invokes a whole group of deities and demons and presents to them the following petition:

> At the request of such-and-such a person, living in such-and-such a place, whose life, because of the stars, is not following its normal course, and who fears that the rapacious stars and the baleful killers do him violence, I recite the sacred texts and I transform and purify these riches[7] in order that you may protect him in his luminous destiny, and that his primordial constellations (*yüan-ch'en* 元辰) may shine forth brilliantly . . .

Following this, the baleful breath which has been incarnated within the sick person is transferred into a substitute body (*t'i-shen* 替身). To do this the priest must first give life to a body of straw or paper by means of "opening the eyes" (*k'ai-kuang* 開光):

> You who were originally a body of paper and are nought but that so long as my brush has not touched you—now that my brush has touched you, behold! you have become a man . . .

Next, the priest establishes a contract between the sick person and the substitute body. By means of twelve red threads (which apparently represent the twelve primordial spirits) he connects the sick person with the substitute body, the torso of which has been wrapped around with Yin and Yang paper money as well as with pictures of the demon responsible for the sickness. The priest then prays to the divine patriarchs,[8] that they may aid him in establishing the contract. Next he cuts the twelve threads with his sword, and in so doing liberates the sick person. By then passing the substitute body three times over the stomach and four times over the back of the sick person, he makes certain of his recovery. At the end, the substitute body is taken outside the house and burned or abandoned, either at a crossroads or by a stream of running water.

During the second part of this ritual the whole gamut of baleful stars is called together, so that offerings and petitions may be presented to them before their expulsion. Among the names on the list are the Nine *Liang* Stars (*chiu liang hsing* 九良星),[9] the Astral Lord of the Five Spirits (*wu-kuei*

5. The *Ling-pao ch'i-jang chi-sung hsiung-hsing chieh-e k'o-i* 靈寶祈禳祭送凶星解厄科儀, pp. 5–16. This text was made available to the author when it was in the collection of K. M. Schipper and labeled Schipper Archive (S.A.) no. 225.

6. The "Killers" (*sha* 煞) are the genies of the earth.

7. This refers to burning paper money, *chih-ch'ien* 紙錢.

8. In the rituals the divine patriarchs are termed either *tsu-shih* 祖師 or *pen-shih* 本師.

9. The name of these demons can be written in various ways: *chiu-liang* 九梁, *chiu-lung*

hsing-chün 五鬼星君), the Astral Lord of the Celestial Dog (*t'ien-kou hsing-chün* 天狗星君), and the Astral Lord of the White Tiger (*pai-hu hsing-chün* 白虎星君). Next come the Astral Lords and Divine Killers (*shen-sha* 神煞) whom one may have offended somewhere, sometime, as at a funeral or marriage, the construction of dwellings and enclosures, the arrangement of the house, or one of the other, less important contingencies of daily life.[10] Then follow the names of other Astral Lords:

> Great Year (*t'ai-sui* 太歲)
> Gate of Mourning (*sang-men* 喪門)

九龍, 九隆, *chiu-lang* 九郎. The name is applied not only to demons. Chiu-lang is the Master of the Law of Lü-shan 閭山法主: see the *San-chiao yüan-liu sou-shen ta-ch'üan* 三教源流搜神大全, paragraph *Lü-shan fa-chu* 閭山法主 (1909 reprint by Yeh Te-hui 葉德輝). Earlier, among the Ai-lao-i 哀牢夷 barbarians, Chiu-lung 九隆 is the Founder-hero: see *Hou Han-shu* 後漢書 116:1026 (Taipei: Hsin-lu shu-chü 新陸書局, 1968). A link seems to have existed between Chiu-liang and the theme of the "Mother with Nine Children" 九子母, which already figures in the *Ch'u-tz'u* 楚辭 ch. *T'ien-wen* 天問, p. 149 (Nanking: Chin-ling shu-chü 金陵書局, 1872).

10. Here is the list of them:

> The Astral Lords of the Terrestrial and Celestial Killers, 天煞地煞星君
> the Astral Lords of the Killer of the Month and the Killer of the Year, 年煞月煞星君
> the Astral Lords of the Killer of the Hour and the Killer of the Day, 日煞時煞星君
> the Astral Lords of the Killer Yang and the Killer Yin, 陰煞陽煞星君
> the Astral Lords of the Happy Killer and the Mournful Killer, 喪煞喜煞星君
> the Astral Lords of the Plundering Killer and the Dream Spirits, 夢神劫煞神君.

Then come the Divine Killers, known and unknown:

> the Divine Killers of Crossroads and Forks, 三叉路頭四叉路尾神煞
> the Divine Killers of Ascents and Descents, 上高落低神煞
> the Divine Killers of the Summits and the Feet of Mountains, 嶺頂嶺脚神煞
> the Divine Killers of the Beginnings and Ends of Roads, 路頭路尾神煞
> the Divine Killers of the Front and Back of the House, 厝前厝後神煞
> the Divine Killers on whom one walks or stumbles, 踏著茂着神煞
> the Divine Killers whom one sees and runs against, 冲着看着神煞
> the Divine Killers whom one bangs and scolds, 犯着嚇着神煞
> the Divine Killers whom one ties and entwines, 圍着縛着神煞
> also the flying Divine Killers of the Flying Soil, 飛土飛煞
> the Divine Killers of the Tombs and the Tomb Spirits, 墓神墓煞
> the Three Divine Killers of the Earth, 地下三煞神
> also the dead Great King and the Small Dead, 大大鬼王細細鬼子
> the Divine Killers who pull out the intestines and draw the stomach, 抽腸挽肚神煞
> the Divine Killers who move about with the days, 逐日占方神煞
> the Divine Killers whom one meets when one drives in stakes and puts up enclosures, 圍籬把栽柱脚神煞
> the Divine Killers whom one meets when one moves the bed, spreads the mosquito net, and replaces old matting, 搬眠床播蚊罩換舊蓆神煞
> the Divine Killers whom one meets when one replaces the old with the new and puts the house in order, 添新換舊收前整後神煞
> also the other ferocious killers and baleful stars of the Five Directions, 五方凶星惡煞.

Official Spirit of the Dead (*kuan-kuei* 官鬼)
Presage of Death (*szu-fu* 死符)
Ruin of the Year (*sui-p'o* 歲破)
Funeral Guest (*tiao-k'e* 吊客)
Talisman of Sickness (*ping-fu* 病符)
Leopard Tail (*pao-wei* 豹尾)
Yellow Banners (*huang-fan* 黃旛)

At the end of this list, Great Year is invoked once again, but now in the form of three different figures: Intendant of the Year (*tang-nien* 當年), Intendant of the Month (*tang-yüeh* 當月), and Intendant of the Day and Hour (*tang-jih tang-shih* 當日當時). From this list one may gain some notion of the baleful stars in everyday belief.

The remainder of the text, dealing with the presentation of the offerings and the expulsion, is composed in a popular style and includes passages which furnish vivid illustrations of the psychology on which the belief is based. The officiant snaps a whip and once again invokes the demons:

> Astral Lord Killers of the Year of the five directions who dwell in celestial palaces, I enjoin you, depart from those celestial palaces. Those of you who dwell in hells, depart from those hells. You who dwell in the mountains, come hither, walking in the clouds and riding up on the mists. You who dwell in the water, depart from the water. I enjoin you all to come here at once. You, Great Killers, seat yourselves above. You, Little Killers, be seated below. For the Great Killers, here are great offerings; the Little Killers will share the remainder among themselves. Let those who have found a place make room for those who have not found one! Let those who have found a bowl pass it to those who have not found one! Let everyone eat his fill of the ten dishes and the eight dishes, and let the full cups and the half-full cups be emptied! Eat and drink till you're drunk . . .

After punctuating the invocation with one more snap of the whip, the officiant continues:

> Eat like pigs, smack your lips: stuff yourselves! And now, drag yourselves to the door and get out! When you came here you were pale; now that you are leaving, you are all red in the face. It has always been the case that those who accept a gift of wine must put up with a bit of joking;[11] those who receive food from someone else must keep calamities away from him. Those who have consumed someone else's meat and wine must give something in return.

After a third snap of the whip, he continues:

> Divine Astral Lord Killers of the five directions, if you want to eat, eat! If you refuse to eat, I, the priest, in accordance with the order of my patriarch, will arrest you!

Once again he snaps his whip, then says:

11. This sentence, 食人酒禮, 受人稽洗, has become as good as a proverb in Formosa.

May the gates of Heaven (*t'ien-men* 天門) open and may the gates of Earth (*ti-hu* 地戶) close; may the gates of men (*jen-men* 人門) stay [open] and may the demons' paths (*kuei-lu* 鬼路) be blocked. [Take care] that I don't smash your hearts, spill your guts, flay you, castrate you [lit., cut out your roots], empty your bellies, annihilate your ancestors, and [take care] that I don't have divine soldiers rush to carry out my orders [that such be done].[12]

After these threats the officiant asks respectfully for the help of the patriarchs in escorting the demons back to where they came from.

First we escort the ferocious demons and the spirits of the earth as far as the exit of the great hall. Next we escort the ferocious demons and evil stars as far as their road. Third, we escort the evil stars as far as the Wheel of Fire (*huo-lun* 火輪), so they may be burnt and transformed. Fourth, we escort the evil stars to return to the citadel of darkness (*yin-fu* 陰府).[13]

Such is the rite celebrated by a Taoist priest, which is in fact much more elaborate than I have been able to show here. There is, for example, the "distribution of the lamps" (*fen-teng* 分燈) which is also part of the *chiao*, the great communal rite of Taoism, and which is intended to summon the auspicious stars (*chi-yao* 吉曜, *hao-hsing* 好星). To light the "lamp" is to cause a guardian star to shine for each family, serving as an antidote to the baleful stars that threaten it.

For the Taoist priest this rite of "Sending Off the Baleful Stars" is a "lesser rite" (*hsiao fa-shih* 小法事), during which he wears the red bonnet of a sorcerer (*fa-shih* 法師), not a "great rite" (*ta fa-shih* 大法事), which would be carried out only by a Taoist priest robed in his sacerdotal garments.

The vernacular rite of *hsieh wai-fang*, which I translate as "Sending Off Afar" or "the Leave-taking Outside [the house]," takes place at a more popular level and does not require the participation of either a priest or a sorcerer. It is undertaken for the same reasons and may be addressed to the same demons, but it is performed by the lay head of the family. He goes outside of the house, in the direction where baleful encounter is thought to have occurred. In case of illness, he requests the remedy from the demon responsible and promises to give him offerings. Three days later, whether or not a cure has been effected, offerings are brought in a winnowing basket to a deserted place far from the house, where there is neither an altar nor a table: they consist of a bowl of rice, a bowl of vege-

12. We find a passage in the same style chanted at the Great Exorcism, *ta-no* 大儺. See J. J. M. De Groot, *The Religious System of China* (Leiden, 1910), 6: 296–97, 319–20; and the explanation by M. Granet, *Danses et légendes de la Chine ancienne* (Paris, 1959), 1: 298–337.

13. This concludes the translation from the work cited in note 5.

tables, the three kinds of sacrificial offerings (*hsiao san-sheng* 小三牲),[14] and three cups of wine. The head of the family returns home and transfers the demon from the body of the sick person to the substitute body by passing the substitute body three times over the stomach and four times over the back of the sick person; then he burns money for deliverance from trouble (*chieh-e ch'ien* 解厄錢), on which is printed the image of the offended demon. The offerings are not to be consumed by those present at the end of the ceremony but must, rather, be thrown away; they have become ill-omened since they were offered in sacrifice (*chi* 祭) to demons, and not "presented as tribute" (*chin-kung* 進貢) to the gods or the ancestors, in which case they would have become auspicious and been consumed.

The first ceremony, a Taoist priestly ritual, is only carried out in serious cases by families who can afford it. The second, a popular rite, is very frequently performed. A Taiwanese family will have recourse to it several times a year in most cases of sickness, domestic discord, accidents while traveling, death, economic crisis, and so on—and it will also be performed as a preventive measure. As soon as the almanac or soothsayer has identified the demons who have caused trouble or who may be likely to cause it—in the coming year, for example—the rites described provide ways to enter into negotiations with them so as to make them avoid the village, family, or individual.

These rites afford an excellent illustration of the way in which Taoist priests, sorcerers, soothsayers, and laymen complement and cooperate with one another in dealing with supernatural danger. They also illustrate the danger seen in baleful stars, the most important of which I shall now discuss one by one. For each of them I shall first present the beliefs and practices now current on Taiwan, as found in the oral tradition, in the theories of the soothsayers, and in protective rituals; then I shall adduce historical texts that reveal the antiquity of the beliefs.

Great Year

Modern Beliefs and Practices

Although in the imperial pantheon T'ai-sui was the powerful protector of the armies, to whom sacrifices were offered before every military enterprise,[15] in popular belief he is an evildoer to be feared by all, whose

14. The three kinds are a fish, an egg, and a piece of pork. One of the first two can be replaced by a piece of beancurd. They are uncooked, which is suitable for demons.

15. See *Ta-Ch'ing t'ung-li* 大清通禮 13:1a–7b and *chüan* 40, *Yün-li* 軍禮 p. 1b (1761). Cf. H. Doré, *Recherches sur les superstitions en Chine* (Shanghai, 1912 and later), 10: 822–32.

anger it is only proper to placate in advance by means of offerings. A statue of T'ai-sui in the temple of Ch'ü-kung Chen-jen 瞿公眞人 in Taipei shows him in the form of Marshal Yin Chiao 殷蛟, son of the last king of the Yin 殷 dynasty,[16] with six arms, three heads, and a vertical eye in the middle of his forehead. He has the horns of a demon, but wears the cap of a Taoist priest; he carries weapons and has a ferocious air. Yet since he dwells in a temple, he must have the character of a protective spirit as well. He is the master of the other baleful stars, controller of the weather,[17] and chief of the Envoys Who Spread Pestilence.[18]

In some of his representations on paper money (*T'ai-sui ch'ien* 太歲錢) he is shown, rather, as a brigand, brandishing a sabre in one hand and in the other a human head that he has just cut off. Here we have without any doubt an angry, offended T'ai-sui, ruling over the directions and the seasons, and one can see why the believer would want to keep him at a distance by means of the rite of "Leave-taking Outside." In connection with this picture of T'ai-sui as a decapitater, the following passage may be quoted from the novel *Shui-hu chuan*, very popular in Taiwan, in which a soothsayer gives the following warning to a worthy: "Venerable Sir, you have always enjoyed good fortune; but this year you have offended the Lord of the Year (Sui-chün 歲星) . . . and in one hundred days you will be decapitated."[19]

The same theme appears even more clearly in a passage of the "Booklet of the Song of the Visit to the Palaces" (*T'an-kung p'u* 探宮簿), a work used by Taiwanese mediums and sorcerers. In this episode, after having passed over the Mountain of Broken Cash (P'o-ch'ien Shan 破錢山), the traveler—that is, the medium—arrives at the Mountain of the Headless Man ("*Tai*"-jen shan 刣人山), where he must pay a toll in order not to be attacked by the general on guard there. The general carries in his left hand a head which he has just cut off; in his right hand he brandishes a sabre. Although the text gives no formal indication of the warrior's name, we may recall that T'ai-sui often holds the rank of "general." What is more, the description of this personage fully corresponds to the effigy of the Great Year which comes from the same place in Taiwan as the text, the town of P'u-tzu 朴子 near Chia-yi.[20]

16. For the legend of Marshal Yin 殷元帥, see *Feng-shen yen-i* 封神演義, chüan 8:28–34, 9:34–37, 63:252–57, 64:257–61, 65:261–67, 66:267, 99:414. (Tainan: Ta-tung shu-chü 大東書局, 1964).

17. See Doré, 10:822–32.

18. In Formosa the pestilence envoys are thought to come by boat. T'ai-sui, as their head, is called "captain" ch'ang-kuan 廠官 or ch'ang-chang 廠長.

19. *Shui-hu chuan* 水滸傳 61:607 (reprinted Taipei, 1968).

20. *T'an-kung pu* 探宮簿, p. 2b. This is an unnumbered manuscript in the Schipper Archive.

When calendrical calculations indicate an encounter with T'ai-sui during the coming year—an encounter that might turn out to be a fire or an illness, or a separation from one's family—it is advisable to perform the rite of "Placation of T'ai-sui" (*an T'ai-sui* 安太歲). Not only will this pacify that fearsome and powerful being; it may even avert the encounter itself. With the family gods present as witnesses, the officiant, who may be either a Taoist priest or a sorcerer, invites T'ai-sui to install himself on the altar of the central hall. While intoning a pacifying prayer, the officiant presents him with offerings of meat, four kinds of fruit, and tea or wine. T'ai-sui's installation on the altar is consecrated by placing either his portrait there or a piece of red paper on which his name has been written. An offering of gold paper (*chin-chih* 金紙) is made to him, which indicates that in this instance he is regarded as a god rather than a demon.[21] Thereafter, on the first and fifteenth day of every lunar month, the family must make offerings to T'ai-sui. Finally, on the last day of the year, the sorcerer or the Taoist priest comes once again to the house to take leave of T'ai-sui by means of a final sacrifice.[22]

This rite of placation is not the only instance of worship that concerns Great Year. In the event of one's having had a baleful encounter with him—that is, in a situation in which he is regarded as a demon whom one has offended—it is necessary to perform the rite of "Leave-taking Outside," in which gold paper is never presented. Rather, T'ai-sui paper alone is burned, together with a substitute body as described above (p. 200).

There is a third ceremony which relates to T'ai-sui. This consists of a trip into the Invisible World (*tsou lu-kuan* 走路關 or *ju-yin* 入陰) with the purpose of ransoming from T'ai-sui, by means of paper money, the *hun* 魂 and *p'o* 魄 souls or the primordial spirits (*yüan-shen* 元神) that he has taken captive. Here are the details of this ceremony, as they are given in the *Chin-ch'ien chou* 進錢呪.

> [The medium] holds in his hand a branch of the peachwood that opens the universe; there is the snap of a metal whip, and he is on the road leading to T'ai-sui. The moun-

21. The custom of offering gold paper to divinities and silver paper to ghosts and demons is also found in Hong Kong and Singapore. On the important phenomenon of religious paper money in Chinese religions, cf. my book, *Monnaies d'offrande et la notion de trésorerie dans la religion chinoise*, Mémoires de l'Institut des Hautes Etudes Chinoises, vol. 1 (Paris, 1975) and reviews in *Journal Asiatique* 264, nos. 3–4 (1976): 486, and *History of Religions*, vol. 17. (February 1978).

22. We owe the information on this ceremony to Mr. Li Lao-chen 李老朕 of Pei-kang 北港. The description of a placation ceremony that is simpler but nearly identical can be found in the *Wan-fa ta-kuan* 萬法大觀 p. 20 (Taipei: Shang-kung wen-hua ch'u-pan she 商工文化出版社, 1969).

tains of the Pitiless Range (*Wu-ch'ing shan-ling* 無情山嶺) fill men with dread, such solitude reigns; spiders have woven their webs there, and his head is covered with them. The cry of the partridge (*chih-ku* 鷓鴣) is heard.[23] [The medium says:] "Pitiless Great Year, accept my offerings.[24] Let them all come, the baleful stars and the ferocious demons, and the auspicious stars as well." When he has got there, Elder Brother [*Ko-ko* 哥哥, the medium] presents paper money. He goes as far as the first gate of Great Year's office, which is guarded by Gate of Mourning and Funeral Guest. He goes as far as the second gate, guarded by Yellow Banners and Panther Tails. Once again he offers paper money: this is the toll. He goes as far as the third gate, guarded by the Mang Spirit and the Robber-killer; then he enters the office of Great Year. The Divine Lord Great Year is truly impressive. "Without a very serious reason, I would not have presumed to come here."

Now is the moment for burning incense on the altar, while invoking the following divinities:

Great Year of the Current Year, Venerable Divinity of Supreme Virtue 當年太歲至德尊神
Marshal Yin of the Great Year 太歲殷元帥
Lady of the Year of the Right 歲右夫人
Great General Wang of the Yellow Banners 黃旛王大將
Great General Hsiung of the Leopard Tails 豹尾熊大將
Vice-envoy Hsieh of the Fei-lien 飛廉謝副使
Great General Wu of the Seven Killers of the Spirit of Metal 金神七煞武大將
Great General Gate of Mourning 喪門大將
Great General Ting, Funeral Guest 吊客丁大將
Great General Chao, Talisman of Death 死符趙大將
Great General Ma, Talisman of Sickness 病符馬大將
Great General Ch'en, White Tiger of the Great Year 太歲白虎陳大將
Divine Lord Ruin of the Year and Destruction of the Year 歲耗歲破神君
Divine Lord Pitiless Dog of Heaven 無情天狗神君

Also invoked are the following vassals of Great Year:

Divine Lords of the Seventy-two *hou* 候
Divine Lords of the Twenty-four Breaths
Envoys of the Current Year Who Spread Crises and Calamities 今年行災使者
Great King, Spreader of Pestilence 行病大王

23. In the Chinese literary tradition the cry of the partridge expresses sadness.
24. Pitiless Great Year 無情太歲 is presumably the god of this mountain.

> King of the Year
> General of the Month
> All spirits of diarrhea and fever, and other baleful stars and ferocious
> killers

Finally, the medium goes on to make the usual libations, and to burn paper money to Great Year. Then he "recovers" (*shou* 收) the patient's souls or primordial spirits which have been appropriated by the demons.[25] We may note that these demons are the subjects of Great Year, whose name comes first on the list given above.

The calendars and books of divination furnish data from which may be foretold the day, month, year, and the direction in which one runs the risk of colliding with T'ai-sui. They also give the means by which one may avoid offending him, or else how one may make up for the offense. This tells us something about the theories that underlie the rites described above. In the *Hsiang-chi pei-yao* we read:

> Great Year is the spirit of the Planet of Wood, which crosses one "palace"[26] every year. That is why it is called "Great Year." When this planet resides (*chu-chao* 主照) above a country, that country cannot be attacked. . . . Where it dwells, the auspicious prevails; opposite it reigns the baleful.[27]

Here we see clearly the ambiguous nature of T'ai-sui: whether he is beneficent or harmful is related to his position in the heavens. His dual character also depends upon his conjunction with other stars:

> If in the quarter that he occupies there are auspicious stars, he brings good fortune; if there are baleful stars, he causes calamities.[28]

Further, according to the same work, the role of Great Year in the spirit world is analogous to that of the emperor in the world of men who, if he has good ministers, causes peace and well-being to predominate, but, if his ministers are bad, unleashes calamities.

There is great diversity in the disasters which Great Year brings. He may turn you into a criminal or make you the victim of a murderer. He

---

25. *Chin-ch'ien chou* 進錢咒 p. 3–4 (S.A. no. 129). This is a manuscript of mediums in P'eng-hu.

26. The Chinese divided the sky into twelve palaces and into five palaces. The twelve corresponded to the twelve cyclical characters and to the Chinese zodiacal signs (Rat = Aries). A man born in the year of the Rat was thus linked to that portion of the sky. As to the fivefold division, the central palace corresponded to the central administration, and the four palaces around it in the four directions corresponded to provincial administrations.

27. *Hsiang-chi pei-yao* 象吉備要 11:1 (reprinted Hsin-chu, Taiwan: Chu-lin shu-chü 竹林書局, 1967); compiled by Wei Chien 魏鑑, preface, 1671.

28. Ibid., 15:4.

may cause the loss of members of your family, or provoke serious illnesses, lawsuits, imprisonment, loss of chattels or of the six kinds of domestic animals, and so on. It could depend on the year of your birth. The *T'ieh-pan shu* notes that, in order to assure his peace of mind, everyone born in the year of the Rat should carry out the ceremony of placation whenever T'ai-sui is residing in the corresponding celestial "palace."[29]

Historical Background

In ancient times belief in T'ai-sui was linked to the planet Jupiter (*Sui-hsing* 歲星), which takes twelve years to complete its cycle: that is to say, it passes through the circle of the twenty-eight constellations in twelve years.[30] Its entrance into any one of these constellations meant that it was exerting its influence over the corresponding (*ying* 應) terrestrial region. Thus, Ssu-ma Ch'ien 司馬遷 notes in the astronomical chapter (*T'ien-kuan* 天官) of the *Shih-chi* 史記: "In those regions over which the Year Star stands, the five grains flourish. In those regions that lie opposite it, there are calamities."[31] Here is already found a theory of divination that is widespread today, as reported in the *Hsiang-chi pei-yao*. The influence of Jupiter's conjunctions with the other four planets is explained in the same chapter of the *Shih-chi*. When Jupiter "encounters the Planet of Earth (Saturn) there is political turmoil and famine. The ruler goes suddenly into battle and is defeated. [If it encounters the Planet of] Water (Mercury), then there is a change in strategy and an alteration in affairs. [If it encounters the Planet of] Metal (Venus), then there is a gathering in white garments (mourning)."[32] It is evident, then, that the current notion of the influence of conjunctions goes back a long way.

According to a Han source, if the Planet of the Year moves too rapidly or too slowly or is not to be seen at a time when it ought still to be visible, it is because the planet has been changed into a "demon-star" (*yao-hsing* 祅星).[33] This notion appears to have some relation to the present-day Taoist belief in the danger which threatens someone whose "palace" becomes the seat of an "invisible star" (*an-yao* 暗曜), a belief that is discussed at the end of this chapter.

29. *T'ieh-pan shu* 鐵板數 Article No. 3023 (Hong Kong, Wan-hsiang shu-chü 萬象書局, 1965).

30. See Leopold De Saussure, *Les origines de l'astronomie chinoise* (Paris, 1930), pp. 403–90.

31. E. Chavannes, trans., *Mémoires historiques de Se-ma Ts'ien* (reprinted Paris, 1967), 3: 401.

32. Ibid., p. 368.

33. This is stated by Meng K'ang 孟康 (early 3d cent.), quoted in the commentary by Yen Shih-ku 顏師古 on *Han-shu* 漢書 26:4a (*Chi-ku Ko* 汲古閣, 1642 ed.).

According to the astrological chapters of the *Shih-chi*, the *Han-shu*, and the *Hou Han-shu*, when the Planet of the Year has been "struck" (*fan* 犯) in one of the constellations of the Five Palaces,[34] there will be a catastrophe on earth, either at the court or in the provinces, depending on the mansion in which the violation has occurred. This is because it is generally considered that the palaces and their constellations correspond to Chinese society and government. The same idea is to be found in most of the dynastic histories.

According to Chavannes, T'ai-sui is "the same thing as the Yin of the Year (*sui-yin* 歲陰). . . . It is the conventional point, the course of which is fixed according to that of the planet Jupiter, but which advances in the opposite direction."[35] In this context T'ai-sui is not the "Year Star," but rather its "shadow." This, however, is an astronomer's conception; in the popular mind, T'ai-sui and Jupiter are identical.[36] In certain Taoist books of the Six Dynasties, however, some traces remain of this initial astronomical conception. We find in the *Cheng-i fa-wen ching-chang kuan-p'in* a "demon in reverse to Jupiter" (*Sui-hsing ni-kuei* 歲星逆鬼), in other words, T'ai-sui.[37] In some almanacs and astrological works, the ideas of inversion and a "shadow" characterize certain baleful stars, such as Lo-hou 羅睺 and Chi-tu 計都.

Religious prohibitions relating to the point of the compass occupied by T'ai-sui were in existence as early as the Warring States period. We read in the *Hsün-tzu* that when King Wu of Chou 周武王 attacked King Chou of Yin 殷紂王 he headed eastward, disregarding the prohibition in current military use, and in so doing found himself face to face with the fearsome Lord Great Year—though this did not prevent him from successfully accomplishing his undertaking.[38] The same anecdote is told in the *Shih-tzu*: the astrologer Yü Hsin 魚辛, having warned King Wu that Great Year was in the North, counseled him to avoid this direction, but the king paid no attention.[39] In these texts we see two orthodox classical authors expressing their opposition to a belief which, in their eyes, was only a groundless superstition.

34. See note 26.

35. Chavannes, 3: 371. Cf. Chavannes, 3: appendix 3, p. 652–66. This interpretation seems to be influenced by Chia Kung-yen 賈公彥 of the T'ang, cf. Gustave Schlegel, *Uranographie chinoise* (Taipei, 1967 reprint), 1: 615–16.

36. The *Tz'u-yüan* dictionary portrays T'ai-sui as the planet Jupiter. In the *Hsiang-chi pei-yao*, 11:1, T'ai-sui is the spirit of the planet Jupiter.

37. *Cheng-i fa-wen ching-chang kuan-p'in* 正一法文經章官品 3:10b (*Tao-tsang* 道藏 [= *TT*] 880).

38. *Hsün-tzu* 荀子 4:11a (Shanghai: Hung-wen chü 鴻文局, 1893).

39. *Shih-tzu* 尸子 3:4b (Taipei: Commercial Press, 1968 reprint).

The *Han-shu* states that in 1 B.C. "when the Shan-yü 單于 [ruler of the Hsiung-nu] visited the court, he was lodged in the P'u-t'ao 蒲陶 Palace in the Shang-lin 上林 Garden. There T'ai-sui manifested his might, and it was declared that this was a mark of respect."[40] The Shan-yü was pleased by this, and subsequently gave assistance to Han troops who had lost their way in the desert. Thus it would seem that the belief in T'ai-sui extended even to foreign tribes.

So widespread was this belief that, during the later Han dynasty, Wang Ch'ung (ca. A.D. 27–100) devoted two chapters of his *Lun-heng* to criticizing it. In the chapter "Against [Beliefs relating to] Temporal Periods" he takes issue with the "vulgar notion" which held that, in the course of leveling or construction works, the spirits of the year and the month are in a position to "devour" in certain directions.[41] If Great Year is in *tzu* 子, he will devour those who were born in *yu* 酉; if the first month begins with *yin* 寅, the lord of the month will devour those who are under the sign *ssu* 巳. If construction work is undertaken in *tzu* and *yin*, families living in *yu* and *ssu* will be doomed. As early as the first century, then, the theme of T'ai-sui was subdivided to correspond to the principal divisions of time—years, months, and days—and the same belief is still found at the present time.

Wang Ch'ung next describes the reactions of those families who believe themselves threatened with being "devoured." They offer sacrifices, after having carried out exorcisms (*ya-sheng* 壓勝), by hanging up objects according to the classification of the Five Elements: metal objects if they

40. *Han-shu* 94:7b.

41. Cf. Bernard Frank, "Kata-Imi et Kata-Tagae, Etude sur les interdits de direction à l'époque Heian," *Bulletin de la Maison Franco-Japonaise*, n.s. 5:2–4 (1958).

live in the west, charcoal if they dwell in the east, and so on. Sometimes the imperiled house is temporarily abandoned. When T'ai-sui is in *tzu* and the houses in that quarter are threatened, a talisman may be installed there to avert the danger; but in that case the evil influence that has been deflected will destroy the houses which lie in the opposite direction, *wu* 午.[42]

In the chapter "Critique of [the Belief in] the Year," Wang Ch'ung attacks the belief relating to the "rule of displacements" (*i-hsi fa* 移徙法), according to which it is quite as deadly to face T'ai-sui as to turn one's back on him. To face him is called "*sui-hsia*" 歲下 (literally, "Great Year descends"); to turn one's back on him is called "*sui-p'o*" 歲破 ("Great Year destroys"). Thus, if T'ai-sui is in the direction *chia-tzu* 甲子 (north), one must go neither toward the north nor toward the south, especially not when taking the most important steps of one's life, such as marriage or the construction of a house.[43]

We may note that by the Han dynasty the principal conceptions relating to T'ai-sui were fixed, and since that time this star has played a very important role in popular belief, Taoist rites, and the imperial cults. Taoist rituals almost always include the Lord Great Year and the General of the Month among the deities, as well as the spirits of the day and hour.

In Six Dynasties Taoism, T'ai-sui was already a great deity. In the *San-t'ien nei-chieh ching* it is stated that in A.D. 157:

> the officers of the court of Han, with the blood of a white horse, wrote in vermilion on tablets of iron an oath sworn before the Three Officers of Heaven, Earth, and Water, and before the General Great Year, always to practice the Right Doctrine of the Three Heavens.[44]

A text in the *Teng-chen yin-chüeh*, compiled by T'ao Hung-ching 陶弘景 (456–536), notes that when one collides with "T'ai-sui [in relation with] one's personal destiny in the current year" 行年本命太歲, it is advisable to invoke the Five Lords of the Earth 制地君 and their hundred and twenty generals who govern the I-ch'uan Palace 宜泉宮, so that they will "annihilate the evils caused by Great Year."[45]

This document is extremely precious, as it enables us to give an approximate date to the text of the *Cheng-i fa-wen ching-chang kuan-p'in* (see n. 37), in which the same passage occurs. It is possible that the passage in this latter work was taken from the text in *Teng-chen yin-chüeh*, which

42. Wang Ch'ung 王充, *Lun-heng* 論衡 23:473–76 (Taipei: Shih-chieh shu-chü 世界書局, 1958).

43. Ibid., 24:492–98.

44. *San-t'ien nei-chieh ching* 三天內解經 A:6a (*TT* 876). This is a fifth-century text.

45. *Teng-chen yin-chüeh* 登眞隱訣 C:20a (*TT* 193).

T'ao Hung-ching compiled in the fifth century. Yet it seems likelier that T'ao borrowed from the *Cheng-i fa-wen*, the date of which should have been much earlier. In it Tai-sui is named "the Great General Great Year" and associated with the Killers of Earth. The circumstances under which one may offend him are associated with the directions and temporal divisions. The text mentions the "lords" created by Taoism in order to destroy the calamities that T'ai-sui is capable of setting in motion. In addition to the Queen Mother of the West and the Lords of Earth, we may note the names of Yü-ching chün 玉竟君, T'ien-ching chün 天竟君, K'ai-t'ien chün 開天君, Yang-fang chün 揚方君, Ch'ang-lo chün 昌落君, and Su-po hsüan-ming chün 素白玄明君. It can be seen that Six Dynasties Taoism adopted the Han beliefs reported by Wang Ch'ung, systematizing and codifying them within the framework of a higher religion.

According to a Taoist text from the end of the T'ang, T'ai-sui "wanders" (*yu* 遊) through the Twelve Palaces of one's individual destiny; here, then, in a tenth-century Taoist text, is a forerunner of the present-day belief in the Twelve Palaces.[46] A Taoist painting attributed to Wu Tao-tzu 吳道子, also of the T'ang (d. 792), shows T'ai-sui—already called Marshal Yin, as he is today—in the guise of the God of Thunder and wearing a necklace of human skulls. This is reproduced in *Zeichnungen nach Wu Tao-tze aus der Götter- und Sagenwelt Chinas* (Munich, 1913, p. 13). Finally, the *I-chien chih* of Hung Mai 洪邁 (1123–1202) records that within the Temple of the Eastern Peak was a hall reserved for the Puissant Lord Great Year 太歲靈君, alongside whom were the deities of the Bureau of Pestilence 瘟司神.[47]

Thus, the present-day belief in T'ai-sui—god of directional prohibitions, master of the seasons, chief of the spirits of pestilence—is based upon a long tradition, the origins of which are still uncertain but which is richly represented in documents. In addition—and still more striking—is the fact that the popular iconography of Taiwan today, and in particular the terror associated with the idea of T'ai-sui as a divine headsman, as he is depicted on the paper money, are related to the gruesome representations of T'ai-sui in Taoist paintings attributed to the T'ang.

White Tiger

Modern Beliefs and Practices

On Taiwan, in plays and popular songs, mention is frequently made of

46. See the *Kuang-ch'eng chi* 廣成集 4:1–17:10 (*TT* 337–39). This work is by Tu Kuang-t'ing 杜光庭 (850–933). The same theory about T'ai-sui can be found in a Taoist work on divination, the *Tzu-wei tou-shu* 紫微斗數 1:1a–3:36 (*TT* 1114).

47. *I-chien chih* 夷堅志 22:4a (Taipei: Hsin-hsing shu-chü 新興書局, 1960).

the star White Tiger (*Pai-hu hsing* 白虎星), a "meeting" with which is a presage of death.[48] This star is an extremely dangerous demon. The almanacs give precise indications concerning its direction and the date of its descent to earth. Pregnant women in particular must avoid going out then, for if they meet him he may well bite the foetus in their womb, which would result in the death of the child and a miscarriage. Men born in the year of the Tiger must not be present at marriage ceremonies or childbirth, nor may they visit newborn children, even the offspring of domestic animals. It is dangerous to have sexual relations with a girl whose pubis is hairless, for she is a White Tiger girl (*Pai-hu nü* 白虎女).

The books on divination are an abundant source of information concerning the powers of the White Tiger. According to the *Wan-fa ta-kuan*, the White Tiger drinks the blood of the members of the family, and scatters their worldly possessions.[49] According to the *Pai-chung ching*, the White Tiger may devour the foetus in its mother's womb, and attack the kidneys, legs, and arms of adults.[50] The *Hsiang-chi pei-yao* states that the crossing of the White Tiger Pass is a presage of the disease "*ching-feng*" 驚風 (a fit followed by convulsions); if it is combined with smallpox, the child will be difficult to cure. He may well injure himself and suffer a loss of blood. A child who has been attacked by White Tiger cries out in terror.[51]

According to the *Ch'i-men tun-chia ch'üan-shu*, should White Tiger enter a house, there will be mourning and laments will be heard. What is

48. Thus, in the "Allegorical Song of Visiting a Lover" *T'an-ko hsiang-pao ko* 探哥相褒歌, p. 4a (Hsin-chu: Chu-lin shu-chü, 1961), a young girl finds her lover sick in bed. Worried, she goes to seek a fortune-teller, who informs her that White Tiger is inexorably drawing near to the person she loves. In the song "A Magical Battle between the Peach Blossom Girl and Chou Kung," *T'ao-hua nü Chou-kung tou-fa* 桃花女周公鬥法 (Taiwan: Chu-lin shu-chü, 1961), Chou Kung is first seen examining the eight characters (*pa-tzu* 八字) of the man who has come to consult him and announcing that he is to die that night because White Tiger is above him, unaccompanied by any auspicious stars (pt. 1, p. 1b). Then he is seen summoning White Tiger to the marriage of the Peach Blossom Girl, which he wishes to ruin: the Tiger will eat the first person to enter the marriage bed. It is Chou's daughter who arrives there first, and White Tiger floods the nuptial chambers with her blood (pt. 3, p. 1a). Today nuptial chambers are red, and red predominates in marriage ceremonies in such a way that even the sight of the color is enough to satiate White Tiger.

The novel "The Conquest of the West by [General] Hsüeh Ting-shan," *Hsüeh Ting-shan cheng-hsi* 薛丁山征西, which is often staged in the theater, portrays the general's father, Hsüeh Jen-kuei 薛仁貴 (the almost invincible hero who conquered Korea at the beginning of the T'ang), as an incarnation of the White Tiger star; and the fortress before which he dies in battle is named the White Tiger Fortress 白虎關.

49. *Wan-fa ta-kuan*, p. 21.

50. *Pai-chung ching* 百中經 p. 34 (Hsin-chu: Chu-lin shu-chü, 1957).

51. *Hsiang-chi pei-yao*, 19:18.

more, lawsuits will result, and one's life will be endangered by battles when traveling.[52] The *T'ieh-pan shu* gives eighteen kinds of encounter (*fan*) with White Tiger, and lists the calamities which result from each: at home, death of husband, wife, parents, or children: outside, meetings with pirates or soldiers in battle, and danger of imprisonment.[53] White Tiger is generally classified among the demons in the Ts'ung-ch'en group,[54] or among the twelve star-gods. He travels through the twelve palaces that correspond to the twelve-year cycle; when he enters the palace of the year of one's birth, it forebodes a crisis. The books on divination are pervaded with this theory: like the calendars, they give precise information not only with regard to the years, days, and hours when there is a chance of one's encountering White Tiger, but also on the directions which it is well to avoid at these particular moments. Thus the *Hsiang-chi pei-yao* warns those born under the sign of Fire against the north (*tzu* 子); those born under the sign of Metal are warned against the east (*mao* 卯); those born under the signs of Water and Earth must avoid the south (*wu* 午); and those under the sign of Wood must avoid the west (*yu* 酉).[55] This prohibition of the *opposite* direction, similar to that which prevails in the case of T'ai-sui, is common to the lore of all the baleful stars.

Many books of divination emphasize the danger involved in celebrating a marriage on days when there is a chance of meeting with White Tiger. If he is crouching on the road 攔路白虎 taken by the marriage procession which accompanies the bride to the house of the bridegroom, he will subsequently be in a position to devour the child in her womb. These books also give the direction of White Tiger which is to be avoided in laying out the marriage bed.[56]

52. *Ch'i-men tun-chia ch'üan-shu* 奇門遁甲全書 (Hsin-chu: Chu-lin shu-chü, 1967). This book of divination is attributed to Chu-ko Liang and Chang Liang. The first comprehensive study of techniques of divination has been written by Ngo Van-Xuyet, *Divination, magie et politique dans la Chine ancienne* (Paris, 1976). It includes a translation of the magicians' biographies in *Hou Han-shu* 112; on the method of *tun-chia* and *ku-hsü*, cf. pp. 190–95.

53. *T'ieh-pan shu*, articles 3038, 3048, 3106, 6308, 8458, 9116, 10043, 10255, 10263, 10300, 10361, 11228, 12091, 12126, 12733, 12851, 12889, 12929.

54. According to the *Hsieh-chi pien-fang shu* 協紀辨方書, a book of divination reprinted by Jui-ch'eng shu-chü 瑞成書局, Taichung, in 1961, the *ts'ung-ch'en* 叢辰 are the ferocious spirits of the year. They are also lucky or unlucky spirits who accompany the hours. For example, Celestial Joy (T'ien-hsi 天喜) and Happiness-Virtue (Fu-te 福德) are propitious stars, whereas Great Exhaustion (Ta-hao 大耗) and Little Exhaustion (Hsiao-hao 小耗) are baleful stars like White Tiger. In modern almanacs one can find the list of auspicious and baleful stars, together with the days and hours that are best to encounter them.

55. *Hsiang-chi pei-yao* 19:18.

56. Since beds in Taiwan are generally fixed to the wall, this practice does not seem to fit in.

The conception of White Tiger found in mediumistic texts hardly differs from that found in the books on divination, as can be seen from the following.

> Once, when you built your house, you offended a killer, and on the occasion of your marriage you offended White Tiger. The demons and ancestral spirits manifest their presence day and night. [Your house] leans toward the East [or] toward the West, [so] you have been unable to obtain descendants. If you do not drive off [the demons] in time by means of sacrifices, in two years your family will have disappeared.[57]

The liturgical manuals of Taoist priests give long lists of the multiple forms assumed by White Tiger, forms that correspond to different times and places. Here is a list of them, drawn from a manuscript manual on sacrifice to the White Tiger:[58]

> Divine Lord White Tiger (*Pai-hu shen-chün* 白虎神君)
> of the Celestial Departments of the world above,
> of the Terrestrial Forests of the world in between,
> of the earth and the heaven, of the Yin and the Yang,
> of the year, the season, the month, the day and the hour,
> of the 72 *hou* 候 (periods of five days),
> of Wood and the east, of Fire and the south . . .
> of the Eight Trigrams and the Nine Palaces,
> of the thunder of the Central Palace,
> of the outside, the inside, front and behind,
> of the year which occupies the dwelling;
> you who enter houses in order to carry out great massacres there,
> who hurl and shoot arrows,
> who enter into one's fate in the course of the year,
> who lie in wait (*chih* 值) by the bed and the door of the dwelling,
> who lie in wait on the road and in the hall,
> behind the stove and in front of the well, etc. . . . .

In the course of this invocation, we find White Tiger associated with other demons and with the five directions:

> Divine Lords White Tiger and Great Year Who Has Charge of the Current Year 值年當年太歲白虎神君,
> Divine Lords White Tiger and Funeral Guest and Gate of Mourning 喪門弔客白虎神君,
> Divine Lord White Tiger of the Despoiling Demons of the Five Directions 五方耗鬼白虎神君,
> Divine Lord White Tiger Crouching on the Road of Kou-ch'en 句陳攔路白虎神君,[59]

57. *Yang Jen-yü chih chin p'ien* 揚仁裕智金篇 6:499 (Taichung: Jui-ch'eng shu-chü, 1963).
58. *Chi-pai hu* 祭白虎 (S.A. no. 101), p. 1.
59. Kou-ch'en 句陳 is in the constellation of the central palace, which is made up of six stars.

Divine Lords White Tiger of the Right and Green Dragon of the Left 左青龍右白虎
神君,

Divine Lords Black Tortoise of the Rear and Vermilion Bird of the Front 前朱雀
後玄武神君,

Divine Lord Serpent of the Centre Who Maintains the House 中央鎮宅騰蛇神君.

It is clear how reassuring such an invocation must be, answering as it does
to dangers issuing from the Three Worlds, the Yin and the Yang, all the
divisions of time and space, and various categories of demons. That helps
to explain why, like the rest of the manual, it is used by Taoist priests to
perform exorcisms.

An old sorcerer of Pei-kang 北港 furnished me with information on a
similar rite of exorcism intended to drive off White Tiger. It is for the most
part like the rite described above (in n. 14), the "Leave-taking Outside,"
only with the special feature that the live "victims" offered in sacrifice,
shrimps or small fish, are to be released at the end of the ceremony in accordance with the Buddhist idea of respect for living creatures. The
money which is burnt must include twelve "knives" (tao 刀) of White
Tiger money, five of Yin and Yang money, and "money for ransoming
life" (mai-ming ch'ien 買命錢).

The text of a prayer to the White Tiger is found in the *Wan-fa tien-
tsang*:

White Tiger, White Tiger, you who make blood glisten, so-and-so has offended you,
Killer White Tiger. We bring you the three kinds of animal offering, wine, cooked
dishes, paper money. Depart with the other ferocious killers, and return to trouble us
no more. You who have now drunk the soup we have prepared for you, take the harmful demons on your shoulders and depart for some other village. You who have now
eaten a piece of beancurd, take the harmful demons on your shoulders and go all the
way to the mountains of T'ang 唐山.[60] You who have eaten an egg, take on your
shoulders the evil spirits; you who have eaten the three victims, take on your shoulders
the evil spirits and harmful demons and go three thousand *li* away. You who have
drunk wine, take on your shoulders the evil spirits and the harmful demons and get
out! Come no more to bite, go away, as far as Luzon and Mindanao! If you leave [the
suppliant] in peace, he will live 120 years. If you go your way, he will live to the age of
120. Leave here once for all, depart hence never to return, come back no more to trouble so-and-so, his life will resume its course, and he will once again find peace.[61]

---

60. "Mountains of T'ang" refers to mainland China. Emigrants in Formosa, Indonesia,
and Indochina call mainland China "T'ang-shan" 唐山.

61. *Wan-fa tien-tsang* 萬法典藏 p. 62 (Taipei: Shang-kung wen-hua ch'u-pan she 商工文化
出版社, 1966). It may be a modern touch that White Tiger is asked to go as far away as the
Philippines, but the expulsion of demons to foreign lands is an archaic theme. The famous
Tung-ching fu 東京賦 of Chang Heng 張衡 (A.D. 78–139), preserved in *Wen-hsüan* 文選 p. 17
(Taipei: Wen-yu shu-chü 文友書局, 1966), states: "The flashing fire gallops as the stars flow.
Let us chase the Red Pestilences to the far-off peoples of the four directions." This passage

We may note the offhand style of this address. By agreeing to consume the offerings, White Tiger has placed himself in a position of inferiority and dependence. Therefore he must put up with the ironic authority of the priest. With its precise geographical references, this ritual seems quite concrete.

The "Tale of the Making of the Bridge," a Taiwanese liturgical manuscript, portrays a scene in the course of which the person threatened by White Tiger passes over a mythical bridge, beyond which the danger no longer exists:

> "Friend, I ask you once again what that pass is called." "That pass is called the Pass of the White Tiger. In the White Tiger Pass you see the two ferocious eyes of White Tiger." "White Tiger, what is the only thing you fear?" "I fear only the sorcerer's dragon horn (*lung-chiao* 龍角)."

The sorcerer performing the rite then blows on his horn and makes the suppliant cross the imaginary bridge.[62]

The *K'o-tse chiang-i*, a divination text, gives a very simple means of keeping away White Tiger on the marriage day, during the installation of the marriage bed, as well as during the construction of a house. One needs no more than an inscription on red paper, stating "the Unicorn is here" 麒麟在此.[63] We know that the Unicorn is an auspicious star considered capable of neutralizing all baleful influences. According to the *Ch'un-ch'iu pao-ch'ien t'u* 春秋保乾圖, Jupiter is able to transform itself into a unicorn.[64] As Jupiter is an auspicious planet for the region under it, we may assume that the beneficent character of the mythical unicorn derives from the star.

Other divination texts give further details. According to the *San-yüan pei-yung pai-chen*, if the spot where one digs a grave is the residence of White Tiger, a day belonging to the Celestial Fire (*t'ien-huo* 天火) must be selected; straw must be placed around the grave and set alight. White Tiger will then flee and do no harm to the descendants of the deceased.[65]

According to the *Hsiang-chi pei-yao*, on the occasion of a marriage White Tiger Great Killer Thunder appears in the principal hall of the house, where the ceremony takes place. This hall is called "the Central Palace" (*chung-kung* 中宮), which is the center that controls the universe.

---

is related to the last episode of the Great Exorcism (*ta-no*), a ceremony held at year's end in the Forbidden City. See Granet, *Danses et légendes*, 1: 228 ff.

62. *Tsao-ch'iao shuo-pai* 造橋說白 p. 11 (S.A., no. 129).

63. *K'o-tse chiang-i* 尅擇講義 2: 14b (Taichung: Jui-ch'eng shu-tien 瑞成書局, 1968).

64. See *Isho shūsei* 緯書集成, vol. 4 B, p. 57.

65. *San-yüan pei-yung pai-chen* 三元備用百鎮 p. 40 (Tainan: Ta-shan shu-tien 大山書局, 1968).

If the couple are not to be destitute of descendants, an animal must be sacrificed and bled there in order to gorge White Tiger. A drum is struck outside the house, and White Tiger, glutted, runs off. As a proverb puts it, "when White Tiger sees blood, he desists [from doing harm]" 白虎見血則止也. The book advises carrying out this sacrifice at the place where, according to the information of the diviner or medium, the marriage procession will meet White Tiger.[66]

The local gazetteer of Feng-shan in the south of Taiwan notes that on the 25th day of the twelfth month, a black duck is killed and offered to the gods. A tiger is made from paper, and daubed on the inside with the blood of this duck or with pig's blood; otherwise, a piece of raw pork is placed inside it. It is afterwards burnt outside the house, and by this act all baleful influences are driven away.[67]

Historical Background

The role of the tiger in Chinese mythology goes back to very ancient times. The tiger motif is frequently found on the bronzes and pottery vessels of the Shang; it is also preserved on a number of wooden objects. During the Eastern Chou the military commander's insignia, the *hu-fu* 虎符, was in the form of a tiger. In many ancient texts reference is made to the strength of the tiger, who devours demons and spectres and protects the living.[68]

The *Li-chi* states: "When the army is on the march, before it goes the Vermilion Bird, behind it the Black Tortoise; on its left, the Green Dragon, on its right, the White Tiger; above it is the star Chao-yao 招搖."[69] This passage refers to the figures represented on the banners. Since Chao-yao is the name of the constellation of the Dipper, White Tiger should also be the name of a constellation. Thus, by the end of the Warring States period, the White Tiger was already one of the four Sacred Beasts (*ssu-ling* 四靈) that were identified with stars. In the *Huai-nan tzu* it is stated that "the West is Metal; its spirit is T'ai-po 太白 ("the Great White One"); its animal is the White Tiger."[70] It symbolizes the destructive

---

66. *Hsiang-chi pei-yao*, 15:3.

67. *Ch'ung-hsiu Feng-shan hsien-chih* 重修鳳山縣志 3:51 (Taipei: Kuo-fang yen-chiu-so 國防研究所, 1968).

68. See, for example, *Shan-hai ching* 山海經 1:7b, 3:11b, 5:7a, 8:6a, 11:5a, 12:2b) Hao i-hsing chien-shu 郝懿行箋疏 1881). On the military tiger insignia, cf. my article, "Hsin-chi hu-fu ti tsai-hsien" 新郪虎符的再現 (The reappearance of the Hsin-chi Tiger *fu*), *Ku-kung chi-k'an* 故宮季刊/*The National Palace Museum Quarterly* 10, no. 1 (1976): 35–77 and plates.

69. *Li-chi* 禮記, *Ch'ü-li* 曲禮 3:8b (Chiang hsi: Nan-ch'ang fu-hsüeh 南昌府學, 1815).

70. *Huai-nan tzu* 淮南子 3:3a (*Chu-tzu chi-ch'eng* 諸子集成 ed.).

force of autumn, in relation to metal as well as to white, the color of mourning. It is the stage of death in the life cycle of all creatures, as expressed in the *T'ai-p'ing ching*, which tells us that:

> All creatures issue from the Great Mystery (*t'ai-hsüan* 太玄); in the middle course of their lives they are in the Great Yang and, when their lives come to a close, they reach the White Tiger. This means that the primordial breath is in the north, and that the White Tiger dwells in the west.[71]

In astronomy, from this period on, White Tiger represented a synthesis of the seven constellations of the West. The astronomical chapter of the *Shih-chi* gives further details on White Tiger's astrological aspect (head, mouth, eyes, shoulders, and limbs) and on his religious functions: punishment and decapitation, but also protection of the army.[72] A Han apocryphal text, the *Ch'un-ch'iu tso-chu ch'i* 春秋佐助期, emphasizes this very function and states that "His spirit bears the name Tsu-chi 祖及 and the byname of Hsü-t'u 虛圖."[73] It seems probable that these precise details of nomenclature are related to the rite of invocation, and may well have some connection with the fact that if one knows the name of a demon or can define his appearance, one nullifies his malevolent power.

From this period on, astronomer-astrologists made the meetings of White Tiger with the Five Planets and shooting stars the subject of the most painstaking observation. Thus the *Hou Han-shu* records that on the day *hsin-mao* 辛卯 of the first month of the first year of the Yung-yüan 永元 reign-period (A.D. 89), a shooting star came forth from the constellation Ts'an 參 (White Tiger), leaving a forty-foot luminous trail behind it, which was a presage of warfare on the frontier—and that, in point of fact, during the sixth month the emperor sent his general, Tou Hsien 竇憲, to attack the Hsiung-nu, and a great victory resulted.[74] The relation of White Tiger to the idea of war is clear. During the Han, official buildings bore his name, such as the White Tiger Hall (Po-hu Tien 白虎殿), where military affairs were discussed; mention is also made of a pavilion of the White Tiger and a White Tiger Gate.[75]

Still in connection with the idea of war, the astronomical chapters of both the Chin and Sui histories state that the seven constellations of the

71. *T'ai-p'ing ching* 太平經 67:1b (*TT* 750).
72. *Shih-chi* 史記, 27:5b, Chavannes trans., 3: 352.
73. See *Isho shūsei*, 4:78.
74. *Hou Han-shu* 21:200.
75. For the White Tiger Hall, see *Han-shu* 82:2a, 84:21a, 97:11b, 98:10b, 99A:37b (Shanghai:Wu-chou t'ung-wen shu-chü 五洲同文書局, 1903); for the White Tiger Gate, ibid., 99A:31b; for the White Tiger Pavilion, see *Hou Han-shu* 3:54.

West are generals who preside over the non-Chinese peoples in the West.[76] The hope is there put forward that these stars will lose their brilliance, which represents their destructive force, so that China will enjoy peace.

Further, the fact that the tiger preys on men influenced the beliefs concerning the constellation of the White Tiger during the Han. The eminent scholar Wang Ch'ung, whose views on T'ai-sui we have already quoted, devoted a chapter of his *Lun-heng* to this subject, under the title "Encountering the Tiger" (*Tsao-hu* 遭虎). Here he states: "Ts'an-fa 參伐 is the constellation of the Tiger, and Hsin-wei 心尾 symbolizes the Dragon. When these stars appear, tigers do harm on earth." Wang Ch'ung also mentions a belief current among soothsayers of the *pien-fu* 變復 school: man-eating tigers represent officials who harm the people.[77] In this case the belief in stars is no more than a reflection of political and social problems.

The *Hou Han-shu* provides information on the belief in White Tiger among the non-Chinese tribes of south China. The five clans which lived in the mountains of Pa 巴 and Nan 南 commanderies (Szechwan and Hupei)—the Pa 巴氏, Fan 樊氏, T'an 暉氏, Hsiang 相氏 and Cheng 鄭氏— had since ancient times offered human sacrifices to White Tiger. According to a myth of these tribes, White Tiger was the transformation of the spirit of Lin-chün 廩君, the legendary hero who had founded their clans. His taste for human blood had to be satisfied with offerings.[78]

Archaeological investigations in this area have brought to light weapons, sword-hilts, and axes which are made in a special style differing from that of the Chinese, and which bear representations of a tiger. These weapons, found in wooden coffin-boats, date from the Warring States period.[79] The myth of the tutelary White Tiger should thus predate this period, and should also be older than our written sources on astrological astronomy. This leads us to a hypothesis: the name of the constellation White Tiger could have originated with these non-Chinese tribes, and the Chinese might have come to associate this constellation with the West at a very remote time, when the center of China was not Ch'ang-an, but

76. *Chin-shu* 晉書 11:11b (Shanghai: *T'u-shu chi-ch'eng*, 圖書集成, 1886 ed.); *Sui-shu* 隋書 20:2b (Shanghai: *T'u-shu chi-ch'eng*, 1886 ed.).

77. *Lun-heng* 論衡 16:333–35.

78. *Hou Han-shu* 116:1023–24.

79. See P'eng Han-chi 馮漢驥, Yang Yu-jun 楊有潤, and Wang Chia-yu 王家祐, "Ssu-ch'uan ku-tai ti ch'uan-kuan tsang" 四川古代的船棺葬, *K'ao-ku hsüeh-pao* 考古學報 2:77–96 (Peking, 1958).

rather a more easterly point. The association with that region would have been reinforced when King Hui of Ch'in 秦惠王 conquered Pa and Shu in 325 B.C., and the chief of the five clans allied himself by marriage to the royal house.[80] It is probable that the custom of sacrificing to White Tiger was known to the Chinese of Ch'in from that time on.

The *Hou Han-shu* mentions a myth that was current among the tribesmen known as Pan-shun Man 板楯蠻, neighbors of the five clans. Under King Chao-hsiang 昭襄王 of Ch'in (306–251 B.C.), a white tiger appeared, followed by numerous other tigers. They overran the regions of Ch'in, Shu, Pa, and Han (Shensi, Szechwan, Hupei), mangling and killing over a thousand people. The king thereupon offered a great reward to anyone who could kill the White Tiger. Among the tribesmen of the district of Lang-chung 閬中 in Pa commandery was a man who knew how to make white arrows out of bamboo. By him the White Tiger was shot and killed. The following passage states that this man was the hero-founder of the seven clans of the Pan-shun.[81] The historical basis for this legend would seem to be the war between the lands of Pa and Shu.[82]

Let us now see the forms that this belief took in Taoism. In the *Ch'ih-sung tzu chang-li*, the section on "Petitions for Assistance in Childbirth" depicts White Tiger being expelled together with the Killer of the Year, the Killer of the Month, and the Killer of the Hour, on account of the harm he causes at the moment of birth.[83] As we have seen above, this notion is still current in Taiwan.

In the *Tao-men k'o-fan ta-ch'üan*, edited by Tu Kuang-t'ing (850–933), in the section "Rituals for placation of the house and deliverance from those whom one has offended" 安宅解犯儀, it is stated that in order to expel White Tiger, one must invoke Hsi-wang mu 西王母, the Queen Mother of the West.[84] The *Ch'ing-wei chieh-e wen-chien* 清微解厄文檢 shows White Tiger related, on the one hand, to the theory of the Five Elements, and on the other, to the host of demons, just as he appears at present in the Taiwanese liturgical manuscripts. Emphasis is placed on the necessity of a blood sacrifice, which enables one to expel White Tiger easily, once he is glutted. This collection gives a method of predicting the arrival of White Tiger according to the cries of dogs and cats: "When a

80. *Hou Han-shu* 116:1024.
81. *Ibid.*, pp. 1024–25.
82. See *Hua-yang kuo-chih* 華陽國志, *Pa-chih* 巴志 1:3, *Shu-chih* 蜀志 3:29 (Shanghai: Commercial Press, 1958).
83. *Ch'ih Sung-tzu chang-li* 赤松子章曆 94:13b (*TT* 335–36).
84. *Tao-men k'o-fan ta-ch'üan* 道門科範大全 42:6b (*TT* 978–83).

dog or cat cries, it means that White Tiger and Funeral Carriage (*sang-ch'e* 喪車) are setting out."[85]

We have seen that White Tiger, just as Great Year, was in very early times considered to be a protector of the armies. Both, however, became basically destructive forces, capable of setting upon anyone in their path. White Tiger is characterized by his thirst for blood, as well as by his attacks on pregnant women and newborn children, whereas Great Year is less specialized.

Dog of Heaven

Modern Beliefs and Practices

Like White Tiger, in the popular imagination the Dog of Heaven is a rapacious and bloodthirsty demon one must avoid meeting, particularly at the dangerous moments which have already been mentioned in the case of White Tiger (marriage, birth, and funerals), as well as in years or on days of which the almanacs give warning based on the duodenary cycle. The popular song "A Magical Battle between Peach Blossom Girl and Chou Kung" (see n. 48), tells how Chou Kung informed his servant that he would meet the Dog of Heaven on the following day, and that he would die.[86]

In a local gazetteer of Foochow, it is said that a newly married woman must not walk beneath the stars at night, for fear of running into the Dog of Heaven.[87] The same prohibition in Taiwan applies, rather, to pregnant women. To the Dog of Heaven, furthermore, is attributed an inauspicious role during eclipses, and it is necessary to beat drums and gongs to save the moon or the sun from his rapacious appetite.

As in the case of White Tiger, the works on divination that have already been quoted, as well as the mediumistic texts, give much information on the calamities caused by the Dog of Heaven, and on the times at which the risk of meeting him is especially great. These works class him, like White Tiger, among the baleful stars. The almanac *Shu-yao li* 樞要曆 states that the Dog of Heaven is the rapacious spirit of the month, and that, on the day when he descends to earth, one must not pray to the deities nor make gifts to them.[88]

---

85. In *Tao-fa hui-yüan* 道法會元 31:8b (*TT* 884–941). This compedium of ritual was made in the Southern Sung.

86. See *T'ao-hua nü Chou-kung tou-fa*, pt. 2, p. 2b.

87. *Fu-chou fu-chih* 福州府志, *Feng-su* 風俗, 4:3b (Taipei, 1969 reprint).

88. Quoted in the *Hsieh-chi pien-fang shu* 協紀辨方書, *I-li* 義例, p. 9a.

The *K'o-tse chiang-i* offers a little-known theory according to which a crisis caused by the Dog of Heaven may be overcome when he is in the vicinity of the stars T'ai-yang ("Yang at its peak") and Ch'i-lin (Unicorn), except on the days *hsü* 戌 in the seventh month and *yin* 寅 in the eleventh. On all other days over which the Dog of Heaven may preside, including the last day of each month, one can more or less escape from his ill-omened domination, and even be married, providing his influence is counter-balanced by T'ai-yang and Ch'i-lin.[89] Danger also lasts for entire years, which vary with the year of one's birth. The *Hsiang-chi pei-yao* sets out correspondences predicting the year when the Dog of Heaven will menace the individual.[90]

The Taoist manuscript entitled "Sacrifice to the Dog of Heaven" presents a list of the diverse forms of the Dog of Heaven which are to be invoked. Some are associated with the five directions and the five elements. In the east the Dog of Heaven is composed of nine stars which form the shape of an ox, colored pale green; its head is in the direction *mao* 卯, its tail in the direction *yu* 酉, its back in the direction *tzu* 子, its belly in the direction *wu* 午, its forelegs in the direction *hsü* 戌, and its hindlegs in the direction *ch'en* 辰. If on their marriage day the bride or groom walks on his head or tail, he will bring about their death or injure them severely. If they march on his body, he will deprive them of offspring. In the south the stars of the Dog of Heaven[91] form a vermilion snake, which brings discord into the family. In the west his seven stars form a snow-colored horse. In the north his twenty-five stars form a pig the color of smoke. In the center he is yellow.[92] Others of his fearsome forms are connected with Yin and Yang, the year, seasons, month, day, and hour.

There is one instance in which he may do the people a service by driving away otters, thus protecting the fish in the ponds. On the days when the Dog of Heaven occupies the ponds, one may dig them and stock them with fish.[93]

The popular exorcism intended to drive away the Dog of Heaven is

89. *K'o-tse chiang-i* 1:19.

90. *Hsiang-chi pei-yao* 19:9 states that a person born in the first year (*tzu*) of the twelve-year cycle will face danger from the Dog of Heaven in the eleventh year (*hsü*); if born in the second year, then in the twelfth; if in the third, then in the first; and so on.

91. There is a lacuna here in the text.

92. *Chi T'ien-kou* 祭天狗, p. 27 (S.A. no. 51). This particular system of relationship between the directions and mythical animals seems to be given in this text alone. It may be linked to an iconographic tradition that is as yet unknown to us. The practice of arranging the stars according to animal figures appears to be connected with the cult practice of lighting lamps during incantations.

93. See the almanac *Ao-t'ou t'ung-shu ta-ch'üan* 鰲頭通書大全 3:22a (Shanghai, n.d.).

similar to the one which we have described in connection with White Tiger, with the difference that here the demons are not expelled but killed. Details are given in the Taoist manuscript last mentioned. Once the offerings have been presented and the contract between the sick man and the substitute is drawn up, the Taoist priest, turning toward the east, sounds the "dragon horn," thus requesting the Great King who Cuts Off the Heads of Demons 斬鬼大王 to come. With him come his horsemen and soldiers, carrying banners of brilliant green. The demons are surrounded and beheaded, and all are destroyed. The same ceremony is repeated toward the south, the west, the north, and the center, which are by this means cleared of Dogs of Heaven, one after the other.[94]

We find in Doré, *Recherches sur les superstitions en Chine*, a picture of an archer shooting arrows of peach-wood to drive away the Dog of Heaven, and the description of a custom which is intended to preserve dead children from him:

> Old crowns of straw are placed on the tombs of children, in order to prevent the Dog of Heaven from coming to devour them. They are, as it were, encircled in their tombs and cannot be removed from them. What is more, the Dog of Heaven takes the crown to be a dog-collar and runs away, for, like the dog in the story, he does not like to be tied up.[95]

Historical Background

The Dog of Heaven has been known since ancient times either as protector of the authorities or as destroyer of armies and scourge of the people. On the one hand, it involves a star in the constellation of the Dragon's Tail 龍尾 which is auspicious for the emperor because it guards the Forbidden Palace (*hou-kung* 後宮), and baleful for the people when it descends to earth.[96] On the other hand, the Dog of Heaven has to do with a comet or meteorite, as is often stated in the dynastic histories. The *Shih-chi* says:

> T'ien-kou (the Dog of Heaven) has the form of a large shooting star. It gives out a sound. When it descends and comes to rest on the earth, it resembles a dog's dropping and a burning fire. When one looks at it from afar, it is like a flash of fire. It bursts forth into the heavens in flames. Its lower part is round and resembles the surface of a field of many *ch'ing*; the pointed upper part is yellow in color. A thousand *li* away an army is defeated and a general killed.[97]

---

94. *Chi T'ien-kou*, pp. 5–12.
95. Doré, vol. 1, fig. 8 and p. 59.
96. See *Ta-hsiang li-hsing ching* 大象曆星經 1:4 (*Han-Wei tsung-shu* ed.). This work is attributed to Kan Kung 甘公 and Shih Shen 石申 of the Han.
97. *Shih-chi* 27:13a, Chavannes trans., 3: 391–92.

Further on there is another passage concerning the scourges which are brought about by this comet: "The Dog of Heaven passed [over the] territory of Liang 梁, battles followed, corpses lay on the earth, blood flowed."[98]

In the *Han-shu*, it is noted that in 6 B.C. "on the *ting-wei* 丁未 day of the first month at sunrise there was in the sky a trail of white vapor, as broad as a piece of cloth and over ten *chang* 丈 (one hundred feet) long, heading toward the southwest while making the sound of thunder . . . It was called the Dog of Heaven." The outcome of this appearance of a comet came three years later: the terrified people fled screaming, an imperial edict ordered the preparation of sacrifices to Hsi Wang-mu, and a rumor was current concerning the imminent arrival of creatures with vertical eyes 從目人.[99] Recourse to Hsi Wang-mu probably had as its aim to neutralize the influence of the Dog of Heaven. This is the first historical reference I have found to a rite for expelling the Dog. As to the vertical-eyed creatures, we should probably consider them to have been demons accompanying it. The Dog of Heaven is mentioned not only in the *Han-shu*, but also some ten times in the *Hou Han-shu*. Whenever this demon appears, he is followed by catastrophes, famine, cannibalism, and so on, and "the people, terrified, flee screaming."

The existence in Han times of magico-mediumistic practices intended to drive off the Dog of Heaven is attested to by Ma Jung 馬融 (79–166) in his celebrated poem *Kuang-ch'eng fu* 廣成賦:

> Let us cross the dwelling-place of the Spirits,
> Let us penetrate into the high places,
> Let us summon by writ the Ling-pao 靈保 [sorcerer or sorceress],
> And let us invoke Fang-hsiang 方相, conqueror of demons.
> May they drive off the pestilences (*li-i* 厲疫),
> May they expell the *yu-hsiang* 蜮祥,
> May they carry off the *wang-liang* 罔兩,
> May they drive away the *yu-kuang* 游光,
> May they condemn the Dog of Heaven to the cangue, and attach the Goat-tombs (*fen-yang* 墳羊).[100]

According to the *Han-shu* and *Hou Han-shu*, the Dog of Heaven is a harbinger of war. It may also be the image of a bad magistrate, hated by

98. Ibid. 27:21a, Chavannes trans., 3 : 408.

99. *Han-shu* 26:15a.

100. Quoted in *Hou Han-shu* 90A: 755. The different categories of demons named are interpreted in various ways by different writers and commentators. See the entries in S. Couvreur, *Dictionnaire de la langue chinoise classique*; M. Granet, *Danses et légendes*, 1: 298–338; and Chiang Shao-yüan 江紹原, *Chung-kuo ku-tai lü-hsing chih yen-chiu* 中國古代旅行之研究 (Taipei: Commercial Press, 1966), pp. 43–58.

the people. The *Wei-shu* tells how, during the period of the Three King-doms, whenever a certain Yang Chih 羊祉, a cruel official, arrived in a province on a tour of inspection, the people cried out: "The Dog of Heaven is descending" (*T'ien-kou hsia* 天狗下).[101]

The astronomical chapter of the *Chin-shu* gives, in addition to the passage from the *Shih-chi*, many other descriptions of the appearance of this comet:

— a hairy star wearing on both sides [of its head] short luminous beams which, when it descends to earth, take the form of a dog.
— a reddish-white beam of light.
— a shooting star brilliant enough to permit identification of a person's face by night. It descends silently, and its feet can hardly be discerned. Outside it is white in color, but inside it flashes like a brazier.

The text gives further details on the scourges brought by these stars:

— armies are destroyed and generals killed.
— within the five camps the troops fight among themselves, and man-eaters turn up.
— in the regions where they descend, blood flows and the ruler loses his position.

In addition, the *Chin-shu* quotes a passage from the *Ching-chou chan* 荊州占, which probably dates from the Han: "In the northeast appear three great stars, white in color, called Dogs of Heaven. When they appear, men eat one another."[102]

It is evident that the demon Dog of Heaven was the author of calamities which vitally afflicted the whole community in a given region. Popular imagination not only associated the demon's image with the arrival of a cruel official. Translating into demonological terms the terror inspired by the subordinates of the emperor's envoy, it created the *ch'eng-ch'eng* 棖棖—agents for doing "dirty work" in the service both of the officials and the Dog of Heaven. Both graphically and phonetically, the *ch'eng-ch'eng* (or simply *ch'eng*) invite comparison with the *ch'ang* 伥 demons. These were souls enrolled in the service of the tigers who had devoured the bodies to which they were originally joined. People who unquestioningly carried out the orders of cruel officials were ridiculed in the popular saying, "to serve the tiger like a *ch'ang*" 為虎作伥.

The *Nan-shih* states that in the sixth month of 514 "rumors spread

101. *Wei-shu* 魏書 89:11a (Shanghai: T'u-shu chi-ch'eng 1886),
102. *Chin-shu* 晉書 12:15 (Shanghai: T'u-shu chi-ch'eng, 1886).

among the people that *ch'eng-ch'eng* were coming to take human livers, lungs, and blood to satisfy the Dog of Heaven. The people were greatly agitated by this, and it went on for twenty days."[103] The *T'ang-shu* tells of something similar in 643 and 744: "Rumors circulated among the people to the effect that officials were sending *ch'eng-ch'eng* to kill people in order to offer sacrifices to the Dog of Heaven. It was said that they were arriving dressed in dog skins and armed with steel claws with which, often under cover of darkness, they took human hearts and livers."[104]

That such rumors were recorded by official historians suggests that offerings to the Dog of Heaven at this period might sometimes have included human sacrifices. But social morality of the time in no wise permitted such cruelties to be practiced openly, and a cult of this nature—if it existed—could only have been practiced in secret, so that in any case we would have no documents on the subject.

The *ch'eng-ch'eng* demons, according to the T'ang text *T'ung-yu chi* 通幽記, are covered with black hair and equipped with teeth and claws as sharp as swords. The same collection tells that during the Chien-chung 建中 reign-period (780–783), cruel demons came from Hunan. They were called Hairy Demons 毛鬼, Hairy Men 毛人, *ch'eng*, and so on. They could change their appearance at will, loved to eat human hearts, and attacked boys and girls. The people were so terrified that they banded together at night, heavily armed, and lighted fires to protect themselves. When one of these demons infiltrated a family, the residents of the neighborhood clanged their bronze utensils and the noise shook heaven and earth so strongly that people dropped dead of fright. The government banned these demonstrations, but without success.[105]

Since the beliefs centering on the Dog of Heaven were terrifying and so widespread as to be mentioned in the dynastic histories, it is no surprise to find them described in more specialized literature, accompanied by practical instructions for avoiding danger. The *Ch'ih Sung-tzu chang-li* discusses the Dog of Heaven in the sections entitled "Dog of Heaven of the Twelve Months" and "Days When the Dog of Heaven Descends." These passages enable one to draw up tables of the correspondences between the Dog of Heaven and dangerous months, days, hours, and directions, and to determine in advance the precautions that must be taken.[106]

103. *Nan-shih* 南史 6:7b (Shanghai: T'u-shu chi-ch'eng 1886).
104. Hsin *T'ang-shu* 新唐書 35:5a (Shanghai: Chung-hua shu-chü, 中華書局 1923).
105. Quoted in *T'ai-p'ing kuang-chi* 太平廣記 339:2690 (Peking, 1957).
106. For example, in the first month, the Dog of Heaven presides and descends on a *hai* day and devours in the direction *ssu*. The cyclical signs change in their usual sequence with

The notion now current in Taiwan that a lunar eclipse is the work of a devouring Dog of Heaven probably goes back a very long way. It is found in an anecdote of Sung times. Yeh-lü 耶律, mother of the Empress Hsiao 蕭 (early 12th cent. A.D.), dreamt that the moon fell on her stomach and then rose up again into the eastern sky, with a blinding light; but when it reached the zenith it was devoured by the Dog of Heaven. Yeh-lü awoke, terrified by her dream, and gave birth to the future Empress Hsiao.[107] The moon being devoured by the Dog of Heaven foreshadowed the destiny of this empress, who was unjustly condemned to death,[108] but this anecdote also reveals that the belief in the Dog's power over the moon already existed at that time.

The present-day belief in the pernicious influence of the Dog of Heaven is very close to that concerning White Tiger. Both are blood-thirsty demons who like to attack embryos. But while White Tiger is sometimes a protector—as he was, especially in his early history—Dog of Heaven never plays that role. It is particularly interesting to note how this demon has been historically associated in the popular mind with cruel officials.

Conclusion

The three baleful stars which we have studied here appear in very early written sources, such as the *Hsün-tzu* and the *Shih-chi*. Of the other stars that have been mentioned (except for the Five Spectres), we find no trace in these early documents.

In ancient times our three baleful stars were actual heavenly bodies: Great Year was Jupiter (or its shadow); White Tiger was the seven-fold White Tiger constellation in the West; and Dog of Heaven was a comet (or a star named "Dog of Heaven"). In current belief, however, their astronomical origin has come to be of secondary importance. Attention is given exclusively to the days and directions that hold the risk of encountering them. Now they are no more than demons.

---

the following months, the direction always being opposite to the day (*Ch'ih-sung tzu chang-li* 2:15a, 14a [*TT* 335]). The Dog of Heaven also descends two signs after Great Year, and they devour together in a direction that is one sign after that. Thus, in a month when Great Year descends on a *tzu* day, the Dog of Heaven will descend on a *yin* day, and they will devour together in the direction *mao*. In that month the propitious hours will be *ssu*, *wei*, and *yu* (*Ch'ih-sung tzu chang-li*, 2:14a). As the first version of the *Ch'ih-sung tzu chang-li* probably dates from the third century, and its latest recension was fixed in the twelfth, it may be presumed that these beliefs were current from the Six Dynasties through the Sung.

107. See *Fen-chiao lu* 焚椒錄, in *Chin-tai pi-shu* 津逮秘書 p. 1a (*Chi-Ku Ko* 汲古閣). The *Fen-chiao lu* was written by Wang Ting 王鼎, a Liao Dynasty official.

108. See *Liao-shih* 遼史 72:12 (Shanghai: Chung-hua shu-chü 1923).

From reading the histories it might appear that the influence attributed to these stars was over administrative and political affairs, initially at a purely regional level. I believe, however, that this impression results from the fact that these documents were the work of court historians. The *Lun-heng*, on the contrary, indicates that in the popular mind their influence was important to the individual. It is true that, among the baleful stars, only Great Year was treated by Wang Ch'ung, but I see no reason why the popular view would have been much different with respect to White Tiger and the Dog of Heaven.

The myth of White Tiger brings up another question. This baleful star is associated with Lin-chün, the hero-founder of some southern tribespeople (see above, p. 217). This might lead us to wonder whether baleful stars may have originated as earthly persons who, after death, were incarnated as constellations by the ancient mind. The founding hero of the Ai-lao tribes of the South, Chiu-lung, was, during the Later Han, only thought to have been their human founder. By Sung times, however, he had become a baleful star, which fits in with our hypothesis.[109] From the Yüan on, the identity of certain individuals with particular stars is attested to in works of popular fiction. The 108 heroic highwaymen of the *Shui-hu chuan*—corresponding to the 36 *t'ien-kang* 天罡 stars and the 72 *ti-sha* 地煞 stars—are presented as baleful stars who have escaped from the Taoist temple where they had been held prisoner by the Celestial Master; their escape caused major disorders.[110]

The belief in the baleful stars had spread before the founding of the earliest Taoist organizations, and they adopted it without adding much of their own. This explains the fact that, in the Taoist Canon and other Taoist writings, there is no systematic theory with respect to this belief.[111] There are simply rituals and collections of petitions (*i-wen chi* 意文集)—an entire arsenal of practices intended to protect the faithful.

As for present-day belief in Taiwan, we have found that it is essentially the same among the people at large and in the more restricted circles of Taoist priests. The priests, however, leave to diviners and mediums the task of foreseeing and predicting the crises which the stars may cause. They limit their own intervention to the performance of the rite in which they are specialists, the "Sending Off the Baleful Stars." This differs in three ways from the one celebrated by laymen: the presentation of peti-

109. On Chiu-lung as founding hero, see note 9. On his role as baleful star, see Hung Mai 洪邁, *I-chien chih* 夷堅志 33:8a (Taipei, 1960).

110. *Shui-hu chuan*, 1:1-3.

111. One exception should be pointed out. The *Tzu-wei tou-shu* (see n. 46) discusses baleful stars in connection with the theory of the Twelve Palaces.

tions, the invitation of the gods as witnesses, and the multiplication of the forms of demons to correspond with the Taoist divisions of time and space (see above, following n. 58), as well as with the various circumstances of life. The priestly rite is far more impressive than the lay; it brings about greater mental security and thus greater efficacy in allaying those anxieties of which the demons are no more than personifications created by the popular imagination. The popular rite of "Leave-taking Outside" is simpler, in that the officient confronts the single demon invoked: there is no need of the gods as witnesses; and the offerings are more modest.

The baleful stars reflect the opposition between the government and the people. Great Year, White Tiger, and the Dog of Heaven are protectors or servants of the authorities. For the people, however, they are usually cruel demons that bring calamities, bloody scourges, and death. White Tiger and Dog of Heaven are now primarily devourers of newborn children and even of embryos. T'ai-sui may sometimes be asked for protection, and in that case people make him offerings of gold paper; otherwise silver paper is used.

In the course of this study, certain recurrent concepts have occurred which, originally taken from astronomy, now have a bearing on the life of the people.

1 Opposition and Accord (ni 逆 and shun 順)

In astronomy a star which follows its normal course, like the planet Jupiter, is an auspicious star. If it moves instead in reverse like Great Year (which goes in the contrary direction to Jupiter), it is baleful.

This belief in baleful stars which proceed by reverse motion is common also in regard to many other stars, such as Yellow Banner, Leopard Tail, Lo-hou 羅睺, Chi-tu 計都, and so on. These stars, the positions of which determine catastrophes unfavorable to those in power—revolutions, coup d'état, assassinations, and so on—were under constant surveillance by court astronomers, in the hope of foreseeing and preventing such events. However, inasmuch as Great Year is linked to the planet Jupiter, he is also an auspicious star protecting the state and individual beings.

2 Collision or Offense (ch'ung 衝 or fan 犯)

According to Meng K'ang 孟康, these technical terms of astronomy are applied when the rays of two stars seven inches apart cross. In the opinion of Wei Chao 韋昭, these terms describe what takes place when one star strikes another on a vertical plane, from below.[112]

112. See Yen Shih-ku's commentary on Han-shu 26:1a.

In present-day belief, these terms have the sense of "bump into" or "strike" in a physical sense, as for example, to offend a high official as he passes on his way, and thus to be liable to imprisonment. A demon when struck will seize the primordial spirits of his victim, who at once falls ill. In the view of diviners, a person "strikes" a demon when the cyclical characters of his birth are in opposition to the cyclical characters of the demon's time and place. One must then neutralize the baleful effects of this opposition in order to limit the harm that would result.

3 Brightness and Darkness (ming 明 and an 暗)

In ancient astronomy if a star disappears from view before the appropriate time, it becomes dangerous on account of its having escaped from control: it is a baleful star. According to the present-day concept, ill fortune may be due to such an invisible star, and the victim is said to be under the sign of a Dark Star (an-yao 暗曜). An individual's health is linked to the luminosity of his Star of Destiny (pen-ming hsing 本命星) in the constellation of the Dipper. Thus, to let a lamp burn during the night in the main hall of the house assures the luminosity of an individual's invisible star and an auspicious destiny to all the members of a family so threatened.

What emerges most clearly from our study is that, since ancient times, a belief in baleful stars has been important in China and has penetrated all classes of society. The way in which imagination has embroidered upon it reflects certain characteristics of Chinese society, and hence should be reflected in our vision of it.

7 Taoist Monastic Life

Yoshitoyo Yoshioka 吉岡義豊

[Editors' note. *Professor Yoshioka had originally planned to participate in the Tateshina conference. In the absence of a paper by him, he agreed that use could be made of his recent book,* Eisei e no negai 永生への願い *("The quest for eternal life"; Kyoto, 1970). The section entitled "The life of monks in Taoism" (pp. 194–228) is presented below in condensed form. It is based on Yoshioka's own observations, from 1940 to 1946, of the largest Taoist monastery in Peking, the Po-yün Kuan 白雲觀. He describes what he discovered in those years, and the use of the historical present tense does not imply that the monastery existed any later than then. Passages in brackets summarize the portions of the text that have not been translated; or they offer editorial interpretation.*]

THE TAOIST EQUIVALENT of the Buddhist monastery is known as a *tao-kuan* 道觀. Taoist temples in general are known as *kuan* 觀 "abbey," *miao* 廟 "temple," *kung* 宮 "palace," *t'an* 壇 "altar," *tz'u* 祠 "shrine hall," *ko* 閣 "pavilion," *tung* 洞 "grotto," etc. Some of these words are also used in the names of Confucian and Buddhist temples.

Taoist temples are of two main types; "public" 十方 and "hereditary" 子孫. Hereditary temples are those in which control is monopolized generation after generation by members of the same subsect. Most Taoist temples fall into this category. They are referred to as "ordinary" 普通 or "small" temples 小道院. Public monasteries are the great Taoist monastic centers which are open equally to the *tao-shih* 道士 (monks or priests) of any school. They constitute a network of major monasteries very similar to the system of public Buddhist monasteries. Public monasteries do not take novices. The tao-shih living in them are itinerant monks who gather from all over China to pursue their Taoist practice, or novices who have come to be ordained.

Among the special privileges accorded public monasteries the most important is the right to build an ordination platform. There the abbot (*fang chang* 方丈), who is equivalent in status to the director (*kancho* 管長) of a chief monastery (*honzan* 本山) of a Japanese Buddhist sect, administers the vows to those tao-shih ready to receive them. Since itinerant monks cannot be recognized as full-fledged tao-shih until they have taken the vows at an ordination ceremony, they use the public monastery to continue their practice while awaiting ordination.

In addition to the hereditary and public categories described above, modern Taoist temples can be divided on the basis of doctrine. The two great sects are known as the T'ien-shih Tao 天師道, or Way of the Celestial Masters, and the Ch'üan-chen Chiao 全眞教, or Doctrine of Complete Perfection. Temples affiliated with the Celestial Masters are, almost without exception, hereditary. The headquarters of this sect are located on Lung-hu Shan 龍虎山 in Kiangsi, where the Celestial Master Chang 張天師 presides. His office has been hereditary from father to son for centuries, which indicates that the tao-shih of this sect, although they formally renounce the world, are not strictly prohibited from wedlock.

Those who do marry, however, are not permitted to live within a proper monastery (*tao-kuan*). Married tao-shih are referred to by a variety of names that emphasize their domestic life or marital ties and distinguish them from tao-shih who spend celibate lives in monastery cloisters. Tao-shih belonging to the Celestial Master's sect do not take the ordination vows. Until the end of the Ch'ing dynasty, all that was required for their full accreditation was a registration certificate 牒錄 bearing the seal of the Celestial Master. After the advent of the Republican government, this system gradually died out and the Way of the Celestial Masters lost most of its sectarian cohesion.

In the Ch'üan-chen sect, on the other hand, a careful distinction is maintained between hereditary and public monasteries. The White Cloud Monastery (Po-yün Kuan 白雲觀), the seat of the Ch'üan-chen sect in Peking, kept a list of twenty-three other Ch'üan-chen monasteries throughout the country that were registered with it as being public, like itself. They were the following:

T'ai-ch'ing Kung 太清宮 (Feng-t'ien)
Ch'ang-ch'ing Kuan 常清觀 (Chi-ning, Shantung)
Pa-hsien An 八仙菴 (Sian)
Lou-kuan T'ai 樓觀臺 (Sian)
Lung-men Tung 龍門洞 (Sian)
Liu-hou Tz'u 留侯祠 (Han-chung, Shensi)

Yü-hung Ko 玉皇閣 (Wuhan)
Hsüan-miao Kuan 玄妙觀 (Wuhan)
Wu-tang Kung 武當宮 (Wuhan)
Ch'ang-ch'un Kuan 長春觀 (Wuhan)
Po-yün Kuan 白雲觀 (Shanghai)
Yu-sheng Kuan 右聖觀 (Ningpo)
Tan-te Kuan 丹德觀 (Ningpo)
Hsüan-miao Kuan 玄妙觀 (Changchow, Kiangsi)
Ch'ing-yang Kung 青羊宮 (Szechwan)
Erh-hsien An 二仙菴 (Szechwan)
T'ien-hou Kung 天后宮 (Tsingtao)
Ch'ung-hsü Kuan 冲虛觀 (Lo-fu Shan, Kwangtung)
Huang-lung Kuan 黃龍觀 (Lo-fu Shan, Kwangtung)
Po-ho Kuan 白鶴觀 (Lo-fu Shan, Kwangtung)
San-yüan Kung 三元宮 (Canton)
Ying-yüan Kung 應元宮 (Canton)
Yüan-miao Kuan 元妙觀 (Hui-chou, Kwangtung)

Sects and Subsects

The two main Taoist sects can be further divided into a multiplicity of subsects. Each has its own sacred verse (*p'ai-shih* 派詩), and it is by such verses that they can be distinguished. The verses are declarations of independence that express doctrinal differences, however slight. Two subsects may have the same name and be almost identical in origin and tradition, but they are treated as independent entities if their verses are different. In principle, each verse is the founder's expression of the essence of his own enlightenment.

The sacred verse of each subsect also serves as an "ideogram genealogy" (*tzu-p'u* 字譜). Tao-shih who stand in lineal succession to the teachings of a particular subsect receive one of the Chinese characters from the verse as part of their religious name. This shows that the tao-shih belongs to a particular subsect and, since the characters are taken in succession starting from the beginning of the first phrase, it is immediately clear to which generation he belongs. In the Lung-men 龍門 subsect, for example, the first four generations were Chao Tao-chien 趙道堅, Chang Te-ch'un 張德純, Ch'en T'ung-wei 陳通微, and Chou Hsüan-p'u 周玄朴. The first four characters of the Lung-men sacred verse read *tao-te-t'ung-hsüan* 道德通玄.

The White Cloud Monastery in Peking has a dual nature. It is a public monastery, the greatest of the Ch'üan-chen sect. At the same time it is the chief monastery of the Lung-men subsect, which was established by Ch'iu Ch'ang-ch'un 丘長春 when he wrote the Lung-men verse in the thirteenth century. The existing White Cloud Monastery centers upon the building known as the Great Hall of Founder Ch'iu, which serves as his mausoleum. In his youth Ch'iu had practiced austerities in the Lung-men mountains. His disciples and their successors, therefore, called themselves "Lung-men" and took as their center the White Cloud Monastery, their founder's burial place.

All tao-shih are equal: in principle, status distinctions do not exist. In the communal life of the monastery, however, the discharging of the various monastic offices calls for varying degrees of responsibility, which are also called for in the monastic regulations or "pure rules" (*ch'ing-kuei* 清規). Besides, although all tao-shih are theoretically equal, within one subsect those ranking higher in the ideogram genealogy are accorded greater respect. Between the twentieth and twenty-first generations of a genealogy, for instance, the relation is that of master 師父 and disciple 法資. If the nineteenth generation is also represented, the relations are those of patriarch 師祖, master, and disciple. Those higher in the genealogy are accorded respect as "seniors." These kinds of vertical relationships based on ideogram genealogy are not restricted to Taoism. They have also been a feature of secular secret societies like the Ch'ing Pang 青幫 and Hung Pang 紅幫, where distinctions between seniors and subordinates, known as "ideogram seniority" 字輩之先輩後輩, were strictly maintained.

There are, then, Taoist monks, monasteries, sects and subsects. In contrast to Japan, however, there are few instances of ties between main temples and branch temples, or of ties of economic dependence between monasteries. Even the great White Cloud Monastery has direct influence over only a very small number of subordinate houses. It has neither the right nor the duty to interfere doctrinally, administratively, or economically in the affairs of monasteries within the Lung-men subsect, much less those of other Ch'üan-chen subsects. With regard to Taoist subsects, it is misleading to overemphasize parallels with Japanese Buddhism. The Taoist subsect is simply the teaching to which a tao-shih wishes to commit himself and the source of the orthodoxy of his lineage.

Sectarian divisions have always been more pronounced in the Ch'üanchen tradition than in the Celestial Masters'. This has resulted from striking differences in the original characters of the two sects. The Ch'üanchen was heavily influenced by Ch'an (Zen) Buddhism. Many of its tao-shih, confident of their spiritual achievements, expressed the content of their enlightenment in sacred verses. When these verses were used and transmitted by disciples, subsects were formed. The establishment of a subsect was an informal process with few restrictions or regulations. For formal recognition, it was sufficient for a tao-shih of that subsect to enroll (*kua-tan* 掛單) in a public monastery and there to have the details of the life of the founder and his sacred verse recorded and dispatched to all other public monasteries. The new subsect was thereby formally recognized.

Relative Strengths of the Various Schools

The strength of any subsect is largely dependent upon the number of tao-shih belonging to it. Size, however, is not the only determinant. Simply because a school is large does not mean that it exerts a correspondingly great influence on society. The quality of human material within it is more important than mere numbers. Any subsect that produces vigorous spiritual leaders can hope to exert a considerable influence in reviving Taoist circles, and even on society at large.

Some small subsects are restricted to a single monastery. In such cases, if a master lacks disciples the sect naturally dies out. In hereditary monasteries the sectarian affiliation changes along with changes in the community. While a monastery is inhabited by Lung-men monks it belongs to the Lung-men sect; if Hua-shan tao-shih should take over, it would become a Hua-shan monastery. Since it is customary for the headship of a monastery to be transmitted from a master to his principal disciple, it is only in exceptional circumstances that the member of one subsect moves in to assume the headship of another. The sectarian affiliations of most Taoist monasteries are therefore fairly stable, and the more populous schools control large numbers of monasteries.

[Here follows a chart based on ordination registers (*teng-chen lu* 登眞錄) kept on file at the White Cloud Monastery in Peking. It shows how many monks were ordained at other monasteries into various sects and subsects in fifteen individual years, the first of which was 1871 and the last 1927. By far the largest number (2, 523) entered the Lung-men subsect. Almost all the large ordinations—those of over a hundred persons—were Lung-men. Second to Lung-men, the subsect ordaining the most monks was Hua-shan (505). Some of the other thirty-nine sects listed have names indicating that they belonged to the Way of the Celestial Masters. There is mention of one person being ordained into the Mao Shan sect in 1924. (Of course, many more persons could have been ordained in the forty-one sects in these years yet not have been listed on the registers kept by Lung-men monasteries.) Yoshioka does not attempt to deal with the many problems raised by this chart.]

Entry into the Ch'üan-chen Sect

There is no fixed age for admission to the life of a Taoist monk. For most tao-shih, however, their religious lives begin between the ages of twelve and twenty. Motives for "leaving the world" are diverse but can be grouped under the following headings:

1. Those with a deep-seated determination to pursue the way of a Taoist immortal;
2. Those who seek a life of seclusion and tranquility;
3. Those from families so poor that they give their sons to a monastery to be brought up and become monks;
4. Those who, because of ill-health or infirmity, feel ill-equipped to cope with the problems of secular life.

Unfortunately, most Taoist monks today seem to fall into categories 3 or 4. One meets few outstanding figures; most have a deficient understanding of Taoism and seem wanting in spiritual vigor.

Anybody wishing to enter the Taoist religious life must find a suitable sponsor. Usually this means going to an ordinary small temple and requesting its tao-shih to act as one's primary master (*tu-shih* 度師). Having secured acceptance by a master, the youth becomes a novice (*t'ung-tao* 童道). During the ceremony in which he does so, he first worships the deities at the altar of the Preaching Hall (*fa-t'ang* 法堂), then offers his respects to the spirits of earlier generations of masters of the sect in the Patriarch's Hall, and finally makes obeisances before his own master. Henceforth the novice allows his hair to grow. He learns the proper manner in which to clean the monastery buildings, to cook, and to receive visitors. At the same time he studies the Confucian *Four Books* and learns to chant the morning and evening liturgy, the *San-kuan ching* 三官經, *Yen-k'ou ching* 焰口經, and *Tou-k'e ching* 斗科經.

When the novice reaches a suitable age, his master chooses an auspicious day to perform the "rites of crown and cloth" (*kuan-chin li* 冠巾禮). The novice's hair is carefully combed and bound up into a top-knot. He is crowned and joins in prayers and celebrations with the tao-shih and other friends of his in the community.

Shortly after "coronation" the novice enrolls in a public monastery where, when the season to take the vows comes round, he participates in the ordination ceremony. He is now a full-fledged tao-shih, free to remain in the public monastery, to pursue an itinerant spiritual pilgrimage, or to return to his master. Men who enter the monastic life in middle age follow a similar course, except that they do not undergo the long novitiate. An auspicious day is chosen and the "crown and cloth" ceremony is performed almost immediately after entry. The same is true for Taoist nuns.

Ordination

For a Taoist monk the taking of the vows is a vital part of his religious life. Formerly the ordination period lasted one hundred days. It was later reduced to fifty-three days. The ceremonies held during this period are conducted at three ordination platforms and consist of:

1. Declaration of essentials (*yao-mu* 要目)
2. Midnight ordination (*shou-fa* 授法) at a "secret platform"
3. Declaration of the hundred-odd articles of the Ch'üan-chen vows.

During the ordination season ordinands are responsible for providing their own living expenses. They must also pay for their robe and bowl (*i-po* 衣鉢), ordination certificate, and kneeling cloth.

Every ordination is presided over by a *ch'üan-chieh lü-shih* 傳戒律師 who holds the rank of abbot (*fang-chang*). He is assisted in administering the vows by a number of senior monks carefully selected for their spiritual insight and experience. [The titles of their offices are given.] With the exception of the ordination instructors (*yin-li shih* 引禮師), there is only one monk for each of the offices. The number of instructors varies with the number of ordinands and may reach as many as ten or twenty. According to the ordination register for the 1927 platform at the White Cloud Monastery, there were six instructors for the [349] ordinands and the presiding abbot was Ch'en Chih-pin 陳至霖, who came from Chih-li. [Here follow the names, titles, and places of origin of 17 of the 31 ordination officers that year, most of whom also came from various localities in Chih-li. Many of the senior ones also had the twenty-first generation name, Chih 至, of the Lung-men sacred verse.]

Above the ordination platform hang effigies of the Three Pure Ones 三清, the principal deities in the Taoist pantheon. Ordinands must be sixteen years of age or over. They will normally have spent at least a year in an ordinary small temple. The names of those ordained are printed in an ordination register. They are "numbered" according to the sequence of characters in the *Ch'ien-tzu wen* 千字文. The first four are qualified to become abbots of large public monasteries. The first two are given a religious pedigree (*fa-chien* 法籤) showing their sectarian lineage. All ordinees receive ordination robes, certificates, eating bowls, and kneeling cloths.

Ordination ceremonies can only be conducted at public monasteries belonging to the Ch'üan-chen sect. Yet tao-shih of the Way of the Celestial Masters are free to participate. Large numbers of tao-shih from this sect began to participate in Ch'üan-chen ordination ceremonies after the Celestial Master ceased to issue his registration certificates. However, even if their performance in the ceremonies is excellent, there seems to be an implicit understanding that they do not have the right to become abbots of public monasteries. This is inevitable as long as sectarian lineages persist.

In the early Ch'ing the number of legally permitted ordinands in any year was in the region of 2,000 and the ordination period was fixed at 100 days. From about 1800 on, the numbers of those actually ordained gradually diminished, until by the late Ch'ing some 500 tao-shih were being ordained each year and the period had been reduced to 53 days. Under the Chinese Republic there was no regulation of the number of ordinands in any year.

Since 1927 the ordination platform at the White Cloud Monastery in Peking has not been in use. Until 1949 this was principally due to economic factors. During the Ch'ing dynasty generous financial assistance from the imperial court sustained the monastery and its platform. After the Republican period began, the monastery had to rely entirely on voluntary support. The ordination ceremonies held in 1927 reportedly cost some 20,000 Chinese dollars (*yuan* 圓). They would have been impossible without the support of wealthy patrons. Once ordination ceased, the Ch'üan-chen sect, like the Way of the Celestial Masters, tended to become a sect in name only, its vitality lost. [Here follows a table of the thirty-one ordinations held at the White Cloud Monastery from 1808 through 1927. In some years the number of monks ordained there exceeded the total of the number recorded at all the other Lung-men monasteries together, in the chart summarized above (p. 233). In 1882, for example, 264 Lung-men ordinees were listed on the registers from other monasteries, whereas at White Cloud alone there were 525.' At its last two ordinations (in 1919 and 1927) the White Cloud Monastery ordained 412 and 349 monks, respectively.]

The Robes and Regalia of the Tao-shih

While I was staying in Peking a group of Japanese sumo wrestlers visited China. The Chinese clerk of a bookshop asked me one day: "There are a lot of Japanese tao-shih visiting Peking these days. What are they doing here?" Puzzled by this mention of Japanese tao-shih, I asked him where he had seen them. "Haven't you seen all those big fellows around the

Tung-tan P'ai-lou?" he said. I was struck by his description of sumo wrestlers as tao-shih. He was right. With their bound-up hair and flowing robes, the wrestlers, in dress at least, truly seemed to be Japanese tao-shih.

One obvious characteristic of the tao-shih is that he lets his hair grow long and binds it up. Over this coil of hair he normally wears a flat cap known as a *hun-yüan mao* 昆元帽 or a *nan-hua chin* 南華巾. His top-knot is held in place by a hairpin made of wood or jade.

The tao-shih's robes are usually blue (*ch'ing-lan* 青藍). In Five Elements thought, *ch'ing* signifies the "vital spirit of the blue (or green) dragon." It is the color of the East and of the element wood. The use of this color is explained as indicating descent from Lord Tung-hua 東華帝君, the founder of the Taoist religion. A tao-shih's robes are not restricted to blue, however. Yellow or purple robes are also worn on ceremonial occasions, or by tao-shih of the status of abbot, but not by anyone unordained. [A table gives the names and specifications of the robes and when they are worn. Many technical details of the various types of headgear follow.]

Only with certain headgear can the crown be worn, as is customary in all ceremonies. The varieties include the Lunar Crown 月冠, Five Peaks 五岳 Crown, Lotus Blossom 蓮花 Crown, Three Terrace 三台 Crown. Made of wood or jade, their use is carefully prescribed. They may not be used by a tao-shih until he has undergone the "rites of crown and cloth" toward the end of his novitiate. The most commonly used is the Lunar Crown. The robes worn by the tao-shih also vary with the kind of crown used, and both are subject to a variety of customary restrictions. The tao-shih—resplendent in gorgeous robes, glittering crown and hair bindings, white stockings, and boat-shaped shoes known as "cloud shoes" or "blue shoes"—is far removed from modern taste. Yet seeing him in this raiment it is easy to believe that he is indeed unworldly, ethereal, even immortal.

The regalia of the tao-shih are also subject to a variety of regulations. His "Immortal's bowls" and kneeling cloth are formally received at the ordination ceremony. The "Immortal's bowls" (*hsien-po* 仙鉢) are made of iron, wood, and lacquer. The iron bowl is used as a cooking utensil on journeys into the mountains in search of herbs. The wood and lacquer bowls are for daily use in the monastery refectory. The kneeling cloth (*Kuei* 規) serves as a prayer mat. It is a piece of scarlet cloth about 1.5 meters long by 80 centimeters wide, with a black border approximately 10 centimeters wide.

The kneeling cloth is employed in three ways: (1) fully opened it is an expression of the most reverent degree of worship; (2) half-folded it is for worship of high-ranking deities; (3) fully folded it is carried over one arm on ceremonial occasions requiring reverence. Its dimensions are similar to those of the kneeling cloth (*chü* 具) used in Buddhist ceremonies and described in such Buddhist manuals as the *P'i-ni jih yung* 毘尼日用.

The above paragraphs describe the costumes of tao-shih belonging to the Ch'üan-chen sect, not those of the Celestial Masters'. In general, tao-shih of the Ch'üan-chen sect emphasize individual practice. They roam the mountains in search of medicinal herbs. To allow for their practice of austerity, their robes are light and simple. Tao-shih belonging to the Way of the Celestial Masters emphasize devotional activities. They devote much of their time to magical incantations, prayers, and festivals. Their robes are correspondingly elaborate. [Here Yoshioka includes a technical description of these robes.]

The Etiquette of Enrollment in the Monastery

In public monasteries itinerant tao-shih from all over the country gather to live a communal life. Their enrollment, a procedure termed *kua-tan* 掛單, is governed by strict regulations. Only if the tao-shih satisfies certain requirements is he permitted to stay. At the White Cloud Monastery, for example, admission is not granted to applicants whose lineage and identity are doubtful or undocumented; who are suffering from severe illness or opium addiction; who are reported to have been expelled from another monastery; who wear outlandish or irregular dress, cut their hair short, or behave strangely; who express heterodox opinions or are suspected of acting as healers, soothsayers, astrologers, or diviners; who are lax in the performance of the daily liturgy; or who are under age.

The etiquette of enrollment involves a searching interrogation. The newly arrived tao-shih first goes to the Public Monks' Hall (*shih-fang t'ang* 十方堂). At the entrance he stops and calls out, "Venerable Supervisor of the Hall, mercy!" When the hall supervisor inside responds, "Mercy," the tao-shih enters the hall to be interviewed by him. He is instructed in those features of the life of the monastery about which he should be familiar and is told its regulations. He is also given a bag, known as a *tan-tai* 裇袋, in which to keep his belongings.

He next goes to the Registration Chamber (*ying-pin fang* 迎賓房) and calls out, "Venerable Registrar, mercy!" Upon the reply of "Mercy," he makes his way into the chamber and prostrates himself three times before the deity of the hall. He then makes "three prostrations for the Venerable Registrar." The registrar greets the new entrant with "one mercy prostration." [Quotation marks indicate that the words are spoken as the acts are performed before the altar.] He next proceeds to ask the new tao-shih in detail about his sect and religious lineage, his age and background, his master and his master's antecedents, his place of entry to the monastic life, his novitiate, and so on. If there are no obvious discrepancies, the registrar records the information on a wooden tablet. The entrant is then asked by the registrar to recite from memory the morning and evening liturgy.

When he has satisfactorily completed this stage, the tao-shih, carrying the wooden tablet, proceeds to the Guest Hall, where he confronts the guest prefect (*chih-k'o* 知客). Before each of the intervening halls, how-ever, he makes three full prostrations, striking his head on the ground each time. At the entrance to the Guest Hall he calls out, "Venerable Guest Prefect, mercy!" At the answer "Mercy" the tao-shih enters. After three prostrations before the hall deity and "three prostrations for the Guest Prefect," another intensive examination of antecedents and creden-tials is carried out. The entrant is required to recite more texts from memory. Any weakness is quickly exposed.

Only when this examination has been completed is the tao-shih given permission to remain in the monastery. He can return to the Public Monks' Hall in a lighter spirit. There, after three prostrations before the hall deity, "three prostrations for the Hall Supervisor," "three prostrations for the Assistant Supervisor," and "three prostrations for all the monks, young and old," the ceremony of enrollment in the monastery ends on a joyful note. The tao-shih unpacks his belongings in a place designated by the hall supervisor. Until he is given specific duties in the monastery, the new entrant continues his spiritual practice under the supervisor's direction. The enrollment procedure takes from two or three hours to half a day to complete.

A number is assigned to each member of the community. In a monas-tery of two hundred tao-shih, for instance, they are numbered from one to two hundred. A newly enrolled tao-shih is given a new number. A tao-shih who has previously belonged to the community and reenrolls is said to "retake his number," although in fact he is given a new one. But his is called a "great number" to distinguish him from those who enroll for the first time and receive an ordinary "new number." A tao-shih who leaves the community is said to "cancel his number."

For monks wishing to reenroll in the monastery after a period of ab-sence the following regulations are enforced:

—Anybody guilty of bad behavior is not to be readmitted.

—Anybody who, during previous residence, withdrew from the monastery before completing half a month there is not to be readmitted.

—Anybody who has "canceled his number" (left the monastery) and yet before half a month has elapsed seeks to "retake his number" is not to be readmitted.

—Anybody who was previously expelled by the abbot or prior (*chien-yüan* 監院) cannot "retake his number" for at least three years.

—Anybody previously expelled by an overseer (*tu-kuan* 督管) or warden (*hsün-chao* 巡照) cannot "retake his number" for at least two years.

—Anybody previously expelled by a manager (*tsung-li* 總理), guest prefect, or superintendent (*chih-shih* 執事) cannot "retake his number" for at least one year.

—Anybody previously expelled by a hall supervisor cannot "retake his number" for at least half a year.

—Anybody whose credentials as a tao-shih have been revoked can never "retake his number."

Punishment of Tao-shih

Tao-shih who break the harmony of the community or disobey the "pure rules" (*ch'ing-kuei* 清規) are punished. The code at the White Cloud Monastery provides that those who commit the offenses indicated below shall receive the following punishments:

1. Prostration for the period of the burning of one stick of incense for:
   —Anybody who does not get up immediately at the morning signal
   —Anybody who fails to attend a community assembly
   —Anybody who is ill-behaved at worship
   —Anybody who leaves the monastery without permission
   —Anybody who leads others into idleness or bad behavior
   —Anybody who is careless about hygiene and sanitation
2. Demotion (*ch'ien-tan* 遷單), which entails being given a lower number and more menial duties, for:
   —Anybody who gathers others about him to chat or gossip
   —Anybody who makes a mistake about signals on the bell and board (*chung-pan* 鐘板)
   —Anybody who is given charge of a hall and fails to keep it clean
   —Anybody who abuses the authority of his office
3. Being ordered to leave the monastery (*ts'ui-tan* 催單) for:

—Anybody who indulges in forbidden foods or wine (*hun-chiu* 葷酒)
—Anybody who neglects his duties
—Anybody who refuses to go on an errand when dispatched
—Anybody who is disrespectful or violent toward his seniors
—Anybody who makes mistakes in office
—Anybody who attacks the failings of others
—Anybody who does not observe the rules of his office
—Anybody who interferes with visitors
—Anybody who engages in practical jokes, quarreling, or fighting
—Anybody who fails to return to the monastery at night
—Anybody who lies about why he did not return to the monastery

4. Expulsion (*k'ai-ko* 開革) for:
—Anybody who does not keep the vows
—Anybody who is lewd or immoral
—Anybody deliberately destroying communal property, who shall be expelled, and also made to pay restitution and be beaten
—Anybody misappropriating monastery funds, who shall, after strict examination, be expelled and also be beaten

5. Referral to the civil authorities for:
—Anybody who instigates riots or unrest within the monastery
—Anybody engaging in arson, who shall be referred to the civil authorities and also be beaten
—Anybody found cheating people of their property
—Anybody found lying in order to secure donations
—Anybody engaging in loose talk about political matters, who shall be expelled and also be beaten
—Anybody breaking the laws of the state, who shall be expelled and also be beaten.

At first new entrants are given such menial positions as gardener, latrine attendant, or pig-keeper. They move up to more senior positions through a series of annual promotions. Yet those who have filled such senior posts as prior, overseer, warden, or guest prefect, must, if they "erase their numbers," become itinerant monks, and upon entering another monastery, begin again there by performing the most menial tasks. This is the rule of the Ch'üan-chen sect. In such cases, however, the time spent in menial roles may be shortened because of a tao-shih's diligence in performing his duties, or simply because of his previous record.

[Here follows a chart showing the titles, though not necessarily the functions, of the thirty-nine offices that existed at the White Cloud Monastery. Many of them were also in use at Buddhist monasteries.]

Reminiscences of the White Cloud Monastery:
  Life without Electric Lights

There were no electric lights at the White Cloud Monastery. During my initial visits to the monastery this simple fact had not struck me. I first noticed it when I entered the monastery on July 1, 1940. The monastery lies only a kilometer west of the Hsi-pien-men Gate in Peking. It is an imposing, densely roofed building, certainly not the kind that one would expect to be without electric lights.

An Shih-lin 安世霖, then thirty-eight years old, was the tao-shih in charge of the monastery. He held both the offices of head monk and prior. He was in the prime of life and full of energy. I told him that I would like to undergo all the formalities of enrollment and be treated exactly as an ordinary itinerant monk. This request was politely refused. I was told that I would always be treated as a guest of the monastery. I later learned that shortly before my arrival there had been a serious dispute within the monastery provoked by a group of tao-shih who opposed the prior. It was probably because of this that they were so cautious in their treatment of a foreigner of unknown origins who had suddenly arrived.

The room to which I was assigned for my stay was the Abbot's Chamber (*fang-chang fang* 方丈房) the innermost monastic building on the left-hand side. The similarly constructed building immediately opposite, on the right-hand side of the complex, was the Prior's Chamber (*chien-yüan fang* 監院房). This was a complete reversal of what I had hoped for. I had wanted to experience the life of the newly entered, low-ranking tao-shih, but here I found myself pressed into the chamber of the highest-ranking monk in a public monastery. Fearing that protest on my part might lead to total exclusion from the premises, however, I accepted my defeat gracefully. At that time, the White Cloud Monastery had no abbot (*fang-chang*). This chamber was therefore reserved for guests.

Li Ch'ung-i 李崇一, the guest prefect, was introduced as the monk responsible for entertaining me. He was then fifty-one years of age. With his luxuriant, flowing white hair, he seemed the very incarnation of an immortal. He spoke to me with affection of Dr. Koyanagi Shikita 小柳司氣太 who had visited the monastery the year before. I learned in subsequent conversations that Li Ch'ung-i had already been living for more than twenty years at White Cloud. At this time he ranked just below the prior in the monastic hierarchy, but in December of the same year he "erased his number" and became an itinerant monk again. Here was a man who could have continued to enjoy a secure and easy life but who chose to relinquish rank and office for the hard life of an itinerant monk. I was impressed. The spirit of the Ch'üan-chen school was not yet dead. The overseer, Pai Ch'üan-i 白全一, and the guest prefect, Li Hsin-lu 李信錄, are two other examples of high-ranking tao-shih I have known who suddenly left to return to the austere life of the lowly itinerant.

In the evening a boy lit the lamp in my room. It was only at this moment that I realized there were no electric lights in the monastery. As a product of modern civilization, I regretted that I had not brought a flashlight with me. I tried to make notes on the many events of the day under the guttering wick. When eventually I looked outside, I found that every other room in the monastery was in pitch darkness. It was already midnight. Every creature, at one with nature, was sleeping. Only one solitary "unnatural" being broke the harmony of life by scribbling notes while he exhausted the flame.

I then realized that in the monastic world the scale of values was reversed, that little significance was attached to artificial, so-called cultural, activities. Taking pride in gathering scraps of knowledge, conducting surveys, doing research—these may be efforts to find some satisfaction or self-understanding in the society of men; but they end, as does life, like the flaring out of a candle. It is better to be embraced in the vastness of nature, to melt into it. Then there is no wasted resistance to life, no useless conflagration. When one's breathing is in harmony with nature, one becomes identical with its very life-flow. The life of the tao-shih at the White Cloud Monastery was the perfect expression of this natural identity. I was suddenly overcome by a sense of hollowness, of humility and sadness at the sharp realization that not only was my body that of an alien but my heart as well. I doused the lamp.

I later learned that, on principle, lights were never used in the monastery. A lamp had been specially provided me as a guest. Since it was certainly odd in this quarter of Peking to have no electricity, I raised the matter with Prior An. He first gave me an economic reason. The cost of lighting such an enormous complex (made up of dozens of buildings covering over three hectares—see p. 250) would be astronomical. Secondly, he explained that, as tao-shih always got up at dawn, the brightening of the Heavens, and went to sleep at dusk, the darkening of the

Heavens, there was no need for electric lights. The economic argument was understandable, and since I had already experienced the second reason for myself, I decided that any further comment would be superfluous and held my tongue.

The Daily Routine of the Tao-shih

When light touched the eastern sky, at 5:30 A.M. in the summer, the morning stillness at the White Cloud Monastery was broken sharply by the striking of a large plank (*pang-tzu* 梆子). It was struck five times, three slow then two quick. This marked the beginning of the tao-shih's day. Silence was observed by those weeding the garden, fetching water, cleaning the halls, or preparing breakfast in the kitchens. The high-ranking tao-shih in the meantime arose and put on formal dress: they combed their hair, washed their faces, and donned their robes, crowns, and ribbons. At 6:30, responding to signals struck on the bell and board, they made their way to the Shrine-hall of the Seven Perfect Ones 七眞殿 to perform the morning devotions.

Normally, morning devotions were attended by the prior and seven tao-shih. The prior acted as celebrant and chanted the scriptures. The signals on the bell and board were fixed, and the same number of each was always given. One ring of the bell was matched by one blow on the board, two rings by two blows, three rings by three blows. On special occasions the great drum might also be used, but daily signals were limited to those given on the bell and board. Never more than three rings on the bell and three blows on the board were given. The words chanted are contained in the *Ch'üan-chen kung-k'o ching* 全眞功課經.

[A list follows of the five texts recited at morning devotions and the four at evening devotions.]

On holidays, the first and fifteenth day of each lunar month, and on the birthdays of the various deities, the monks recited in addition the *Yü-huang ching* 玉皇經, *San-kuan ching* 三官經, *Chen-wu ching* 眞武經, and other scriptures. The first two were also recited in temples of the Way of the Celestial Masters.

After the recitation of the scriptures another signal was given on the plank (in the morning and at midday it was on the plank, in the evening on bell and board). At this signal the tao-shih assembled in front of the Shrine-hall of Founder Ch'iu; then, in two files led by the guest prefect on duty, they entered the refectory. When they reached the entrance, a bowl-

244

shaped gong (*ch'ing-tzu* 罄子) was sounded. The morning meal began. Regulations governing behavior in the refectory were strict. Conversations and glancing at one another were absolutely forbidden. At the head of the hall was an altar for the worship of Wang-ling-kuan 王靈官. On the left and right sides two long tables were placed face to face down the length of the hall.

All tao-shih stood at their places while an offering was first made to Wang-ling-kuan. A single rice bowl was placed on a small round tray. Then the cantor (*ching-shih* 經師), who stood facing the altar on the right, struck a hand-chime (*yin-ch'ing* 引罄) and began to chant. All the monks followed him in reciting an opening and a closing grace (*Kung-yang chou* 供養呪 and *Chieh-chai chou* 結齋呪). When these were finished, the tao-shih standing to the left of the prior's seat raised the tray to eye level, set the offering down on a table before the altar, and retired to his place. The prior, guest prefect, superintendent, and cantor then left the hall. The remaining tao-shih sat and began their meal. When the meal was over, they bowed once and left the hall.

The abbot's chair was set between the niche of Wang-ling-kuan and the offering table behind the prior's seat. When an abbot was in residence he sat there. The space behind the altar was used for storing eating utensils. Inside the main part of the refectory, framed verses commemorating ordinations were hung from the ceiling at one end of the hall. These were verses written by tao-shih to extol the virtues of the [former] abbots. On the eastern and western walls hung two plaques inscribed with large characters reading *T'ai-shang kan-ying p'ien* 太上感應篇 and *Wen-ch'ang ti-chün yin-chih wen* 文昌帝君陰隲文. These were both originally the titles of basic texts of popular Taoism. Their presence here indicated that they were now revered by monk and layman alike.

After the morning meal the *Yü-huang ching* was chanted in the Lecture Hall. Tao-shih then formed "education classes" 教育班 to listen to a lecture. Formerly there had been no such educational provision. The morning lecture had recently been introduced by Prior An Shih-lin. Instruction covered such works as the *Four Books* and the *Five Classics*, together with more specialized topics in the history of Taoism. There were about three hours of lectures in the morning, which were followed by the midday meal. The afternoons were allotted to the duties of the various offices and to private study or religious practice. Bell and board were sounded again at about 6:30 P.M. to signal the evening meal. After the meal the tao-shih rejoined their education classes for a period of instruction in the chanting of scriptures under the direction of the cantor. (I attended one or two of these sessions. However, not only did I understand nothing that was going on, but my presence interfered with the studies of the tao-shih, so I soon stopped going. Now, in retrospect, I regret that I did not persevere.)

Speaking of chanting of the scriptures I used to own a copy of the *Pei-tou yen-ming ching* 北斗延命經 dating from the period 1119–25 of the Northern Sung dynasty. Once, when Prior An came to visit me in my temporary residence, I showed it to him. He smiled and said, "At the White Cloud, too, we have a scripture dating from the Yüan dynasty." This was news. My eyes lit up, and I asked for the name of the scripture. He pointed to a verse (*yün-wen* 韻文) in the *Pei-tou yen-ming ching* and said, "Listen, I'm going to chant this," and recited it by heart. "Well, did you recognize the White Cloud's Yüan dynasty scripture?" he asked gleefully. I was nonplussed, but could not help smiling at his innocent delight. This way of chanting seems to have been handed down at the White Cloud Monastery since the Yüan dynasty. If my visit had been in these days, I would have tape-recorded it. Unfortunately, at that time, in the midst of war, all I could do was listen to it.

At nine in the evening there were more signals on the bell and board. Henceforth it was possible to loosen one's robes and relax. The tensions of the day were over. Tao-shih strolled about the monastery and its environs. I sometimes persuaded Prior An to join me in a stroll. People we met whispered, "It's the old monk (*lao-tao* 老道) of the White Cloud Monastery." They stared with puzzled expressions, however, at the small bespectacled individual in Taoist robes beside him—a tao-shih blessed not with flowing hair but with a balding crown!

Just in front of the White Cloud Monastery stood the thirteen-story pagoda of the T'ien-ning Ssu 天寧寺, a famous architectural legacy from the Liao dynasty. The bronze bells suspended from each of the corners of its thirteen octagonal tiers made a clear, soothing sound when touched by the wind. Heard from within the monastery, they added an elegant tone to summer evenings. One might even have been misled into thinking that this pagoda had been built for the White Cloud Monastery.

At ten there was another signal on the plank. It was a warning to make ready for bed. Continental summer evenings were long, and it was not until ten that the heavens darkened. During the night, tao-shih known as night wardens made the rounds of the monastery every two hours, striking their wooden clapping sticks.

The above timetable is for the summer months. Since life at the White Cloud Monastery was regulated by the sun, the daily timetable changed in the winter. Meals were then taken only twice a day, morning and evening. I have already mentioned that ordinary monks took their meals in the refectory. The food was prepared under the supervision of the monastery cook in the main kitchen. The meals of the prior, guest prefect, and other high-ranking tao-shih were prepared in a separate kitchen by a "high cook" (*kao-tsao* 高灶). When the senior monks had guests, they would take their meals together with them. Otherwise they ate individually in their own rooms. All food within the monastery was vegetarian. The high cook of the small kitchen at the White Cloud while I was there was renowned as a master of vegetarian cooking. Unlike the other monks, senior tao-shih ate only two daily meals, summer and winter, at eleven in the morning and six in the evening.

The daily menu and the amounts of ingredients to be used were carefully fixed. If any dishonesty was detected, the offender was severely punished. The morning and evening meals taken by ordinary tao-shih in the refectory consisted of a bowl of congee and one plate of pickles shared by every two monks. The midday meal consisted of a portion of corn bread 玉米粉 and fried vegetables for each, with a plate of pickles shared by two. Since this was purely vegetarian cooking, anybody not used to the diet would have had difficulty adjusting to it. On the first and fifteenth day of each month, flour was used in the bread for the midday meal, on the basis of one catty (*chin*) per person. It was dark, poor-quality flour. For the regular meals in the senior monks' dining room, congee or noodles were used. Vegetable dishes were only served when guests were present and were limited to a maximum of four plates. This is far removed from the luxurious Japanese image of vegetarian cooking.

The Ceremony of the Airing of the Books

July 1, 1940, the date on which I first entered the White Cloud Monastery to stay, corresponded to the first day of the sixth month according to the lunar calendar [*sic*]. I had a particular reason for choosing this day. I was hoping to see the ceremony of the airing of the books at the monastery. In the Peking area, the week from the first day of the sixth month of the lunar calendar was given over to airing household items. It was said that clothes or books aired at this time would escape moths and mildew for the coming year. The White Cloud Monastery possessed the only surviving copy of the famous Ming edition of the Taoist Canon. During this week the precious work was taken from its sealed repository and brought out for airing ceremonies. For anyone anxious to see the canon, to miss this opportunity would mean waiting another whole year.

It is said that these ceremonies originated in response to a request 祈願 from the court during the Ch'ing dynasty. Starting on the first day of the sixth month, the monastery used to be decorated with pennants and streamers, and there was an elaborate inauguration ceremony. Throughout each of the six following days one-sixth of the canon used to be recited. This corresponded to the ceremony of reciting the long version of the *Prajñāpāramitāsūtra* held in Buddhist monasteries. However, when I was there, the monks at White Cloud just placed long tables on the porch of the Pavilion of the Three Pure Ones, where the canon was stored, and twenty of them turned the pages of the volumes briskly with bamboo spatulas. There were a total of 5,385 *chüan*. Starting at seven in the morning and working for two hours or so, the monks completed the "airing" in three days.

This Taoist Canon was published between 1924 and 1926 by photocopy in 1,120 volumes (*ts'e* 冊) by the Commercial Press in Shanghai. Hsü Shih-ch'ang 徐世昌 and Fu Tseng-hsiang 傅增湘 were sponsors. This photocopy edition was the source of the 1962 edition, published by I-wen Publishing Company in Taiwan. The Taoist Canon, which was formerly almost inaccessible to scholars, is now, thanks to the photographed edition, generally available. Had the original White Cloud edition been lost, the documentary study of Taoism would be virtually impossible. Here is an example of the preservation of a rare religious tradition by the White Cloud Monastery. Through this act alone the monastery has proven to be a precious cultural treasure for Taoism.

While I was in Peking I visited the monastery whenever I had time to spare, and I stayed there at will. Prior An also visited my rooms in the city. The first time he visited me, I wondered how I was going to entertain a Taoist monk who was accustomed only to a vegetarian diet. I asked him point blank, "Can you eat meat and fish?" "Yes," he replied. I was relieved but asked, "But what about the pure rules?" He replied: "In the monastery we observe the rules strictly. When we go out, we have to be more relaxed. There are occasions when tao-shih are away from the monastery on business for a fortnight or a month at a time. If one tried to stick to a vegetarian diet, without suitable eating places one might starve to death. Even on one-day visits to the city, since it isn't easy to find restaurants serving vegetarian meals, one would have to go without food all day. In practical terms it's impossible to stick strictly to the rules when outside the monastery." What he said was so obvious that I kicked myself for my stupid dogmatism.

During the Great East Asian War I sometimes met White Cloud tao-shih who could say "hello" or "thank you" in Japanese and who averred that they wished to learn more. I told them not to; their Japanese would sound funny and be out of character.

When the war ended everything fell apart. I vacated Peking at the end of April 1946, leaving behind all the notes, documents, and manuscripts which I had so painstakingly gathered. Those Japanese involved in cultural activities in Peking at the time formed a small association to negotiate with the Chinese authorities for the right to take the documents and the results of our research back to Japan. We were told that we could not take any document containing so much as a single Chinese geographical or personal name! In effect, this meant that we could take absolutely nothing: cultural documents containing no reference to Chinese people or places do not exist. I felt great affection for the Taoist robe I had worn during my stay at the White Cloud but sadly threw it away, since it was likely to provoke suspicion at the checkpoints.

In postwar Japan I lived for several years on a basic diet of potato roots and abstinence. During this period, about two years after my return, I heard from a friend who was still living in Peking of the violent death of An Shih-lin. He had been burned to death in the garden in front of the Shrine-hall of Founder Ch'iu by a militant faction in the monastery. This report was substantiated by a photograph and clipping from a Peking newspaper. I was shocked and saddened. I have already mentioned the dispute which had occurred just before my first stay at the monastery. In this incident Prior An and his supporters had expelled from the monastery some members of an opposing faction. These tao-shih had remained in Peking awaiting an opportunity for revenge. It is not hard to imagine that in the disturbances of the postwar period they were able to egg on militants within the monastery to accomplish their own private ends.

In the early Yüan dynasty, shortly after the death of the founder Ch'iu Ch'ang-ch'un, members of the Ch'üan-chen sect engaged in a debate with Buddhists before the Chinese emperor. The Taoists were worsted, with the result that the texts of their sect were judged apocryphal 僞 and burned. This incident put an end to attempts to establish the sect as one with roots in the general populace. From then on it developed as a docile monastic entity serving the state. This tradition was preserved at the White Cloud Monastery. The burning to death of An Shih-lin, ironically enough in front of the founder's hall, meant that the tao-shih of the Ch'üan-chen sect had themselves rung down the curtain on monastic Taoism—an act that coincided with the start of one of the greatest revolutions in Chinese history.

Floorplan of White Cloud Monastery

白雲觀平面図

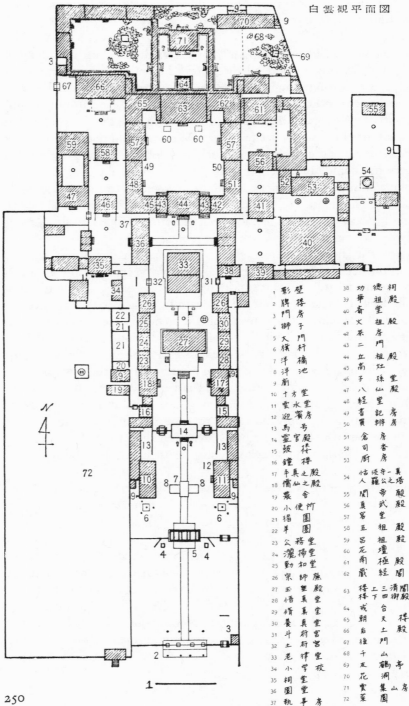

N

250

1 影壁
2 牌樓
3 獅子
4 門
5 旗杆
6 橋
7 池
8 洋廁
9 洋廁
10 十方堂
11 雲水堂
12 迎賓房
13 馬號
14 靈官殿
15 鐘樓
16 鐘
17 辛真之殿
18 備仙舍
19 農
20 小便所
21 豬圈
22 羊圈
23 公務堂
24 灃佛堂
25 勤和堂
26 宗師殿
27 玉皇殿
28 悟真堂宮
29 修真堂宮
30 養真府堂
31 斗府律校
32 土學堂
33 老律堂
34 小
35 祠園
36 祠軌
37 房

38 祠殿
39 殿
40 德祖堂祖房門
41 齋火茶二祖灶
42 丘高孫仙堂
43 子八仙堂
44 記辦
45 經書房
46 房
47 房香房
48 倉司廚
49 怡寺公帝
50 羅人閣真
51 寫五花
52 呂花藏
53 昌極經
54 真塔殿殿
55 武堂祖壇
56 真閣殿間
57 清御殿
58 三四天門
59 台上下
60 樓殿亭
61 後山洞集
62 戒朝
63 禪
64 千友花寶菜
65 山房
66 千鶴洞集園
67 山房
68 後
69 花
70 寶
71 菜
72 園

[Editors' note on floorplan. *Yoshioka states that the premises of the White Cloud Monastery covered 10,000 tsubo, or about 3.3 hectares. On a map of Peking published by the Map Publishing House, Peking, in April 1957, the compound is clearly shown, and according to the scale used, it measured about 300 by 220 meters. This would contain over six hectares, or fifteen acres. Except for the compounds of temples of the state cult (like the Temple of Heaven), the White Cloud Monastery appeared to be the religious institution with the largest premises, as shown on this map. In any case, Yoshioka has not exaggerated its size.*]

Key to Floorplan of White Cloud Monastery

1 Spirit wall (*ying-pi* 影壁)
2 Ornamental entry (*p'ai-lou* 牌樓)
3 Gatehouse
4 Stone lions
5 Main gate
6 Flagstaffs
7 Sea bridge
8 Pond
9 Toilets
10 Public monks' hall (*shih-fang t'ang* 十方堂)
11 Itinerant monks' hall (*yün-shui t'ang* 雲水堂)
12 Guest reception room (*ying-pin fang* 迎賓房)
13 *Ma-hao* 馬號
14 Shrine-hall of Ling-kuan 靈官殿
15 Drum tower
16 Bell tower
17 Shrine-hall of Feng-chen 豐真殿
18 Shrine-hall of the Confucian Immortals 儒仙殿
19 Farm shed
20 Urinals
21 Pigpen
22 Sheep pen
23 Business room
24 Janitorial room (*sa-sao t'ang* 灑掃堂)
25 Workroom
26 Ancestral Master's porch (*tsung-shih wu* 崇師廡)
27 Shrine-hall of the Jade Emperor
28 Hall for Awakening to Perfection 悟真堂
29 Hall for Cultivating Perfection 修真堂
30 Hall for Fostering Perfection 養真堂

31 Palace of the Treasury of the Dipper 斗府宮
32 Palace of the Treasury of Earth 土府宮
33 Hall of the Discipline of Lao-tzu [?] 老律堂
34 Small school
35 Hall of Ancestral Worship
36 Garden hall
37 Functionaries' room 執事房
38 Hall for the Worship of Meritorious Ancestors 功德堂
39 Shrine-hall of Patriarch Hua [Tung?] 華祖殿
40 Refectory (*chai-t'ang* 齋堂)
41 Shrine-hall of the Fire Patriarch 火祖殿
42 Tearoom
43 Second gates
44 Shrine-hall of Patriarch Ch'iu [Ch'ang-ch'un] 丘祖殿
45 High kitchen
46 Hall of lineal disciples [?] 子孫堂
47 Shrine-hall of the Eight Immortals
48 Hall of the Scriptures 經堂
49 Secretaries' room 書記房
50 Purchasing room 買辦房
51 Storeroom
52 Finance office [?] 司香
53 Kitchen
54 Burial Pagoda of the *chen-jen* Lord Lo 恬淡守，真人羅公之塔
55 Shrine-hall of Kuan-ti 關帝殿
56 Shrine-hall of Chen-wu 真武殿
57 Guest hall
58 Shrine-hall of the Five Patriarchs 五祖殿
59 Shrine-hall of Patriarch Lü 呂祖殿

60 Flower stands 花壇
61 Shrine-hall of Nan-chi 南極殿
62 Pavilion of the Taoist Canon 藏經閣
63 Pavilion of the Three Pure Ones (ground floor) 三清閣 Shrine-hall of the Ssu-yü (second floor) 四御殿
64 Ordination platform 戒台
65 Ch'ao-t'ien Lou 朝天樓
66 Shrine-hall of Hou-t'u 后土殿
67 Rear gate
68 [Garden of] the Thousand Mountains 千山
69 Yu-ho T'ing 友鶴亭
70 Flower cavern 花洞
71 "Room of the mountains where many monks gather" 雲集山房
72 Vegetable garden

8 The Formation of the Taoist Canon

Ninji Ōfuchi 大淵忍爾

[Editors' note. *A preliminary version of this paper was sent to the 1968 conference on Taoist studies at Bellagio, Italy, which Professor Ōfuchi was unable to attend. (He did attend the conference at Tateshina.) In its finished form, the paper was first published as "Dōzō no seiritsu"* 道藏の成立, Tōhōgaku 東方學 38:49–57 (September 1969).]

THE TERM Tao-tsang 道藏, or Taoist Canon, designates the comprehensive collection of scriptural, scholastic, and historical texts of the Taoist religion. The Taoist Canon is comparable to the Tripiṭaka (*San-tsang* 三藏), or Complete Scriptures (*I-ch'ieh ching* 一切經) of Buddhism, in that both collections comprise sacred books—revealed scriptures—as well as discursive and historical treatises, all under a comprehensive title. The sense of the word *tsang* in *Tao-tsang* evolved from its Buddhist technical meaning (as a translation of the Sanskrit *piṭaka*, "receptacle" for containing the scriptures) to that of "body of learning" (as exemplified in the expression "corpus of the doctrine," *fa-tsang* 法藏), until it finally came to designate the scriptural texts themselves.

Despite this development in meaning, however, it would appear that the original sense of the term, in Taoist usage, was simply that of a receptacle for storage of Taoist scriptural texts. The ensemble of scriptures themselves were commonly referred to as the "Scriptures of the Taoist Canon" (*Tao-tsang ching* 道藏經) or, still more precisely, as the "Complete Scriptures of Taoism" (*I-ch'ieh tao-ching* 一切道經). It was only from the Sung dynasty onward—from the tenth century—that the expression "Scriptures of the Taoist Canon" (*Tao-tsang ching*) was shortened to "Taoist Canon" (*Tao-tsang*), with the sense that it retains in common usage today of "the ensemble of Taoist texts."

The internal organization of the canon breaks down into seven sections, the Three Tung (*San tung* 三洞, "Three Vaults" or "Caverns"), followed by four lesser units, the Four Supplements (*Ssu fu* 四輔). Each of the Three Tung is further divided into twelve subsections (*shih-erh pu* 十二部). This organizational schema was first fixed sometime during the Six Dynasties period[1] and remained unaltered for nearly a thousand years until about 1447, when it served as the guiding principle of the final printed canon. The persistence of this classificatory terminology and arrangement naturally reveals more about the continuing *form* of successive canons over the centuries than about their *contents*, which were not mutually identical.

Insofar as we may judge from extant documents, the central conception of the Three Tung has been a fundamental characteristic of the Taoist Canon from the very beginning. If we were to define the Taoist Canon as the whole ensemble of Three Tung and Four Supplements, then the first canon might be said to have been completed at the moment when all these elements were brought together. If, however, we take the idea of the Three Tung as being the essential factor in the canon's formation, then it is the creation of the Three Tung that must be regarded as the initial step in the making of the first Taoist Canon.

The Contents of the Three Tung

The Three Tung are those divisions of the canon known respectively as *Tung-chen* 洞眞, *Tung-hsüan* 洞玄, and *Tung-shen* 洞神. Each of these divisions originally grew up around a particular scripture or group of scriptures. The scriptures of Shang-ch'ing 上清 formed the original nucleus of the *Tung-chen* section. The Ling-pao scriptures 靈寶經 were at the core of the *Tung-hsüan* section. The *Tung-shen* section was built around the *Scripture of the Three Sovereigns* (*San-huang ching* 三皇經). However, no historical documents remain that indicate clearly what the nature of the Three Tung was at the time they were first put together. What we do know about this subject derives from statements in such works as the *Supreme Register of Ts'ang-yüan, a* Tung-chen *Scripture of the Most High* (*Tung-chen t'ai-shang ts'ang-yüan shang-lu* 洞眞太上蒼元上錄, *TT* 1031), a text of uncertain date, but probably Six Dynasties,[2] and the *General Mean-*

1. See Fonds Pelliot, Tun-huang manuscript 3001, "Sung fa-shih shih-erh-pu i-ts'an" 宋法師十二部義殘 (provisional title) and another text derived from it, the *Tung-hsüan ling-pao hsüan-men ta-i* 洞玄靈寶玄門大義, pp. 18b10–19b2 (*TT* 760). With regard to these two texts, see my "Tonkō zankan sansoku" 敦煌殘卷三則, in *Fukui hakushi shōju kinen Tōyō Shisō Ronshū* 福井博士頌壽記念東洋思想論集 (Collected studies on East Asian thought in honor of Fukui Kōjun on his sixtieth birthday; Tokyo, 1960), pp. 109–27.

2. The name of this scripture appears in the *Shou-fa ch'ih-chai p'in* 受法持齋品 of the North-

ing of the Gateway to the Mysteries (*Hsüan-men ta-i*, *TT* 760), dating from the very beginning of the T'ang.[3]

As for the three different categories of scriptures which individually composed the Three Tung, we have the statement of A.D. 570 by the Buddhist polemicist Chen Luan 甄鸞, writing in north China. When mentioning "the scriptural catalogue of Lu Hsiu-ching 陸修靜 (406–477)," he cites as representative titles from it "the Shang-ch'ing scriptures in 186 *chüan* and the *Tung-hsüan* scriptures 洞玄經 in fifteen *ch'üan*."[4] Further, the *Preface to the Three Tung Scriptures* (*San-tung ching hsü* 三洞經序) by Master Ko (dates unknown) cited in a work completed around 700, the *Pivot of Meaning in the Taoist Religion* (*Tao-chiao i-shu*, *TT* 763),[5] refers to

ern Chou Dynasty *Wu-shang pi-yao* 無上秘要 encyclopedia 47:10a6 (*TT* 773). There are quotations from this scripture in *I-ch'ieh tao-ching yin-i miao-men yu-ch'i* 一切道經音義妙門由起, pp. 31b10–32a4 (*TT* 760) and in *Tao-chiao i-shu* 道經義樞 2:2b2sq (*TT* 763).

3. This work is quoted in *Yün-chi ch'i-ch'ien* 雲笈七籤 6: 1a5–3a2 (*TT* 677–702) where it is called *Tao-men ta-lun* 道門大論. This is just another name for the same book. [Its full title is *Tung-hsüan ling-pao hsüan-men ta-i* 洞玄靈寶玄門大義.]

4. See *Hsiao-Tao lun* 笑道論, in *Kuang hung-ming chi* 廣弘明集 9, *Taishō Tripiṭaka* T, LII 2103, 9:151b6–9.

5. *Tao-chiao i-shu* 道教義樞 2:3b9 (*TT* 763). On the author and date of this text: the *Tao-chiao i-shu* was purportedly compiled by the Taoist Meng An-p'ai from Ch'ing-hsi 青溪道士孟安排集 (cf. 1:1) Yoshioka Yoshitoyo 吉岡義豊 and Kamata Shigeo 鎌田茂雄 have reached different conclusions as to the date of this text. Yoshioka concluded that it was written around the middle of the seventh century, basing his estimate on his discussion of the general situation between Buddhism and Taoism at that time: see his *Dōkyō to Bukkyō* 道教と佛教 (Taoism and Buddhism; Tokyo, 1959), 1: 309–50. Kamata concluded that the book was from the early eighth century, basing his estimate on the book's relation to Buddhist thought: see his *Chūgoku Bukkyō shisōshi kenkyū* 中國佛教思想史研究 (Studies on the history of Chinese Buddhist thought; Tokyo, 1968), pp. 199–217.

The name of Meng An-p'ai appears in the inscription on the *Ching-chou Ta-ch'ung-fu kuan pei* 荆州大崇福觀碑, (Stele of the Ta-ch'ung-fu temple in Ching-chou) preserved in the section on epigraphy in *Hu-pei t'ung-chih* 湖北通志 96:2360b–61a. (Shanghai: Commercial Press, 1934), [The *Hu-pei t'ung-chih*] notes that the text [of this inscription] was taken from the Sung edition of the *Wen-yüan ying-hua* 宋本文苑英華 and quotes from a *Chin-shih ts'un-i k'ao* 金石存佚考 that its author was Ch'en Tzu-ang 陳子昂 of the T'ang Dynasty. However, this inscription is mentioned neither in the common Ming edition [of the *Wen-yüan ying-hua*], nor in the *Ch'üan T'ang Wen* 全唐文, nor in Ch'en's collected works. Considered in terms of its content, the inscription clearly belongs to the era of the Empress Wu 武后 (684–704). It discusses the project to construct at this spot a Taoist temple (*tao-kuan* 道觀) in honor of Wu Shih-[huo?] 武士彟, the empress's father, who had been governor-general of Ching-chou, and states that in A.D. 699 the temple was imperially granted the name Ta-ch'ung-fu Kuan 大崇福觀. On this occasion, the Taoist Meng An-p'ai appears to have played an important role.

Ching-chou is the present Chiang-ling *hsien* 江陵縣 in Hupei. The geographical work *Yü-ti chi-sheng* 輿地紀勝 65B:10b (1849 ed.) of the Southern Sung Dynasty, in its section on Chiang-ling *fu* 府, mentions neither the temple nor the stele, but reports that in 1206 a *Stele of the Governor General of Ching-chou, Wu Shih- (huo?), of the T'ang Dynasty* 唐武士彟都督荆州碑 was accidentally excavated and that it had been broken into pieces. It is probable

Lu Hsiu-ching's catalogue as *Master Lu's Catalogue of Scriptural Writings of the Three Tung* (*Lu Hsien-sheng San-tung ching-shu mu-lu* 陸先生三洞經書目錄).

Those who revered the various Shang-ch'ing scriptures belonged to the group which later came to be known as the Mao Shan 茅山 school, from the name of the mountain in Kiangsu where the Shang-ch'ing movement began. To this group belonged the eminent Taoist scholar, T'ao Hung-ching 陶弘景 (456–536); and from the book called *Declarations of the Perfected* (*Chen-kao* 眞誥, *TT* 637–40), which he compiled and annotated, we learn that the principal text among the Shang-ch'ing scriptures was the *Ta-tung chen-ching* in thirty-nine sections (*chang*) 大洞眞經三十九章 (*TT* 16–17).[6] In a late fourth-century hagiographic text emanating from the same movement,[7] this scripture is said to have been the ultimate text which Lord Huang-lao bestowed upon his disciple Chou I-shan 周義山; by means of the *Ta-tung chen-ching* Chou was able to "ascend to heaven in broad daylight." Finally, in the *Preface to an Annotated Catalogue of Scriptures of the Shang-ch'ing School* (*Shang-ch'ing yüan-t'ung-ching mu-chu hsü*

that after the T'ang ruling house recovered power, this monument met the same fate as the whole Wu clan.

Incidentally, the *Shui-ching chu* 水經注 32:409 (*Shih-chieh shu-chü* 世界書局 ed.) in the section on the Chü River 沮水 states: "The Chü River runs southward to the west of Lin-chü *hsien* 臨沮縣 [northwest of today's Tang-yang]. The waters of the Ch'ing-hsi [stream] 青溪水 flow into it. The latter comes from Mt. Ch'ing 青山 to the west of [the seat of Lin-chü] *hsien*. . . . Because its source is at Mt. Ch'ing, it is named Ch'ing-hsi 青溪. If you trace it to its headwaters, you will marvel at the high precipices. Sheng Hung-chih 盛弘之 [of the Liu Sung, in his *Ching-chou chi* 荆州記] states . . . 'Beside the springs *tao-shih* have built many huts for retreat.'"

The section on Yüan-an *hsien* in Hsia-chou in the eastern circuit of Shan-nan 山南東道峽州遠安縣 in *T'ai-p'ing huan-yü chi* 太平寰宇記 147:76 (*Chin-ling shu-chü* 金陵書局 1882 ed.) states: "The Ch'ing-hsi is 65 *li* south of [Yüan-an] *hsien*. Its source is at the foot of Mt. Ch'ing-hsi 清溪山. Its flow does not vary winter or summer. The *Kuei Ku hsien-sheng chuan* 鬼谷先生傳 (Biography of Master Kuei Ku) says: 'In Ch'u 楚 there is the Ch'ing-hsi 清溪. Its vertical descent is 8,000 feet 下深千仞 and its waters are marvelous and efficacious 靈異.'"

[Summing up all this information, we can say:] The Lin-chü *hsien* mentioned in the *Shui-ching chu* is this Yüan-an *hsien* 遠安縣 [mentioned in the *T'ai-p'ing huan-yü chi*]. The Ch'ing-hsi is a branch of the Chü River, which flows into the Yangtze to the west of Chiang-ling [today's Sha-shih]. Since, as we have seen, it is said that many a tao-shih practiced spiritual retreats in this area, the author of the *Tao-chiao i-shu* could well be the Meng An-pai of this stele's inscription. Therefore, although the date of the book is hard to ascertain, it would not be too grossly mistaken to place it at about 700. It was Ch'en Kuo-fu 陳國符 who discovered the importance of this inscription: see his *Tao-tsang yüan-liu k'ao* 道藏源流考 (Researches into the origin of the Taoist Canon; Peking, 1963), p. 2.

6. See *Chen-kao*, 5:3a4 (*TT* 637) and 19:10b10 (*TT* 640) and elsewhere. This is also clear from the *Ta-yu miao ching* 大有妙經, p. 3a7 (*TT* 1026), a far older text of the same sect, which will be mentioned below (p. 262).

7. *Tzu-yang chen-jen nei-chuan* 紫陽眞人內傳, p. 16b10 (*TT* 152).

上清源統經目註序), which dates from about 500,[8] mention is made of a "*Ta-tung chen-ching* in thirty-one *chüan*." We may consequently assume that the name of the *Tung-chen* section of the canon derives from the title of this scripture, the *Ta*-TUNG CHEN-*ching*.

We know from two sources[9] that the Ling-pao scriptures were the principal component of the second division of the canon, the *Tung-hsüan* section. What is more, among the early Taoist texts cited in fascicle 773 of the *Wu-shang pi-yao* (*TT* 678–779), a Taoist encyclopedia completed in 583 in north China, many bear the classificatory term *Tung-hsüan* prefixed to their titles. It is significant that the names of all these texts appear in the catalogue of Ling-pao scriptures which is preserved in a manuscript from Tun-huang.[10] This demonstrates the identity of the Ling-pao scriptures with the contents of the *Tung-hsüan* section of the canon.

Finally, there are also early indications that the third of the Three Tung, the *Tung-shen* section, was based on the *Scripture of the Three Sovereigns* (*San-huang wen* 三皇文 or *San-huang ching* 經). Once again, in the late sixth-century *Wu-shang pi-yao* (43:1a4) we find citations from the *Tung-shen San-huang ching* 洞神三皇經. The association of the *Scripture of the Three Sovereigns* with the *Tung-shen* section is further corroborated by the scriptural catalogue (*Ta-yu lu-t'u ching-mu* 大有籙圖經目 or *Tung-shen ching-mu* 洞神經目) contained in the *Rites of the Most High of the* [*Scripture of the*] *Three Sovereigns of* Tung-shen (*T'ai-shang tung-shen San-huang i* 太上洞神三皇儀, *TT* 565).[11]

There is thus every reason to suppose that from its first occurrence the expression "Three Tung" meant *Tung-chen* (the scriptures of Shang-ch'ing), *Tung-hsüan* (the Ling-pao scriptures), and *Tung-shen* (the scriptures of the Three Sovereigns, San-huang). If such were the contents of the Three Tung, and if we may consider their formation as being tanta-

8. See my book *Dōkyō shi no kenkyū* 道教史の研究 (Studies in Taoist history; Tokyo, 1964), pp. 266–67. The preface is to be found in *Yün-chi ch'i-ch'ien* 4:2a9 (*TT* 677).

9. These two sources are the *T'ai-shang san-chiu su-yü nei-chou chüeh-wen* 太上三九素語內呪訣文, in the *Ta-yu miao-ching*, pp. 41a5–46a2; and the *Chen-kao* 13:1a7–8 (*TT* 639). The latter, in the commentary on the phrase *feng-ming Tung-hsüan* 諷明洞玄 states: "It [*tung-hsüan*] is not what people today call the *Tung-hsüan ling-pao ching* 洞玄靈寶經."

10. [*Ling-pao chung-meng ching-mu* 靈寶中盟經目] in *San-tung feng-tao k'o-chieh i-fan* 三洞奉道科誡義範, 5 (Pelliot 2337). There are various views as to the date of composition of this manuscript, but it was probably complete by the end of the seventh century at the latest. It is to be found in the *Tao-tsang*, where its title is *San-tung feng-tao k'o-chieh ying-shih* 三洞奉道科誡營始 (*TT* 760–61).

11. Although the date of composition of this scripture is not clear, I would estimate that it was written during the T'ang dynasty.

mount to the creation of the first Taoist Canon, we must now inquire more closely into the significance of the concepts which they embody.

The Significance of the Three Tung

This problem may first be approached from another perspective: why was it really found necessary to assemble a systematic collection of Taoist scriptures? This question furnishes a logical point of departure precisely because it is difficult to see how the need for such a collection could have arisen within the context of early religious Taoism.

The essential condition for the creation by Taoists of a Taoist canon must have been a common sense of identity as Taoists. But in fact what was conspicuously lacking in early Taoism was any shared belief on the part of the faithful in a definite founder, or any well-defined body of doctrine which they considered to represent the teachings of such a founder, as was the case with Christianity, Islam, and even Buddhism. Consequently, although during the early stages of the religion (ca. A.D. 150–600) there may have existed a number of doctrines which later came to be known as "Taoism," the people who held these beliefs were organized in separate groups regardless of the degree of actual similarity there may have been in the nature of their respective beliefs or in the form of their several organizations.

Thus, for example, the Way of the Great Peace (T'ai-p'ing Tao 太平道) and the Way of the Five Pecks of Rice (Wu-tou-mi Tao 五斗米道, which later became the Way of the Celestial Masters, or T'ien-shih Tao 天子道) came into being within a fairly short time of one another toward the end of the Later Han, and indeed seem to have been similar in many ways. Yet the former in the east and the latter in the west were quite distinct organizations, and there is no trace of any affiliation between them. Somewhat later, the Mao Shan school, which took the Shang-ch'ing scriptures as textual authority, did have some initial connection with the Way of the Celestial Masters. But the real development of the movement, as described in early historical accounts, was wholly independent of the older organization.[12]

The case of the other great textual movement in the south, that of the Ling-pao scriptures, appears to be quite similar in this respect.[13] Whether or not the historical accounts of the origins of the Shang-ch'ing and Ling-

12. See *Chen-kao*, ch. 19 (*TT* 640) and such works as the *Shang-ch'ing yüan-t'ung ching-mu chu-hsü* 上清源統經目註序 in *Yün-chi ch'i-ch'ien*, 4:1a4 sq. and the *Shang-ch'ing-ching shu* 上清經述, in ibid. 4:6a8.

13. See the *Ling-pao ching-mu hsü* 靈寶經目序, in *Yün-chi ch'i-ch'ien*, 4:4a3, the *Tao-chiao i-shu* 道教義樞, 2:1a–7b (*TT* 763), and *Chen-kao*, ch. 19.

pao scriptures are entirely factual is beside the point here. What is important for our present purpose is to take note of the fact that these scriptural texts provided the authority for two distinct movements, and, what is more, that the historical narratives themselves emphasize the very separateness of their respective traditions.

In north China, meanwhile, the teachings of the successful court Taoist, K'ou Ch'ien-chih 寇謙之, as described by the *Treatise on Buddhism and Taoism* in the *History of the Wei Dynasty* (*Wei-shu Shih-Lao chih* 魏書釋老志), were a purified form of the doctrines of the Way of the Celestial Masters. In this sense his movement could be described as a continuation of the earlier organization. Yet it is also stated that what must certainly be regarded as K'ou's basic text, the *Articles of a New Code to be Chanted to Yün-chung Musical Notation* (*Yün-chung yin-sung hsin-k'o chih chieh* 雲中音誦新科之誠),[14] was bestowed upon him directly by Lord Lao the Most High (T'ai-shang Lao-chün 太上老君). This gives to K'ou's movement the unmistakable look of an independent body of doctrine newly initiated by himself, rather than a return to the older Way of the Celestial Masters. What is more, K'ou's movement makes no reference to the Shang-ch'ing school, which by then (ca. 425) was already flourishing in the south.

Such being the case [with three quite distinct scriptural movements in operation by the second quarter of the fifth century, two south of the Yangtze and one in north China], it is highly unlikely that any spontaneous pressure from within could have conferred on these separate schools a sense of unity or common identity. The political separation of north and south China which obtained at the time would seem to be still another factor in favor of disunion. In view of all this we are obliged to assume that there was no intrinsic probability of an effort being made to form a systematic collection of the canonical texts emanating from these various schools.

Yet the Three Tung did come into being, even though to the scriptures they contain are still attached historical accounts of their different respective origins. We must therefore suppose that a sense of community did indeed develop among persons who venerated one or another of these distinct bodies of scripture. Further, it seems logical to conclude that, since there was no cogent internal pressure which might have fostered this development, it must have come into being as a response to similar activities taking place outside of these Taoist communities—that is, among the Buddhists.

It is a well-known fact that Buddhism, which first entered China at

14. See Mather chapter, p. 107.

about the beginning of the Christian era, began to achieve its thorough infiltration of Chinese society—particularly that of the upper classes—from about the fourth century. In my view, the sense of community that arose among members of religious movements who had in common their indigenous Chineseness more than anything else, was a reaction to this increasing penetration by the foreign religion.

If my view is justified, when did this development take place? As far as can be determined from extant documents, the expression "Three Tung" makes its appearance in connection with the most eminent Taoist of the Liu Sung Dynasty, Lu Hsiu-ching (406–477). He signed his *Preface to a Catalogue of Ling-pao Scriptures*,[15] dated 437, as "Lu Hsiu-ching, Disciple of the Three Tung" 三洞弟子陸修靜, and the term "Three Tung" alone is also to be found in his *Exposition of the Ritual of the Most High for Transmission of the Ling-pao [Scriptures] of Tung-hsüan (T'ai-shang tung-hsüan ling-pao shou-tu i-piao* 太上洞玄靈寶授度儀表, *TT* 294). Yet how much earlier than 437 was the expression in use?

In considering this problem it seems necessary to look more closely at the concept of the Three Tung. The term itself is generally thought to be an imitation of the usual designation of the Buddhist Canon, the "Three Receptacles" (*San-tsang* 三藏). However, the organization of the Three Tung of the Taoist Canon in no way corresponds to the tripartite division of its Buddhist counterpart, although, as we have remarked, both canons share the fact of being comprehensive collections of the scriptural and other literature of their respective traditions.

The contents of the Three Receptacles are *ching* 經 (*sūtra*), *lü* 律 (*vinaya*), and *lun* 論 (*abhidharma*)—three different genres of literature rather than the scriptures of three different historical movements. Further, for studying the classification of Buddhist scriptures in China, we possess the evidence furnished by a succession of scriptural catalogues. From an examination of these documents, it is clear that though there was, quite early on, a twofold division of scriptures according to whether they belonged to the Great or Small Vehicle (Mahāyāna or Hinayāna), the characteristic tripartite division of texts into the *ching-lü-lun* pattern does not appear before the Sui dynasty catalogue of Buddhist texts, that is, the *Chung-ching mu-lu* 衆經目錄 (A.D. 594).

We may express this in another way by saying that prior to the time of the great translator Kumārajīva (344–413), most of the texts translated into Chinese had been scriptures (*sūtra*) of either the Greater or Lesser

15. See the listing "*Ling-pao ching-mu hsü* 靈寶經目序, in one *chüan*, compiled by Lu Hsiu-ching" in the *I-wen lüeh* 藝文畧 of the *T'ung-chih* 通志 67:788b (*Shih-t'ung* ed.).

Vehicle. It was only subsequently, from the fifth century, that texts of the other two categories, monastic rules (*vinaya*) and doctrinal treatises (*śāstra*), began to be translated in large numbers. As this process continued, there gradually came into existence a comprehensive tripartite division of Buddhist literature into Three Receptacles. Under these circumstances, it is quite inconceivable that Chinese popular religion should long before the end of the Six Dynasties have been so greatly influenced by the notion of a Tripiṭaka as to produce the Three Tung.[16]

In fact, the use of the expression "Three Tung" in early Taoist writings ought not to be compared with the Three Receptacles, but rather with another Buddhist technical term, the Three Vehicles (*san ch'eng* 三乘, *triyāna*). These Three Vehicles are, in ascending sequence, those of the Auditors (*śrāvaka*), the Pratyekabuddhas, and the Bodhisattvas, and they are identified with the Lesser, Middle, and Greater Vehicles, respectively.[17] What is more, the expressions "Three Vehicles" and "Three Tung" are occasionally used in Taoist texts as virtual synonyms, for example, in the following passage:

> The Three Tung and the Three Purities (*san ch'ing* 三清) are the Three Vehicles. There are twelve sections of scriptures and precepts in each of the Three Vehicles, making a total of thirty-six sections wherewith they save incalculable numbers of gods and men. As to the study of the Three Tung, the Superior Tung is the Great Vehicle, the Middle Tung is the Middle Vehicle, and the Lesser Tung is the Small Vehicle.[18]

16. The term *San-tsang* 三藏 (*Tripiṭaka*) is used also in senses other than its primary reference to the principle of classification of Buddhist texts—as, for example, in the religious title "Master-of-the-Doctrine San-tsang" 三藏法師 [during the T'ang]. *San-tsang* was already in use at the end of the Eastern Chin. The title "Disciple of the Three Tung," previously mentioned (*san-tung ti-tzu*) 三洞弟子, is not unrelated to the "Master-of-the-Doctrine San-tsang." Therefore, leaving aside the question of earlier times, *San-tung* and *San-tsang* were connected with one another at a later period. If, however, one is discussing the classification of the scriptures, one should view the term in different frames of reference.

17. For example, the *Shih-Lao chih* 釋老志, in the *Wei-shu* 魏書 114:3a (*Erh-shih-wu shih* 二十五史 ed.), states: "There are three kinds of men who become holy sages of the first rank. Because their root karma 根業 is very different, we speak of them as belonging to three vehicles—the Auditor's Vehicle, the Pratyeka Vehicle, and the Great Vehicle. . . . People with incipient roots belong to the Small Vehicle. . . . People with middling roots belong to the Middle Vehicle. . . . People with superior roots belong to the Great Vehicle."

18. *Tung-chen t'ai-shang ts'ang-yüan shang-lu* 4a8–9, 6a3–5 (*TT* 1031). [In the passage quoted in the text, the Three Purities 三清 refer to the Three Taoist heavens, Yü-ch'ing 玉清, Shang-ch'ing 上清, and T'ai-ch'ing 太清—Translator's note.] The *Hsüan-men ta-i* pp. 1a3–8 (*TT* 760) states: "As for the [sets of] scriptures in twelve sections they are equivalent to the wonderful classics of the Three Vehicles 通三乘之妙典 and are penetrated by the great standards of the seven sections. . . . Therefore the *Cheng-i ching* 正一經 says: 'Each of the Three Vehicles has been arranged into twelve sections. . . . As for the [sets of] twelve sections, their significance is equivalent to the Three Vehicles.'"

We can see that, as a result of their assimilation to the Three Vehicles, the Three Tung were associated with a grading in three degrees, Great, Middle, and Small; and that among the three basic divisions of the Taoist Canon, the *Tung-chen* section occupied the highest place. This, in my view, is the most important feature of the concept of the Three Tung.

In connection with this point, we must here take note of a passage from a book that has been mentioned earlier [in nn. 6 and 9], the *Tung-chen t'ai-shang su-ling ta-yu miao ching* 洞眞太上素靈大有妙經 (*TT* 1026). The name of this book is found in the *Esoteric Life of the Perfected Immortal of Tzu-yang* [see n. 7], which is presumably to be dated no later than the end of the fourth century. The scripture is also cited in T'ao Hung-ching's *Concealed Instructions for Ascent to Perfection* (*Teng-chen yin-chüeh* 登眞隱訣, 1:3a, *TT* 193), which means that it must at all events have been composed before the end of the Liang (A.D. 556). It is thus one of the older components of the Shang-ch'ing scriptures. In the following passage of the *Ta-yu miao-ching*, as cited in the sixth-century Taoist encyclopedia *Wu-shang pi-yao*, we find a series of statements that set forth a concept basically identical with the idea that the Three Tung were equivalent to the Three Vehicles:

> The Most High said: "All study must proceed upward from below; it must be put into practice with due account being taken of the proper sequence. One must neither skip nor abridge, lest by so doing he fail to conform to the celestial statutes. The scriptures have their Three Categories (*san p'in* 三品), as the Tao has its Threefold Perfection (*san chen* 三眞). 'The Secret Writing of the Three Sovereigns' of the celestial texts in great characters, the Register of the Nine Heavens, the Tao of the Yellow and White . . . form the lowest category. The *Ling-pao Tung-hsüan* [scriptures], which came into being at the same time as the Primordial Beginning . . . are the marvels of the middle category, which may even be studied by mere terrestrial immortals (*ti hsien* 地仙). The Taoist scriptures of Shang-ch'ing, and the hidden writings of T'ai-tan (*T'ai-tan yin-shu* 太丹隱書), three hundred precious titles in all, with nine thousand valuable instructions, are the uppermost category, that of the Superior Perfected (*shang chen* 上眞); they are the personal library of the Jade Emperor . . . the instructions of the highest degree. . . ."[19]

Here we see clearly that the Scripture of the Three Sovereigns is taken to be the lowest category of text; the *Ling-pao Tung-hsüan* scriptures are considered the intermediate class; and the scriptures of Shang-ch'ing are placed in the highest position. Thus, these three groups of scriptures not only bear the name of "Three Tung," but also they embody the very concept of the Three Tung as three consecutive "vehicles." We may there-

---

19. *Wu-shang pi-yao*, 42:4a–b (*TT* 773). The same passage appears in the text of the *Ta-yu miao-ching* p. 44a2–44b1 (*TT* 1026).

fore assume that this classification of Taoist writings, in which the Shang-ch'ing scriptures occupy the most prominent position, must have been the work of members of the Shang-ch'ing school, for whom these were the principal texts, and also must have been compiled under the influence of the Buddhist concept of the Three Vehicles. If such was indeed the case, then this development must have occurred sometime after the first appearance of the Shang-ch'ing scriptures, from about 364, and before Lu Hsiu-ching's main period of activity. In other words, the first canonical arrangement of Taoist scriptures according to this tripartite principle of organization must have taken place toward the end of the fourth or the beginning of the fifth century.[20]

These years correspond precisely to one of the most remarkable periods of activity in the whole history of Chinese Buddhism. This was the era of the famous scholars Tao-an 道安 (312–385) and Hui-yüan 慧遠 (334–416), and of the great translator Kumārajīva (344–413). By this time a large number of Buddhist scriptures had been either translated or fabricated, and a point had been reached where it was necessary to classify them systematically. It was Tao-an who most exerted himself in the collection and arrangement of scriptural texts. As a result of these activities, in about 374 he drew up the first comprehensive catalogue of Buddhist sacred writings, the *Systematic Catalogue of the Scriptures* (*Tsung-li chung-ching mu-lu* 綜理衆經目錄). Not long afterward, early in the fifth century, Tao-liu 道流 and Chu Tao-tsu 竺道祖 produced their *Catalogue of the Scriptures* (*Chung-ching lu* 衆經錄) in four *chüan*, and in the northwest Seng-jui 僧叡 wrote the *Catalogue of Scriptures of the Second Ch'in Dynasty* (*Erh-Ch'in chung-ching mu* 二秦衆經目). Rather later in the fifth century, again in the south, there appeared the *Special List of Scriptures* (*Chung-ching pieh-lu* 衆經別錄) in two *chüan*.

It was under such circumstances, and in response to this activity among the Buddhists, that a sense of cohesion developed among indigenous movements which had never before felt themselves to share any common bond. It was, therefore, against the shared background of not being Buddhist that there arose what we could almost designate "a concept of the Three Tung," with its principal emphasis on the Shang-ch'ing scriptures. The arrangement in sequence of the literature of these groups resulted in the scriptures of the Three Tung.

20. Some scholars posit that the creation of the *San-tung* was due to Lu Hsiu-ching. However, he had the closest relationship to the Ling-pao scriptures and played merely a minor role in the Shang-ch'ing scriptural tradition. It is hard to believe that he was the one who created the *San-tung*, which bear the stamp of a Shang-ch'ing viewpoint.

Among the texts that were originally involved in the formation of this collection, the Shang-ch'ing and Ling-pao scriptures developed in rather close relationship to each other. This may be deduced from such early historical documents as T'ao Hung-ching's postface to the *Chen-kao* (ch. 19, 20), which arose out of the Shang-ch'ing school at Mao Shan, and Lu Hsiu-ching's preface to his catalogue of Ling-pao scriptures (*Yün-chi ch'i-ch'ien*, 4:4a3). The third of the triad of canonical texts, the *Scripture of the Three Sovereigns*, was reportedly revealed to Pao Ching 鮑靚. This shadowy figure is said to have been the teacher of Hsü Mai 許邁 (300–348), the elder brother of Hsü Mi 許謐 (303–373), one of the central personalities in the Shang-ch'ing movement. What is more, the text of this scripture was transmitted by Ko Hung 葛洪 (283–343).[21]

Both the Ko and Hsü families lived in the town of Chü-jung 句容, Kiangsu, and were related by marriage over several generations (*Chen-kao, ch.* 20). Further, the Shang-ch'ing scriptures were for the most part transmitted by members of what had been the old aristocracy of the former Kingdom of Wu 吳, to which the Kos and the Hsüs belonged. Its great families lived in the region of Chiang-nan 江南, south of the Yangtze, before the coming of the Chin dynasty; and their position in Eastern Chin society was somewhat lower than that of the powerful aristocrats from the north who had emigrated to south China [after 316]. The original Shang-ch'ing literature assumed its definitive form with T'ao Hung-ching at the end of the fifth century.

Oriented as they were toward the interests of an aristocratic group, the Shang-ch'ing scriptures played no great part in any missionary activity aimed at the general public. Yet their influence on the time was probably all the greater on that account, since the dominant culture of the age was in some sense aristocratic. There is, in any case, no doubt of the intellectual capabilities of the movement's representatives. The situation of both the Ling-pao scriptures and the *Scripture of the Three Sovereigns* appears to have been more or less similar, as they too were transmitted largely by members of the old southern aristocracy, and thus seem to have developed under circumstances analogous to those of the Shang-ch'ing scriptures.

All this suggests an added significance to the fact that it was these particular texts that composed the Three Tung: it must have been due to something more than the Buddhist concept of the Three Vehicles. Instead, the arrangement of the canon must at first have been realistic, closely corresponding to the current position of the Shang-ch'ing school, at a

21. See *Yün-chi ch'i-ch'ien* (*TT* 678), in the sections *San-tung ping-hsü* 三洞并序 and *San-tung p'in-ko* 三洞品格, 6:1a–12a.

time when tripartite systems of classification were most in fashion. This, I believe, is the way in which the earliest form of the Taoist Canon came into being.

Yet, these considerations notwithstanding, there was evidently considerable partiality in the arrangement, when viewed in historical terms. A prime example of this may be seen in the total omission from this schema of the canonical writings of the Way of the Celestial Master, the titles of which are frequently mentioned, for example, in the *History of the Chin Dynasty*. We know from the biographical sections of the standard histories that the Way of the Celestial Masters already had a canonical literature of its own.[22] The *Treatise on Buddhism and Taoism* in the *History of the Wei Dynasty* (*Wei-shu* 114:25a9) mentions the "texts of petitions to the celestial officials" (*t'ien-kuan chang-pen* 天官章本). A fragmentary Tun-huang manuscript, written probably in the sixth century, contains a large part of the commentary on the *Lao-tzu* attributed to Chang Lu 張魯, the *Lao-tzu Hsiang-erh chu* 老子想爾注.[23]

This fact shows clearly the special conditions surrounding the creation of the concept of the Three Tung—the milieu of a particular group of "schools"—originating in and perpetuated among the old aristocracy of south China. Yet, though this particular systemization now appears to be far from an objective reflection of the relative importance of the different schools, it seems to have been a necessary stage in the process by which these separate schools eventually acquired a sense of cohesiveness. Considering these facts, we might be led to anticipate what eventually followed: the need for a revision of the concept of the Three Tung and the subsequent admission of a greater variety of scriptures into the canon. In the emergence of the Four Supplements (*Ssu fu*) we have what appears to be the most obvious example of this process of modification.

The Origin of the Four Supplements

The Four Supplements are those portions of the canon entitled *T'ai-hsüan* 太玄, *T'ai-p'ing* 太平, *T'ai-ch'ing* 太清, and *Cheng-i* 正一. When listed in this order, the first three are considered as being ancillary to the *Tung-*

22. See, for example, the biography of Chang Lu 張魯 in *Wei-chih* 魏志, 8:42b–49b (*Erh-shih-wu shih* ed.); the biography of Liu Yen 劉焉 in the *Hou Han-shu*, 105:1a–5b (*Erh-shih-wu shih* ed.); the biography of Chang Tao-ling 張道陵 in Ko Hung's *Shen-hsien chüan* 神仙傳, 4:16a–17b (*Tao-tsang ching-hua* 道藏精華 4.4 ed.)

23. The fact that this commentary actually must have been written by Chang Lu, is discussed in my article "*Rōshi Sō-ji chū* no seiritsu" 老子想爾注の成立 (The composition of the Hsiang-erh Commentary on the *Lao-tzu*) *Okayama shigaku* 岡山史學 (Okayama Journal of History) 19:9–31 (1967).

chen, Tung-hsüan, and *Tung-shen* sections, respectively, while the *Cheng-i* division is described as supplementing all three Tung. Thus the arrangement of the Four Supplements is subsidiary to that of the Three Tung.[24]

San tung 三洞	*Ssu fu* 四輔
1. *Tung-chen* 洞眞	1. *T'ai-hsüan* 太玄
2. *Tung-hsüan* 洞玄	2. *T'ai-p'ing* 太平
3. *Tung-shen* 洞神	3. *T'ai-ch'ing* 太清
	4. *Cheng-i* 正一

The *T'ai-hsüan* section is based upon the *Lao-tzu* (the *Tao-te ching* 道德經). The central text of the *T'ai-p'ing* section is the *T'ai-p'ing ching* 太平經, the successor to the famous work of the Later Han dynasty, the *T'ai-p'ing ch'ing-ling shu* 太平清領書. The *T'ai-ch'ing* section contains writings on alchemy, the class of literature which Ko Hung held to be of the greatest value, whereas the *Cheng-i* section is made up of the canonical texts of the Way of the Celestial Masters. It is obvious that all of these scriptures are in fact older than the texts around which the Three Tung were created.

The earliest reference to the Four Supplements is considered to be the *Scriptural Catalogue of the Seven Sections of the Jade Apocrypha of Master-of-the-Doctrine Meng* (*Meng fa-shih yü-wei ch'i-pu ching-shu mu* 孟法師玉緯七部經書目), mentioned in *Tao-chiao i-shu* (2:3b9, *TT* 763). Master Meng seems to have been a contemporary of T'ao Hung-ching, active during the Ch'i and early Liang. Since the "Seven Sections" of his scriptural catalogue apparently refer to the Three Tung and Four Supplements, the first mention of the latter would have been at about the beginning of the sixth century, if not before. No extant documents reveal how much earlier they may really have been, nor whether they might even have been compiled at the same time as the Three Tung.

If, however, the Three Tung did originate as the result of a process such as the one we have suggested above (pp. 258–65), it seems most likely that the Four Supplements were a later addition. It is highly improbable that the idea of a group of four categories supplementing the Three

24. *Yün-chi ch'i-ch'ien* 6:19b2–6 (*TT* 678) quotes the *Cheng-i ching-t'u k'o-chieh p'in* 正一經圖科戒品 as follows: "The *T'ai-ch'ing* scriptures supplement the *Tung-shen pu* and deal with the work of immortals under the rubric of alchemy. The *T'ai-p'ing* scriptures supplement the *Tung-hsüan pu* and deal with the work of the Perfected under the rubric of the *Chia-i shih-pu* 甲乙十部 [the "text in ten sections named after the Celestial Stems"—the *T'ai-p'ing ching*]. The *T'ai-hsüan* [scriptures] supplement the *Tung-chen pu* and deal with the work of Holy Sages under the rubric of the *Scripture in Five Thousand Words* [the *Tao-te ching*]. The *Cheng-i fa-wen* 正一法文 [正一部] takes the Way and its Power as the main theme, exalts the Three Tung, and propagates the Three Vehicles." This entire section of *Yün-chi ch'i-ch'ien* seems to be quoted from the *Hsüan-men ta-i*.

Tung would have been the initial conception; and the rather haphazard system of correspondences established between the two groups appears to support this impression. There is, finally, the mention of Lu Hsiu-ching's fifth-century catalogue as the *Catalogue of Scriptural Writings of the Three Tung* (p. 260, above), suggesting that, in Lu's time, the Taoist Canon comprised the Three Tung alone.[25]

If we are justified in this assumption, then we might consider the Four Supplements as having their origin in a kind of movement of reform or reevaluation [at the time of the Liang dynasty]: the result of efforts to bring both the concept of the Three Tung and the contents of the canon into greater conformity with the actual facts. It must be admitted that we know absolutely nothing of the real substance of this movement. Yet it seems highly probable that at its core lay a basic awareness of resistance to Buddhism. The outcome of this, as we have already seen, was to be the definitive form of the Taoist Canon, within which the principal emphasis remained on the Shang-ch'ing scriptures.

If the conclusions here put forward are correct, one might estimate that the Four Supplements were added to the Three Tung at about the beginning of the sixth century, approximately a hundred years after the Three Tung themselves came into being. We might then conclude that within the space of a century the Taoists' sense of cohesiveness and their awareness of themselves as Taoists had gradually broadened. The formation of first the Three Tung, then the Four Supplements, is a concrete manifestation of this fact. It was during the same period that the basic structural principles of the Taoist Canon were established, and that the canon was brought to completion, at least for a time. Subsequently, the constant increase in the richness and diversity of its contents and the gradual relaxation of the clear-cut rules which had originally governed classification resulted in the comparatively chaotic collection that the Taoist Canon is today.

25. *Master Lu's Catalogue of the Scriptures of the Three Tung* (*Lu hsien-sheng San-tung ching-shu mu-lu*) is quoted in the *Preface to the Scriptures of the Three Tung* (*San-tung ching-hsü* 三洞經序) by Master-of-the-Doctrine Ko 蓋法師 (which, in turn, is quoted in *Tao-chiao i-shu* 道教義樞 2:3b7–8 [*TT* 763]). This same passage by Master-of-the-Doctrine Ko is also the text which mentions the *Meng-fa-shih yü-wei ch'i-pu ching-shu mu* 孟法師玉緯七部經書目 composed during the Liang dynasty (cf. above, p. 266). [This whole complex of texts is interrelated and probably very old.] The *Tao-chiao i-shu* [dated ca. A.D. 700, cf. n. 5 above] is based on the *Hsüan-men ta-i* (*TT* 760; composed end Sui, beginning of T'ang, cf. above, p. 255 and n. 3). [As we have seen, cf. n. 1], the *Hsüan-men ta-i*, in turn, is based on the [even older] *Sung fa-shih shih-erh pu i-ts'an* 宋法師十二部義殘 [Tun-huang, Pelliot 3001]. Therefore we can assume that the passage by Master-of-the-Doctrine Ko [quoted in the *Tao-chiao i-shu*] also originally figured in the Tun-huang text by Master-of-the-Doctrine Sung, and consequently is very old.

9 Taoist Studies in Japan

Tadao Sakai 酒井忠夫
Tetsurō Noguchi 野口鐵郎

TAOISM, MUCH LIKE CONFUCIANISM, is a cultural composite drawn from the Chinese people and Chinese society. Taoism incorporates elements of philosophy, thought, religion, superstition, popular life, manners, customs, morality, literature, art, science, and so on. It has played a significant role politically, socially, and culturally throughout Chinese history. Compared to Confucianism, the relationship of Taoism to the Chinese masses is so close that we can consider Taoism to be the national religion of China, indispensable for understanding the Chinese people and their society.

Given this many-faceted nature of Taoism, then, any study of the subject must perforce deal with these several factors separately. Yet, if such scholarly investigation is to be truly scientific, it must attempt to view its object both in its "horizontal" relation to the other component elements of Taoism as well as in terms of the broader total historical "vertical" flow of political, social, and cultural phenomena. The same may be said to apply to studies in Confucianism and Buddhism, and to other socio-historical research.

Taoist studies in Japan, as in other countries, did not originally incorporate the kind of comprehensive approach described above. Research tended to focus on the above-mentioned individual components of Taoism—especially philosophy, thought, religion, superstition, custom, and so on—but not in terms of their interrelation with each other. The earliest work, moreover, was done mainly by Sinologists whose primary interests were the Chinese classics, Chinese Buddhism and Chinese Buddhist history, and by connoisseurs of things Chinese. Consequently, a considerable amount of research tended to treat Taoism from a Confucian or a Buddhist standpoint or to view it in relation to the latter two orthodoxies, which made it not uncommon for Taoism to appear as heretical or secular. Another common approach to Taoism was in terms of its thought, philosophy, or religious beliefs; alternatively, it might be studied as a variety of superstition.

Since the Meiji period, Japanese efforts to understand China and its people have been characterized by an attitude of mystery and curiosity. Of course a certain exoticism had long been a feature of studies done by Western diplomats, missionaries, and businessmen resident in China; and despite the social and cultural heterogeneity of their various countries, they tended to view Chinese culture as something different from their own and thus retained a degree of objectivity.

Japan, however, for reasons not unrelated to its political advocacy of such pan-Asian concepts as *dōbun dōshu* 同文同種 (same script, same race) and *Ajia wa itsu nari* アジアは一なり (Asia is one), showed little inclination to adopt the Western approach to China as a distinct cultural and social entity. Instead, the Chinese and Japanese cultures were considered in Japan to be essentially the same—that is, Chinese culture was taken to be the progenitor of Japanese culture. In the modern period, however, it was Japan, as the advanced country, whose culture was felt to be superior. There was a sense of curiosity about what the Chinese culture of the past—the source and inspiration of Japanese culture—had really been like. And, as Taoism was a particularly obscure part of that culture, it was a likely focus for the curious scholarly mind and came to be treated accordingly.

The above, then, may be taken as the general trend of this first period of study, extending from Meiji through Taishō and into the early Shōwa reign. The work produced during this period, even when it dealt with broader subjects than Taoism, Confucianism, and Buddhism (such as Chinese philosophy, thought, and ethics, or literature, science, and history), remained limited to its particular focus, rarely seeking to relate its subject to other currents in Taoism or Chinese religion. Scholars of Chinese history, in particular, almost without exception, failed to consider Taoism in relation to political and social phenomena.

Here we should mention those few whose pioneering contributions to Taoist studies during this early period of development deserve to be highly praised.

Hattori, Unokichi 服部宇之吉. "Fūsui-ron" 風水論 (On geomancy), "Zensho ni tsuite" 善書について (On morality books), and "Kandai hōshi no henkon-jutsu" 漢代方士の返魂術 (The art of recalling the soul [practiced by] Han dynasty *fang-shih*). In *Shina kenkyū* 支那研究 (China studies). Tokyo, 1926, Pp. 466–513.

Kōda, Rohan 幸田露伴. *Dōkyō shisō* 道教思想 (Taoist thought). Tokyo, 1936, 40 pp.

Koyanagi, Shigeta 小柳司氣太. *Tōyō shisō no kenkyū* 東洋思想の研究 (Studies on East Asian thought). Tokyo, 1934, 623 pp.

———. *Hakuunkan shi* 白雲觀志 *Fu Tōgaku-byō shi* 附東嶽廟志 (White Cloud Monastery annals and annals of the Temple of the Eastern Peak). Tokyo, 1934. 388 pp.

———. *Zoku Tōyō Shisō no kenkyū* 續東洋思想の研究 (Studies on East Asian thought, no. 2). Tokyo, 1938. 418 pp.

———. *Rō Sō no shisō to dōkyō* 老莊の思想と道教 (Taoism and the thought of Lao-tzu and Chuang-tzu). Tokyo, 1942. 392 pp.

Takeuchi, Yoshio 武內義雄. *Rōshi genshi* 老子原始 (Tracing the origin of Lao-tzu [the man and the book]). Tokyo, 1967 (1st ed., 1926). 356 pp.

Tokiwa, Daijō 常盤大定. *Shina ni okeru Bukkyō to Jukyō Dōkyō* 支那に於ける佛教と儒教道教 (Buddhism, Confucianism, and Taoism in China). Tokyo, 1930. 750 pp.

Tsuda, Saukichi 津田左右吉. *Dōka no shisō to sono tenkai* 道家の思想と其の展開 (Taoist thought and its evolution). Tokyo, 1927. 639 pp. (2d ed. as vol. 13 of *Tsuda Saukichi zenshu* 津田左右吉全集 (Collected Works of Tsuda Saukichi) Tokyo, Iwanami, 1964. 581 pp.

———. "Shinsen-shisō no kenkyū" 神僊思想の研究 (Studies on the immortals) in *Tsuda Saukichi zenshu.* Tokyo, Iwanami, 1939. Pp. 172–333.

Tsumaki, Chokuryō 妻木直良. "Dōkyō no kenkyū" 道教の研究 (Taoist studies). *Tōyō gakuhō* 東洋學報 (East Asian Studies), Tokyo, 1.1:1–56; 1.2:20–70 (1911); 2.1:71–75 (1912).

———. "Nihon ni okeru dōkyō no kenkyū" 日本に於ける道教の研究 (Study on Taoism in Japan). *Ryūkoku gakuhō* 龍谷學報 (Journal of the Ryūkoku University), Kyoto, 306:23–44 (1933); 308:71–85 (1934).

Although some of the volumes listed above, Koyanagi's and Kōda's for instance, were published in the 1930s and 1940s, almost all of the essays they contain date from before 1930. These early studies, of course, manifest the tendencies described above, although the latter were also apparent in a number of works written during the succeeding period. There were also works (especially those of Koyanagi and Kōda) which did strive to relate Taoism to coexisting religious and cultural phenomena, thus including many elements that were to be significant in later Taoist studies. It was toward the end of this period that some of the most important contributions to Taoist studies were made; these consisted notably of the publication of the Taoist Canon (*Tao-tsang* 道藏) and the exploitation of the literary finds at Tun-huang and other places in western China.

Between 1923 and 1926, the Han-fen-lou Publishing Company 涵芬樓書局 in Shanghai published photolithographic versions of the regular Taoist Canon and the Wan-li Supplement *Wan-li Hsü Tao-tsang* 萬曆續道藏, an event which served as a stimulus to Taoist studies both in Japan and abroad. Between 1907 and 1911, several works related to Taoism had been among the finds discovered in Tun-huang by Westerners such as Pelliot, by Japanese such as Tachibana Zuichō 橘瑞超, and by the Chinese themselves. The manuscripts discovered, as they were gradually utilized, proved to be of immense value in the dating of scriptures in the Taoist Canon, whose authenticity had been difficult to verify. It was not until after World War II, however, that the results of these developments became truly significant for the study of Taoism, though the Tun-huang region finds had generally become available for use as research materials as early as the 1930s. Special recognition is due in this connection to Ōfuchi Eshin 大淵慧眞 of Japan, whose pioneering work in photographing materials in the libraries of Peking and Paris as early as 1929–30 paved the way for their further exploitation.

The direction of Taoist studies began to change gradually, following the Manchurian Incident in September 1931. The political situation created a growing demand for knowledge about China and the Chinese people. Interestingly enough, at this time there was a feeling in some circles of the Japanese intelligentsia that Taoism was the most significant source of such knowledge.

This turning point, then, marks the beginning of the second period of Taoist studies. The demand for knowledge about Chinese culture and about Taoism as an integral part of Chinese life and society gave rise to new studies of Taoism in its political and social manifestations. These efforts, which were centered in the Research Department of the South Manchurian Railway (Minami Manshū tetsudō kabushiki kaisha Chōsabu 南滿洲鐵道株式會社調查部) and the East Asia Institute (Tōa Kenkyūsho 東亞研究所),[1] stimulated in turn a new campaign to study Chinese Buddhism and Taoism from the standpoint of Chinese history. The tendency to see Taoism within the full context of Chinese history marked a significant methodological step toward a comprehensive study of Taoism, an approach, as we have noted, not often evident in the first period.

The instrumental organization here was the "Society for the Historical Research of Chinese Buddhism" (Shina Bukkyō-shi Gakkai 支那佛教

史學會), formed in 1936. In the view of the association, "traditionally the history of Buddhism has been a history of religious sects." In order to remedy this, the association proposed that the fields of study be expanded to include "historical understanding," a knowledge of "geography," and "the study of almanacs," in addition to the accumulation of extensive historical data: see Ogasawara Senshū 小笠原宣秀, "Shōwa jūichinen no Shina Bukkyō-shi Gakkai tembō" 昭和十一年の支那佛教史學會展望 (Profile of the Chinese Buddhist History Association in 1936), *Shina Bukkyō shigaku* 支那佛教史學 (Journal of the History of Chinese Buddhism), 1.1:131–38 (April 1937). The majority of Japan's Taoist scholars of this period were members of this association, including Fukui Kōjun 福井康順, Kimura Eiichi 木村英一, and Itano Chōhachi 板野長八 in the field of thought and philosophy, and Tsukamoto Zenryū 塚本善隆, Takao Giken 高雄義堅, Ogasawara Senshū, Nogami Shunjō 野上俊靜, and Michihata Ryōshū 道端良秀 in the field of Buddhist history.

Also during this period began the rise of Chinese folklore studies, influenced by the work of Yanagida Kunio 柳田國男. The aforementioned Research Department of the South Manchurian Railway and the East Asian Research Institute, along with the members of the Chinese Buddhist History Association, gave new direction to Taoist studies by seeking to approach Taoism from a comprehensive perspective. These groups did field work on the religion and life of the masses in the villages and cities of north and central China. A representative result of these efforts, almost all of which were written up after World War II, was *Chūgoku nōson kankō chōsa* 中國農村慣行調查 (Investigations of Chinese agricultural customs), 6 vol. (Tokyo, 1952–58), which incorporated field work devoted to Taoism and folklore. The most important contributors, after Koyanagi Shigeta, were Yoshioka Yoshitoyo 吉岡義豊, Nagao Ryūzō 永尾龍造, Naoe Hiroji 直江廣治, Sawada Mizuho 澤田瑞穂 Igarashi Kenryū 五十嵐賢隆, and Takizawa Shunryō 瀧澤俊亮, all of whom had accumulated a good deal of valuable data. Some of the representative achievements of individual scholars at this time follow:

Hirano, Yoshitarō 平野義太郎. "Dōkyō no keiten" 道教の經典 (The scriptures of Taoism) and "Kōkakaku" 功過格 (Ledgers of merit and demerit). In his *Dai Ajia shugi no rekishiteki kiso* 大アジア主義の歴史的基礎 (Historical basis for Pan-Asianism). Tokyo, 1945. Pp. 220–44.

Igarashi, Kenryū 五十嵐賢隆. *Taiseikyū-shi* 太清宮志 (Annals of the T'ai-ch'ing Kung). Mukden, 1938. 287 pp.

Nagao, Ryūzō 永尾龍造. *Shina minzokushi* 支那民俗誌 (Records of

Chinese folklore). Vol. 1, Tokyo, 1940, 672 pp.; vol. 2, Tokyo, 1941, 883 pp.; vol. 6, Tokyo, 1942, 857 pp.

Sakai, Tadao 酒井忠夫. *Kindai shina ni okeru shūkyō kessha no kenkyū* 近代支那に於ける宗教結社の研究 (Study of religious societies in modern China). Tokyo, 1944. 309 pp.

Tachibana, Shiraki 橘樸. *Shina shisō kenkyū* 支那思想研究 (Studies in Chinese thought). Tokyo, 1936. Pp. 39–222.

————. *Dōkyō to shinwa densetsu* 道教と神話傳說 ([Religious] Taoism, myths and legends). Tokyo, 1948. 286 pp.

Takizawa, Shunryō 瀧澤俊亮. *Manshū no gaison shinkō* 滿洲の街村信仰 (Popular beliefs in Manchurian towns and villages). Shinkyō, 1940. 299 pp.

Yoshioka, Yoshitoyo 吉岡義豊. *Dōkyō no jittai* 道教の實態 (The actual state of Taoism). Peking, 1941; reprinted Kyōto 1975. 431 pp. (In both cases published without the name of the author.)

Another important feature of this period was the introduction through translation of a number of European and American studies, including those of Arthur H. Smith and Henri Doré, as well as Max Weber's *The Religion of China: Confucianism and Taoism* (Tübingen, 1922; trans. H. H. Gerth, New York, 1951). A Japanese annotated version of the whole *Chinese Repository* [Canton, 1832–51] was also published (*Shina sōhō* 支那叢報; Tokyo, 1943).

The third period of Taoist studies in Japan may be said to extend from the end of World War II to the present. During the postwar period, scientific study advanced in all areas of learning. Taoism was no exception. There had been the beginnings of comprehensive systematic research during the war itself, but the majority of scholars, once the war was over, chose to rework and supplement the research and field studies on society and culture which they had done in China during the war. The result was a succession of major works. The valuable materials that had been collected during the war were used to advantage, such as the "precious scrolls" (*pao-chüan* 寶卷), the morality books (*shan-shu* 善書), and the encyclopedias for daily use (*jih-yung lei-shu* 日用類書). These studies flourished amidst the general mood of enthusiasm for Chinese popular culture. The emphasis tended to be on popular Taoism rather than on philosophical or monastic Taoism. Also studied for their connection with the life of the people were the almanacs. The work of Moriya Mitsuo 守屋美都雄 is noteworthy in this area, as is, for example, his *Chūgoku kosaijiki no kenkyū* 中國古歲時記の研究 (A study of old records of annual observances in China), Tokyo, 1963, 492 pp.

The Taoist Canon and the Tun-huang finds were meanwhile being used extensively. Most of the work done was not limited to Chinese and Taoist historical studies (that is, to a "horizontal" association of several fields, such as thought, philosophy, religion, literature, and science), but was rather aimed at a historical "vertical" flow of cultural, political, and social phenomena centered on Taoism. In particular, there was a call for comprehensive research in individual academic fields, including the leading areas of specialization in the postwar period—in other words, for what was known as studies of marginal aspects (*Grenzgebiet*) or, more, recently, by the more inclusive term "interdisciplinary studies." Two examples will suffice to illustrate this:

Furuno, Kiyoto 古野清人. *Genshi shūkyō no kōzō to kinō* 原始宗教の構造と機能 (The structure and function of primitive religion). Yokohama, 1971. 380 pp.

Yabuuchi, Kiyoshi 藪內清. *Chūgoku chūsei kagakugijutsushi no kenkyū* 中國中世科學技術史の研究 (Studies on the history of technology in medieval China). Tokyo, 1963. 540 pp.

The trend apparent in the humanities toward comprehensive research became apparent in Taoist studies as well. Thus, in 1950 the Japan Society of Taoistic Research (Nippon Dōkyō Gakkai 日本道教學會) was formed. The role played by the Taoist scholars belonging to the former Society for the Historical Research of Chinese Buddhism was thus transmitted and perpetuated. The journal of the Japan Society of Taoistic Research, *Tōhō shūkyō* 東方宗教 (the Journal of Eastern Religions) began to come out the next year, in 1951. It included the following statement of purpose, indicative of trends in Japanese Taoist research in the postwar period:

> We consider that Taoism is recognized as a religion encompassing the whole of Chinese life. Its importance must be evident to every East Asian specialist, particularly to the Sinologist. In view of the growing tendency to do systematic research on China, Taoist studies can no longer be ignored. Therefore, with our colleagues, we have organized the Japan Taoist Studies Association. Its task will not be easy. Research on Taoism is in itself a vast and complex field, but also it cannot effectively lead to any full understanding without broad, associated research into other East Asian religions and parallel research in other disciplines. After a detailed investigation of the present condition of Taoist studies, we have decided to adopt an integrated approach from various directions. It is our aim thereby to win for Taoist studies the place they deserve in Sinology.
>
> The association has started this journal in order to record the fruits of our studies. It has been named *Tōhō shūkyō* 東方宗教 (Journal of Eastern Religions) rather than *Dōkyō kenkyū* 道教研究 (Taoist Studies) in order to emphasize the relationship with East Asian religions in general. Taoism has had an important influence on East Asian culture and is related, in one way or another, to the totality of East Asian religions,

folklore, customs, and annual festivals, with all of which we intend to deal, as well as with the problem of culture in everyday life.[2]

This statement emphasizes "horizontal" integration of Taoist studies but makes no mention of a "vertical" approach to politics, society, and culture. The horizontal approach is no less scientific than the vertical approach, but in the study of Taoism, which has developed and been transformed with the development of Chinese society, the vertical approach becomes much more important and effective. And, in fact, the statement quoted above reflects only one dimension of postwar Japanese research on Taoism, for studies were done in history and the social sciences both during and after the war, as seen, for example, by the historical studies listed earlier.

The following are representative of major achievements in Taoist studies since 1945:

Fukui, Kōjun 福井康順. *Dōkyō no kisoteki kenkyū* 道教の基礎的研究 (Basic studies in Taoism). Tokyo, 1957. 452 pp.

———. *Tōyō shisōshi kenkyū* 東洋思想史研究 (Studies in the history of East Asian thought). Tokyo, 1960. 397 pp.

Kanaya, Osamu 金谷治. *Rō Sō teki sekai—Enanji no shisō* 老莊的世界—淮南子の思想 (The world of Lao-tzu and Chuang-tzu: the thought of Huai-nan tzu). Kyoto, 1959. 259 pp.

Kimura, Eiichi 木村英一. *Chūgoku minshū no shisō to bunka* 中國民衆の思想と文化 (Thought and culture among the Chinese populace). Tokyo, 1947. 164 pp.

Kubo, Noritada 窪德忠. *Kōshin shinkō no kenkyū* 庚申信仰の研究 (Studies of the *keng-shen* beliefs). Tokyo, 1962. 1,149 pp.

———. *Kōshin shinkō no kenkyū—tōsho hen* 庚申信仰の研究—島嶼編 (Studies of the *keng-shen* beliefs in the islands). Tokyo, 1969. 652 pp.

Miyakawa, Hisayuki 宮川尚志. *Rikuchōshi kenkyū—shūkyō-hen* 六朝史研究—宗教編 (Studies in Six Dynasties history—vol. 2: Religion). Kyoto, 1964. 417 pp.

———. *Rikuchō shūkyōshi* 六朝宗教史 (A religious history of the Six Dynasties period). Tokyo, 1974. Revised edition.

Ōfuchi, Ninji 大淵忍爾. *Dōkyō-shi no kenkyū* 道教史の研究 (Studies in the history of religious Taoism). Okayama, 1964. 547 pp.

———. *Tonkō dōkei mokuroku* 敦煌道經目錄 (Catalogue of Taoist manuscripts from Tun-huang). Kyoto, 1960. 123 pp.

Sakai, Tadao 酒井忠夫. *Chūgoku zensho no kenkyū* 中國善書の研究 (Studies on China's morality books). Tokyo, 1960. 485 pp.

Sawada, Mizuho 澤田瑞穗. *Zōho Hōkan no kenkyū* 增補寶卷の研究

(Studies of "precious scrolls"). Tokyo, 1975. 461 pp.

———. Kōchu Haja-shōben 校注破邪詳辯 (A critical edition of the *P'o-hsieh hsiang-pien*). Tokyo, 1972. 260 pp. On heterodox religions. Sub-title reads "Source material for the study of religious groups among the Chinese populace."

Tsukamoto, Zenryū 塚本善隆. *Gisho shakurōshi no kenkyū* 魏書釋老志の研究 (A study of the "Treatise on Buddhism and Taoism" in the *Wei-shu*). Kyoto, 1961. 544 pp. Includes an annotated translation into Japanese.

Yoshioka, Yoshitoyo 吉岡義豊. *Dōkyō no kenkyū* 道教の研究 (Studies in Taoism). Kyoto, 1952. 344 pp.

———. *Dōkyō keiten shiron* 道教經典史論 (Historical treatises on the Taoist scriptures). Tokyo, 1955. 484 pp.

———. *Dōkyō to Bukkyō* 道教と佛教 (Taoism and Buddhism) Vol. 1, Tokyo, 1958, 596 pp.; vol. 2, Tokyo, 1959, 407 pp.; vol. 3, Tokyo, 1976, 384 pp.

Yoshioka, Yoshitoyo 吉岡義豊. *Eisei e no negai—Dōkyō* 永生への願い—道教 (The desire for everlasting life—Taoism). Kyoto and Tokyo, 1970. 271 pp.

The above are only examples of the work of these and other authors, who have published numerous articles as well. There are also not a few works devoted to Chinese philosophy and Chinese Buddhist history which contain sections dealing with Taoism.

In the foregoing we have attempted to give an overview of the history of Taoist studies in Japan, divided into three periods. A full bibliography[3] would show that during the first period, works on the Three Religions and on thought and philosophy were particularly numerous. These works, on the whole, achieved their educative and methodological goals. However, they cannot be said to offer a comprehensive and systematic approach to Taoist studies. In general, during all three periods the historical approach has prevailed. There has been a relatively large number of studies that attempt to view political and social factors in relation to history, not always satisfactorily. Quite a lot has been published, for example, on the Way of the Five Pecks of Grain (Wu-tou-mi Tao 五斗米道) and the Way of Great Peace (T'ai-p'ing Tao 太平道), for example:

Miyakawa, Hisayuki 宮川尚志. "Kizoku, gōzoku to dōkyo" 貴族, 豪族と道教 (Aristocracy, gentry, and Taoism). *Rekishi kyōiku* 歷史教育 (Historical Education), 14.5:59–66 (1966).

Ofuchi, Ninji 大淵忍爾. "Kōkin no ran to Gotobeidō 黄巾の亂と五斗米

道 (The rebellion of the Yellow Turbans and the Five-Pecks-of-Grain Sect). In *Iwanamikōza Sekai Rekishi*, 岩波講座世界歴史 (World History, ed. Iwanami Shoten 岩波書店). Tokyo, 1970. Vol. 5, pp. 23–52.

――――. "Chūgoku ni okeru minzoku shūkyō no seiritsu" 中國における民族宗教の成立 (The formation of ethnic religion in China). *Rekishigaku kenkyū* 歴史學研究 (Journal of Historical Studies), 179:4–11; 181:4–11, 37 (1955). "Ethnic religion" refers to popular Taoism.

Such papers have often left unresolved many important points relating to actual Chinese social and political conditions.

The study of the Ch'üan-chen Sect (Ch'üan-chen Chiao 全眞教), considered in terms of its political and social implications, has been carried on in China as well as in Japan.

Ch'en Yüan 陳垣. *Nan-Sung-ch'u ho-pei hsin Tao-chiao k'ao* 南宋初河北新道教考 (New Taoist [sects] in the northern provinces at the beginning of the Southern Sung dynasty). Peking, 1941. 112 pp.

Kubo, Noritada 窪德忠. *Chūgoku no shūkyō kaikaku* 中國の宗教改革 (Religious reformation in China). Kyoto, 1967. 206 pp.

Other religious groups have been an additional topic important to Taoist studies even when they are not immediately related to Taoism. Studies of the Maitreya Sect, Manichaeism, the White Lotus Sect, the T'ai-p'ing Rebellion, the Boxer Rebellion, and so forth, have made good progress, as can be seen from the following:

Ichiko, Chūzō 市古宙三. "Giwadan no seikaku" 義和團の性格 (The nature of the Boxers). *Kindai Chūgoku kenkyū* 近代中國研究 (Studies of modern China). Tokyo, 1948. Pp. 243–67.

Kojima, Shinji 小島晋治. "Taiheitengoku to nōmin" 太平天國と農民 (On the *T'ai-p'ing-tien-kuo* and peasants). *Shichō* 史潮 (Journal of History), 93:44–76; 96:1–30; 97:85–102 (1965–66).

Kubo, Noritada 窪德忠. "Sōdai ni okeru Dōkyō to Manikyō 宋代における道教とマ二教 (Taoism and Manichaeism during the Sung). In *Wada hakushi kokikinen Tōyōshi ronsō* 和田博士古稀記念東洋史論叢 (East Asian studies in honour of Dr. Wada Sei on the occasion of his seventieth birthday). Tokyo, 1961. Pp. 361–71.

Noguchi, Tetsurō 野口鐵郎. "Min Shin jidai no Byakurenkyō 明清時代の白蓮教 (The White Lotus Sect during the Ming and Ch'ing). *Rekishi kyōiku* 歴史教育 (History Education), 12.9:26–34 (1964).

Shigematsu, Shunshō 重松俊章. Tō Sō jidai no Miroku kyōhi 唐宋時代の彌勒教匪 (The Maitreya Sect during the T'ang and Sung periods). *Shien* 史淵 (Fukuoka), 3:68–103 (1931).

———. "Tō Sō jidai no Manikyō to makyō mondai" 唐宋時代の末尼教と魔教問題 (On the problem of Manichaeism and spirit-cults during the T'ang and Sung). *Shien* 12:85–143 (1936).

———. "Sō Gen jidai no kōkingun to Gen matsu no Miroku Byakuren kyōhi ni tsuite. 宋元時代の紅巾軍と元末の彌勒白蓮教匪について (The Red Turbans during the Sung and Yüan, and the Maitreya and White Lotus sects at the end of the Yüan). *Shien* 史淵, 24 : 79–90 (1940); 26:137–54 (1941); 28:107–26 (1942); 32:81–123 (1944).

Beyond presenting the facts, many of these essays interpret the phenomena they discuss as social movements of the peasant class. The result has been increased attention to the religious aspects of popular mass movements, and this has meant a significant contribution to the study of Taoism in its role as a Chinese popular religion. Religious groups found their bases in the social organizations of the peasantry and general populace.

Future studies of religious groups may be expected to investigate aspects of the people's religious consciousness within the context of a broader treatment of peasant and popular organizations and of class structure. We have already indicated the importance of the "precious scrolls" (*pao-chüan*) as a source used since the war for the study of Chinese religious groups. Utilization of this source has been advanced by Yoshioka Yoshitoyo, Sawada Mizuho, and Sakai Tadao.

Sawada, Mizuho, 澤田瑞穂. *Hōkan no kenkyū* 寶卷の研究 (A study of *pao-chüan*). Nagoya, 1963. 255 pp. Earlier version of work cited above.

Yoshioka, Yoshitoyo 吉岡義豊. "Kindai Chūgoku ni okeru hōkanryū shūkyō no tenkai" 近代中國における寶卷流宗教の展開 (The development of the religions producing "precious scrolls" in modern China). *Shūkyō bunka* 宗教文化 (Studies on Religious Culture), Tokyo, 3:1–64 (1950).

The "precious scrolls" have been especially useful as a source for literary history, but their relation to religious groups has not been given much attention except in the case of the Wu-wei Sect.

Sakai, Tadao 酒井忠夫. "Min matsu ni okeru hōkan to Muikyō" 明末における寶卷と無爲教 (*Pao-chüan* and the Wu-wei Sect at the end of the Ming Dynasty). In *Chūgoku zensho no kenkyū* 中國善書の研究 (Studies of the *shan-shu*). Tokyo, 1960. Pp. 437–85.

Sawada, Mizuho 澤田瑞穂. "Raso no Muikyō" 羅祖の無爲教 (A study of the Wu-wei Sect founded by Lo-tsu). *Tōhō shūkyō* 東方宗教 (Journal of East Asian Religions), 1:44–63 (1951); 2:44–58 (1952).

Historical studies of Taoist orders and religious sects have covered not only the Ch'üan-chen and Cheng-i 正一 sects, but also the alchemical Chin-tan Tao 金丹道, the "Way of the Golden Elixir":

Imai, Usaburō 今井宇三郎. "Kintan Dōkyō kenkyū—Nan Sō no dōshi Haku-gyokusen no shisō" 金丹道教研究—南宋の道士白玉蟾の思想 (A study of Chin-tan Taoism—On the philosophy of Pai Yü-ch'an, a Southern Sung Taoist). *Tōkyō kyōiku daigaku bungakubu kiyō* 東京教育大學文學部記要 (Bulletin of the Tokyo Kyōiku University Faculty of Letters), 8:91–126 (1963).

Miyakawa, Hisayuki 宮川尙志. "Ryū Itsumei no *Goshin-chokushi* ni tsuite" 劉一明の悟眞直指について (A Study on Liu I-ming's *Wu-chen chih-chih*—'The gist of the *Wu-chen p'ien* 悟眞篇' by Chang Po-tuan 張伯端). In *Okayama Daigaku Hōbun-gakubu gakujutsu kiyō* 岡山大學法文學部學術紀要 (Transactions of the Okayama University Faculty of Letters), 3:49–58 (1954).

Although these studies have attempted a comprehensive approach, taking up alchemy and Taoism along with various aspects of thought and philosophy, much remains to be done. Another focus of postwar study has appeared in work done on the Ching-ming chung-hsiao Sect by Akizuki Kan'ei:

Akizuki, Kan'ei 秋月觀暎. "Kyoson kyōdan to Jōmyōchūkōdō ni tsuite" 許遜教團と淨明忠孝道について (The Hsü Hsün Sect and the Ching-ming chung-hsiao Tao). *Dōkyō kenkyū* 道教研究 (Taoist Studies), 3: 197–235 (1966).[4]

———. "Jōmyōdō-kyōgaku kanken—Ju-Butsu-Dō sangyō kankei o chūshin ni" 淨明道教學管見—儒佛道三教關係を中心に (My personal views on the doctrines of the Ching-ming Sect of Taoism, with special reference to the relations among the three teachings—Confucianism, Buddhism, and Taoism). *Tōhō shūkyō*, 35:20–35 (1970).

The Ching-ming chung-hsiao Sect, along with the Ch'üan-chen Sect and other Taoist groups of the Sung period, arose against the background of early modern Chinese society and politics, and reflected the growing relationship between the Three Religions. Its singular nature requires particularly comprehensive research, which takes into account politics, society, thought, and religion; and, as in the case of the morality books (*shan-shu*), it should be closely linked with research on popular Taoism.

There have been a great many studies of "thought and philosophy" in Japan, China, and elsewhere. However, in almost all the work devoted to Chinese thought itself, there has been little effort to relate it with Taoism.

Conversely, the coming task in the field of Taoist studies is to determine the way to benefit from its many valuable achievements in thought and philosophy. One important problematical aspect of Taoism has been how to interpret the thought of Lao-tzu and Chuang-tzu in view of their numerous associations with religious Taoism. Such scholars as Koyanagi Shigeta and, in the postwar period, Kimura Eiichi, have already begun work in this direction, and most recently, there has been the research on the *Lao-tzu Hsiang-erh Commentary* by Fukui Kōjun and Ōfuchi Ninji.

Fukui, Kōjun 福井康順. "Rōshi-Sōjichū kō—kōsen o shudai to shite" 老子想爾注考—校箋を主題として (On [the authenticity of] a commentary on the *Lao-tzu*—the *Lao-tzu Hsiang-erh-chu*). *Waseda daigaku daigakuin bungakukenkyūka kiyō* 早稻田大學大學院文學研究科紀要 (Bulletin of the Graduate Division of Literature of Waseda University), 13:1–20 (1967).

Kimura, Eiichi 木村英一. *Rōshi no shin kenkyū* 老子の新研究 (A new study of the *Lao-tzu*). Tokyo, 1959. 633 pp.

Koyanagi, Shigeta 小柳司氣太. *Rō Sō no shisō to dōkyō* 老莊の思想と道教 (Taoist religion and the thought of Lao-tzu and Chuang-tzu). Tokyo, 1942. 392 pp.

Ōfuchi, Ninji 大淵忍爾. "Rōshi-Sōjichū no seiritsu" 老子想爾注の成立 (The composition of the *Hsiang-erh* Commentary on the *Lao-tzu*). *Okayama shigaku* 岡山史學 (Okayama Journal of History), 19:9–31 (1967).

Nevertheless, a general comprehensive treatment of the relation between philosophical and religious Taoism has yet to be undertaken. The Tao has above all been studied as a Confucian or Taoist Tao; there has been little, if any, attempt to elucidate the relation of the Tao of the thinkers to the Tao of the people—in other words, to discover how the Tao and religious Taoism were connected. As the religion of the Chinese people, Taoism contains within it the ethical basis of their life, consciousness, and behavior. The people's consciousness and thought were first enunciated by their rulers—the upper-class intellectuals—who recorded them in their writings. We have not yet answered such questions as: "Just how were popular consciousness and beliefs recorded, not only by later literati but by the early philosophers and sages?" and "By what process did the consciousness and beliefs of these intellectuals become those of the masses?" When issues such as these have been clarified, Taoist studies will be correspondingly advanced. Yet it seems that little of this type of research is being carried out in Japan.

Popular beliefs, customs, festivals, and so forth, survive in the life and consciousness of the people. On these subjects there has been a rather large amount of research. It is over the undercurrent of such popular beliefs that specifically Taoist beliefs have taken shape. For instance, beliefs in gods of the soil, as they developed into gods of agriculture and gods of hell, allow us to grasp the history of popular life, religion, and mass society. Yet a comprehensive approach to the study of either official shrine-gods or popular earth-gods has yet to be developed.

Considerable attention has been given to the spread of individual popular beliefs: Kubo Noritada's study of the *Keng-shen* cult (see above, p. 276) and Li Hsien-chang's study of Ma-tsu are major achievements, also significant for understanding the spread of Taoist beliefs in Japan.

Li Hsien-chang 李獻璋. "Maso densetsu no gensho keitai" 媽祖傳說の原初形態 (Original forms of the legend of Ma-tsu). *Tōhō shūkyō*, 11:61–82 (1956).

———. "Mintei no taigai senyu kara mitaru Maso no denpa—toku ni Tei Wa no seiden ni okeru reigen ni tsuite" 明廷の對外宣諭から見たる媽祖の傳播—特に鄭和の西征における靈驗について (Diffusion of the Ma-tsu cult as seen after the Ming dynasty decree on overseas travel—treating especially the miracles accompanying Cheng Ho's Western expeditions). *Chūgoku gakushi* 中國學誌 (Sinological Researches), 1:113–39 (1964).

Two other studies on the spread of Taoist beliefs in Japan are:

Naba, Toshisada 那波利貞. "Dōkyō no Nihonkoku e no ryūden ni tsukite" 道教の日本國への流傳に就きて (The introduction of Taoistic religion into Japan), pt. 1, *Tōhō shūkyō* 1. 2:1–22 (1952); pt. 2, ibid., nos. 4–5: 58–122 (1954).

Shimode, Sekiyo 下出積與. *Nihon kodai no jingi to Dōkyō* 日本古代の神祇と道教 (Deities of ancient Japan and Taoism). Tokyo, 1972. 294 pp.

Investigation of the Taoist scriptures, beginning with the *Lao-tzu*, *Chuang-tzu*, and the *T'ai-p'ing ching*, has advanced in the postwar period, in part given impetus by the literary finds in Tun-huang and elsewhere. Fukui Kōjun, Yoshioka Yoshitoyo, Ōfuchi Ninji, and others have made outstanding contributions to the study of the evolution and composition of the Taoist Canon, as well as of the scriptures it contains. The field is often split on the question of the dating of these scriptures, with some tending to place their composition earlier, whereas others, on the basis of intensive textual criticism, prefer to date them later. For example, in his article "*Taiheikyō no ichi kōsatsu*" 太平經の一考察 (A study of the *T'ai-p'ing ching*), in *Tōyōshikai kiyō* 東洋史會紀要 (Bulletin of the Association for East Asian History) 1:91–136 (1935) and 2:141–78 (1936), Fukui Kōjun concluded, after a detailed philosophical investigation, that the existing *T'ai-p'ing-ching* was a forgery made during the Liang or Ch'en dynasties (502–589). A most important work on the *T'ai-p'ing ching* is Yoshioka Yoshitoyo's "Tonkō bon Taiheikyō to Bukkyō" 敦煌本太平經と佛教 (The Tun-huang manuscript of the *T'ai-p'ing ching* and Buddhism), in his *Dōkyō to Bukkyō* 道教と佛教 (Taoism and Buddhism; Tokyo, 1970), 2:7–161. Such disagreements about dating, because of the intricacy of the problems involved, are likely to continue. In any case, research on all types of Taoist scriptures must be carried forward.

The main work on monasteries, monks, and ritual, after that of Koyanagi, has been done by Igarashi Kenryū and Yoshioka Yoshitoyo. In the postwar period, field surveys in Taiwan and Hong Kong have been supported by research funds from the Japanese Ministry of Education.

As a popular religion, Taoism contains a variety of elements. The relative strength of superstition and folk beliefs has tended to obscure the scientific elements inherent in Taoism and has led, in fact, to a tendency to consider Taoism as remote from science. In the past, Taoism has been the victim of repressive policies aimed against superstition and heresy by successive dynasties upholding a bureaucratic Confucian ideology. In the modern period, both the Kuomintang and the Communist Party, in spite of their differing political philosophies, have joined in denouncing Taoism and superstition. However, the Communist Party has also stressed the popular democratic consciousness to be found in Taoism and in Chinese popular fiction (*T'ung-su hsiao-shuo* 通俗小說) and has noted the role of Taoism in China's cultural heritage of science.

Taoism included various practical arts (*fang-chi lei* 方伎類) such as medicine, pharmacology, alchemy, sexual hygiene (*fang-chung* 房中), and Taoist sorcery, as well as pseudo-sciences like astrology, geomancy, and calendar-making. The "practical arts" were closely connected with the purposes of religious Taoism. Alchemy, for example, was a Taoist method of attaining immortality. The pseudo-sciences, on the other hand, seem often to have been independent of religion and to have been considered academic fields. For instance, calendar-making in China was a prerogative of the sovereign, studied by each dynasty; and in the standard histories a particular section is devoted to it (the *lü-li chih* 律歷志). Within the Taoist framework, the pseudo-sciences functioned as sciences; yet precisely here they often took forms that we would be most likely to call superstitious.

Research on the history of Chinese science seeks to relate science and religion, but its emphasis is, of course, on the substance of science itself. However, the work of Watanabe Kōzō, Yoshida Mitsukuni, and others, has given due consideration to science's relationship with Taoism.

Watanabe, Kōzō 渡邊幸三, "Tō Kōkei no *Honzō* ni taisuru bunkenga-kuteki kōsatsu" 陶弘景の本草に對する文獻學的考察 (A textual study of T'ao Hung-ching's *Pen-ts'ao*). *Tōhō gakuhō* 東方學報 (East Asian Bulletin), Kyoto, 20:195–222 (1951).

Yoshida, Mitsukuni 吉田光邦. *Renkinjutsu—senjutsu to kagaku no aida* 錬金術—仙術と科學の間 (Alchemy—between Taoist sorcery and science). Tokyo, 1963. 220 pp.

The future should see progress in the joint efforts of Taoist specialists and specialists in the history of science. One result of cooperative research on East Asian medicine and Taoism already achieved has been KAZMAC.[5]

In the above I have touched on selected points in the present problems and future prospects of Taoist studies. To conclude I should like to discuss the problem of data retrieval and bibliography for research on Taoism in Japan. Taoism is a cultural composite incorporating a variety of elements. Accordingly I have set up the following ten categories, based on these elements as well as on the content and methodology of the research.

1. General Works on Taoism
2. Historical Studies
3. Popular Beliefs, Folklore, Almanacs, Taoism and Literature
4. Taoism and Science
5. The Three Religions
6. Thought and Philosophy
7. Scriptures and Documents
8. Dissemination of Taoism
9. Monasteries (*tao-kuan*), Monks (*tao-shih*), Ritual, Festivals
10. Academic Trends

These categories are tentative. Depending on the content of a particular work, it may fall into several categories. I have, however, arbitrarily assigned each work to a single category in a bibliography published elsewhere:

Sakai, Tadao, *Dōkyō kenkyū bunken mokuroku* (Nihon) 道教研究文獻目錄(日本) (Bibliography of Taoist studies in Japan). Tokyo, 1972. 94 pp.

In compiling this bibliography I consulted the following works.

Chūgoku shisō, shūkyō, bunka kankei ronbun mokuroku 中國思想宗教文化關係論文目錄 (Bibliography of studies in Japan of Chinese thought, religion, and culture). Tokyo, 1960. 331 pp.

Hōbun rekishigaku kankei shozasshi Tōyōshi ronbun yōmoku 邦文歷史學關係諸雜誌東洋史論文要目 (Bibliography of studies in Japanese of Oriental history). Tokyo, 1936. 362 pp.

Tōyōgaku bunken ruimoku 東洋學文獻類目 (Annual bibliography of Oriental studies). Kyoto, 1961–.

Tōyōshi kenkyū bunken ruimoku 東洋史研究文獻類目 (Bibliography of Oriental studies). Kyoto, 1934–60 (annual).

In my bibliography I have included books, academic reviews, and articles published by Japanese, as well as articles by foreigners in Japanese scholarly journals. I have also included translations of foreign books published in Japan, though omitting all book reviews and speeches. I have not confined myself strictly to Taoism. For example, under the heading "Historical Studies" are works dealing with peasant and popular movements and the secret societies, which, since they are related to popular life and religious consciousness, should be useful in any comprehensive study of Taoism.

I hope that Western readers of Japanese may benefit from such bibliographical efforts, even as we have benefited from bibliographies of Western work on Taoism.[6]

Editors' Notes on Sakai article

1. Most of the materials collected by these research centers are in the Library of Congress, Washington, D.C. Some are in the Japanese Diet Library.

2. See *Tōhō shūkyō* 1.1 :i–ii (1951). Here and often below the editors have changed the author's translation of *tōhō* and *tōyō* from the usual "Oriental" to "East Asian," since what is being referred to are the religions of East Asia, not of South or Southeast Asia nor of the Middle or Near East, all of which are covered in the conventional usage of "Oriental." Similarly, alterations have sometimes been made in the official English translation of the names of Japanese associations.

3. See Introduction, note 28.

4. *Dōkyō kenkyū* is a serial appearing irregularly under the editorship of Yoshioka Yoshitoyo and Michel Soymié. It has been put out by different publishers, the latest volume (vol. 4, 1971) by Henkyōsha 邊境社, Tokyo.

5. KAZMAC or OMRON is an acronym for *Tōyō igaku butsuri ryōhō jidō shindanki* 東洋醫學物理療法自動診斷機. At Tateshina, bilingual offprints that described this computer were distributed. The first was by

Ōshima Yoshio 大島良雄 of Tokyo University's Department of Physical Therapy and School of Internal Medicine. Its English title was "Computer Diagnosis in the Fields of Acupuncture and Moxibustion" (*Shinkyū ryōiki ni okeru jidō shindan* 鍼炎領域における自動診斷), *Journal of the International Congress of Acupuncture and Moxibustion*, Tokyo (1966). The second offprint was by M. Yamamoto 山本通隆, M. Uemura 上村幹夫, and K. Yaida 矢井田光一, all of Tateishi Electronics Company 立石電機 株式會社, and was entitled "Oriental Medicine Data Processing Apparatus (KAZMAC)." It appeared in *Omron Technics* 6.1:1–10 (March 1965). Also distributed was a brochure describing the company's model OMRON Type TOC-1 (KAZMAC). Researchers at Tokyo, Tokyo Kyōiku, and Waseda universities were said to have taken part in the development of this computer, which apparently operates like the diagnostic computers found in some Western hospitals but is fed with information used in diagnosis by traditional Chinese and Japanese doctors.

6. Professor Hisayuki Miyakawa has kindly brought to the attention of the editors the following works on Taoism that have appeared in Japanese since the Tateshina conference:

Fukunaga, Mitsuji 福永光司. "Dōkyō ni okeru kagami to tsurugi—sono shisō no genryū" 道教における鏡と劍—その思想の源流 (The mirror and sword in Taoism—the origin of their idea). *Tōhō gakuhō* 東方學報, Kyōto, 45: 59–120 (1973).

Kani, Hiroaki 可兒弘明. "Minshū Dōkyō no shūhen" 民衆道教の周邊 (Around popular Taoism). Part 1: "*Fu-luan* or Chinese automatic writing. Its history and present practice," *Shigaku* 史學 (Historical Studies), 45.1: 57–88 (1972); Part 2: "The relation of the Chinese puppet theaters to popular Taoism," Ibid. 45.2: 53–82 (1973); Part 3: "Chinese paper charms in the changing society of Hong Kong," Ibid. 45.3: 1–46 (1973) (in Japanese).

Kominami, Ichirō 小南一郎. "*Kan Butei naiden* no seiritsu" 「漢武帝內傳」 の成立, 上 (Formation of the *Han Wu-ti nei-chuan*, pt. 1). *Tōhō Gakuhō* 東方學報, Kyoto, 48: 183–227 (1975).

Kubo, Noritada 窪德忠, *Dōkyō shi* 道教史 (History of Taoism). Tokyo, 1977. 440 pp.

Masuda, Fukutaro 增田福太郎. *Shin. kyū chūgoku no shinkō to hyōshō* 新. 舊中國の信仰と表象 (Beliefs and their representations in old and new China). Tokyo, 1974. 292 pp.

Sanaka, Sō 佐中壯. *Sengoku. Sōsho kan no shinkō to gijutsu no kankei* 戰國. 宋初間の信仰と技術の關係 (Studies relating to [Taoist] beliefs and

technics from the Warring States period to the early Sung [10th cent.]).
Ise, 1975. 320 pp.

We would like to add Professor Miyakawa's reference to three other
important studies, prior to 1972, published in places where they might
escape the attention of specialists in Taoism.

In 1938, the Japanese governor-general of Taiwan launched a campaign
to abolish indigenous Chinese temples and shrines on the island. On this
event exists a short book:

Miyazaki Naokatsu 宮崎直勝. *Jibyōshin no shōten* 寺廟神の昇天 (The
ascension of the gods of [Buddhist] monasteries and [Taoist] temples).
Taipei, 1942. 111 pp.

There are two studies on the interaction of Taoist and Buddhist thought
by a renowned Buddhologist:

Kamata Shigeo 鎌田茂雄. "Chōkan no kegon to Rō Sō shisō" 澄觀の華嚴
と老莊思想 (The Hua-yen philosophy of Ch'eng-kuan and the thought
of Lao-Chuang). *Chūgoku kegon shisōshi no kenkyū* 中國華嚴思想史の研
究 (Studies on Chinese Hua-yen philosophy). Tokyo, 1965. pp. 253–
322.
———. "Butsudō ryō shisō no kōryū" 佛道兩思想の交流 (The Interaction of Buddhist and Taoist Thought). Part 1 of his *Chūgoku Bukkyō
shisōshi kenkyū* 中國佛教思想史の研究 (Studies in the history of
Chinese Buddhist thought). Tokyo, 1968. Pp. 11–256.

Index